D1288523

future is one way to develop a modicum of confidence that there will be a future, and get young people committed on a long-term basis to helping solve or ameliorate major issues facing the society at various levels (local to international).

Finally, of course, we need to conduct additional surveys of people's perceptions of the future every year or every two years to monitor trends and, based on the results, hopefully to take some constructive actions. After all, what is at stake is the future of our children, grandchildren, and their children – and our society.

THE STATE OF THE GARDEN STATE

Edited by
MICHAEL P. RICCARDS

Preface by
GEORGE E. HALL

Hall Institute of Public Policy – New Jersey
2006

A publication in the series: New Jersey 2020

Printed by Walsworth Publishing Company, Inc., Marceline, Missouri.
Dennis Paalhar, *Publishing Consultant*
Dust jacket photo courtesy of Richard Lee

CONTRIBUTORS

Sherry Glied, Ph.D.
Professor and Head of the Division of Health Policy and Management, Mailman School of Public Health, Columbia University, New York, New York. She has also co-authored the article "Medicaid in New Jersey: Options for Reform" with Michael Sparer, Ph.D., and Megan Vanneman, MPH.

George E. Hall
Founder of the Hall Institute of Public Policy and President, Founder, and majority shareholder of The Clinton Group, Inc., New York, New York.

Robert P. Haney, Jr., Esquire
A partner of the law firm Covington and Burling and is based in the firm's New York Office. He is a Board Member of the New Jersey City University Foundation and is also President of the Citizens' Council on Affordable Higher Education.

Glenda Kirkland, Ph.D.
Coordinator of the Political Science Department and Assistant Professor of Public Administration, Bloomfield College, Bloomfield, New Jersey. She is also the Executive Director of Isaiah House, East Orange, New Jersey.

Richard A. Lee
Director of Communications of the Hall Institute of Public Policy, and formerly was Deputy Director of Communications to Governor James McGreevey and Acting Governor Richard Codey. He is a Ph.D. candidate in Media Studies at Rutgers University, New Brunswick, New Jersey.

Thomas John Locke, Ph.D.
Director of Curriculum, Cherry Hill Public Schools, Cherry Hill, New Jersey. He was an elementary principal, middle school assistant principal, and previously taught English for six years in East Brunswick, New Jersey.

Donald B. Louria, M.D.
Professor and Chairman Emeritus of the Department of Preventive Medicine, School of Medicine and Dentistry of New Jersey, Newark, New Jersey, and the author of numerous articles on a variety of topics.

Karyn Malinowski, Ph.D.
Dean of Outreach and Extension Programs, Rutgers Cooperative Research and Extension and Director of the Equine Science Center, New Jersey Agricultural Experiment Station, Rutgers University, New Brunswick, New Jersey.

Brendan O'Flaherty, Ph.D.
Professor in the Department of Economics, Columbia University, New York, New York. His most recent textbook, "City Economics" (Harvard University Press), is the first such study written by a New Jerseyan since 1980.

Michael P. Riccards, Ph.D.
Executive Director of Hall Institute of Public Policy. He was formerly the Public Policy Scholar at the College Board in Washington, D.C., and a college president at three institutions.

TABLE OF CONTENTS

PREFACE

This anthology, *The State of the Garden State*, is the first occasional publication by the Hall Institute of Public Policy – NJ in the series *New Jersey 2020*. The mission of the Hall Institute is to encourage debate and dialogue on the major issues and challenges facing the State of New Jersey. It is our hope that such explorations will help lead to solutions to some of those difficulties. We all have a vested interest in furthering a high quality future for our children and ourselves.

All of these major pieces of work have been featured on our website, www.hallnj.org, and I urge you to visit our site often as its range grows and its opinion pieces multiply. The solicitation and publication of those web pieces offer immediate and topical responses on salient issues. I have been especially pleased by the numerous favorable reactions from my fellow citizens, both in New Jersey and across the nation, to the website. Now, some of those pieces are reprinted here for more intense scrutiny and debate.

No work such as this is possible without the active assistance of scholars, opinion makers, and other interested citizens who are willing to expose their views to the light of day. I am grateful to the authors in this journal anthology and to the many more who believe in the mission and purpose of the Hall Institute of Public Policy – NJ.

Sincerely,
GEORGE E. HALL
Founder

FOREWORD

The Hall Institute of Public Policy in New Jersey is a non-partisan, not-for-profit research center, in Trenton that explores the nature and dimensions of policy issues that impact on the state and the nation. The Institute, founded in 2005 by George E. Hall, reflects his commitment to the use of knowledge to further solutions to our common challenges. Public policy is a society's response to its economic, social, political, and cultural developments, which, in turn, creates priorities for the whole society.

This volume looks at the "State of the Garden State," as New Jersey has branded itself since 1876. It is the first publication in the Hall Institute's *New Jersey 2020* series. This volume starts off with a preface by the Institute's founder, which outlines the mission and purposes of the center and the nature of this publication. My introduction focuses on the historical origins and consequences of the state of New Jersey with an emphasis on the problems of state identity, urban machines and bosses, the need for transparency in its politics, and the lack of a statewide media. For New Jersey, to a large extent, geography is destiny – since the state is located between two great cities, New York City and Philadelphia.

Being so densely populated in some areas, New Jerseyans frequently debate the question of urban sprawl. Brendan O'Flaherty, a professor of economics at Columbia University and a resident of New Jersey, provides a comprehensive view of urban sprawl, and in the process examines many of our assumptions about taxation policy, land use, recreational space, transportation, water consumption, and even race relations. His treatment of urban sprawl challenges the reader's understandings of how we do our public business. Then, in a case study, Professor O'Flaherty focuses on the state's largest city, Newark, and how it can, again, emphasize its economic uniqueness and the value of its geographic location. The case study is clearly meant as a mandate for change, especially in the use of tax breaks in the city.

His colleague at Columbia University, Professor Sherry Glied of the Mailman School of Public Health, and her associates have completed a major, three-part series commissioned by the Hall Institute. Two of those reports, which are included here, examine the increasingly important issue of medical care coverage. Glied provides one of the most comprehensive reviews of New Jersey's programs and federal policies that affect New Jersey citizens under Medicare and Medicaid. Even with New Jersey's comparatively generous coverage under Medicaid, Glied shows the continuing need for care in certain areas, especially within segments of older residents and the poor population.

The state and its cities face an increasingly vexatious situation in dealing with the homeless, especially since the early 1980s. To examine that social dilemma, Professor Glenda Kirkland of Bloomfield College presents a data-grounded model that allows us to interpret, track, predict, and make decisions about the homeless problem. But there are disagreements about what causes homelessness – does it result from disturbances and inequalities in the housing and economic sectors of our economy, or does it reflect more individual pathologies. There is also no real agreement about how many homeless people there are, or even the definition of what it means to be homeless.

One of the most controversial and far-reaching pieces of federal domestic legislation is the "No Child Left Behind Act." The act is intended to set up long-term benchmarks to further educational accountability. That legislation reflects the continuing concern about American education since the critical "Nation at Risk" report came out during the Reagan Administration. Thomas John Locke, Director of Curriculum in the Cherry Hill school district, looks at NCLB's goals and objectives through extensive, in-depth interviews with the leadership of a large New Jersey school district. He finds a deep commitment to the ideals of educating every student, but also honest discussions of the real world difficulties that administrators and teachers have to confront every day. Locke reports on how, in response to NCLB, the district became very exam-oriented, especially in two key subjects, language arts and mathematics, and how it dealt with community opposition when it moved quickly to implement special intervention efforts for struggling students. The long-term consequences of NCLB in the district and in the nation are still unclear and will be for some time.

Higher education has had, generally, very strong support from the people of New Jersey who accept the view that a college education is the very engine of social mobility and economic development in this state and nation. But Robert Haney argues that a steady increase in tuition and fees, especially at public institutions, presents a real danger to those social objectives. He maintains that tuition should be capped at a reasonable rate, and that there should be an augmented state commitment to need-based assistance for prospective students.

In a different vein, an interesting area of economic concern with significant environmental impact is the horse racing industry. New Jersey is highly dependent on leisure and entertainment, especially through its tourism business. But being the most urbanized state in the nation, it must be very sensitive to the protection and preservation of its open land, parks, and agricultural spaces. One of the consequences of a healthy horse racing industry, in the expert opinion of Dean Karyn Malinowski, director of the Equine Science Center at Rutgers University, is the dedication of large acreage to the care and training of racehorses. It is an interesting perspective on the importance of having open spaces that can also be productive.

Also, in terms of leisure and economic benefits to the state, New Jersey's shore and its ocean-fronting areas are, obviously, a great resource to the state, attracting people interested in commercial fishing, boating, and general recreational usage. The Jersey shore has in history and popular lore an enormous impact on people of all ages who wish to enjoy the waters and the beach lifestyle, but as New Jersey becomes more urbanized, it experiences development pressures to curtail rules and regulations and to allow more growth and multiple use. To protect the ocean, the Coastal Ocean Coalition formed a task force and presented to Acting Governor Richard Cody a series of recommendations to create a tough, integrated strategy to protect, preserve, and restore the coastal areas. Those recommendations are presented here in summary form.

On a more personal level, opinion polls provide us with interesting data on social and political attitudes, and give us a snapshot of opinions. Dr. Donald Louria, professor emeritus at New Jersey School of Medicine and Dentistry, summarizes a study that shows we are rather optimistic when it comes to our lives and futures, but not as optimistic for the nation as a whole. Those opinions, of course, are very much dependent on the types of events and personal experiences that inform our judgments. In a second provocative essay, Dr. Louria predicts that the United States is headed for a future that includes extra-longevity, including life spans that may reach as much as 120 years. He warns of the enormous impacts that such life spans could have on our health, work, economic security, and retirement systems.

In order to understand these and other public policy issues, it is important to have a diversified and informed mass media. Richard Lee, Director of Communications at the Hall Institute of Public Policy, explains how the media, especially the print media, is now highly concentrated in the hands of a few large chains, and how their editorial policies and, indeed, their coverage are often influenced by corporate and advertising concerns. Given this situation and the fact that New Jersey has few statewide organs of information, citizens have very limited knowledge of the day-to-day operations of the state government.

Taken individually and together, these essays help to provide us with a clearer understanding of some of the major public policy concerns that face the State of New Jersey in the twenty-first century. Knowledge is indeed power, and widespread dissemination of information is essential to a functioning, healthy democracy. This truth drives the mission and commitment of the Hall Institute of Public Policy.

MICHAEL P. RICCARDS
Trenton, NJ 2006

HOW NEW JERSEY
BECAME NEW JERSEY

By
Michael P. Riccards

Benjamin Franklin once humorously commented that New Jersey was a keg with two spigots – an obvious reference to the colony being located between the two large cities of Philadelphia and New York City. Actually, the area was formally split in two with the royal gifts to Lord Berkeley and Sir George Carteret. Eventually each had a charter or constitution, with West Jersey reflecting, at times, the easy tolerance of the Quakers. Still, for a while, even the united colony had two capitals, mirroring the early division. That split influenced other decision makers as well – for example, in 1808 Pope Pius VII divided the area of New Jersey into two regions to be assigned to the dioceses of Philadelphia and New York. (Issacson, 2004; Riccards, 2005a).

New Jersey was extremely important also as a battlefield during the American Revolution, with General George Washington waging four major battles and 90 smaller battles there. The battles of Trenton and Princeton in 1776 and 1777 were instrumental in reviving the Continental Army and its lagging fortunes. (Ellis, 2005; Salmore and Salmore, 1998).

The early colonial constitution of 1776 exhibited many of the characteristics of the other American colonies. As Thomas Jefferson once remarked, all patriots were Whigs in temperament – that is, they supported a weak executive with political power being concentrated in a strong legislature. Some states like Pennsylvania even had a committee performing the executive functions. It is interesting to note that when the Founding Fathers created a new national government in 1787, they avoided the New Jersey and Pennsylvania models and looked more toward Massachusetts and New York with their stronger executives. (Riccards, 1987). New Jersey's William Livingston, governor from 1776 to 1790, was a fairly weak executive, lending the office his personal prestige rather than vice versa.

The governor's term then lasted only one year, and he had little in the way of veto power. The weakness of the governorship actually paralleled the historic weaknesses and the overall insignificance of New Jersey state government. That government provided very few services, and the major drain on its resources was the state penal system. The state lacked broad-based state taxes, mainly relying on fees paid by the powerful railroad interests throughout much of the nineteenth century. (Bernstein, 1972).

Until recent decades, New Jersey politics and government were characterized by the following major factors:

1) A weak state governor;
2) No broad-based state taxes;
3) A prevailing view of localism;
4) Strong county-based machines in both parties;
5) Rather extensive homogenous ethnic communities, even in parts of the urban areas;
6) The lack of a clear and respected state identity; and
7) The absence of a statewide media.

Many of these factors are still apparent in state life. Although I have argued that New Jersey is comparatively "clean" and its politics transparent, there is still a widespread view that the state's politics have been and are riddled by extensive corruption – in both parties at all levels. Thus, an eighth characteristic often identified is widespread corruption. (Riccards, 2005b).

Overall then, the question is: How did New Jersey become New Jersey?

I. The Local Units

The late Alan Karcher, member of the New Jersey state assembly from 1973 to 1990 and Speaker from 1982-1985, authored a classic study of New Jersey government that focused on the reasons for such extensive localism. He insisted that localities grew up for economic reasons, sheer political egotism, and diverse social and cultural causes. In 2003, then-governor James McGreevey observed that New Jersey had more local governments per square mile than any other state in the Union, more than Arizona, Delaware, Hawaii, Maryland, Nevada, New Mexico, Rhode Island, and Wyoming combined. A third of those municipalities in New Jersey had fewer than 5,000 residents. Today, a good deal of the explanation for localism is the desire of suburbanites to create and control their public schools. New Jersey has more public school districts per capita than states much larger in size, with over 600 such districts in place; about half of those school districts do not even have one high school. Governor McGreevey also noted that 172 school districts have only one school building; 143 school districts have fewer than 500 students; and 23 school districts do not have even a single school building! Many of these suburbanites left the New Jersey and New York urban areas in order to provide a better education for their children. While few New Jerseyans have a strong sense of loyalty to their state, they do seem deeply committed to their schools' athletic teams and achievements. Property taxes, now the highest in the nation, still heavily undergird the school systems, even after the efforts at educational equalization pushed by the state supreme court. (Karcher, 1998; McGreevey, 2003).

The highly regarded political scientists – Barbara Salmore and the late Stephen Salmore – have characterized New Jersey as a prime example of suburban politics coming of age. They point out the preeminence of Philadelphia and, especially, of New York City in the life of the state, and indeed, in the very definition of New Jersey. The earliest manifestations of New Jersey population growth hugged those two neighboring cities. Even today, New Jersey news and politics are overshadowed by those two great cities and their media outlets. New Jersey citizens are probably more able to name the mayor of New York City than the mayor of Newark or the two United States Senators from New Jersey. (Salmore and Salmore, 1998).

In some ways New Jersey, except in per capita income, is like West Virginia. That state's major growth areas are near the cities of other states – Pennsylvania, Maryland, Virginia, and Ohio. The major media outlets come from Pittsburgh, not Wheeling, and Washington D.C., not Martinsburg. The last part of each state to be developed was the middle area or interior.

Once a long commute to New York City was Summit; now people are commuting from Mercer and Ocean Counties to the City. There is little leisure time left for state politics or state culture. Local school board politics is, for some people, the real focus of state politics. The absence of a strong print and electronic media has another consequence – it severely limits the ability of political candidates to connect to New Jersey constituents, or, if they do, they must pay for media in the very expensive markets of Philadelphia and New York City. In one sense, cable television and the state's public television station have somewhat muted that effect, but not totally. One of the persistent problems that New Jersey politicians have, especially novices, is the lack of name recognition, thus the advantages that incumbents enjoy – even those who have run before and lost. (Salmore and Salmore, 1998).

The innate conservatism of localism has been accentuated in the past by the peculiarities of what is often called "little federalism." The national government provides for equal representation of each state in the U.S. Senate, regardless of population. This has been called the Great Compromise of 1787. But most states, including New Jersey, adopted that model by establishing constitutionally a state senate in which rural counties counted as much as the large populous urban counties. The result was a legislature that was often more conservative and more Republican than the population would reflect. Also, county parity reinforced the role and importance of county political machines, many controlled by political bosses or powerful autonomous chairmen. Then, in 1962 and in 1964, the U.S. Supreme Court ruled respectively in Baker v. Carr and Reynolds v. Sims that such arrangements violated the equal protection clause of the U.S. Constitution. Ironically, the high court could do nothing about the U.S. Senate, which is embedded in the original constitution of the nation. The result in New Jersey was the decline of the power of rural areas, but the population by then had begun to shift to the suburban areas, and so the Republicans were competitive once again with the Democrats. Also, the old county machines in some areas went into marked decline, but were succeeded by more sophisticated organizations.

II. The Machines and the Bosses

The history of county machines in New Jersey is a special chapter in state and national history. At the turn of the twentieth century, two of the northern counties – Hudson and Essex – each embraced a fifth of the state's residents. Half of Hudson County lived in Jersey City; two-thirds of Essex lived in Newark. (Salmore and Salmore, 1998). The political operations of the counties were reinforced by the services they provided to various ethnic groups. Since the state government was so meager, there were very few good patronage jobs at that level, and the focus for job seekers was the county governments. Actually, the urban machines often represented the cause of political reform in New Jersey life.

In the late nineteenth century, the state was, for all practical purposes, run by the powerful operators of the Camden and Amboy railroad line that went from Jersey City through to Camden. Then in 1871, the Camden and Amboy leased its property and rights of way to the influential, but out-of-state, Pennsylvania Railroad, thus losing some of its local support. Later, other railroad lines would be developed, especially down the New Jersey shoreline. Since Jersey City, a national railroad terminus, was so important, the Republicans in Trenton limited Hudson County politicians' control of Jersey City, and the rest of Hudson County by creating independent boards and commissions that oversaw the railroad operations. Both political parties though, on the state level, catered to the railroad interests, which led to a very weak state government and a governorship that was often headed by men who actually lived in New York City! New Jersey also earned the disdain of good government forces across the country when it welcomed the trusts or holding companies that had been prosecuted elsewhere. Political offices often went to agents of the Pennsylvania Railroad, the Prudential Insurance Company, and Elizabeth Gas and Electric. (Salmore and Salmore, 1998).

It is argued by some historians that the new Progressive movement in New Jersey triumphed with the election in 1910 of Woodrow Wilson, the president of Princeton University. Betraying the bosses who elected him, Wilson pushed hard for a new reform agenda and was remarkably successful, at first. But his sights were set higher, and New Jersey never really had a Progressive movement of the magnitude or duration of New York, California, or Wisconsin. Although Wilson was a brilliant orator and a magnetic leader, the major change in the political landscape came not from the Progressives but from a notorious political figure in New Jersey – Frank Hague. (Rapport, 1961; Link, 1947).

Born in a poor Irish-Catholic family in Jersey City, Hague took over control of the Democratic machine in Hudson County in 1913, and waged an effective battle at the local and state levels against the railroad interests and the CIO labor unions, which he believed were Communist-run. He was crude, corrupt, and authoritarian, and not above using the Jersey City police to persecute his enemies. But Hague was also a towering figure in the national Democratic Party and a very able pleader for welfare programs for his constituents. At one point he built the world's third-largest public hospital in Jersey City. (Dorsett, 1977).

Hague ran the Democratic machine until 1947, when he voluntarily retired to Florida and New York City, where he continued to oppose the railroad interests. The Hague machine controlled vast numbers of patronage jobs by assessing 3% to 40% of an officeholder's salary for the organization. He was able to curtail Republican effectiveness in the county and elsewhere, including that of governors in Trenton. When reform Democrats ran for the governorship, Hague did not support the Republicans as much as he simply did not turn out the Hudson County Democratic vote. His position was accentuated by his association with Franklin Delano Roosevelt's administration. (Dorsett, 1977).

In 1932, Frank Hague, like most of the northeastern bosses, supported Catholic Al Smith of New York for president, a legendary figure who rose from the streets of New York City to the governorship of that state. But when FDR won the Democratic nomination for president in 1932, Hague promised to turn out the largest political rally in American history, and to FDR's amazement he did just that. In 1932, 1940, and 1944, FDR was heavily dependent on the huge Hudson County majorities that Hague delivered, which allowed the president to carry the swing state of New Jersey. Only in 1936 with his enormous national landslide was FDR not dependent on the Hudson County pluralities. Roosevelt, a patrician in his personal lifestyle, looked the other way at Hague's illegal activities, and his New Deal employment programs swelled the patronage ranks of the county machine. Hague, not the governor, was the go-to-guy in New Jersey, especially in the eyes of the Democratic president and the state leaders. (Dorsett, 1977). Although Hague was only one county chairman, he had enormous influence over the other Democratic chairs in Essex, Passaic, and Middlesex counties.

When state experts and out-of-state commentators speak of New Jersey county machines, corruption, and patronage, they are still referring to the world of Frank Hague and his successor John V. Kenney. Yet in some ways, Hague's influence has not been fully recognized. Novelist Frank O'Connor immortalized boss James Curley of Boston in his novel, *The Last Hurrah*, as the archetype urban machine leader, but, as FDR realized early on in 1932, Curley talked a good game; Hague delivered again and again. (Beatty, 1992; O'Connor, 1956).

The Republicans added their own county bosses to the mix in that period of time. The most well known were Arthur Vanderbilt in Essex County and the long-lasting Senator Frank "Hap" Farley, whose career spanned the period from 1941 to 1972. (Salmore and Salmore, 1998). Farley was supposed to have "held back" enough votes in the Atlantic City area to overcome the Democratic majorities in Hudson and Essex counties so as to elect the revered Clifford Case to the U.S. Senate in 1954.

It is a common historical judgment that the New Deal provided a system of entitlements that ironically destroyed the Democratic urban machines. The story in Hudson County, though, is much more complicated, as Hague astutely used federal programs actually to strengthen his machine. Also, it is often asserted that the role of the electronic media curtailed the sway of the machines by allowing candidates to go over the heads of the bosses to reach the people. (Rapport, 1961). But that is not necessarily so. In southern New Jersey, for example, George Norcross is still a major party figure, and Jon Corzine's large personal contributions to county organizations, in his words, were meant as much to undergird the county Democrats as to support the "causes" he believes in. Lastly, the ability of the Democratic bosses to pluck out of comparative obscurity men of the caliber of Richard Hughes and Brendan Byrne, for example, who became fairly good governors, speaks well of their judgment – at least some of the time. Back then, men and women of modest means could still climb up the political ladder with the help of political machines; it is now fairly hard for them to afford the world of media politics, especially in expensive media markets.

III. Taxation

The American Revolution was, to a large extent, fought because of taxes levied by the British Empire. Historically, Americans love liberty and deplore taxes. And nowhere has that disdain reached the level it has in the state of New Jersey. As has been seen, New Jersey state government in the nineteenth century was a modest affair, spending money mainly for prisons, for housing the insane, and for a few other nominal social services. As late as the twentieth century, the state really had a limited income stream provided by the taxes of the railroads and some other corporations. New Jersey politicians protected those interests to a large extent, because they paid the bills. Also the state gave little money to the localities in that period of time, and therefore demanded little of them in return – another reason for the intense parochialism that characterizes the state.

In the mid-1950s only three states, including New Jersey, had neither a state sales tax, nor a state income tax. Most of the revenues in New Jersey came from excise taxes and fees and some corporate taxes. Earlier, when a modest 2% sales tax was pushed in 1935 by Republican Governor Harold Hoffman, it was repealed after enormous popular outrage. Of course, property taxes rose, as did the use of public authorities to build turnpikes and other improvements through the use of bond issues. New Jersey consistently opposed a statewide income tax, even when supported by popular governors. In 1965, Governor Richard Hughes proposed such a tax in order to aid the cities, which were then in racial turmoil, but the Essex County Democratic leader opposed such a levy because of popular feelings, and consequently it did not pass the Assembly. Republican Governor William Cahill also had no support from his party leaders when he proposed an income tax. (Salmore and Salmore, 1998). After defeating Hughes' proposal for an income tax, the legislature, though, did approve a 3% sales tax in 1966, which exempted food and clothing. Cahill raised it from 3% to 5%.

Then in 1973, in the Robinson v. Cahill case, the state supreme court found that school funding relied too heavily on property taxes – so extensively that it was, in fact, unconstitutional. Democratic Governor Brendan Byrne, with the court's decision as a spur, moved for a broad-based income tax. The rate was a modest 2% to 2.5%, but the resentment was so staggering that Byrne had to wage a rather skillful public relations campaign to get reelected, and he had to explain contritely that he had abandoned his no tax pledge, which he made when he first ran for governor because of the dire circumstances. Republican Tom Kean, later running for governor, denounced the income tax, and then raised both income and state taxes when he was governor during the financially difficult early years of the 1980s. (Salmore and Salmore, 1998). No fate was more bitter for a tax-raising governor than that suffered by James Florio, who, on assuming office in 1990, had to deal with a huge deficit on top of other school funding problems arising from the beginnings of the Abbott v. Burke cases. The new governor proposed a major increase, doubling the state income tax to 7% and the sales tax to 7% Florio insisted that the revenues would be used to lower property taxes for all but the wealthy and to provide major funding for urban schools. The legislature made some changes in the proposal, and then passed the levies, and the statewide uproar was shrill and very pronounced. Even United States Senator Bill Bradley, who refused to comment on the increases, was almost defeated by a then-unknown Republican. Florio's party in the off-year races lost control of both of the houses of the legislature by substantial majorities and lost even the governor's home area of Camden. Eventually, Florio was defeated for reelection, clearly a casualty of the anti-tax forces. (Salmore and Salmore, 1998). Ironically, today, New Jerseyans are indeed being heavily taxed, often for programs and problems they had fled the cities to avoid.

The constitution of 1947 has provided New Jersey with a model constitution, and, in a departure from its early days, with one of the strongest governorships on paper in the nation. The governor is the only statewide elected official, and, increasingly in a post-World War II era, most states, including New Jersey, have been run by what are called "executive-centered coalitions." The governor has created the political agenda to a large extent, with occasional and important intrusions by a very activist state supreme court. It has been the governors who pushed for broad-based taxes to meet new needs.

Running against Florio was the woman who nearly defeated Bill Bradley, Christine Todd Whitman. Reared in a wealthy Republican family, her major campaign pledge was simply to cut taxes as President Ronald Reagan had done nationally. But unlike the federal government, the state government is mandated to balance its budget. Whitman defeated Florio in a very close election, and then proposed a 30% cut in the state budget. She merged some departments, abolished others, and pushed for reforms in the expensive state pension systems.

But to balance a precarious budget and to cut taxes, Whitman had the state recalculate assumptions about the pension funds and their growth rate. She also proposed a huge state bond issue to borrow money to close future gaps in the pension funds. Like her predecessors, Whitman had to wrestle with the increasing disparities in funding public education, as well as more court decisions challenging the current set-up. In addition, popular discontent focused on another perennial issue in New Jersey – auto insurance rates – which were heavily regulated and which, in the public mind, became associated with the state government. (Salmore and Salmore, 1998).

In her second election, Governor Whitman defeated Woodbridge mayor James McGreevey by only about 1% of the popular vote. Whitman was probably assisted more by name recognition than anything else, despite the growing animosity in both parties to her candidacy. So, New Jerseyans have historically hated taxes – except now they have considerable grounds for such a sentiment.

IV. Corruption in the Garden State

New Jersey media and political leaders insist that their state is comparatively more corrupt than others in the Union. I have argued elsewhere that this state is in fact comparatively clean, but the recent string of indictments in both parties by the federal attorney provides some support for continuing concerns. There are surely some egregious examples of corruption (and some rather petty ones as well), and so what explains them beside human venality and greed? It has been argued by the state's Chamber of Commerce, for example, that New Jersey's extreme localism and small government units, further non-accountability as well as multiple opportunities for corruption. There are over 1,000 taxing authorities in this state, which lends to numerous vantage points for influence peddling. If this is so, then many large mega-cities, like New York City and Chicago, should be relatively corruption free, and that surely is not the case. (Riccards, 2005b). There is also an argument made that New Jersey is one of the few states that allows multiple office-holding, a practice abolished at the federal level by the Founding Fathers in 1787. Plural office holding is supposed to bring with it conflicts of interest, but that is an unproven assumption.

New Jersey corruption is due to a large extent to a different set of opportunities. First, there are still large building developments, flexible zoning, and expansive economic opportunities in the profile of the state. Bribes, kickbacks, and extortion are handmaidens, often, of avoiding bureaucracy, non-competitive bidding, and endless rules and regulations. Second, interest groups and private agents "pay to play," that is, they contribute time, money, and connections to candidates, especially with the decline of old line parties and the costs of skyrocketing political advertising. People rarely give to candidates because of civic engagement; they seek to buy access, believing that access can (but not necessarily) lead to favorable action by elected and appointed officials.

Lobbyists have two major assets for elected officials – money, usually in the form of campaign contributions, and detailed knowledge of legislation and regulations. Money and knowledge are the great modern sources of power. New Jersey, like the federal government, has pushed for campaign regulations and public financing, but, at both levels, the changes have not won out. And the loopholes are large indeed. The county organizations and the state party committees have become, in a sense, fundraising arms of the candidates, especially incumbents or those in leadership positions. Frank Hague has been replaced by the $1,000-a-plate dinner.

Reformers have run hard into court decisions that express reservations about curtailing political expression, including the giving of money. Thus, First Amendment rights are pitted against clean elections. Which is more important for a functioning democracy? Hard corruption is easy to deal with – an official who takes $10,000 for favorable treatment by a builder or a product distributor – but what of a company that is one of the few in an area, and wins a non-competitive contract? Also, Americans have not been too enthusiastic about public funding for all elections. Who pays for elections, especially if we curtail the use of personal and family contributions to a candidate? And if we do not, are we saying that one must be rich – very rich – to play in the first place?

When reformers moved to crush machine politics, they accelerated the importance of interest group liberalism and its ability to influence public policy. This is only one of the unintended consequences of good government progressivism in New Jersey and at the federal level. Also "pay to play" is not simply about banks and railroads, it is the teachers' union, public interest advocacy groups, gun control advocates, and environmental clubs and agencies. Some associations may provide a more precious commodity than money – manpower to ring doorbells, mail appeals, staff phone banks on Election Day. That is why the unions have been so effective, especially the teachers' unions. Are they also paying to play? One of the largest structures on the right side of West State Street across from the state house is the headquarters of the New Jersey Educational Association. (Lowi, 1979; Riccards, 2005a).

Are our politicians less honorable as a group than corporate leaders, union leaders, lawyers, bishops, or college presidents? Power corrupts us all. What is critical is to establish checks and balances to curtail our lesser natures. Perhaps New Jersey needs a separately elected attorney general, an independent procurement administrator, an autonomous Federal Reserve-type board to oversee the expensive pension system and to set benefits without the interference of the politically myopic legislature or governor, and a long-term, non-reappointable inspector general looking at local contracts and zoning appeals. (Shorto, 2005).

V. Identity

It is clear that New Jerseyans do not have a sense of identity and pride the way that Texans or Massachusetts citizens do. For so long, the state seemed to revolve around Philadelphia and New York City, just as Ben Franklin observed a long time ago. Nonetheless, that same argument has been made that there is no sense of identity for New York as well. People identify with Brooklyn or Buffalo, but not with the state of New York. That lack of identity is even more reflected in the New Jersey regional news media. Coverage of state politics is very spotty, even among major newspaper outlets. Except for New Jersey public television, there is little prolonged exposure to New Jersey life, culture, and politics. Because the state's identity is lacking, there is little competition against the impulses of localism that are rampant in this state. One can see that reality in football, where local people are more excited about what happens Saturday afternoon at the Irvington High game than at the state university. This is not Illinois or Ohio or West Virginia. Perhaps the New York Jets and Giants have given New Jersey some refracted glory in football statewide, even with their New York names. (Karcher, 1998). If there is excessive localism revolving, now, mainly around the school system, a lack of strong statewide media outlets, and a part-time legislature, how can one understand the need for a statewide agenda and the consequences of a party's positions? The new Hall Institute of Public Policy is one of the few nonpartisan, non-advocacy think tanks in the entire state.

As Alan Karcher has shown, history and political circumstances explain much in the chronicle of this state. And so, too, does geography and demographics. But politics is important. It is a form of organized and usually civilized conflict, whereby opinions, organizations and ideas compete. The difference is that, in general, in a democracy, one's attention span is limited and one's information is inadequate, especially for complicated matters. Those limitations are even more apparent when a state lacks the institutional apparatus to command the public's attention and make it focus on stubborn facts and harsh alternatives. The problem with democracy is that it takes so much time, dedication, and work. That is why freedom is so in peril here and across the globe.

References

Baker v. Carr, 369 US 186, 1962.

Beatty, Jack. 1992. The Rascal King: The Life and Times of James Michael Curley, 1874 to 1958. Reading, MA: Addison-Wesley.

Bernstein, David. 1972. "William Livingston: The Role of the Executive in New Jersey's Revolutionary War." New Jersey in the American Revolution, II. Trenton History Symposium, 1993, 12-30. Based on his "New Jersey in the American Revolution: The Establishment of a Government Amid Civil and Military Disorder, 1770-81." Ph.D. Dissertation, Rutgers University, 1970

Dorsett, Lyle. 1977. Franklin D. Roosevelt and the City Bosses. Port Washington, NY: Kennikat Press, Chapter 7.

Ellis, Joseph. 2005. His Excellence. New York: Vintage.

Issacson, Walter. 2004. Benjamin Franklin: An American Life. New York: Simon and Schuster.

Karcher, Alan. 1998. New Jersey's Multiple Municipal Madness. New Brunswick, NJ: Rutgers University Press.

Lee, Richard. 2005. "The Propaganda Model Is Alive and Well in New Jersey." Hallnj.org website.

Link, Arthur. 1947. Wilson: Road to the White House. Princeton: Princeton University Press.

Lowi, Theodore. 1979. The End of Liberalism. New York: W. W. Norton.

McGreevey, Governor James E. November 2003. Speech to the New Jersey League of
Municipalities. Source: Richard Lee, Hall Institute of Public Policy-NJ.

O'Conner, Frank. 1956. The Last Hurrah. Boston: Little Brown.

Rapport, George. 1961. The Statesman and the Boss. New York: Vantage Press.

Reynolds v. Sims, 37 US 535, 1964.

Riccards, Michael P. 1987. A Republic If You Can Keep It: The Foundation of the
American Presidency, 1700 to 1800. Westport, CT: Greenwood Press.
Chapters 1 and 2.

Riccards, Michael P. 2005a. St. Vincent Martyr Parish: 200 Years of Faith. Marcelen,
MO: Walsworth. Chapter 1.

Riccards, Michael P. August 22, 2005b. "New Jersey and the Public Trust." Hallnj.org
website.

Salmore, Barbara G. and Stephen A. Salmore. 1998. New Jersey Politics and
Government. Lincoln, NB: University of Nebraska Press.

Shorto, Russell. October 2, 2005. "All Political Ideas Are Local."
New York Times. 58.

CHAPTER ONE

URBAN SPRAWL

By
Brendan O'Flaherty

Sprawl is a symptom. A host of state and federal policies encourage development that is too sparse, and activities that are too harmful to other people. We could all lead better lives if these policies were reformed. The current valid concern about sprawl gives New Jersey a good opportunity to make these reforms.

What reforms? To name a few: reducing homeowners' tax preferences, taxing paved land, instituting pay-per-mile motor vehicle insurance, encouraging parental sharing of school costs, replacing property taxes with land value taxes, imposing a double-strict liability standard for most traffic accidents, introducing pollution-based gasoline taxes, creating smaller urban schools, charging insurance fees for developments likely to be hit by floods and hurricanes, building better parks, implementing marginal cost pricing of water and sewer services, instituting highway congestion pricing, and performing statewide integration maintenance efforts. Many of these reforms would have the added bonus of relieving the state's current fiscal distress, and all of them would allocate our resources better.

Unfortunately, few if any of these reforms are now being discussed seriously. Instead of addressing these problems, our leaders are now addressing the symptoms. This will not work. Even if it could make the settled areas of the state smaller and denser (and it probably will not), the cost of doing so would be excessive. A lot of this excessive cost would be borne by poor people. Sprawl requires a broad-based approach, not a single-minded reliance on regulating new construction.

This essay begins with a general exploration of what people mean, and what I will mean, by the word "sprawl." Then I will discuss why sprawl has benefits, and why it has costs. After that will come a discussion of good ways to reduce sprawl, followed by a discussion of bad ways.

Section 1: What is it?

I have seen the word sprawl used many different ways, but always pejoratively and always referring to land use. So, in order to stay close to current usage, I will have to define sprawl as some sort of bad land use practice.

That is where the consensus seems to end. Sometimes sprawl means that metropolitan areas take up too much land (Toms River is too far from Newark for people to be commuting); sometimes it means that development is too sparse (townhouses are better than McMansions); sometimes it means that open land is better for the neighbors than development (building houses on the abandoned Kernan's Quarry parcel in South Orange was called sprawl). These possible definitions are different, and sometimes even contradictory. Sparseness and size are the same only if population is fixed, but population is hardly fixed. This is especially true in New Jersey, which is a small state with more people in either the New York or Philadelphia metropolitan areas. Moving vans go over rivers easily. Keeping Kernan's Quarry vacant makes South Orange sparser, and so these uses contradict each other. If the people who might live in Kernan's Quarry would live in Hunterdon County if it were to remain vacant, preserving the quarry makes the metropolitan area bigger, too.

Thus, common usage gives us no coherent definition of sprawl. There are two academic definitions (sparseness and size), and one colloquial definition (added congestion, broadly defined). The size definition does not seem to be a New Jersey issue. A size problem means that people are living in New Jersey who really should be living in Arizona or Fuji. These are problems we would generally call immigration problems of involving problems of barriers to moving to Arizona – not New Jersey problems. That is why I do not think about size as a New Jersey sprawl problem.

Thus, I take sprawl to mean either "excessively sparse development in a metropolitan area" or "excessively inharmonious land use patterns within a metropolitan area."

Both of these definitions have merit, and we will see that they are complementary. The sparseness definition seems to be most concerned with where the edge of development is located, while the congestion definition seems to be most concerned with what is happening inside the edge of development. The link is that you cannot get the edge of development to be in the right place unless the right things are happening inside the edge, and vice versa.

So we will pay attention to sprawl in both the academic sense and the colloquial sense.

"Excessively" is in both definitions to capture the pejorative aspect of "sprawl" in common usage. But I need to be more precise. Fortunately, neoclassical economics has a readily available way of making pejoratives explicit: the idea of potential Pareto improvements. A potential Pareto improvement is a change that makes some people better off, and maybe other people worse off, but the winners could compensate the losers for all of their losses, and still be better off than they were before the change. So, I will say that a land use pattern is excessively sparse if changing to some other, feasible, denser land use pattern would be a potential Pareto improvement.

What is really going on here? What are New Jerseyans really worried about when they say they are concerned about "sprawl?" This is an issue that has emerged in the last 10-15 years – even though cities have been spreading out in New Jersey since about 1860. Tables 1 and 2 provide a different look at what has been happening in New Jersey since 1990.

Table 1 shows that car usage has risen substantially. More, bigger vehicles are spending more time going faster on American and New Jersey roads.

Table 2 shows where the new people and new cars are going in New Jersey. The county with the greatest growth in population per square mile is Hudson; Union, Middlesex, and Bergen are the next three. For growth in household motor vehicles, Hudson is also the leader, followed by Middlesex, Bergen, and Somerset. The greatest growth per square mile has been occurring in Hudson and the near suburbs, not in the exurbs.

Now remember that "sprawl" is an issue for a large number of New Jerseyans – and only a small number of New Jerseyans live close to any edge of development. Thus, it seems that New Jerseyans mainly care about sprawl not because houses are being built in the Highlands, but because traffic is crawling, the mall is crowded, and property taxes are high – my colloquial definition. Notice that this inference explains why people in South Orange, for instance, use "sprawl" to complain about the development of Kernan's quarry. In common usage, sprawl is what is happening close to home, not at the edge of the metropolis.

Contrary to the scare stories, New Jersey is not running out of space. To fill up New Jersey even to the density of Essex County would require 46.6 million people, roughly the combined 2002 populations of Texas and Florida. At current growth rates, that will not happen for another 200 years or so. And remember that Essex has vast amounts of open space – the Big Piece meadows; South Mountain, Eagle Rock, and Mills reservations; the seaport and airport; the East Orange watershed and the Canoe Brook reservoirs. A large portion of Essex land is devoted to mansions in Short Hills, Essex Fells, Livingston, and North Caldwell.

The story, instead, is that resources are being mismanaged throughout the state, not just at the edge of development. That is why dissatisfaction is widespread. And that is why the remedies affect everyone.

Section 2: Why is density bad?

In keeping with common usage, I have *defined* sprawl as something bad: if it were not bad, it would not be sprawl. So if it exists in New Jersey, we should look for ways to get rid of it. But defining something does not make it real. To show that there is sprawl in New Jersey, you have to show not only that development is sparse, or that development is sparser than it used to be, but you also have to show that a denser alternative could make everyone better off (after suitable compensation). You cannot just say, "It's ugly."

Modern sparse development brings many benefits. Up until a hundred years ago, dense cities were killers: Urban historian, Paul Bairoch, concluded that in Western Europe and North America, "Around 1800-1830, life expectancy at age 15 was probably lower by some 20-30% in the city than in the country." (Bairoch, 1988).

While industrialization contributed to this difference, the main culprit was density. According to Wrigley (1969), "It was in the bigger cities that mortality was so very high. Many of these big cities were not heavily engaged in the new industries, but were administrative and commercial centers. Paris, Berlin, Marseilles, and Liverpool all had high death rates and low expectation of life though none was a typical product of the industrial revolution in a narrow sense. Wherever there were large cities there were slum areas with very high densities of population and severe overcrowding which allowed diseases like tuberculosis to spread very widely and exposed children and young people to a great range of infectious illnesses."

Survivors were wasted and stunted. American soldiers in World War I were shorter on average than their counterparts in the American Revolution, and urbanization is mainly responsible. Conscripts from Tokyo were among the shortest soldiers in the Japanese Army at the beginning of the 20th century.

Thus, public health reformers fought passionately to make cities less dense – through housing codes, parks, and transportation improvements, primarily. One of the goals in constructing the New York City subway, for instance, was to move people out of the Lower East Side and spread them out over the farmland of the Bronx and south Brooklyn. What planners today might call sprawl, reformers a century ago called health.

Cities, even outside the US, have been as healthy as the countryside for the last half-century, and so fighting disease is probably no longer a good reason to decrease density, although there is no guarantee that this happy situation will continue forever as new diseases emerge. (Both conventional warfare and terrorism continue to make cities more dangerous, however. The more dispersed New Jersey's population, the fewer the expected number of casualties from a terrorist attack or a bombing run.) The point is not that we should deconcentrate population further to cut tuberculosis rates; rather we should not automatically label any decrease in density as a disaster.

One of the best contemporaneous reasons to think that New Jersey neighborhoods are not excessively sparse is that many people like living, working, and playing in those environments – and they like it well enough to pay for a great many of the costs associated with this lifestyle. Many people like privacy; they like big backyards for their children or places to store a motorboat; they like roomy houses where they can invite a multitude of friends; they like working without elevators and having lunch on a lawn with their co-workers; they like driving; they like Home Depot, Seven-Eleven, and Target; and they like their mornings to be very quiet. Not everybody likes all these things; I do not, for instance. But many people do, and satisfying their desires is very important.

To be sure, people did not always live this way, but a big reason why is that they did not have the opportunity. Twentieth century inventions like trucks, powerful automobiles, frozen food, and television have made this lifestyle possible (and cheap). Glaeser and Kahn (2003), for instance, show that countries with less automobile access and higher gas prices have more compact cities. Lives in the 21st century should not resemble lives in the 19th.

Decentralized living has other benefits as well, besides the ability to live and work far from neighbors. High densities and slow growth appear to be correlated with racial segregation. (Glaeser and Kahn, 2003; Kahn, 2001); racial mixing is more common when people spread out.

Finally, it is not at all clear why we should be concerned about the loss of some alternative uses of land if sparseness makes metropolitan areas bigger. In general, the less land devoted to agriculture in the United States, the better. The federal government subsidizes agriculture heavily, and many crops are protected from foreign competition by tariffs and quotas. We would all be better off if farmers got lump sum payments from the federal government, so that they did not have to run their farms anymore, marginal farms could shift to more productive uses like housing or factories, and consumers were allowed to buy products from low-cost producers in places like Brazil and Ghana. This change would also reduce many forms of pollution. Less farmland is good news, not bad.

Section 3: Why we may not have enough density

Privacy, integration, gardens, freedom from infection, and having a place to store your motorboat are all fine things, and sparse metropolises probably make them easier to obtain, but they are only a few of the many fine things in life. Our policies may be giving us too much of these, and not enough of the other fine things.

I can make this argument without appealing to any special esthetic judgment. Rather I will show that various subsidies and taxes allow people to make decisions without realizing the full benefits and costs of those decisions. As a result, these decisions often lead to more costs, in the aggregate, than benefits. Preventing these ill-advised decisions is a potential Pareto improvement.

In this section I will show numerous policies that are leading people to make ill-advised decisions to gravitate to sparse environs. These decisions lead to sparser metropolitan areas. In other words, this section will show – indirectly – that there probably is sprawl in New Jersey, as I have defined it.

A. Driving

Through its motor vehicle insurance and tort liability policies, its rock-bottom gasoline tax, and its fetish about removing tolls, New Jersey has induced its motorists to drive far more than they should, and in times and places where they should not. The fixed cost of owning a properly registered and insured motor vehicle is high, but, once you have one, you are essentially free to cause all the havoc, delay, and destruction you please, while bearing only a tiny portion of the true costs of your activities.

Pollution, accidents, and congestion are the primary external costs that driving causes. We will discuss each in turn.

Motor vehicles now pollute less for each mile they are driven than they used to, but they still pollute. Small and Kazimi (1995) estimated average pollution costs per mile at about three cents in the early 1990s, with most of the harm arising from the effects of particulates on human health. Cars are somewhat cleaner today than new cars were in the 1990s, but the Small-Kazimi estimates omitted (intentionally) the cost of global warming. The costs of pollution in New Jersey are also likely to be above the national average, because New Jersey is densely populated, and, its residents are, relatively speaking, highly compensated. Some pollutants, particulates especially, do not travel far from where they are emitted, and so affect more people when the tailpipe they come from is in New Jersey than when it is in New Mexico. Since wealthier people are able to pay more for their health, you would also have to compensate New Jerseyans more than, for instance, New Mexicans, before they would voluntarily agree to be subjected to the same illnesses.

Thus, it does not seem unreasonable to think that the average mile driven in New Jersey causes three to four cents worth of pollution damage, with some driving causing much more harm. For a vehicle that gets 20 mpg, that works out to 60-80 cents per gallon.

The New Jersey gasoline tax is 14.5 cents a gallon (only Alaska, Georgia, and Wyoming had lower rates in 2005) (American Petroleum Institute), and the tax on diesel is 17.5 cents a gallon (six more states had lower rates). The federal excise tax is 18.4 cents a gallon. Thus, New Jersey motorists pay 32.9 cents a gallon for gasoline, 35.9 cents a gallon for diesel. They mainly have to pay less than the pollution damage they cause, and so they do not make the right decisions about how much to drive. Sometimes they drive when the aggregate harm is greater than their personal benefits.

This calculation, however, leaves out the costs of accidents. Driving is the main cause of accidents; accidents never occur between two parked cars. Any (one-car or two-car) accident could have been avoided if one of the drivers had stayed home; thus, each driver is a "but-for" cause of the accident, and each should bear the full cost of the accident. Otherwise, people will drive too much (and too carelessly).

Motorists buy insurance, so, in some sense, they bear some of the cost of the accidents, but they buy it in the wrong way – a way that does not give them proper incentives to exercise care. My argument is about efficiency, not equity. Once you have paid your insurance bill, you can drive as much or as carelessly as you want. Cohen and Dehejia (2003), in fact, show empirically that mandatory liability insurance, such as that in place in New Jersey, increases traffic fatalities.

To be sure, New Jersey motor vehicle insurance is not entirely without incentives for less driving and safer driving. But these incentives are very weak.

When you buy insurance, the company asks how long your commute is, and bases its rates partly on this information. But the categories they use are rather crude, the sensitivity of rates to this information is rather small, and almost no one ever verifies. Most importantly, trips to and from work accounted for only 17.7% of daily person-miles by private vehicle in 2001. (Hu and Reuscher, 2005, table 17). Insurance companies in New Jersey do not ask about non-work driving.

Insurance rates also depend on points, and points sometimes depend on accidents. But the incentives are a lot weaker than they should be. When I totaled a car worth $10,000, destroyed several sections of guardrail, and backed up traffic on I-81 for an hour, thereby adding at least another several thousand dollars to the cost of my mistake, my insurance rates went up by a few hundred dollars for a few years. If I had killed someone, the insurance consequences for me would not have been a lot worse.

So, while saying that New Jersey insurance provides no incentives for less driving or safer driving is not true, it is not a bad approximation.

What are the costs per mile of accidents? Like pollution, the costs vary by time and place. Night driving is more dangerous than day driving, and roads like Route 22 and Route 46 more dangerous than lightly traveled residential streets. Edlin estimates that an additional mile of driving generates 12.7-14.8 cents in accident costs at the average time and place in New Jersey. A mile in New Jersey gives you a lot more things to bump into than an average mile in the nation, and those things are more valuable. This cost is above and beyond the cost of pollution. It works out to almost $3 per gallon of gas.

Finally, there are congestion costs. What is relevant here are not the congestion costs that I bear as a driver, but the congestion costs I impose on other drivers. Not all driving in New Jersey is under congested conditions, but some of it is, and every driver who enters a traffic jam makes the experience worse for all the drivers behind him. Congestion can be very expensive. Pozdena (1988) for instance, estimated that a mile driven under congested conditions in the San Francisco Bay Area imposed about 65 cents worth of costs (delay and gas) on other motorists on central urban freeways, 21 cents a mile on suburban highways.

Congestion costs come in two varieties. First, there are what I call "pure bottleneck costs." Suppose that the number of vehicles that can pass over a particular stretch of road or pass through a tunnel in any minute – the rate of throughput – is fixed, but more drivers than that number want to pass over that stretch of road. Think of the Garden State Parkway when construction or an accident knocks out a lane, or the New Jersey Turnpike where it narrows in central Jersey, or the Goethals Bridge between New Jersey and New York, where six or seven lanes of traffic have to merge down to two. Once you reach the bridge or the roadwork or the point where the Turnpike narrows, you resume normal speed; the delay arises because you have to wait to arrive at the bottleneck.

With a bottleneck, if I go through at 8:48 A.M., I preclude your doing so; that is the cost I impose on the rest of the world. If I were vaporized, someone else would gain a lot by using my slot, or a lot of other people would gain a little by waiting slightly less or adjusting their schedules slightly. Bottleneck costs are probably the predominant ones in New Jersey; they are the traffic jams you can identify with a cause.

The other variety of congestion costs come from reductions in maximum throughput; I call these degradation costs. Every stretch of a road has a maximum throughput and an ideal speed. If very few cars are on the road, they can travel fast, but few of them will pass a line in the road in any minute, because there are not many of them. If very many cars are on the road, they will be packed in tightly, but they will not be able to drive fast, and so once again very few of them will pass a line in the road in any minute. Throughput is maximized at some happy medium of volume and density.

If traffic volume exceeds maximum throughput and another vehicle enters the road, gaps decrease and everyone has to slow down. If any vehicle were to be vaporized, everyone else could drive faster – that is the degradation cost of driving on a congested highway. Think of the mysterious slowdowns that sometimes occur on the Parkway, or the general slog of Route 22 or Route 46.

So drivers in New Jersey take many trips that they should not – trips where if they had to bear the full cost they would decide against it.

If driving is priced too low, then some decisions based on the opportunity to drive will be faulty. If people have to pay 20 cents a mile for pollution and accident costs, they are going to be more reluctant to live five miles from the nearest grocery store or school than if they have to pay only 1.6 cents per mile for gas tax. An employer will also be reluctant to locate her offices far from where her workers and potential workers live, if getting there will be very expensive for them.

B. Mass Transit

Virtually everything I said about cars applies to mass transit, too. When riders pay less than the social costs they impose, they take too many trips and induce developers to build metropolitan areas that are too sparse. Calculating the marginal social cost of a mass transit trip is hard, though, and explaining it would take up a great deal of space. Peak-hour commuters to New York probably pay well below marginal cost, but whether other riders do is not so clear. Since very few trips are made by mass transit, it is not a big issue in discussing sprawl.

C. Houses and Land

The way the federal government treats housing also encourages sprawl. Federal income tax rules, as presently constituted, pay upper income families, especially, to invest in housing rather than in other productive assets. As a result, the U.S. has too much housing; marginal long-term gross rates or return on investments in owner-occupied housing are well below gross rates of return for investments in corporate plant and equipment and in education, but people keep investing in owner-occupied housing because the taxes are lower.

Several provisions of the income tax code favor owner-occupied housing. The most important is the exemption for the imputed income from owner-occupied housing. Suppose you have $600,000. With that money you could either buy a nice house in New Jersey or corporate bonds that would pay you, say, 5% interest – $30,000 a year. With that $30,000 you could rent a very nice apartment at $2,500 a month – in a world without income tax. The correct decision is to buy the bond if you like the apartment better than the house, and buy the house if you do not. Let us say you like the apartment better – then you should buy the bonds.

But the income tax system may dissuade you from doing so. If you buy the bonds, you have to pay tax on the interest. Suppose your marginal tax rate is 33%. Then you have only $1,675 left over every month to rent the apartment. If you buy the house, you do not have to pay income tax on anything – even though the house is providing you, each year, with valuable services that you would otherwise have to buy on the market (this is what is meant by the "imputed" income). So unless you can find an apartment renting for $1,675 a month or less that you like as much as the $600,000 house, you will buy the house.

Notice that if you could strike a deal with the government to pay $12 a year for the right to buy the bonds and rent an apartment for $2,499 a month, everyone would be better off. The government would get $12 a year instead of the zero it gets when you buy the house, and you get to live in an apartment you like better than the house.

This argument applies at the margin, too. Suppose I have a choice between investing in bonds and using the proceeds to finance vacations, or investing in building an in-ground swimming pool. Even if I would prefer the vacations to the pool in a world without taxes, I may end up choosing the pool, because the federal government will tax the vacations but not the pool.

This argument ignores capital gains, but capital gains make the situation worse. Capital gains on most assets are taxed, but not on houses. (More precisely, it is almost impossible to owe capital gains taxes on the sale of a primary residence).

The deductibility of property taxes is commonly listed as a third way in which the federal tax system favors owner-occupied housing. Really, though, there would be nothing strange about this provision if the imputed income from homeownership were taxed. An office building, for instance, deducts property taxes from the income from the building – but the owner counts rents as income. The problem is that the imputed income from owner-occupied housing is not taxed.

A fourth way that the income tax system favors owner-occupied housing is indirect: through the exemption of imputed income from spousal services. If a woman hires a butler, he has to pay income tax on his earnings, but if she marries him and pays him an allowance, he can keep it all. Since spousal labor is untaxed, other goods that are complementary to spousal labor are purchased more than they would be in a neutral tax system. Spousal labor is used primarily for raising kids, shoveling snow, taking out garbage, and going shopping. Most of these activities are complementary to housing, and shopping is complementary to housing far from stores. So more housing is purchased than would be if spousal services were not exempt.

For all of these reasons, Americans, in general, and New Jerseyans, in particular, buy more housing than economists would like. Since homeowners tax preferences are more valuable for taxpayers in higher brackets and New Jerseyans are among the richest taxpayers in the nation, these subsidies are especially big in New Jersey.

There are three links to land use. First, part of the cost of housing is the cost of land. If the federal government pays for a large part of the cost of your land, you will buy more land. The more land people buy for their houses, the sparser the metropolitan areas. Voith (1999) has worked this argument out in detail and estimated the effect.

Second, part of the cost of owning a car is storing it somewhere, and houses store cars as well as people. So homeowners' tax preferences are garage-owners' tax preferences, too. Because houses make car storage cheaper, they make car ownership cheaper, and people own more cars. The more cars homeowners own, the more they drive, and the more of that driving is socially wasteful. Some homeowners' tax preferences exacerbate the problems we examined in subsection A.

Finally, to the extent that stay-at-home spouses spend their time driving around, the link to sprawl is direct. A household that had to pay the federal government 33% of the value of dad's time whenever he drove the kids to soccer practice, or 33% of the value of mom's time whenever she went to Home Depot, would think twice about living far from everything.

D. Medicaid

Medicaid rules also encourage people to buy and expand their ownership of housing. If an elderly couple lives in an apartment, and one partner (the "community spouse") has to spend virtually all of her assets before Medicaid will start paying for a nursing home. If they live in a house they own, the community spouse does not have to sell the house, although she still has to spend down the other assets. The more you put into a house you own, the less you are required to spend on a nursing home, and the more your children can inherit.

E. Employer-Provided Parking

Employer-provided parking does not count as workers' income. This encourages employers to provide free parking, even when workers would be happier with more money, instead. Free parking encourages driving, and driving encourages firms and workers to locate far from each other. Ninety-five percent of commuters who drive to work get free parking. (Shoup, 1997).

F. Fannie Mae and Freddie Mac

These two companies were originally started by the federal government, but are now private. They are mainstays of the secondary mortgage market: they buy mortgages from originators like retail banks and loan companies, and they sell securities backed by anticipated payments on the mortgages. In May 2005, Fannie Mae had about $1.5 trillion in mortgage-backed securities outstanding. (Fannie Mae, 2005, Monthly Summary, www.fanniemae.com-/ir/pdf/monthly/2005/053105.pdf), and Freddie Mac had about $1.2 trillion outstanding. (Freddie Mac, 2005, Monthly Volume Summary: May 2005, www.freddiemac.com/investors/volsum/pdf/ 0505mus.pdf).

Although there is no explicit statement that the federal government stands behind Fannie Mae and Freddie Mac securities, many investors believe that the federal government would step in if either were in danger of default. They are "too big to fail." As a result, investors are willing to lend money to these companies at lower rates. The lower borrowing rates allow the companies to make more profit, but they also partially translate into lower rates for borrowers. Passmore (2003) estimated that borrowers paid about $60 billion a year less in interest because of these guarantees. Thus the implicit guarantee diverts capital from more productive investments. This is another reason for over-investment in housing – and the attendant over-investment in land and garages.

G. Property Tax

The property tax in New Jersey consists of two separate taxes: a tax on the value of improvements and a tax on the value of the land. The tax on the land value does not cause sprawl; I will note in the next section why it is a very attractive tax. The tax on improvement value, however, causes sprawl.

The reason is fairly simple, and Brueckner, (2001) gives a more rigorous and sophisticated explanation. Development is a decision about how much capital to put on each piece of land. When improvements are taxed, the profit-maximizing quantity of improvements to put on each piece of land falls: three-family houses become more attractive than four-family houses, eighteen-story office buildings become more attractive than twenty-story ones. This is a distortion: the developer would be better off and the government no worse off if the developer could pre-pay all the property taxes on a three-family house and then be allowed to build whatever he pleased – a four-family house in particular.

Land with capital per unit than is optimal is my definition of sprawl; so taxes on improvements cause sprawl.

H. Antiquated School Systems

Historically, education has been a magnet that drew people into cities, towns, and other dense living arrangements. Paris, for instance, grew up as a college town, and it is hard to think about Beijing, New Delhi, Boston, or New York without thinking about their universities.

Dense cities have great advantages for elementary and secondary education, too. Children – small ones especially – are very hard to transport. The more children per square mile, the easier it is to assemble a class of any size, and the more different classes you can assemble, the greater the variety available for each student to choose among. In South Orange you can find both bilingual Mandarin and Montessori nursery schools within walking distance of the village center; most less dense towns probably have neither. Variety is valuable because kids have different interests, inclinations, and abilities, and parents have different goals for their children. The more variety, the better the final match is likely to be. Cities have natural advantages as places to educate children.

Those natural advantages, however, are wasted if the school systems in densely populated areas do not offer a rich variety of options. For this argument, the institutional form that that variety takes is not important: vouchers, charter schools, magnet schools, even curricular variety within a school building work equally well.

Measures that enforce uniformity within urban school districts therefore cause sprawl. I do not know how widespread such measures are. The most obvious example is high-stakes testing. If every school has to be the same, density loses its natural advantage.

I. Average Cost Pricing

Many regulated and governmental utilities in New Jersey engage in average cost pricing. The city of Newark, for instance, tries to set its water rates by adding up all its water-related costs, including overhead and debt service, and dividing by the volume of water it thinks it will sell. The Passaic Valley Sewerage Commissioners do the same thing. When the State sets rates for regulated public utilities, it often attempts to engage in a similar exercise, since this is how you arrive at an allowable expected profit.

These prices are the wrong prices to charge, and they lead to sprawl. The argument is basically the same as the argument about taxes on improvements. Prices should equal marginal cost rather than average cost. With marginal cost pricing, consumers will use all those units of service for which their benefits exceed the costs of a production, and no more. Average cost pricing keeps some consumers from enjoying services in a way that would make everyone better off. Suppose I spend $2 billion to build a bridge that only 20 people have any desire to use, and you are one of those people and are willing to pay a dollar to cross it. If I ask you for $100 million, I will not get it, and the services of the bridge will be wasted. But if I ask for 50 cents, I will get it, and the services of the bridge will not be wasted. Both of us will be better off than if I had asked for $100 million.

How does average cost pricing cause sprawl? Suppose a developer is trying to decide how many units of housing to build on a particular parcel. Under marginal cost pricing, the buyers of the houses that the developer builds will pay only for the additional loads they place on the utility systems. With average cost pricing, the house buyers will pay for those costs plus a share of the overhead and debt service. The more the developer builds, the greater the share of overhead and debt service her house buyer will be responsible for. Clearly she will build more sparsely, under a system of marginal cost pricing, because she is forced to pay for a greater share of overhead, and in effect, "punished" for density.

Average cost pricing makes metropolitan areas too sparse.

J. Flood and Hurricane Insurance

When a hurricane hits the shore, a disaster will be declared, and state and federal dollars will be used to help both communities and residences rebuild. No law says that this is how the state must respond, just as no law says that a hurricane will hit the shore in the next five years. But everyone knows both things will happen.

Building at the shore thus imposes costs on the state government. The more people build at the shore, (and the less sturdily they build), the more the state has to pay when the next bad hurricane hits. This is just like the external costs of driving or dumping garbage. As long as people who live in areas subject to natural disasters (the largest and most frequent disasters in New Jersey are hurricanes) do not pay actuarially fair insurance, and can expect disaster relief, too much development will occur in these areas.

K. Stormwater

Stormwater run-off causes a variety of harms. Floods can wreak havoc on structures and landscapes and endanger lives. Detritus of various kinds, including motor fuels/fertilizers, can be swept into water courses and pollute them. Diseases spread when biologically active waste, including material from septic tanks and sanitary sewers, gets washed throughout the state.

Nature delivers the rain, but does not determine what happens when it hits New Jersey. A good portion of the rain that falls on forests, farms, and open land gets absorbed in the earth and does not contribute to the immediate run-off. But rain that falls on pavements, roofs, and other impermeable surfaces runs off quickly and presents the kinds of hazards that we described above.

Pavement creates faster run-off, and faster run-off creates harm, and so New Jerseyans build and maintain more pavement (and other impermeable surfaces) than they should. To the extent that multi-story buildings produce less run-off per unit of housing or production, encouraging run-off like this creates sprawl.

Of course, no New Jersey developer would accept the simple description of current policies I gave above. Major developments today must meet stringent run-off standards and include all sorts of retention basins and other infrastructure to make sure that they do not cause flooding. But newly built major developments are only responsible for a small subset of the pavement in New Jersey.

The model ordinance that the New Jersey Department of Environmental Protection publishes, for instance, applies only to new developments that disturb more than an acre of land, and requires that only 80% of runoff in hard storm be retained.

More importantly, state regulations do not affect existing properties. My driveway is at least 40 years old, but it generates just as much run-off as a similar-sized driveway that was four days old. Any day I want, I can hire a contractor to rip it up and put down grass. Every day that I fail to rip it up is a day that I take a chance on flooding my neighbors and everyone downstream on the Rahway River. No government official has ever asked me to mitigate this hazard (in fact, ripping it out might get me in trouble for not maintaining an off-street parking space); no one has ever taxed me for it; and I suspect no one ever will. I will continue to wreak havoc.

L. Amenity Values

People enjoy being around forests, fields, and other open space, even when they do not own them. Development makes these people worse off, but the market does not force developers to recognize the costs they impose in this fashion. Thus, open space is too cheap, and too much of it gets used.

Just as all driving is not equally noxious, open space differs greatly in amenity value. Not a lot of research has been done on this topic. Kremer (2001), for instance, speculates that amenity values are greatest for land that can be seen from roads.

Nechyba and Walsh (2004) provide some evidence that what people value most highly are moderate-sized expanses of open space, reasonably close to their houses. Thus, it is not obvious whether proper accounting for the amenity values of open space would lead to sparser or denser metropolitan areas.

M. Crime and Flight-from-Blight

Instead of maintaining that some resources are over-used, another set of arguments maintains that NJ metropolitan areas are too sparse because some resources are under-used. These arguments are often called flight-from-blight: because cities like Camden, Newark, and Trenton are so crime-ridden and the schools are so poor, people are forced to build McMansions in Hunterdon County; fewer households would move to Hunterdon County if Trenton were safer and its schools better.

As stated, this argument is mainly wrong, but contains a grain of truth. It is wrong because, in the long-run, the population of Hunterdon County depends on how attractive Hunterdon is, relative to the rest of the world, not relative to Trenton. There are large numbers of people who do not have to live in New Jersey; they can live in New York, Pennsylvania, Florida, Nebraska, Santo Domingo, or Fiji. Blight in Trenton causes too few people to live in Trenton; it does not cause too many people to live in Hunterdon. That is why the stated argument is mainly wrong.

However, I have not defined sprawl as "too many people in Hunterdon." I have defined it as "too few people in Trenton." But I have not shown that crime and similar problems cause too few people to live or work in Trenton.

Some types of violent crime are highly concentrated in cities, murder and robbery especially. In 2003, 58.3% of New Jersey's robberies occurred in just eleven of the older cities, which contained only 14.5% of the population.

Camden reported 827 robberies, while Cherry Hill, with more jobs and a population only slightly less, reported only 40 robberies (New Jersey State Police, 2005). Crime also has been shown to reduce city population (Cullen and Levitt, 1999).

The missing step is whether reducing crime in cities would be a potential Pareto improvement. The fact that crime is higher in cities than in suburbs does not, by itself, indicate that it is too high. For instance, if you live in a city, walk to dinner, eat in a restaurant, and drink in a bar, and then walk home, you expose yourself to burglary (because your home is empty), robbery (because you are walking on the street), theft (when you lose sight of the valuables you are carrying), and assault (when somebody starts a fight at the bar). By contrast, if you live in a suburb, eat dinner at home, and drink on your patio, you expose yourself to none of these crimes.

The question about whether there is "too much" crime in cities is equivalent to the question of whether there are cost-effective strategies to reduce crime that are not being used now. That is an important question, but beyond the scope of this paper. If there are strategies like that, then, until they are implemented, New Jersey cities will be too sparsely populated.

N. Poor Governance

The argument here is similar to the argument about crime, but the data are even more meager. If the cities that should be most densely populated are governed more poorly than they should be, then these cities will be more sparsely populated than they should be. Surely the spectacle of Newark giving 24 acres of its most valuable land and over $240 million of its money to a team that sometimes plays hockey is enough to raise serious questions about the quality of governance. But this is just an anecdote, and one can easily accumulate anecdotes of poor governance from any quarter of the state – or of the nation. No good evidence is available on this question.

State law, however, has some systematic biases that may make older cities too sparse. New Jersey has two different laws about how municipalities dispose of real property they own. One of them, the Local Land and Buildings Act (NJSA 40A:12-1 et seq.), covers most towns most of the time. It prescribes a careful bidding process to make sure the town gets the highest price. Of course, auctions also have a tendency to steer property to its most valuable use and away from cousins of city council members. The other law, the Local Redevelopment and Housing Law (NJSA 40A:12A-1 et seq.) (LRL), gives the town extraordinary discretion in choosing who will receive land, and what they will pay for it. The LRL was part of urban renewal in the 1950s and 1960s, and so was designed primarily for the older cities. Its use has spread considerably, but mainly to older suburbs like Lodi and Bloomfield. Before the LRL can be invoked, an area must be found to be "blighted" – a term of art where being densely developed, and developed a while ago, helps make an area qualify.

You can look at the LRL either idealistically or cynically, but either view leads to the conclusion that it makes cities too sparse. If you think New Jersey cities are governed by philosopher-kings, the LRL says that those philosopher-kings can encourage any activity they think is in the public interest, but the easiest and, often, only way they can encourage it is by giving away free or reduced-price land that cannot be resold easily. As a result, you will get too much land being given. A town that wants to encourage restaurants, for instance, cannot subsidize them directly and let them decide how best to combine productive inputs; it has to give them free land. The result is restaurants that use more land than they would if the town could subsidize them directly. That is sprawl.

On the other hand, if you think New Jersey towns are run by crooks who are motivated only by a desire to take care of their friends and by fear of going to prison if they are caught, you will still reach the same conclusion. All evil has to flow through the narrow channel of land giveaways. A town that wants to make a restaurant owner rich cannot hand the treasury over to him directly and let everyone operate productively; it has to give him free land. That is still sprawl.

O. Too Much Zoning

Another governance issue concerns suburbs, especially those that are mostly, though not completely, developed. Here, the problem is town governments that are responsible to the majority of their constituents, and zone at densities that are too low. Fischel (1985) has developed this argument at greatest length.

The basic problem here is that zoning is not fungible. Think about a highly developed town and a large undeveloped parcel. If that parcel were to be developed intensely, many newcomers would benefit from being in the town. Let us assume that they would benefit a great deal – they would be closer to their jobs and to recreation areas, their children would gain by being in a better environment, they would like living in the well-designed new houses the developer was planning. Since they would benefit a great deal, they would be willing to pay a great deal, and so the developer would be willing to pay the parcel's current owner a great deal. So, prospective newcomers would gain a great deal from intense development, and these benefits are manifested in the high price the current owner would get for the parcel.

On the other hand, most current residents would probably lose something from intense development. Immediate neighbors might lose the opportunity to walk in the woods, and they might be placed in greater danger of flooding. Most people in town would encounter more traffic, and schools would be more crowded. Crime might rise. If the newcomers were less wealthy than the current residents, average school test scores might decline, the quality of stores might decrease, and the address might lose some of its cachet.

The newcomers could provide external benefits, too. The town center might now be able to support a Thai restaurant or two pizzerias, a chess club might form, and the local high school might add electives and enjoy more athletic success. With more eligibles to choose among, voters might be able to elect better town officials. Babysitters and store clerks, too, might be easier to find. These possible benefits are not usually cited in these discussions.

If the benefits of the newcomers exceed the losses to the current residents, intense development is a potential Pareto improvement. But if town officials represent their constituents and obey the law, the project will not be built. If zoning could be sold, the newcomers (through their representative, the developer) could buy the right to live in the town, compensate the current residents, and everyone would be better off. Since that is not legal, the town will be sparser than it should be.

Where the newcomers go, because they cannot complete this Pareto-improving deal, is immaterial. In the short run, they are probably more likely to move further out than to go to Newark or Camden, and, in the long run, they are almost certain to end up in Westchester, Iowa, or Guangzhou. In the long run, partially developed suburbs end up sparser than they should be, and that is sprawl.

Of course, development professionals might object that developers have a wide variety of ways to make the payments I claim are impossible – that zoning can be sold after all. Towns can charge impact fees, require all sorts of work to be done off-site as well as on-site, or collect bribes. But these mechanisms are all just extremely clumsy imitations of the kind of smooth, direct payments that theory requires in this case to avoid sprawl. Impact fees cannot compensate for the costs that have nothing to do with public capital; developer-provided facilities are likely not to be worth as much to every resident of the town as the money that went into building them; and bribes are wrong. Saying that these transactions create a market for zoning is like saying your promises to your cat are legally binding contracts.

After all, if you could buy and sell zoning, then zoning would have no impact on the physical configuration of the state.

P. Segregation

New Jersey includes some of the most racially segregated metropolitan areas in the nation. Out of the 50 metropolitan areas in the nation with the largest black populations, the Newark metropolitan area (Essex, Union, Morris, and Warren counties) ranked fifth in black-white residential segregation. Of the 50 metropolitan areas with the greatest Hispanic populations, Newark ranked second in Hispanic-(non Hispanic) white segregation, Bergen-Passaic ranked eighth, and Middlesex-Somerset-Hunterdon ranked 17th. New Jersey has five metropolitan areas – the three mentioned plus Jersey City (Hudson County) and Trenton (Mercer County) – and all of them have greater Hispanic-white segregation than the national average. Only Middlesex-Somerset-Hunterdon and Trenton have lower black-white segregation than the national average, but only 20% of the New Jersey African-Americans who live in metropolitan areas live there (Logan, 2001; Lewis Mumford Center, 2005).

Income differences are responsible for very little of this segregation. Table 3 shows that segregation among middle-income households in New Jersey is just as great as segregation in the total population. If income differences caused racial segregation, households at every income level would be pretty much integrated. More sophisticated analyses (e.g. Sethi and Somanathan, 2001; Bayer et al., 2004) come to similar conclusions: black-white segregation would not be greatly reduced by income equalization.

For land-use purposes, it is also important to note that segregation is not random. African-American neighborhoods, in particular, tend to be closer to the center of metropolitan areas than neighborhoods predominantly inhabited by non-Hispanic whites. Data to support this contention is available on a national level (Massey and Denton, 1993). I have not seen formal calculations for New Jersey, but this state does not appear to be an exception to the national generalization.

There is good reason to think that a more integrated residential pattern would be a potential Pareto improvement.

For African-Americans, abundant evidence indicates that centralization and segregation produce harmful effects. Growing up in a more segregated metropolitan area makes African-American young adults less likely to complete high school, more likely to be single parents, and more likely to be without employment (Cutler and Glaeser, 1997). Segregation and centralization also make African-American women more likely to bear low-birth-weight (LBW) babies (Ellen, 2000b).

Centralized neighborhoods make it hard for many African-Americans to commute to the jobs they are most likely to get. Centralization probably makes finding those jobs hard, too. For instance, even though East Orange is very close to the center of Newark, the average East Orange worker had a commute of 33.6 minutes in 2000 – as opposed to 29.4 minutes for the average worker in Morris County and 33.5 minutes for the average worker in Hunterdon County.

Very little evidence that I am aware of indicates that segregation and centralization of minorities makes whites better off, although integration appears to make whites more likely to be robbery victims. Living in less segregated metropolitan areas has no effect on white education, single-motherhood, employment, or LBW experience. Nor does having a pool of minority labor nearby seem to help employers and landowners in the central part of metropolitan areas. Mills (1985) found that jobs left central cities faster in the metropolitan areas where African-American residences were more centralized.

The pattern of segregation and centralization was not produced by a neoclassical market, and is not maintained by one. Therefore, we cannot start with a presumption that no government intervention can improve upon it. It was created by terrorist attacks on blacks entering white neighborhoods, by realtor cartels and federally mandated underwriting standards, by sloppily drawn racial covenants, and by the concentration of public housing for blacks in black neighborhoods. The pattern is maintained, in part, by continuing coercive activities to keep minorities out of some white neighborhoods, but largely by externalities. The race of a family moving into a neighborhood in New Jersey affects many other families' willingness-to-pay to live in that neighborhood, and so there is no reason to believe that laissez-faire will optimally allocate families to neighborhoods.

The neighborhoods immediately surrounding the center of a major American metropolitan area are a scarce and valuable resource. They should be densely populated by households for whom access to the center is most valuable (for either work or fun or both), and for whom the costs of density are lowest, relatively speaking. Some of these people are rich, and some of them are poor. It is almost impossible to believe that all of them are of the same race.

How does this situation affect sprawl? One major effect may be to make these central neighborhoods less dense than they would otherwise be. If race and ethnic origin are the criteria for entry into the neighborhoods, rather than skills and proclivity, then many of the families that live in these neighborhoods will not take advantage of the unique advantages they offer, and infrastructure designed to exploit those advantages will not be developed.

Consider mass transit for instance. Mass transit works best when large numbers of passengers want to travel from about the same origin to about the same destination at about the same time. If the Weequahic neighborhood in Newark is full of people who live there because of its convenience to downtown Newark, bus service will be frequent and fast (because expresses will be popular). This service will attract even more of the people who work in downtown Newark, or who enjoy the arts there, and also enhance the attractiveness of downtown Newark. These households will need few cars.

But in fact, only 44% of workers from Weequahic (zip code 07112) work in Newark, and bus service is poor. In all, only 41% of workers who live in Newark work in Newark. (By contrast, 92% of the workers who live in New York City work in NYC; 77% of workers who live in San Francisco work in San Francisco.)

Since there is no great residential concentration in Newark of people who work in Newark, there is no great concentration anywhere, and no opportunity for downtown Newark to benefit from superior mass transit. (This is one mechanism for the Mills correlation between black residential centralization and job suburbanization.) The entire Newark metropolitan area is less dense than it would be if race were less important in determining where people lived.

Of course, an argument can also be made that segregation and discrimination make metropolitan areas denser by constricting African-American and Hispanic opportunities to buy housing. In this view, discrimination in mortgage markets makes it hard for minorities to buy land-intensive single-family houses; and realtor discrimination and fear of harassment keep minorities out of low-density neighborhoods on the fringe of the metropolitan areas. Discrimination constricts minority residential demand; if minorities had the same opportunities that non-Hispanic whites enjoy, they would spread out like everybody else.

I have some doubts about the force of this argument. If segregation were created primarily by the constriction of minority demand, then quality-adjusted housing prices in minority neighborhoods should be greater than quality-adjusted housing prices in mainly white neighborhoods. Before 1960, this was probably the case. After 1970, most studies have found the opposite: that housing costs more in white neighborhoods than in minority neighborhood (Chambers, 1992; Cutler, Glaeser; and Vigdor, 1999; Gablinger, 2003). These studies are not definitive, since many minority neighborhoods have characteristics like very few, if any, mainly white neighborhoods. But it is pretty clear that in New Jersey, at this time, there is no premium for living in a minority neighborhood. The predominant form of discrimination seems to be the extraordinary unwillingness of whites to think about moving to neighborhoods like Weequahic or towns like East Orange, not the difficulties that minorities face in moving to white neighborhoods. Since whites outnumber minorities and outspend them in the housing market, a conclusion like this is quite plausible.

Thus, it appears that more integrated residential patterns would probably reduce sprawl, but no one can be sure.

What Should Be Done?

Thus, we have seen that many ill-advised policies and practices make metropolitan areas sparser than they would otherwise be. What should be done is obvious; the bad policies should be replaced by better policies. In this section I will outline a few of these better policies.

Will these better policies result in more compact development? Probably, but I am not sure whether the land-use difference they will make is great. Nor do I care. If all of the best policies were implemented and New Jersey grew only a tiny bit less sparse, it would demonstrate that sprawl was a small problem to begin with, not that stronger policies were required. Policies are the problem, not density.

The goal is not to find policies that make development less sparse. Such policies are easy to find: randomly executing motorists on the southern stretches of the Garden State Parkway, for instance; or carpet-bombing new developments in Hunterdon County; or never allowing another new sewer hook-up. The goal is to find policies that make life better.

A. Traffic Accidents

Most two-car accidents could have been avoided if EITHER driver had acted differently. Even if one driver acted in a clearly negligent fashion and the other driver drove alertly and carefully, no accident would have occurred if the careful driver had stayed home and played with the cat instead of venturing forth to pick up a pizza for dinner. So, even the more careful driver should be responsible for the full cost of the accident; otherwise he will lack the correct incentive to stay home and play with the cat.

The legal standard that holds both parties responsible for the full cost of the accident is called "double strict liability." By contrast, the current standard in New Jersey, "comparative negligence," says, essentially, that you are free to crash into anyone at all, provided that the other party is more reckless than you are, and your driving is not absurd. Establishing double strict liability is the first stop to meaningful motor vehicle insurance reform.

Since, under double strict liability, each party pays the full cost of an accident, money is left over after everyone has been compensated. What happens to this money? To get people to drive the right amount, what happens to this excess does not matter, as long as it is not used in any way that encourages driving. The obvious solution is to give the excess to the state or local governments reduce distorting taxes, like those on improvements. Under some circumstances, the fund of excess payments is exactly enough to pay for construction of an optimally safe road system, freeing funds now used for road construction for other purposes.

Other aspects of motor vehicle insurance should be reformed, too, even if double strict liability is not implemented. The treatment of traffic deaths is particularly appalling. If your negligent driving kills someone, you are liable for the financial losses and the grief that the decedent's survivors suffer, but you are not responsible for the loss that the decedent himself suffers from having his life cut short. The difference is not trivial. Negligent drivers or their insurance companies generally pay under a million dollars for traffic deaths, while well-developed literature in economics shows that, in making risky decisions, modern Americans act as if they valued their lives at a $5 million-$7 million (Aldy and Viscusi, 2003). That is the magnitude of the penalty that drivers involved in fatal accidents should pay.

Who would get this money, since the decedents, is no longer around to receive it? Again, receipt does not particularly matter. To get incentives right, it is more important to give than to receive. But this money could also go to state and local governments.

The final problem with New Jersey motor vehicle insurance is the treatment of pain and suffering. The pain and suffering that both parties endure is a real cost of the accident, but in many cases the parties to an accident do not have to pay for it.

In particular, even without double strict liability, even if I negligently hit a motorist who has elected "verbal threshold" insurance coverage, I will not be responsible for that motorist's pain and suffering. Her insurance company will not pay her for it, and so will not seek recovery from me. I should have to pay for her pain and suffering no matter what her relationship with her insurance company is. She should have the right to waive receipt of this money, but she should not have the power to remove my obligation to pay it.

Would these reforms make motor vehicle insurance cheaper? Almost certainly no. But they would reduce accidents, especially if they were accompanied by the insurance reforms described below, and they would reduce taxes. The combination of fewer accidents and lower taxes would more than compensate motorists for more expensive motor vehicle insurance.

B. Pay-Per-Mile Motor Vehicle Insurance

Motor vehicle insurance should depend on how much you drive and what conditions you drive under. Two technologies for implementing pay-per-mile insurance have been proposed.

Pay-at-the-pump is the older proposal. Every gallon of gas would come with insurance coverage for the driving it empowers. When you buy the gas, you buy the insurance. Different risk classes of drivers would pay different rates per gallon. This could be arranged through credit card sales. Your per-gallon insurance charge could be encoded on your credit card. If you paid cash, you would be treated as a 17-year-old male. Liability rules could discourage low-risk drivers from filling the cars of high-risk drivers.

Conceivably, gas stations in different parts of the state could levy different per-gallon insurance charges to reflect geographic variation in accident rates. But since most motor vehicles can drive from High Point to Cape May on a single tank of gas, it is not clear that meaningful geographic variation could be achieved. Out-of-state motorists and out-of-state gas stations would also present a challenge unless neighboring states undertook the same reform.

One additional advantage of pay-at-the-pump is that it eliminates the problem of uninsured motorists. Some motorists would still be uninsured, but their cars would not go anywhere.

The more modern technology uses global positioning systems (GPS) to monitor directly the mileage of insured vehicles. Several insurance companies have actually implemented GPS technology on a small-scale basis. Crossing state lines is not an issue with GPS, and many important refinements can be made. Night driving, for instance, is much more dangerous than daytime driving, and GPS can make that distinction.

If pay-per-mile is such a great idea, why have motor vehicle insurance companies not adopted it on their own? One reason is that much of the technology that could make it work well is relatively recent (probably some of the most crucial technology has not been invented yet). A deeper reason is that, without double strict liability rules, individual insurers have almost no incentives to rein in driving by their relatively safe drivers. These drivers will be involved in many accidents that pay-per-mile could eliminate, but those accidents will mainly involve cars insured by other companies. Without double strict liability, a large portion of the benefits from reduced driving by any company's insured motorists will accrue to the benefit of other companies. Double strict liability and pay-per-mile work together.

Edlin (2002) estimates that, in New Jersey, the combination of double strict liability and pay-per-mile insurance (even without a night differential) would produce a net efficiency gain of about $1 billion a year. Gasoline and insurance would cost more for most people, but the benefits from lower taxes and fewer accidents would be greater.

C. Gasoline Tax

The gasoline tax is probably best used as a tax on pollution, even though it is a fairly crude instrument for this purpose. (Capital costs for roads probably should be paid for from the other half of double strict liability, congestion payments, and possibly land taxes. Because road damage depends on the cube of weight per axle, repairs should be financed from truck and bus gasoline taxes.) This would make the tax 60-80 cents a gallon, as compared with the current 32.5 cents a gallon.

It may also be possible to improve this tax. Because there are large differences among cars in pollution per gallon, those who buy gas with credit cards could receive discounts for driving cleaner (per gallon) cars. These differences could even be verified in the regular bi-annual emissions testing process.

If GPS for insurance caught on, drivers could also get rebates on their pollution tax payments for driving under conditions where their emissions were less costly. Probably this would mean that burning a gallon of gas on crowded city streets would be more expensive than doing the same on empty country lanes, since some pollutants do not travel far, and the most costly aspect of pollution is its effect on human health. I do not know whether this differentiation would increase or decrease population concentration: driving in cities would be less attractive, but breathing in cities would be more attractive. As usual, though, my ultimate concern is well being, not land use.

D. Congestion Pricing

The degradation costs of congestion could be eliminated fairly easily by intelligent traffic engineering. Traffic is metered onto freeways in California, for instance, and into the Route 46 circle in Netcong. General application of more up-to-date versions of this technology could probably eliminate degradation congestion from New Jersey highways. Once you got on the Garden State Parkway or Route 287 you would travel at a good speed – but you might have to wait to get on. Pure bottleneck congestion would replace degradation congestion.

The technology to address pure bottleneck congestion, which we think of even now as the predominant form in New Jersey, also exists: congestion pricing. Congestion pricing requires that tolls vary smoothly so that each driver pays the social cost of her trip – the delay she imposes on everyone behind her, which would be eliminated if she decided not to go. Congestion pricing eliminates waiting, just as a system of reservations at a desirable restaurant eliminates waiting. The value of time wasted on waiting is converted to money that the toll authority collects and then can use for good purposes (or bad). (Arnott, de Palma, Lindsey, 1994.)

Various forms of congestion pricing are being used throughout the world. London and Singapore have crude restrictions on rush hour travel, while more sophisticated systems are in use in Minnesota, Houston, San Diego, Orange County, Norway, and France. Airlines and football teams (it costs a lot more to get into the stadium when the Giants are playing than when they are not) have been using congestion pricing for decades.

The purpose of tolls is not to make drivers pay for the roads, but to make them pay for the costs they impose on other drivers. My driving on the Parkway today does not make the construction of the Parkway either more or less expensive. Therefore the cost of constructing the Parkway should be irrelevant to my decision whether to go to the Shore today. Accordingly, tolls should be zero when roads are not congested.

Tolls, of course, should be collected by high-speed EZPass, as they are, for instance, at the new toll plazas on the Garden State Parkway. New Jersey is only about a decade behind the times with this technology. There is no reason to have any toll barriers.

What about drivers without EZPass? Essentially, they should be subjected to large fines for driving on tolled roads. You cannot drive an ox-cart or ride a bicycle through the Lincoln Tunnel or down Route 80. You cannot even drive a car without headlights, brake lights, or mufflers. You should not be able to drive a vehicle without EZPass either. Out-of-state drivers or those who fear Big Brother should be able to buy smart cards at the nearest gas station (you cannot drive on the Turnpike without gasoline, either).

What effect will congestion pricing have on sprawl? Probably none, directly. Trips will cost more money but take less time at peak hours; and off-peak will just be cheaper. Indirectly, though, reducing the costs of congestion makes dense development easier.

E. Mass Transit

If drivers bear the full marginal costs of their trips, there is no reason for mass transit riders not to do the same (unless collection costs are too high). New Jersey Transit might still lose money, which probably should be raised through taxes on land near train stations and bus stops, but not that much. Fares should act like congestion tolls – much bigger than they are now during peak hours, and essentially nothing off-peak. This is almost the exact opposite of what happens now, since most peak riders buy monthly tickets and essentially ride for free.

F. Homeowners' Tax Preferences

The obvious solution here is to repeal homeowners' tax preferences, a reform that would be very popular with economists. At the very least, they should be limited to households with minor children. These are federal issues, however.

In the absence of federal action (a fairly safe assumption), New Jersey can try to correct for some of the inadequacy of the income tax. For instance, the state income tax can recognize imputed income from owner-occupied houses and tax it, possibly at rates higher than regular income is taxed. Again, families with minor children might be exempted.

New Jersey might also tax capital gains on houses. This is an especially good revenue source, because it is close to a land tax. The New Jersey tax should probably be at the federal capital gains rate. One might object that house capital gains are already taxed through higher property taxes (if towns revalue property fairly frequently, which they do not), or that estimating capital gains net of home improvements would require too much paper work. An alternative might be to assume that, every year, every house in a town appreciates at the same rate, and tax this capital gain every year (or allow homeowners to deduct the loss). This approach addresses the property tax issue, because an individual's property taxes increase only to the extent that her property appreciates in value faster than the town average. The administrative burden would be considerably less, though not insubstantial, since the state would have to estimate only 566 numbers, and the law of large numbers would increase the relative accuracy with which these numbers were estimated. Annual payment would reduce the shock and make the tax more predictable, but there is no reason why homeowners might not be allowed to opt to defer payment until a house was sold.

The Medicaid issue should be resolved by allowing the community spouse to protect a fixed asset amount that is independent of whatever house she currently owns or rents. Such a policy removes the incentive to own housing rather than other assets but allows the community spouse to maintain her independence. The amount should be something like the median purchase price for a one-bedroom apartment in the county or metropolitan area. Those who wanted to stay in owner-occupied housing of greater value would have to reduce their equity to this level through mortgages or liens. Renters could keep this money in a bank account or other investment vehicle.

G. Parking

California addressed the incentives for driving to work through a "parking cash-out program." In 1992, that state required certain employers to offer workers a choice between free parking and cash. Cash-out substantially reduced the number of solo drivers and substantially increased ride-sharing and mass transit usage. Women and minorities gained the most (Shoup 1997). New Jersey should imitate California.

H. Land Taxes

Since taxes on improvements lead to sprawl and taxes on land do not, taxes on improvements should be reduced and taxes on land raised. This is an old idea; Henry George espoused it in *Progress and Poverty,* the best-selling secular book of the 19th century, and was almost elected mayor of New York City in 1886. Australia, New Zealand, Taiwan, and some cities in Pennsylvania, for instance, tax land more heavily than improvements. Oates and Schwab (1997) found that taxing land more heavily in Pittsburgh contributed substantially to dense development.

In New Jersey, land tax is probably a more pressing issue in cities than in suburbs. To a large extent in developed suburbs the property tax acts like a land tax, because land is a high proportion of a property's value, and the extent of improvements is governed as much by the zoning code as by the market (Fischel, 1998; Hamilton, 1975). In New Jersey's cities, neither condition obtains.

Therefore, the New Jersey constitution should be amended to allow cities to tax land at higher rates, and funding should be given to Rutgers University to improve assessments of land.

I. Better Schools

The recent implosion of the state's bizarre effort to buy land and build huge new schools in Abbott districts provides an opportunity to start over and build smaller schools. If there is another round of funding (which seems likely to be required by the Supreme Court ruling), it should concentrate on smaller schools. Aside from taking advantage of what cities actually offer, smaller schools reduce the amount of contiguous land that has to be acquired, and so reduce the potential for skullduggery. Perhaps the next program could be constrained to retrofitting existing buildings (including those not originally built as schools), and purchasing single parcels. If you have to acquire multiple parcels and demolish buildings, the school you are building is probably too big.

The state should also drop its subsidies for student transportation. The least painful way of doing this is to freeze the amount each school board is receiving at its current level.

J. Marginal Cost Pricing

Whenever possible, the state and municipalities should move away from average cost pricing, especially for water, since many land use arguments are about preserving land for water. (Preserving land for water that should not be used makes no sense, and without good prices, New Jersey is not likely to be using the right amounts of water.) Public authorities are among the major purveyors of water and the major treaters of sewage, and so could adopt marginal cost pricing almost immediately.

K. Water

Water is a valuable resource, but not infinitely valuable. The average value of water consumption is much greater than the marginal value of water consumption; some uses of water are necessary for survival while others are close to frivolous. The latter are more affected by small changes in price and availability than the former. The latter also use more water than the former: lawn care uses more than 40 times as much water as direct human consumption.

Clean water can be produced by many different technologies. Seawater can be desalinated, moderately dirty water can be purified, used water can be recycled, and pure water can be piped from North Jersey, Canada, or anywhere in between. We do not have to use the same technology we used in 1950.

Marginal cost pricing of water is very important. In a drought, the marginal cost of water is very high: water I use today may not be available for life-saving purposes next month, or it may have to be replaced by water trucked in from Canada. That is why the price of water should be very high in a drought. Water drawn from an aquifer that is not being replaced may also be very costly, and should be priced accordingly. Insurance can be provided, either publicly or privately, to people who are worried about sharp spikes in water prices.

Most importantly, marginal cost pricing encourages conservation before and during droughts. Prices rise gradually as conditions worsen, encouraging people to start conserving before a drought emergency, when they would normally be told to stop watering their lawns. The more conservation, the less capacity is needed. Since per capita water consumption is rising slowly, if at all, indicating that New Jersey population is not growing fast. In addition, New Jersey has lost forever many water-intensive manufacturing industries, so there is no need for significant growth in water supply capacity. With appropriate conservation, there might be no growth whatsoever in per capita water consumption for many years.

But even with no growth in total capacity, it is not at all obvious that we should keep using the water supply technology of a century ago. Even without scientific progress, the right technology to use at any moment depends on the relative prices of the possible inputs at that time.

A century ago, pipes were expensive, and land 10 or 20 miles from major cities was very cheap. The relative prices of pipes and nearby land are radically different today. So it is not obvious to me that we should continue getting water from the same places and in the same ways that our great-grandfathers did. We do not get food or fuel or wood from the same places we did a century ago; why should we still get water that way?

The city of East Orange is an interesting illustration. East Orange owns about 2,300 acres in western Essex County and eastern Morris County that it uses for water. Land in Short Hills, Livingston, and Florham Park, the relevant towns, sells now for at least $20 per square foot. So East Orange could sell its land for around $2 billion, invest this money at a 5% rate of return, and have $100 million a year to replace the water it was getting. What could it do with $100 million? Newark is four times as populous, and has a lot more industry, including Anheuser-Busch, but collected less than $35 million in 2004 – RETAIL – for all the water it used. So for $10 million or $20 million a year, East Orange could probably purchase wholesale all the water it uses now (possibly even from Newark, since the current combined populations of Newark and East Orange are about 100,000 less than the 1950 population of Newark). The resulting savings would almost be enough to eliminate the property tax in East Orange forever.

The purpose of this illustration is not to argue that East Orange should sell its entire watershed tomorrow. The purpose is to show that the people of East Orange are paying a very high price for keeping Short Hills, Livingston, and Florham Park green, and that they could probably find a cheaper way to supply themselves with water.

With the Highlands Preservation Act, New Jersey seems to have made it a matter of public policy to supply as much water as people imagine they could want, and to do it using obsolete and probably inefficient technology. That does not seem wise.

L. Zoning and Schools

One of the reasons that many towns try to discourage residential construction is that houses bring kids, kids go to school, and school costs money. To the extent that parents who live in these houses would be willing to pay for the schools their kids attend (or the towns they left would be willing to pay to get rid of them), this reaction is inefficient. If the local supermarket had to give out free food to any resident who showed up at its door, it, too, would lobby against every proposal to build houses.

To reduce this pressure and allow more houses to be built in appropriate places, the law should be changed so that a larger fraction of a school board's revenue depends on the number of pupils it enrolls. The straightforward way of doing this is to tax parents for a portion of the costs of educating their kids (this tax should be independent of whether the children are actually enrolled to discourage dropping out). Alternatively, the state could establish a fairly high per-pupil grant as part of the state-aid formula.

The two mechanisms could be combined by establishing a per-pupil state grant, and then taxing parents on the state level based on the number of school-age children. This state mechanism could allow poor parents to pay less (or nothing) per child.

M. Floods and Hurricanes

When a hurricane hits the state, the government responds compassionately and helps as much as possible. Even though this sort of behavior can create bad incentives, the state cannot help but act in this fashion. But compassion does not have to create bad incentives.

The key is careful planning before a crisis. The state should levy a recovery fee on land likely to flood. The amount this fee would generate in a decade would be the actuarially fair estimate of the costs of disaster relief associated with that land. Inhabited land would generate more than uninhabited; uninsured properties more than insured. The fee would appropriately discourage people from building in areas likely to flood.

Once the fee was in place, some developments would no longer be viable. The state should be willing to buy out these developments to create parks. This is one of the cheapest and most efficient ways of providing easily accessible parkland. Land that floods every year or two is a lousy place for a house but a great place for a park.

N. Stormwater

The obvious solution to the stormwater problem is to tax pavement and other impermeable surfaces. The tax would be levied on a square foot basis. It would be higher in areas where run-off posed more of a danger, either to other structures or to water supplies, and lower where it posed less. Taxpayers could get credit for retention basins and other protections against run-off. Although most of these problems are probably local, the state should probably levy the tax. Local governments and school districts create vast amounts of pavement (road and playgrounds, for instance), and rain falls on public pavement the same way it falls on private.

Notice that pavement taxes also discourage employer-provided parking.

O. Parks

Most modern Americans like parks and open space, and they like them nearby. People were not always like this, but we are richer now, more conscious of health and exercise, more appreciative of what we think of as natural. These are long-term trends that have been operating for over a century and a half, and there is no reason to think that they will abate any time soon. The desires to maintain Kernan's quarry and the Halper farm in Piscataway free from development were not aberrations.

Since the demand for parks is largely a local demand, counties and municipalities seem to be the appropriate agents to meet that demand. Essex County residents do not benefit much from preserving the Halper farm; nor do Middlesex residents gain much from preserving Kernan's quarry. Large developers and condominium associations can also produce local parks.

Because some private goods are substitutes for parks, towns may find themselves in sub-optimal, under-parked equilibria. Backyard swimming pools and swings, for instance, are substitutes for a town swimming pool (or a private swim club) and for a playground. If everyone has a backyard swing, no one will want to go to a playground, even though everyone would be better off if no one had a backyard swing and everyone went to the playground. Only if a large fraction of people in concerted fashion switch to the playground will the backyard equilibrium ever be abandoned.

What can be done about the under-supply of local parks? Note, first that measures that encourage homeownership exacerbate this problem. A single owner of many properties can be large enough to reach the tipping point by herself.

Second, the state could tax park-substitutes like backyard swimming pools, backyard swings, driveway basketball hoops, backyard tennis courts, and lawns. This move would make assembling the critical mass to switch to a park equilibrium easier.

Finally, the critical mass story and the statement that the park-equilibrium was better than the no-park equilibrium were just possibilities; I know of no data to support them. Researchers should work on this question.

People also seek extraordinary park experiences like those offered by High Point, Batsto, Liberty State Park, and the Palisades. These parks are rightly state responsibility.

Some of these parks are overcrowded at peak times, like summer Sundays.

Many of the people who use these parks might want to use parks closer to home if those parks were better. If Harrison had better local parks, fewer people might travel from there to Lake Hopatcong for barbecues. State parks are another substitute for local parks.

The obvious solution to overcrowded state parks is congestion pricing – high entry fees at peak times, and essentially nothing off-peak. Beijing, for instance, requires entry fees at almost all parks, except in the early morning hours. Since many peak-hour park users are children, and park use is something of a "merit good," this idea in its raw form probably will not work in this country.

A better alternative is to charge peak-hour fees, but bill the towns or counties that the visitors come from, not the visitors themselves. This will give the towns and counties better incentives to develop local parks. The fees will also help maintain and expand the state parks.

A good system of local parks may economize on land; homeowners may not need a backyard big enough for a tennis court if the local park had better courts; people may be willing to live in small apartments if their children can play safely nearby. In other words, these recommendations might reduce sprawl. But no evidence is available on this question. Simply "preserving" an unused piece of land like Kernan's quarry, which is nice but not a substitute for any land use, does not reduce sprawl in this sense.

P. Amenities

People also appreciate open space that they cannot enter, although, once again, they appreciate it more when it is near where they live or work rather than somewhere far distant. Paying owners an annual fee to keep their land relatively open is therefore not a bad idea. The fee should be higher the more people gain from the openness, and lower the more other subsidies are being heaped on the land. Thus, subsidies should be higher for land that is near roads (Kremer 2001), that has with easements for hikers, and closer to densely populated areas. Subsidies should be lower for farms.

These kinds of modest annual subsidies can also solve the problem of destructive adult recreational uses: golf, skiing, hunting, ATV riding, snowmobiling, mountain-biking, and possibly fishing. These activities should largely be kept out of public parklands, in order to encourage entrepreneurs to develop private preserves. The open-space subsidies will legitimately assist these preserves.

Notice that I am advocating annual subsidies, not transfer of development rights (TDR). The annual subsidies would fall and rise as the estimated benefits of the open space fell and rose, and the owner could opt out at any time. Those who enjoy the open space should pay for it, and if it is no longer worth paying for, it should not be open. I do not want to bind the hands of future generations.

TDR's, by contrast, are permanent. Future generations get the open land, even if they would rather have the money. Since I have no idea what the future will be like this, seems rather shortsighted. Maybe the New Jerseyans of 2050 will decide to devote all of their efforts to preserving the Amazon, or will all want to live in Warren County and use Hudson County for recreation.

The argument for TDRs instead of annual subsidies is that development is irreversible, and we, who are wise, should protect the people of 2030 from the stupid shortsightedness of people in 2020. In fact, development is reversible. The Northeast has more forest today than it had in 1800, and Batsto and Liberty State Parks are wonderful. But even if it were not, the argument still fails. Suppose 2020 politicians are foolish and shortsighted, but the citizenry of 2030 is clamoring for open space. Then, long-sighted 2020 property owners will anticipate the high payments they will receive in 2030, and keep their land open, even though they receive nothing in 2020. Irreversibility is no problem as long as property owners look after their own interests.

Q. Poor Governance

The redevelopment portions of the Local Redevelopment and Housing Law should be repealed. Instead, local governments should have useful tools like land taxes, pavement taxes, and marginal cost pricing of utilities. Most of the arguments for "economic development" activities are that they avoid particular instances of distortions. For instance, consider the fiscal argument for eminent domain: the town should take the trailer camp and sell the land to a hotel because the hotel will generate more property tax. This argument evaporates in a land tax regime.

It is better to reduce the distortions than to design ways to get around them selectively and surreptitiously.

R. Integration

Since a more integrated society would probably be better for African-Americans, possibly better for Hispanics, and probably not worse for whites, trying to create one is a worthwhile endeavor. Integration may increase density, too.

Anti-discrimination laws are the traditional tools for reducing segregation. These laws cover a small segment of the market – owner-occupied houses are exempt – and they cover behavior by sellers and intermediaries – Realtors and mortgage lenders. They do not cover buyers, and so they do not attack the most pervasive discrimination in the New Jersey housing market today – the almost universal refusal of whites even to search in primarily minority neighborhoods.

Because of this restriction, these laws serve mainly to facilitate minority entry into primarily white neighborhoods and to allow minorities better access to mortgages. Thus, they promote integration in white neighborhoods and, in the short run, reduce demand in minority neighborhoods. Empirically, the effect on segregation has not been strong: Collins (2003) found that the existence of fair housing laws had no impact on segregation in the 1960s, while Gablinger and Virabhak (2003) found that states with stronger laws in the 1990s had somewhat less segregation.

These laws, though, almost certainly reduce density. Primarily, they increase the quantity of housing minorities purchase in the long run; they allow minorities to live in neighborhoods with bigger houses and bigger lawns; and, in the short run, they make minority neighborhoods more sparsely populated by lowering demand. Anti-discrimination laws are probably good policies, but not a way to reduce sprawl.

Integration maintenance programs hold more promise for this purpose, especially if they become widespread. These are local programs that subsidize entry of under-represented groups into neighborhoods, promote understanding, and engage in outreach and publicity on the benefits of integrated living in particular towns. Only a small number of towns nationwide operate these programs, with the South Orange-Maplewood program being the best known in New Jersey. Ellen (2000a) provides a detailed discussion of the strengths and weaknesses of these programs.

Integration would probably be better promoted if these programs operated on a metropolitan level rather than a local level; so would the efficient allocation of people to towns. Many people probably want to live in an integrated setting, but do not want to live in South Orange or Maplewood (they would rather be near the shore, for instance, or want their kids to learn religious Christmas carols in school). The more different types of town are integrated – conservative towns as well as liberal, shore towns as well as leafy, car towns as well as train towns – the more households can find an integrated town that they want to live in, and the better the matches between households and towns.

A world in which only South Orange and Maplewood have an integration maintenance program is a probably far from optimal. It distorts location decisions, and concentrates integration-seekers in a single spot rather than spreading them around where they could promote more integration.

On the other hand, a state-run integration maintenance program would probably be a disaster. People want to know that the community they are thinking about moving to promotes integration, not some state government bureaucrats who cannot be found after 5 o'clock.

The obvious compromise is a system of state grants to community integration maintenance programs – like state grants to arts and cultured organizations. The state should strive for variety in funding these programs – it should not just be Montclair, Teaneck, and Englewood.

In particular, the big anti-sprawl payoff from integration maintenance may come from programs in towns like East Orange and Lawnside, and neighborhoods like Weequahic and Vailsburg. Integration maintenance, here, means encouraging whites to move in or stay. In the past, efforts to bring whites into cities have been anti-black – urban removal in Newark, for instance, and they failed. Why should people in Weequahic want white neighbors? Because it will increase property values (the resounding reason why South Orange-Maplewood residents support integration maintenance). You cannot cut off 90% of potential buyers for your house and expect to see it be worth a lot.

What should not be done?

I have now set forth a more than ample agenda for fighting sprawl. I have left out a few minor recommendations (e.g., banning automobile collision insurance because it encourages careless driving) because of space. But I have also left out many of the ideas most closely associated with sprawl: sewer hook-up moratoriums, state plans, smart growth, and urban growth boundaries. These ideas are not part of my agenda. They do not correct the underlying problems, and they often make them worse.

Let us go back to some of the underlying causes of sprawl and see how this works out. For instance, suppose the underlying cause of sprawl is excessive crime in cities. The obvious solution is to reduce crime in cities, not to ban exurban development that would let people avoid crime. The state should be apprehending criminals, not serving up victims for them.

But perhaps I am being too sanguine here; perhaps for some reason cities cannot or will not adopt cost-effective, crime-fighting policies. In the absence of first-best policies, do second-best policies call for restricting exurban development? Obviously not. Whatever the reason, if crime is rampant in some location, and people can leave that location, they should be permitted to do so. Restricting development is not even a second-best solution in this case.

What about sprawl caused by excessive driving? Development restrictions at least work in the right direction with this problem, but their effect is at best minuscule compared with direct measures like pay-per-mile insurance, gasoline taxes, and congestion tolls. It is like trying to fight global warming by leaving a single ice cube on your windowsill every night.

Development restrictions – for instance, setting a line at the edge of a metropolitan area beyond which development is prohibited – reduce travel by eliminating trips that would have crossed the boundary line. If everyone has to live and work within 30 miles of downtown Newark, then no one will take any of the shopping or commuting trips that would have begun or ended more than 30 miles from downtown Newark. Since some of these trips would have been wasteful, the restriction can produce some gain.

But development restrictions do, at best, nothing about the excessive trips made inside the boundary, and so they do not sufficiently increase density within the boundary. Stopping development in Hunterdon County will not in the least deter my Maplewood neighbors from driving their SUVs a half mile, pass a school, to buy a bagel. Thus, development restrictions do not directly affect the vast majority of excess trips.

In fact, these restrictions may worsen the harm that these trips cause. In short run models with fixed populations, the remaining trips are made under more congested conditions and with more people around. If Hunterdon County development were arrested and my street in Maplewood had two-family houses on it instead of one-family houses, the bagel-seeking SUVs would get to poison twice as many people.

Thus, development restrictions are a very, very poor substitute for direct measures to regulate motor vehicles. Recent simulation models have demonstrated this result rigorously: Brueckner (2005) in a standard urban model with centralized employment and commuting trips only, Anas and Rhee (2004) in a more modern model with decentralized employment and many kinds of trips.

Perhaps the best case can be made for development restrictions as a way of preserving open space. Even here, much better strategies are available: open-land subsidies are likely to work a lot better at pinpointing the land that should and should not be open. Placing open land on the fringes of metropolitan areas, for instance, flies in the face of what we know about the type of open space people value, and encourages even more driving.

Economists (Weitzman 1974, for instance) have studied at some length the sorts of situations in which rules work better than subsidies and taxes, and preserving open space is not one of them. Both subsidies and rules work equally well when the government has perfect information about costs and benefits, and so the question is, when do rules work better with imperfect information? The answer is that rules work better when the marginal harm the government is trying to avoid escalates much more swiftly at some points than at others. Thus, because the second car in an intersection at a given instant causes a lot more harm than the first, governments use rules (traffic lights and stop signs), rather than prices, to regulate intersections. And because the 80th person in a large meeting room is much more likely to cause life-threatening congestion in the event of a fire than the 30th, the fire department uses a rule: "Occupancy by more than 70 persons is prohibited." On the other hand, when the harm caused by a marginal unit is more or less constant, taxes and subsidies work better. Every license plate costs the state the same amount to produce, and so each gets sold for the same amount.

The arguments given for open space preservation are much closer to the equal-marginal harm type than the first. Every acre developed causes about the same losses in natural beauty and ecological diversity; it causes about the same losses in water purity and creates about the same need for filtration. One more house in the Pine Barrens is not going to cause them to shrivel up and die; that's why parks are often developed around a few existing buildings, and they contain rangers' houses and Boy Scout camps. In general, then, subsidies will do a better job at preservation than prohibitions.

The evidence also indicates that development restrictions are inequitable, not just inefficient. Their costs are disproportionately borne by poor people in the form of greater housing costs and restricted access to housing.

Quigley and Raphael (2004), in a survey of housing affordability, cite over a half dozen empirical studies that link development restrictions to higher prices, less construction, or both. Malpezzi and Green (1996), for instance, find that rents in the bottom quartile are more than a fifth higher in highly regulated metropolitan areas than they are in relatively unregulated metropolitan areas, everything else being equal. Somerville and Mayer (2003) show that affordable housing units are more likely to "filter up" and become unaffordable when constraints on new building are strong. Most of the empirical evidence supports the contention of Malpezzi and Green that anything that produces more houses produces more housing for poor people.

One might object, of course, that many of the proposals I make in this paper may also hurt poor people. That is probably true. But there are two mitigating factors. First, many of these policies help poor people – like the reductions in motor vehicle pollution and stormwater floodings. Second, all of them create more benefits than costs (unlike many of the development restrictions), and so make it easier to compensate losers, no matter who they may be.

Conclusion

Many, many productive steps can be taken to reduce the kind of sprawl that New Jerseyans care about – wasteful degradation of the environment throughout the state, not just in the Highlands or the Pine Barrens. Most of the measures I have discussed are not on anyone's political agenda, but they are more efficient, more effective, and probably more equitable than anything that is getting attention now. The present strategy of combining a Draconian approach to new construction with laissez-faire in every other area will leave New Jersey less populous, and leave its poor people with worse housing. It will also not do much about the real environmental problems the state faces. We need a broad-based approach.

References

Aldy, Joseph and Viscusi, W. Kip. 2003. "The Value of a Statistical Life," National Bureau of Economic Research working paper w10199.

Anas, Alex and H. J. Rhee. 2004. "Curbing excess sprawl with congestion tolls and urban boundaries." Unpublished working paper, SUNY- Buffalo.

Arnott, Richard, André de Palma and Robin Lindsey. 1994. "The Welfare Effects of Congestion Tolls with Heterogeneous Commuters," *Journal of Transport Economics and Policy:* 139-161.

Bairoch, Paul. 1988. *Cities and Economic Development: From the Dawn of History to the Present.* Translated by Christopher Braider. Chicago: The University of Chicago Press, p. 234.

Bayer, Patrick, Robert McMillan and Kim Ruehrer. 2004. "Residential Segregation in General Equilibrium," *Yale Economic Growth Center*, discussion paper 885.

Brueckner, Jan K. 2005. "Urban Growth Boundaries: An Effective Second-Best Remedy for Unpriced Traffic Congestion?" Unpublished working paper, Department of Economics, University of California, Irvine.

Brueckner, Jan K. 2001. "Urban Sprawl: Lessons from Urban Economics," in *Brookings-Wharton Papers on Urban Affairs.* William G. Gale and Janet Rothenberg Pack, eds. Washington, D.C.: Brookings Institution Press, pp. 65-89.

Chambers, Daniel N. 1992. "The Racial Housing Price Differential and Racially Transitional Neighborhoods," *Journal of Urban Economics* 32: 214-232.

Cohen, Alma and Rajeev Dehejia. 2003. "The Effect of Automobile Insurance and Accident Liability Laws on Traffic Fatalities," National Bureau of Economic Research working paper w9602.

Collins, William J. 2003. "The Housing Market Impact of State-Level Anti-Discrimination Laws, 1960-1970," National Bureau of Economic Research working paper w9562.

Cullen, Julie Berry and Steven D. Levitt. 1999. "Crime, Urban Flight, and the Consequences for Cities," *Review of Economics and Statistics* 81: 159-169.

Cutler, David, and Edward Glaeser. 1997. "Are Ghettoes Good or Bad?" *Quarterly Journal of Economics* 112 (3): 827-871.

Cutler, David, Edward Glaeser, and Jacob Vigdor. 1999. "The Rise and Decline of the American Ghetto," *Journal of Political Economy* 107 (4): 455-506.

Edlin, Aaron. 2002. "Per-Mile Premiums for Auto Insurance," working paper E02-318, University of California- Berkeley.

Ellen, Ingrid Gould. 2000a. *Sharing America's Neighborhoods: The Prospects for Stable Racial Integration.* Cambridge, MA: Harvard University Press.

Ellen, Ingrid Gould. 2000b. "Is Segregation Bad for Your Health? The Case of Low Birth Weight," *Brookings-Wharton Papers on Urban Affairs* 1: 203-238.

Fischel, William A. 1985. *The Economics of Zoning Laws.* Baltimore: Johns Hopkins University Press.

Fischel, William A. 1998. "The Ethics of Land Value Taxation Revisited: Has the Millennium Arrived Without Anyone Noticing," 1-23 in Dick Netzer, ed., *Land Value Taxation: Can It and Will It Work Today?* Cambridge, MA: Lincoln Institute of Land Policy.

Gablinger, Ynon 2003. "The Extent and Nature of Discrimination in Housing." Ph.D. dissertation, Columbia University.

Gablinger, Ynon and Suchin Virabhak. 2003. "Discrimination in the Housing Market: What Can We Learn from Inter-State Differences in Fair Housing Laws," mimeo, Department of Economics, Columbia University.

Glaeser, Edward and Matthew Kahn. 2003. "Sprawl and Urban Growth," *National Bureau of Economic Research*, working paper w9733.

Hamilton, Bruce W. 1975. "Zoning and property taxation in a system of local governments," *Urban Studies* 12 (June): 205-211.

Hu, Pat S. and Timothy R. Reuscher. 2004. *Summary of Travel Trends: 2001 National Household Survey.* Accessed at http:// nhts.ornl.gov/2001/pub/STT.pdf

Kahn, Matthew E. 2001. "Does Sprawl Reduce the Black/White Housing Consumption Gap?" *Housing Policy Debate* 12 (1): 77-86.

Kremer, Michael. 2001. "Comment," in *Brookings-Wharton Papers on Urban Affairs.* William G. Gale and Janet Rothenberg Pack, eds. Washington, D.C.: Brookings Institution Press, pp. 93-94.

Lewis Mumford Center for Comparative Urban and Regional Research. 2002. Metropolitan Racial and Ethnic Change – Census 2000, Data." Accessed at http://mumford.albany.edu/census/data.html.

Logan, John. 2001. "Ethnic Diversity Grows, Neighborhood Integration Lags Behind," Lewis Mumford Center, SUNY-Albany. Accessed at http://mumford.albany.edu/census/WholePop/Wpreport/MumfordReport.pdf.

Malpezzi, Stephen and Richard K. Green. 1996. "What has happened to the bottom of the U.S. housing market?" *Urban Studies* 33 (10): 1807-20.

Massey, Douglas S. and Nancy Denton. 1993. *American Apartheid: Segregation and the Making of the Underclass.* Cambridge, MA: Harvard University Press.

Mills, Edwin S. 1985. "Open Housing Laws as Stimulus to Central City Employment," *Journal of Urban Economics* 17: 184-188.

Nechyba, Thomas and Randall P, Walsh. 2004. "Urban Sprawl," *Journal of Economic Perspectives* 18 (4): 177-200.

New Jersey State Police. 2005. "Crime in NJ: 2003 Uniform Crime Report." Accessed at www.njsp.org/ info/ucr2003/ index.html.

Oates, Wallace E. and Robert Schwab. 1997. "The Impact of Urban Land Taxation: The Pittsburgh Experience," *National Tax Journal* 50 (March): 1-21.

Passmore, Wayne. 2003. "The GSE Implicit Subsidy and the Value of Government Ambiguity," Federal Reserve Board of Governors, working paper 2003-64, Washington DC.

Pozdena, Randall J. 1998. "Unlocking Gridlock," Federal Reserve Board of San Francisco Weekly Letter, December, 1-5.

Quigley, John and Steven Raphael. 2004. "Is Housing Unaffordable? Why Isn't It More Affordable?" *Journal of Economic Perspectives* 18 (1): 191-214.

Sethi, Rajiv and Rohini Somanathan. 2001. "Racial Income Disparities and the Measurement of Segregation," Barnard College working paper 01-07.

Shoup, Donald C. 1997. "Evaluating the Effects of Cashing Out Employer Paid Parking: Eight Case Studies," *Transport Policy*, 4(4): 201-216.

Small, Kenneth A. and C. Kazimi. 1995 "On the Costs of Air Pollution from Motor Vehicles," *Journal of Transport Economics and Policy*, January.

Somerville, C. Tsuriel and Christopher Mayer. 2003. "Government Regulation and Changes in Affordable Housing Stock," *Economic Policy Review*, Federal Reserve Bank of NY, (92), 45-63

Voith, Richard. 1999. "Does the federal tax treatment of housing affect the pattern of metropolitan development?" *Business Review*, Federal Reserve Bank of Philadelphia. March/ April, pp. 3-16.

Weitzman, M. 1974. "Prices vs. quantities," *Review of Economic Studies* 41 (4): 477-491.

Wrigley, E. A. 1969. *Société et population*. Collection l'Univers des Connaissances. Paris.

Table 1

Recent Growth in Vehicle Miles of Travel (VMT)

Area	Unit of obs.	Period	Annual growth rate	Decadal growth rate
U.S.	Household	1990-2001	1.40%	14.9%
N.J.	Person	1997-2002	1.27%	13.5%

Sources: U. S. : Hu and Reuscher, 2004, table 3. N. J.: U.S. Bureau of Transportation Statistics, 2005, table 05-03; accessed at www.bts.gov/publications/state_transportation_profiles/.

Table 2

Growth Per Square Mile in Population and
Household Vehicles by County

County	Population growth per mile 1990-2004	Household vehicle growth per mile 1990-2000
Hudson	1138.2	415.7
Union	369.2	37.5
Middlesex	365.9	111.4
Bergen	331.5	103.2
Passaic	255.6	47.3
Somerset	251.0	101.5
Ocean	188.7	97.5
Monmouth	176.2	100.4
Mercer	174.6	73.2
Essex	146.3	26.1
Morris	142.5	57.5
Gloucester	128.5	65.4
Atlantic	79.1	25.6
Burlington	67.9	33.9
Camden	60.5	38.9
Warren	51.4	25.7
Hunterdon	51.1	
Sussex	40.8	22.4
Cumberland	26.8	0.3
Cape May	22.3	26.7
Salem	0.2	4.5

Source: U.S. Bureau of the Census: 1990 Census, 2000 Census, 2004 Population Estimates. Area is land area. Population growth is difference between estimated population of July 1, 2004 and census population of April 1, 1990. Household vehicle growth is difference between estimated household vehicles April 1, 2000 and April 1, 1990.

Table 3

Residential Segregation in New Jersey, 2000: Indices of Dissimilarity

	Black-White		Hispanic-White	
	All	Mid-Income	All	Mid-Income
Newark	80.4	81.9	65.0	62.7
Bergen-Passaic	73.2	75.5	57.8	55.5
MSH*	52.0	58.5	52.2	52.5
Jersey City	65.7	73.4	44.8	46.3
Trenton	64.0	62.2	54.0	54.4
Average U.S.	65.1		51.6	

*Middlesex-Somerset-Hunterdon

An index of dissimilarity between group A and group B is the minimum proportion of group A members who would have to move in order to create a pattern where the proportion of group A members is the same in every neighborhood.

"Neighborhood" means census tract.

"White" means non-Hispanic white.

The Newark metropolitan area is the counties of Essex, Union, Morris, and Warren. The Jersey City metropolitan area is Hudson County. The Trenton metropolitan area is Mercer County. Metropolitan areas are listed in order of declining African-American population.

"Middle income" means a household income between $10,000 and $60,000 in 1999.

U.S. indices of dissimilarity are from Logan (2001). Metropolitan indices of dissimilarity are from Lewis Mumford Center (2002).

CHAPTER TWO

Newark As A Case Study

By
Brendan O'Flaherty

On July 1, 2006, Newark City Clerk Bob Marasco swore in a newly elected mayor and city council. The challenges those winners will face could well be obscured in the flurry of charges, counter-charges, treachery, and outrage that usually marks Newark politics. Before that begin, it is good to note what the challenges will be.

Immediate Challenges

1. Curbing bloat at the top

The mayor and council were sworn in at noon, and the council convened its organizational session. At that session, the city will have to decide whether to continue its current bloated, compensation for top elected and appointed officials, or to become like a normal, mid-sized city.

Compensation for the mayor of Newark in 2005, for instance, was $186,985 – considerably above the salary of the governor of New Jersey. The last time a national survey of mayoral salaries was published, 1997, Newark came in third, behind only Chicago and New York, and well ahead of such large cities as Los Angeles, Houston, and Philadelphia. Day-to-day operations in Newark are the province of the business administrator, whose 2005 compensation was $172,965, only slightly less than the governor's $175,000. The council president's compensation was $97,085, and the average council member received $81,920. The mayor and most council members have other paying jobs as well, often full-time. Each council member has a staff of five, costing the taxpayers roughly $280,000 per council staff in salary alone. The mayor and council also get generous budgets for meals, travel, and entertainment. They drive city-owned automobiles (mainly SUVs), powered by city-supplied gasoline, and protected by city car insurance. Newark spends about five times as much per capita as Jersey City does on its city council, even though both cities are about the same size, and have about the same form of government.

Bloat-at-the-top does not cost Newark taxpayers a lot of money, but it costs Newark's government a lot of credibility. You cannot tell city workers that they should go an extra mile to help the public when they can see that "those officials" are going an extra mile to fleece the public. You cannot tell citizens that they should make sacrifices like attending community meetings, watching their neighbors' kids, or cleaning up after their dogs, when those officials are obviously making no sacrifices whatsoever – and enjoying the best-paid job those officials will ever have. Newark's top officials are going to need a lot of help if they are going to deal successfully with the challenges the city faces, and that help will not be forthcoming if potential helpers rationally conclude that assistance redounds chiefly to the benefit of elected officials and their greedy henchmen.

Reducing bloat-at-the-top will improve Newark's image in Trenton, too, and Newark can definitely use assistance from state government. But whether improved image translates into more support from the legislature is an open question.

2. Salvaging something from the arena debacle

I do not know how deeply the city will be legally and physically committed to the construction of a new arena for the New Jersey Devils, but it is never too late to stop throwing good money after bad and never too early to bandage a bleeding wound.

The city signed a deal with the Devils under which the team's owners get 24 acres of prime downtown real estate and over $240 million in public money. In return, the Devils are supposed to pay a few million dollars a year in rent – eventually – but that money goes to the Newark Housing Authority, not the city. The Devils are supposed to "contribute" $100 million to the project, but that contribution has not been seen yet, and it may never show up in any form that a normal person (or even an economist) would recognize as a "contribution."

The project was not competitively bid, and no marketing study was ever completed. One of the strongest empirical regularities in economics is that professional sports venues spur no development. Newark is throwing $240 million and 24 acres of prime land down a rat hole.

Since an arena is far from the highest and best use of this land and this money, there is some deal could that stops the arena and make everyone better off. Because of the contracts that have already been signed, that deal will probably let the Devils walk away with a sizeable sum of money in their pockets. (Such a deal would not be necessary if the citizen suit against the fiscal procedures that were used in setting up the arena is successful in voiding these contracts.) Some mistakes can never be erased. But they do not need to be exacerbated.

3. Avoiding falling off the budget cliff

Newark faces substantial budget shortfalls during the next mayor's term because the city has been spending at an unsustainable level for the last two years, and due to existing commitments, almost certainly will continue to do so for the first half of 2006. The city has recently reached a settlement with the Port Authority for $450 million, but about half of the money in this settlement will be gone when the newly elected mayor takes office.

Newark owns the land on which the airport and seaport are located and leases it to the Port Authority. Part of that lease is a "most-favored nation clause." Newark's deal with the Port Authority has to be at least as favorable as New York City's. In 2004, New York renegotiated its agreements for JFK and LaGuardia airports, and it became apparent that Newark would get a large but indeterminate sum of money. Negotiations have recently concluded, and Newark will get $450 million.

This is a lot of money, but not enough to match the stepped-up spending that the anticipated settlement caused. In 2004, Newark faced a budget gap of $40 million. It closed this gap by borrowing $40 million against the anticipated settlement. The gap grew to $60 million in 2005, and the remedy was the same: borrow another $60 million, on top of the $40 million from 2004. In 2006, we can anticipate a gap of at least $80 million, bringing the total draw on the settlement to at least $180 million.

That seems to leave $270 million. But $50 million of this balance is not really money: it is just a promise by the Port Authority to spend this money in capital improvements at Newark Airport over the next five years, and they were going to do this anyway. The rest of the money comes partly in 2006, and then in $40 million installments, once a year, between 2007 and 2011.

That means the problems start in 2007 and get progressively worse. Assume that the cost of running Newark city government goes up by $20 million a year – about 4%. This amount is slightly less than the historical average, and does not account for some likely serious problems (large increases for pensions and schools, for instance), as well as any expensive initiatives. Then the city faces gaps of $40 million in 2007, $80 million in 2008, $100 million in 2009, $120 million in 2010, $140 million in 2011, and $200 million in 2012. These are all relative to current revenue and spending patterns.

The basic problem is that Newark is now treating a one-time windfall like a recurring revenue. The windfall is a big one, so this illusion can continue for a dangerously long time. But the mayor who takes office in the middle of 2006 has to confront the 2007 and 2008 budget gaps immediately.

4. UMDNJ and NHA

Federal investigations are currently revealing that two of Newark's largest government agencies – the University of Medicine and Dentistry of New Jersey (UMDNJ) and the Newark Housing Authority (NHA) – have both been seriously mismanaged. The U.S. attorney has taken over UMDNJ's fiscal operations, and the U.S. Department of Housing and Urban Development (HUD) is thinking about doing something similar with the NHA.

Both agencies are vital to Newark. UMDNJ runs the largest hospital, the largest mental health center, and the cities emergency medical system. It is deeply involved in public health, and is also the largest employer in the city. The NHA operates or funds over 12% of the city's housing stock, controls countless acres of land, and is doling out the Devils' generous subsidies. The city cannot be healthy with these agencies sick.

The city government has more direct responsibility for the NHA than for UMDNJ, which is part of state government. But even UMDNJ can be influenced by the mayor's "bully pulpit," and by the city government's direct contracts, land use regulations, police powers, and redevelopment authority.

Long-term Challenges

1. Crime

Overall reported crime has gone down in Newark, as it has throughout the country, but remains distressingly high, especially as compared with other cities in the metropolitan region. The Bronx, Brooklyn, Jersey City, Paterson, and Elizabeth are all considerably safer than Newark. Camden and some of Newark's inner-ring suburbs are more dangerous, but "safer than something" is not the right criterion on which to judge a city. There are 566 towns in New Jersey, and so a city cannot be called successful merely by avoiding being dead last.

Table 1 provides the basic details, for three important index crimes: murder, robbery, and motor vehicle theft.

Table 1: Crime Rates, 2004

	Murder	Robbery	MV Theft
Newark	3.09	5.07	21.08
Brooklyn	0.93	3.48	2.63
Bronx	0.92	3.66	3.21
Jersey City	0.96	6.02	7.24
Paterson	0.66	4.15	7.45
Elizabeth	0.81	3.85	13.34
Camden	6.05	10.3	17.0
East Orange	2.46	8.19	18.20
Irvington	4.33	12.62	20.53

Murder rate is per 10,000 estimated population; robbery and motor vehicle theft are per 1,000 population. "Motor vehicle theft" for New York is "grand larceny – automobile." (For New Jersey, statistics are from the New Jersey State Police, Uniform Crime Reports, section 6, "Crime in the Cities." For New York, crime statistics are from the New York Police Department, Compstat. 2004 population is from the Division of City Planning, as accepted by the Census Bureau.)

Compared with the other major urban areas in the metropolitan area, Newark is extremely dangerous. The murder rate is more than triple that anywhere else, and the motor vehicle theft rate is more than double that of any place else except for Elizabeth. Only on robbery is Newark in the same ballpark as the other places; in fact, Jersey City has a higher robbery rate, although the four other cities are below Newark. Of these three crimes, robbery is the one least likely to be reported to police, and the one for which police have the greatest discretion in classification.

Urbanity – the kind of easy coming and going in most places at most times that draws people to great cities – cannot be achieved with murder, robbery, and motor vehicle theft rates like Newark's.

2. Health

Age-adjusted mortality and morbidity rates are not available separately for Newark, but Newark is at the epicenter of the ongoing North Jersey minority health disaster.

In 2002, the age-adjusted mortality rate for African-Americans in Essex County was 1,098.8 per 100,000. The corresponding rate for whites was 777.2 (slightly higher than white rates in Morris, Bergen, and Somerset counties). What does this difference of 321 deaths per year per 100,000 mean? Most studies show that modern Americans are willing to pay $5,000-7,000 to avoid a 1% chance of death a year. Thus black Essex County residents would be willing to pay $15,000-20,000 a year each to have white Essex County mortality experience.

Nationally, most of the racial difference in age-adjusted mortality is due to three serious, widespread diseases – heart disease, cancer, and stroke. But that is not true for New Jersey. While each of the big three accounts for a difference of around 30 per 100,000 in age-adjusted mortality, a fourth cause does, too: HIV. The black HIV mortality rate for New Jersey for 2002 was 40.0 and the white was 3.8. The gap was bigger than the gaps for stroke and cancer, and almost as big as the gap for heart disease.

HIV in New Jersey is different. Nationally, the black HIV mortality rate was 20.8, about half the New Jersey rate. This difference was confined to blacks. Among blacks, 5.2% of New Jersey deaths were due to HIV, as compared with 2.7% of national deaths. But among whites, New Jersey wasn't much different from the rest of the nation: 0.4% of white New Jersey deaths, as opposed to 0.3% of white national deaths.

Newark alone cannot address every aspect of this disaster. Needle exchange and needle legalization, for instance, are being held up by the state legislature (but parts of Newark's legislative delegation are among the most active obstructionists). Historically, though, public health has been largely a municipal responsibility. The greatest public health victory in American history, the sanitation revolution between 1890 and 1920, was largely the work of city governments.

The mayor of Newark, for instance, controls the federal Ryan White funds for much of North Jersey. Reducing HIV mortality is not mysterious – it has been done in many other places many other times.

Newark city government has also traditionally controlled the funds to treat sexually transmitted infections (STIs). STIs are probably very important in the spread of HIV. The rate of transmission – the probability that a sexual partnership between an HIV-positive person and an HIV-negative person will infect the HIV-negative person – turns out to be an incredibly powerful parameter when you simulate an HIV epidemic. That is pretty good, but obviously non-experimental, evidence that indicates that untreated STIs increase the rate of transmission.

3. Jobs

Newark has been losing jobs pretty steadily for over 40 years. Jersey City, the Bronx, and Brooklyn have been gaining jobs in recent years. Table 2 compares the six urban areas on private sector jobs covered by unemployment insurance.

Table 2: Covered Private Sector Employment, 1986-2003

	Newark	Bronx	Brooklyn	Jersey City	Paterson	Elizabeth
1986	100	100	100	100	100	100
1991	90	98	98	92	88	86
1995	90	102	102	107	85	85
2000	——	106	109	——	——	——
2003	88	——	——	124	75	83

1986 = 100

Source: For New Jersey, Department of Labor and Workforce Development (earlier, Department of Labor and Industry. For New York, Department of Labor. New York does not publish covered employment data for counties in metropolitan areas after 2000.

Adding jobs is not absolutely crucial for the economic well-being of Newark's citizens. In almost every town in New Jersey, the majority of residents work outside the municipal boundaries, and Newark is no exception. But Newark is extraordinarily well-suited to be a hub of productive activity. Making it a sort of Toms River North is wasteful, even though doing so might enrich a few developers.

4. Information technology

Multi-factor productivity has been increasing at a rate of about 1.1% a year since 1995, a rate unseen in over a generation, and rarely achieved in American history (http://data.bls.gov/cgi-bin/surveymost). Information technology is changing how Americans live – and what they should expect of their city governments. Some cities, like Philadelphia, for instance, are trying to make the entire town a wi-fi hot spot. This might be visionary, or it might be ridiculous. Newark's leaders are going have to decide how to respond.

5. Trade reorientation

Newark is America's major hubs for international trade. The confluence of a major seaport, major airports, major rail yard, and several major highways is rare in this country, if not unique. The volume of trade passing through this hub has grown sharply in the past 15 years. Between 1991 and 2003, the number of container-equivalents shipped through the Port of New York (of which Port Newark-Elizabeth is the major component) more than doubled, while the number of motor vehicles handled rose by almost 80% (Port Authority trade statistics at www.panynj.gov/commerce/tradestatsframe.html). The vast majority of these cargo movements are now imports.

This trade pattern, however, is unsustainable in the long run. It has been maintained by the willingness of Asian central banks to purchase large amounts of dollar-denominated bonds and thereby allow the U.S. to continue to consume more than it produces. This willingness is not boundless, and sooner or later these purchases will abate, the dollar will depreciate, and the U.S. trade deficit will turn around.

When that happens, American seaports will have to turn around, too. They will have to import less, and export more. Since manufactured goods are the main products that can be exported, and manufacturing is more concentrated than population, east of the Mississippi than population, East Coast ports are likely to bear the brunt of the export expansion. (64.4% of U.S. population in 2002 was east of the Mississippi, as compared with 68.1% of manufacturing payroll, according to the 2002 economic census.) Newark is the largest seaport on the East Coast.

This is basically good news for jobs in Newark, good news for businesses, and good news for payroll taxes. But the turnaround will not happen painlessly and automatically. Infrastructure has to accommodate it. Even now the port is congested, and plans are under discussion to rebuild roads to bring in more trucks. Newark does not need more air pollution, more traffic accidents, or more noise. The challenge for the next administration will be to protect Newark citizens' legitimate interests without being obstructionist. That is a fine line.

Resources

Considering these challenges, why would anyone (other than someone looking for a very nice paycheck) want to govern Newark? Newark has some unusual strengths and opportunities. It would be a serious mistake to see

Newark as a rust-belt relic, a creature of the 19th century unsuited for the 21st. Characterizing some cities that way might be accurate, but it is not Newark.

1. Abbott

State Supreme Court decisions in the *Abbott v. Burke* case have brought about massive changes in the Newark school system. The recent school construction fiasco was hardly surprising – it is hard to think of a way to spend more money with less educational result than to buy land and build buildings. But Abbott programs have made major changes in pre-kindergarten education and in operational funding.

Thanks to Abbott, Newark is now approaching universal pre-kindergarten education, and many of the programs are of high quality. Unlike school construction, pre-school education works. Many studies have shown that high-quality programs produce cognitive and non-cognitive gains, and some studies have shown positive results for moderate- and low-quality programs.

Abbott funding has also underwritten a major expansion of after-school programs, which at one time had virtually disappeared in Newark. After-school programs have no demonstrated relationship to cognitive development, but they make life easier for parents, and probably reduce property crime. And kids like them.

Abbott has also changed the regular school day. Newark schools in 2003-2004 spent $14,826 per pupil, considerably above the state average of $11,903 (this is the state education department's calculation in its school report cards). Test scores have improved at the elementary level, but not yet at the secondary level. Much of the money has gone, as it should, into parts of school life that do not show up on reading and arithmetic tests.

Abbott's effects have been indirect, too. Abbott may have played a role in the recent residential building boom, for instance. In non-Abbott districts, municipal spending has to go up when new houses add pupils to the schools, but in Newark more pupils mean more state dollars, not more local money. It should not be surprising that Newark has encouraged residential development more than other towns have. Abbott-funded school improvements may also have made those houses more attractive to buyers.

Abbott has also provided major relief to the city budget. The local contribution to running the city schools has remained capped at $80 million since 1991. This figure represents less than a tenth of the school budget, now. Because Newark spends less than $2,000 per pupil in local money and because it has not had to worry about raising its school contribution, the city was able to spend more money in many areas over the last 15 years (taxes went up, too).

While the state may start asking for a larger contribution at some point, Abbott will probably mean for the next administration what it has meant for the past decade: that it will not have to use local taxes for the vast majority of educational expenditures. Abbott might also mean educational improvement. These two facts present real substantive opportunities for Newark's leaders.

2. New Jersey

Newark is a poor city, but it is embedded in one of the richest, best-educated states in the nation. That has to help.

3. New York

Newark is not an isolated city, like Detroit or Cleveland. It has to come up with its own reasons to get people to visit or live there, and has to make sure that it provides everything necessary for a metropolitan area. Instead, Newark is part of the New York metropolitan area, the most productive agglomeration of economic activity the world has ever seen. Newark does not have to create its own excitement; it is an integral part of the greatest excitement on earth at this time. (This is another reason why chasing sports teams is stupid.)

4. Watershed

Newark owns 48 square miles in North Jersey, which it uses for part of its water supply. The land is not now providing benefits to Newark citizens commensurate with its value.

5. Library

The Newark Public Library has a long history, a reputation for professionalism, and good ties to the community. It is also well-linked to the libraries at the states colleges and universities. One of the challenges Newark faces is giving its citizens and businesses good access to information – defined by 21st century standards. The library's century of experience in bringing information to citizens and businesses is a good foundation for meeting that challenge.

Conclusion

No one who takes office will have a cushy job. But the challenges can be surmounted; Newark has a lot going for it. The winners in the city's 2006 should be held to high standards; excuses should not be accepted easily. Low expectations will, unfortunately, confirm themselves.

> *Disclaimer: I was not a neutral party in the Newark election. However the views expressed in this paper are my own, not necessarily those of any other person or organization.*

CHAPTER THREE

The Health Care System of New Jersey in 2005:
A Snapshot

By
Sherry Glied

The health care system of New Jersey is of considerable importance to the State. About 11% of the State's GDP is spent on health care. (Center for Medicaid and Medicare Services, 2000). The health care sector employs 7.2% of the State's workforce. (Kaiser Family Foundation, 2005). The state government spends over 13% of its budget on health care services. (New Jersey Department of the Treasury, 2006). In this paper, we describe the organization of health care financing and delivery in New Jersey, and assess the outcomes of the New Jersey health care system in terms of access, costs, and health status.

I. Socioeconomic Characteristics of New Jersey

Population characteristics affect the utilization of health care. People 65 and over use, on average, 3.3 times as much health care as do those 19-64. (Keehan, Sean P., et al., 2004). The demographics of New Jersey are comparable to those of the United States. Twenty-six percent of the population is younger than 18 years, 61% is between 19-64, and 13% is above 65 (about 1 percentage point above the national average). (Kaiser Family Foundation, 2005).

Economic characteristics also affect health care system usage. Higher income individuals tend to be healthier than lower income people, implying that they require fewer health care services. At the same time, higher income people generally spend just a little more on health care services than do lower income people with the same health conditions. Looking across nations, however, higher income countries spend much more on health care – about 1-1.6% more on health care for each 1% increase in GDP – reflecting greater endowments of health care technologies and services. Higher income jurisdictions are also able to support more generous health care assistance programs. New Jersey is a high-income state. Only 28% of NJ residents have incomes below 200% of the federal poverty level, considerably below the national average of 36%. (Kaiser Family Foundation, 2005). Thus, we would expect it to be healthier than average, support a more generous health care assistance system than average, and spend slightly more per capita on health care services.

II. Health Care Finance in New Jersey

In the United States as a whole, 16% of health care costs are paid by consumers out-of-pocket. The remainder is paid through private and public insurance and by government purchase. (Center for Medicaid and Medicare Services, 2005). Figure 1 describes the distribution of health insurance in New Jersey and in the United States.

Large Group Insurance

Most privately-insured residents of New Jersey obtain their coverage through their employers. For the 59% of New Jersey workers who are employed by firms of 100 workers or more, insurance is generally provided in the large group insurance market. Forty-six percent of all New Jersey residents obtain their coverage in this market. (Glied, Sherry, 2002-2004).

Large firms may either insure their coverage through an insurance carrier or through self-insurance. Large national insurance carriers – Aetna, Oxford, United Healthcare – sell coverage in New Jersey and the state has a Blue Cross Blue Shield plan, Horizon Blue Cross Blue Shield of New Jersey. In many states, the State Blue Cross plan has been converted from a not-for-profit to a for-profit plan, usually with some compensation to the state. In 2003, the New Jersey legislature passed a law permitting such a conversion to take place. (Mays, Glen P., et al., 2005). To date, Horizon has not taken advantage of this legislation.

The state government plays a limited role in the large group insurance market. All plans sold by insurers in the State must be registered by the State insurance department and must comply with state health insurance benefit mandates. Mandates may require coverage for specific health care services, or require insurers to reimburse services provided by certain classes of providers. NJ has enacted 30 mandated benefits, requiring firms to cover treatment for alcoholism, biologically-based mental illness, maternity, and a range of other conditions, similar to those mandated by most other states. (New Jersey Department of Banking, 2005). The State recently created a mandate review commission to assess the mandates currently in place. (Forum Institute for Public Policy, 2005).

Large firms may self-insure and escape state regulation altogether. Self-insurance places more risk on the firm, but because of the provisions of ERISA (the Employee Retirement and Income Security Act, 1974), self-insured plans are exempt from state insurance mandates. Mandates, likewise, do not apply to self-insured plans where the employer is responsible for the claims but uses an insurer or third-party administrator to process claims. Self-insurance is less prevalent in the Northeast than in other areas of the country, and the number of self-insured establishments in New Jersey is significantly lower than the national average. (Fox, K., et al., 2001). The lower rate of self-insurance implies that public regulation of the group insurance market will have a relatively greater impact in New Jersey.

Small Group Insurance

Employees of smaller firms (those with 100 or fewer employees) are significantly less likely to be offered health insurance coverage than are those in larger firms. Lower rates of coverage are particularly prevalent in firms with many low-wage and/or part-time employees. These patterns also hold in New Jersey, but small establishments in New Jersey are somewhat more likely to offer coverage than are small establishments in other states. (Fox, K., et al., 2001). About 11% of all New Jersey residents obtain health insurance coverage through small firm employers. (Glied, Sherry, 2002-2004).

Small firms rarely self-insure their health benefits, so they are subject to all state mandates. In many states, as in New Jersey, governments have also taken deliberate actions to improve health insurance coverage among small employers. The State's Small Employer Health Benefits Program, administered by the State's Department of Banking and Insurance, went into effect January 1, 1994. Under the program, employers with 2-50 full-time employees, who had not previously held coverage, must purchase plans from a menu of standardized offerings offered by all insurance carriers in the State. Plans offered through the program must apply modified community rating, adjusting premiums to reflect the age, gender, and location of employees of each participating firm, but not the health status of these employees. Moreover, carriers participating in the program must have a medical loss ratio of 75% or higher – that is, pay out 75% or more of premiums in the form of health care benefits. (New Jersey Department of Banking and Insurance, 2005).

The Small Employer Health Benefits Program was been quite successful. Between 1994 and 1997, nearly 150,000 people were newly enrolled in the program, about 15% of whom were previously uninsured. Enrollment remains high, but premiums for small employers are now the second highest in the nation, leading to interest in reforming the program. (Cantor, Joel, 2005).

Government Employees

The State Health Benefits Program (SHBP), administered through the State Department of Treasury, provides health benefits to state employees, participating local employees, and their dependents. (New Jersey Department of the Treasury, 2005). About 420,000 people, nearly 5% of the population, obtain health insurance through a government employer (including federal and local government employees). (Glied, Sherry, 2002-2004). The State also operates an Employee Prescription Drug Plan offered to active state employees and their eligible dependents. The cost of health benefits in the program has been escalating rapidly, placing significant pressure on the state budget. (New Jersey Department of the Treasury, 2006).

In some jurisdictions, notably the federal government and the government of California, employee benefit programs have been a locus of "managed competition" style health reform (through the Federal Employees Health Benefits Plan, FEHBP, and the California public employees plan, CalPers, respectively). This has not been the case in New Jersey, where state employees have a choice of only three plans: a traditional indemnity plan, an HMO plan, and a Point-of-Service plan.

Non-Group Insurance

Nationwide, relatively few Americans obtain insurance coverage in the non-group (or individual) insurance market. Just under 300,000 people, less than 4% of New Jersey residents, obtain coverage in this market. (Glied, Sherry, 2002-2004). In New Jersey, the non-group health insurance market has been the focus of considerable policy attention. The State's Individual Health Coverage Program (IHCP), begun in 1993, requires carriers to offer standardized, open enrollment, fully community-rated individual coverage (premiums may not vary by age, sex, or health status). All carriers operating in New Jersey must participate in the IHCP, either by selling coverage or by paying a share of the losses incurred by those carriers that do sell individual policies. (Swartz, Katherine, et al., 1999).

The IHCP was initially quite successful, attracting both carriers and subscribers. (Swartz, Katherine, et al., 1999). Since 1998, however, the program has lost ground and has faced rising premiums and declining participation. Enrollment fell by more than half between 1995 and 2001, and premiums have been rising rapidly. (Monheit, Alan, C., et al., 2004). Current enrollees in the program are substantially older than the average enrollee in the employer market. Young, healthy subscribers have been priced out of the market, a pattern seen in other community-rated states. (Monheit, Alan C., et al., 2004). A recent analysis suggests that reform of this program, through a shift from pure community rating to a modified age-rating system might double enrollment in the program, while increasing premiums by about 15% for current subscribers. (Monheit, Alan C., et al., 2005).

Medicare

About 625,000 people in New Jersey are insured through Medicare. (Glied, Sherry, 2002-2004). Medicare is a federal program, which provides health insurance coverage to aged and disabled people in all the states. It includes both the traditional fee-for-service component and a range of Medicare Advantage options. While the traditional fee-for-service component is uniform across the states, the available Medicare Advantage options vary by state. In New Jersey, there are currently 19 Medicare Advantage Plans offered with varying benefits. (Medicare, 2005). Medicare Advantage plans may enter and leave the state market each year. In 2002, the sudden exodus of several Medicare Advantage (then Medicare+Choice) plans left 53,000 Medicare enrollees in New Jersey without coverage. (Medicare+Choice Plan Withdraws, 2002).

Medicare's new pharmaceutical coverage component, legislated through the Medicare Modernization Act of 2003, will, for the first time, provide pharmaceutical coverage to Medicare enrollees. Under the program, Medicare will take over responsibility for providing pharmaceutical benefits to beneficiaries enrolled in both Medicare and Medicaid. In New Jersey, this means that the Federal government will take on responsibility for beneficiaries currently receiving benefits through the State's $400 million Pharmaceutical Assistance for the Aged and Disabled (PAAD) program. (New Jersey Department of the Treasury, 2006). The State will be required to continue making financial contributions to these beneficiaries through the program's maintenance of effort provisions. (Forum Institute for Public Policy, 2005).

Medicaid

Medicaid is an entitlement program that provides health insurance for over 900,000 low-income New Jersey residents. The costs of Medicaid are divided between the federal and state government, using a federal matching rate that is based on state income. The current Federal match rate in New Jersey is 50%. (Kaiser Family Foundation, 2005). Medicaid in New Jersey is administered by the State's Department of Human Services. Table 1 describes Medicaid in New Jersey and nationally.

People are eligible for Medicaid in New Jersey if they meet three requirements: residency in the State, citizenship in the United States (or qualified alien status), and financial resources below eligibility levels. Other legal residents who are not United States citizens may be eligible for Medicaid if they have emergency medical needs. Medicaid beneficiaries include those eligible for all services under the NJ Medicaid program, those eligible under the Medically Needy program, and those eligible under the Home and Community-Based Services Wavier Programs. The latter two options provide a more limited range of services. (New Jersey Department of Human Services, 2005).

NJ Medicaid is mandated to provide certain services, including inpatient and outpatient hospital treatment, lab tests and X-rays, early and periodic screening, diagnostic and treatment services, home health care, physician services, nurse-midwife services, assistance with family planning and any necessary supplies, and nursing facilities for people over 21. There are also many optional services available to beneficiaries enrolled in specific programs. In addition to these benefits provided to individuals, state Medicaid programs make "disproportionate share" payments to hospitals that care for large numbers of Medicaid and uninsured patients (discussed below). (New Jersey Department of Human Services, 2005).

New Jersey's Medicaid program differs considerably from the national program. State Medicaid payments per enrollee averaged $5,437 in 2001, well above the United States average of $4011. About 42% of New Jersey Medicaid spending is for acute care (inpatient hospitalizations, physicians/lab/X-rays, outpatient services, prescribed drugs, and managed care); 44% is for long -term care (facilities for the mentally retarded, nursing homes, and home health); and

14% is for disproportionate share payments. By contrast, Medicaid nationally spends a much higher fraction – about 58% – of costs on acute care, 36% on long-term care, and only 5.3% of costs on disproportionate share payments. The demographics of the New Jersey program also differ from those of the national program, with a smaller share of beneficiaries in New Jersey being children under 19 (51%), compared to the nation as a whole (59%). (Kaiser Family Foundation, 2005).

New Jersey Family Care

New Jersey's FamilyCare program, begun in 1998, provides health insurance coverage to children in low-income, uninsured families with incomes above 133% and below 350% of the Federal Poverty level (that is, above the cutoff for Medicaid). (New Jersey FamilyCare, 2005). Those in families with incomes above 150% FPL are required to pay monthly premiums (varying between $17-$113.50 per month) and copays for health services.

Research comparing participation in insurance programs across states suggests that the imposition of premiums tends to lower participation. Research in New Jersey confirms that it has been difficult to enroll and retain children whose families are required to pay premiums in order to participate. (Silow-Carroll, S., et al., 2002). Today, about 15% of the potentially eligible children in New Jersey (those with incomes below 350% FPL) remain uninsured. (Glied, Sherry, 2002-2004).

In 2001, FamilyCare expanded to include certain low-income adults, but the program was rapidly oversubscribed and has since been closed. (Draper, Debra A., et al., 2001). Current adult enrollment in FamilyCare is less than one-half of the 2001 level. New Jersey also offers a Premium Support Program, which subsidizes family contributions to employer-sponsored insurance if the subsidies cost the State less than the cost of enrolling children in the state FamilyCare program. (Silow-Carroll, S., et al., 2002). The FamilyCare program covers a somewhat more limited set of benefits than does Medicaid. (Fox, M., et al., 2002).

The FamilyCare program spent just over $160 million in 2005. Coverage for children under FamilyCare is financed, in part, by the federal government, which pays 65% of the cost through the State's Child Health Insurance Program. The State has financed its share of contributions to FamilyCare with a combination of tobacco settlement funds and expected employer funds from the Premium Support Program. (New Jersey FamilyCare, 2005).

Managed Care in New Jersey

New Jersey ranks 17th in the nation in managed care enrollment, a relatively low ranking given the State's high population density (a factor that generally increases participation in managed care). (Draper, Debra A., et al., 2001). About 25% of all New Jersey residents are enrolled in some form of managed care program. (Kaiser Family Foundation, 2005). HMO plans are offered by the state employee health benefits plan, the Small Employer Health Benefits

Program, and the Individual Health Coverage Program. Increases in rates in the Individual Health Coverage Program have led to a shift toward enrollment in the HMO options in that program over time. About 70% of New Jersey Medicaid beneficiaries are enrolled in HMOs, somewhat above the national average (61%). (Kaiser Family Foundation, 2005). New Jersey regulates the HMO market very stringently, monitoring plans' financial status, level and promptness of payment to providers, and quality. (Draper, Debra A., et al., 2001).

Direct State Payments

The Medicaid Disproportional Share (DSH) program enables states to make extra Medicaid payments to hospitals with a high percentage of Medicaid and uninsured patients. Under the federal Medicaid DSH program, states have discretion in determining hospitals' eligibility for DSH payments: hospitals must receive DSH payments if their low-income utilization exceeds 25% and may receive designation if the Medicaid utilization rate is at least 1% of total bed days. In New Jersey, at a minimum, each hospital with a Medicaid inpatient hospital utilization rate that is one standard deviation above the mean Medicaid utilization rate for hospitals receiving Medicaid payments in the State receives DSH. (New Jersey Department of Health and Senior Services, 2005). The Medicaid DSH program is administered by the State's Department of Health and Senior Services.

Hospital Care Payment Assistance Program

The New Jersey Hospital Care Payment Assistance Program provides free or reduced charge care to certain patients receiving inpatient or outpatient services at hospitals in New Jersey. Payment assistance is available to uninsured New Jersey residents who are not eligible for other insurance coverage and have incomes below 200% of the Federal poverty level (for free care) and below 300% of the federal poverty level (for subsidized care). (New Jersey Department of Health and Senior Services, 2005).

Payments under the hospital care payment assistance program totaled over $500 million in 2005. The State's health care subsidy fund, financed through a variety of means, including payroll taxes, surcharges on ambulatory surgical centers and HMOs, cigarette taxes, and general revenues, is the source of this funding. (New Jersey Department of the Treasury, 2006). Charity care reimbursements through the payment assistance fund cover about 50 cents for every dollar of care provided to uninsured patients. (Greenwald, L. D., 2004).

Pharmaceutical Assistance and Other Public Insurance Programs

New Jersey also operates several means-tested health insurance programs aimed at aged and disabled residents. The Pharmaceutical Assistance and Senior Gold programs pay for prescription drugs for certain low-income residents. As noted above, these programs will soon be replaced by the Medicare Part D pharmaceutical program. A small hearing aid assistance program provides some reimbursement toward the cost of hearing aid equipment. (New Jersey Department of Health and Senior Services, 2005).

III. Health Care Delivery in New Jersey

Health care is big business in New Jersey. The five largest pharmaceutical companies in the nation have their headquarters in the State. The State's hospitals employ over 150,000 people, and are particularly important as a source of employment in the large urban centers. (Glied, Sherry, 2002-2004). Over 18,000 physicians practice in New Jersey. (Cantor, J., et al., 2005).

Hospitals

New Jersey has 78 hospitals. Almost all of these hospitals – 95% – are private, not-for-profit institutions. New Jersey has very few (three) for-profit hospitals and only one public hospital, Newark's University Hospital. This distribution is atypical. At the national level, about 16% of hospitals are for-profit, and 23% are public. (Kaiser Family Foundation, 2005). New Jersey's regulations on hospital ownership make it very difficult for for-profit hospitals to establish themselves in the State. (Health Care Finance, 2003). The state's suburban nature leaves it with few large cities to support public hospital systems. Instead, the State's hospital payment assistance program and disproportionate share program mean that not-for-profit community hospitals act as safety net providers for the poor and uninsured.

New Jersey hospitals experienced substantial over-capacity (and low occupancy rates) in the early 1990s. The later 1990s saw a wave of hospital consolidations, closures, and hospital system formation. Two large hospital systems, St. Barnabas and Atlantic Health System, now dominate. (Mays, Glen P., et al., 2005). These and other systems can exert countervailing bargaining power, leading to improvements in hospitals' financial situations – and rising insurance premiums.

New Jersey's hospital utilization rates resemble national averages. Beds per capita (2.69) are slightly below the national average; hospital admissions (128 per 1,000 population) and inpatient days (712 per 1,000 population) are just above the national average. (Kaiser Family Foundation, 2005). Average length of stay for non-Medicare patients at 4.831 days is consistent with the national average, while New Jersey Medicare patients have longer than average stays. (New Jersey Department of Health and Senior Services, 2005).

Throughout the 1980s and until 1992, New Jersey used a centralized hospital rate-setting system to establish hospital prices. Like all other rate-setting states, except Maryland, it deregulated the hospital rate-setting system as managed care penetration increased. At the same time, New Jersey substantially reduced subsidies for hospital care for the uninsured, which had been financed through a 19% surcharge on all hospital bills. As a result, state funding for charity care decreased from $700 million in 1992 to $350 million in 1996. (Volpp, K. G. M., et al., 2003).

New Jersey hospitals face increasing pressure to improve quality. Several studies suggest that the State's hospitals under-perform relative to national norms. (Mays, G. P., et al., 2005). The State does particularly poorly in measures of end-of-life care. New Jersey decedents have the highest probability in the nation of dying in hospital, are very likely to spend part of the last six months of their lives in intensive care units, and are likely to be seen by 10 or more different physicians. (Center for the Evaluative Clinical Science, 2000). The State now monitors and publishes risk-adjusted hospital performance in bypass surgery, and offers a website that permits consumers to compare hospitals using several measures of quality. (See http://web.doh.state.nj.us/hpr/). Employers are also actively engaged in hospital quality improvement. The Leapfrog Group, a group of large employers, has established a set of widely publicized quality standards. Eight hospitals in New Jersey report that they fully met at least one of the nine quality leaps of the Leapfrog Group, three have come close to completing all of them, and none has completed all of them. Another five have made partial progress toward at least one goal. (Leapfrog Hospital Survey Results for New Jersey, 2005).

Hospital Staffing

Hospitals in the United States and other developed countries tend to face cyclical nursing shortages. Finding sufficient numbers of nurses to staff hospitals is likely to be a growing problem as the baby boom ages and requires more hospital care, the nursing workforce ages, and many currently practicing nurses retire. New Jersey has a relatively robust nursing workforce, with about 86 registered nurses per 10,000 population (slightly above the United States average of 78 per 10,000), but it is estimated that the State will be short 19,600 registered nurses by 2010 unless further action is taken. (Kaiser Family Foundation, 2005). In 2002, the State legislature created the New Jersey Collaborating Center for Nursing to develop and disseminate information about the State's nursing workforce and to make recommendations to address future problems. Enrollment in New Jersey's schools of nursing has been increasing moderately over the past two years, but many of the nursing schools are now operating above capacity. (Dickson, G., et al., 2005).

Supply of Physicians

New Jersey has a relatively large supply of patient care physicians. The patient-physician ratio in the State stands at about 300:1, while the national average is slightly over 350:1. Primary care physicians make up about 40% of all physicians in New Jersey, comparable to the national average. (Canton, J., et al., 2005).

New Jersey has the highest concentration of international medical graduates (primarily immigrant physicians who trained outside the United States and Canada) in the nation. Over 40% of physicians practicing in the state trained abroad, about the same proportion as in New York State. Nationwide, just over one-fifth of the physician workforce trained abroad. (American Medical Association, 2005). International medical graduates often staff hospitals and provide services in disadvantaged areas that are not attractive to domestic graduates.

New Jersey has three medical schools, including one school of osteopathic medicine. All three schools are part of the University of Medicine and Dentistry of New Jersey. Together, they admit about 920 students each year, with preference given to residents of New Jersey. All three schools are subsidized by the State. (New Jersey Department of the Treasury, 2006).

According to the American Medical Association (AMA), twenty states, including New Jersey, face a crisis because of rapid increases in malpractice insurance premiums. There were slightly more claims per active physician (20.1 per 1000 physicians) in New Jersey in 2003 than the national average (18.8), and average claims payments ran about 10% above the national average. (Kaiser Family Foundation, 2005). These systemic problems were exacerbated by the failure of a large malpractice insurer in 2002. (Mays, Glen P., et al., 2005).

The AMA indicates that some physicians in the affected states are either leaving practice in the State altogether or have ceased to perform high-risk procedures. New Jersey has considered, but not yet passed, tort reform laws that would limit the liability of physicians. Instead, in 2004, the State implemented a malpractice subsidy program, financed through assessments on physicians and lawyers, which provides a subsidy toward premium costs.

Nursing Homes

There are 338 nursing homes in New Jersey. About 3.8% of the population over 65 resides in nursing homes in New Jersey, the same as the national average. Nursing home occupancy rates are high, with about 87% of beds occupied at any given time. (Kaiser Family Foundation, 2005).

Medicaid pays about 65% of nursing home costs in the State. (Kaiser Family Foundation, 2005). The state Medicaid program also runs a home care program intended as an alternative to nursing home use. New Jersey's home care program is much smaller than the national average, accounting for less than one-fourth of total long-term care expenses (compared to over one-third nationally). Kaiser Family Foundation, 2005).

IV. Health Care System Outcomes

The "products" of the New Jersey health care system include access to health care services, health care costs, and health status outcomes. New Jersey tends to do about average nationally on most of these outcomes.

Health Insurance

Overall health insurance coverage patterns in New Jersey are somewhat more favorable than the United States average (see figure 1). A somewhat higher than average share of the State's population holds employer-based insurance (62% vs 54%), slightly fewer hold individual, non-group insurance (3% vs 5%), somewhat fewer are enrolled in Medicaid (9% vs 13%), and slightly fewer are uninsured (14% vs 16%). (Kaiser Family Foundation, 2005).

As is the case nationally, uninsurance rates in New Jersey have been rising since the late 1990s. The State's uninsurance rate fell to 12.1% in 1999, and has since risen nearly two percentage points. Most of this increase has come through a decline in employer-sponsored coverage since the late 1990s, as health care costs increased and the labor market weakened. (United States Census Bureau).

Most uninsured people in New Jersey, as nationally, have low incomes. Fifty-eight percent of the uninsured in New Jersey have incomes below 200% of the Federal poverty level, compared to 66% in the nation as a whole. A greater proportion of New Jersey households earning between 200% and 349% of the Federal poverty level is uninsured than is the case nationally. This is likely a consequence of high health care costs and high general costs of living in the State. (Fox, M., et al., 2002).

The highest rates of uninsurance are found in the densely populated urban areas of northeastern New Jersey, and, consistent with the demographics of these areas, a higher than average proportion of these uninsured African-American, compared to the nation (19% vs. 15%). (DeLia, D., et al., 2004).

Uninsurance rates in New Jersey, as well as nationally, are highest for young adults and lower for children and those aged 40-64. Children are more likely to have access to Medicaid or New Jersey FamilyCare. Older adults are more likely to hold employer-sponsored insurance or to qualify for Medicare because of a disability. Uninsurance rates tend to be higher for single adults than for married couples, because of lower household incomes and the lack of access to spousal coverage. (DeLia, D., et al., 2004).

Costs of Care

The total cost of health care in New Jersey in 2000 amounted to over $37 billion. Personal health care expenditures comprised 10.8% of the State's gross product, somewhat below the 11.7% national figure. The lower share of health care in the State's GDP reflects the State's higher than average income – not the lower than average health care costs. Per capita health care costs in New Jersey in 1998 averaged $4,197 per person, 11% above the national average of $3,759. (Center for Medicaid and Medicare Services, 2000).

Employers in New Jersey routinely pay more for health insurance than do employers elsewhere in the nation. In a 1998 survey of 40 states, employers in New Jersey paid the highest premiums for single plans and third highest for family plans, and there is no indication that these relatively high premiums have since fallen. Small businesses pay particularly high rates, with premiums up to a third higher than the national average. (Fox, K., et al., 2001).

New Jersey establishments are more likely to offer at least one plan with no employee coverage contribution than is the case nationally, with nearly 60% of establishments offering at least one single plan without an employee contribution requirement in 1998. (Fox, L., et al., 2001). Like their counterparts nationally, however, employers in New Jersey have responded to these high premiums by raising required employee contributions for single and family coverage. (Fox, M., et al., 2002). These increases tend to lead some employees, particularly younger and/or low-income employees, to decline participation in employer-sponsored plans.

Health Status

The relationships between the characteristics of a health care system and the health of the population itself are complex and ambiguous. An area with poor underlying population health characteristics, for example, may spend a great deal on health care services and appear to be obtaining little value for its disproportionately high expenditures. Conversely, an area with high average incomes and good health habits may spend relatively little on health care services, even if these services are inefficiently organized and excessively costly. New Jersey is a relatively prosperous state, and we would expect it to have better than average outcomes even if its health care system only exhibited average performance.

New Jersey's public health system is very fragmented. Each of the State's counties operates its own local public health system, so that there were 578 operating Boards of Health in 1998. (Bovbjerg, Randall R., et al., 1998).

Births

There are about 115,000 babies born in New Jersey each year. Slightly more than 75% of mothers received prenatal care in the first trimester of their pregnancies, a figure similar to that in most large cities in the Northeast, but below rates in California and Texas. As elsewhere, black, non-Hispanic mothers, unmarried mothers, and less educated mothers were more likely to receive late or no prenatal care. Just under 8% of infants born in New Jersey are of low birth weight (less than 2500 grams), a rate that is comparable to the national average. Again, black, non-Hispanic mothers and teen mothers have the highest rate of low birth weight babies. (New Jersey Department of Health and Senior Services, 2002).

Deaths

Life expectancy at birth in New Jersey in 2002 was 78.1 years, slightly better than the national average of 77.6 years. The age-adjusted death rate in New Jersey is about 808.8 per 100,000, below the United States average of 845.3 per 100,000, but above the rates in New York (783.3) and Connecticut (762.4).

(Center for Disease Control, 2004). As is the case nationally, males and non-Hispanic blacks in New Jersey have higher than average age-adjusted death rates (38% and 31% higher than females and whites, respectively) and lower than average life expectancy (80.4 years for females vs. 75.6 for males; 78.6 for whites vs. 72.9 for blacks). (New Jersey Department of Health and Senior Services, 2002).

The leading causes of death in New Jersey, as nationally, are heart disease, cancer, stroke, chronic respiratory disease, and unintentional injuries. Together with the next five causes of death – diabetes, septicemia, influenza and pneumonia, kidney disease, and Alzheimer's disease – these conditions account for over 80% of all deaths in New Jersey each year. (New Jersey Department of Health and Senior Services, 2002).

Many deaths in New Jersey are related to behavioral and social factors. Unintentional injury – mainly automobile accidents – accounted for 2,599 deaths and was the third leading cause of death for males. There were 415 firearm-related deaths in 2002. About half of these firearm-related deaths were homicides and almost all of the remainder were suicides. Nearly 900 New Jersey residents died of drug-related causes in 2002, and nearly 500 died of alcohol-related causes. All of these causes of death are substantially more prevalent among men than among women, explaining a portion of the life expectancy gap between the sexes. (New Jersey Department of Health and Senior Services, 2002).

Health Behaviors

One of the main contributors to all four of the State's leading causes of death is cigarette smoking. New Jersey residents are slightly less likely to smoke than the national average (18.9% vs. 22.5%). As is the case nationally, smoking rates in New Jersey are higher among men than among women and higher among whites than among blacks. (Kaiser Family Foundation, 2005).

The main public policy instrument available to address high smoking rates is cigarette taxes. The tax rate on cigarettes in New Jersey is $2.40 per pack, the second highest state rate in the nation (after Rhode Island, at $2.46). (Princeton University Policy Research Institute, 2005).

An increasingly important disease risk factor in the United States is obesity. About 19% of New Jersey residents are obese with a body mass index of 30 or greater, and a further 34% are overweight, below the 21% and 35% national averages. Rates for each of the major population subgroups (males, females, whites, blacks, and Hispanics) are also slightly lower in New Jersey than nationally. (Kaiser Family Foundation, 2005). Obesity rates in New Jersey, as in the United States overall, have been rising recently. It is not yet clear what public policy remedies are effective and appropriate in addressing the rising rate of obesity either nationally or in any area.

By the end of 2004, 32,746 people were reported living with HIV/AIDS in New Jersey. More than three-quarters of this group were minorities and more than one-third were female. Nearly 70% are over age 40. Injection drug use and sexual contact are the main modes of exposure to HIV infection in the New Jersey population, with sexual contact rising as a source of exposure. (New Jersey Department of Health and Senior Services, 2004). New Jersey is one of only six states in the nation to outlaw syringe exchange programs. (Jacob, Riki, et al., 2003).

V. Overall Assessment

In a ranking of state health care systems, New Jersey would likely appear as a solid performer in the second tier of states. While not a dramatic innovator, like Minnesota, Maine, or Massachusetts, it has taken a series of steps to expand coverage and has experimented with a variety of strategies to keep costs down.

That said, the State's ambitions often seem to exceed its actions. For example, the expansion of health insurance to children and parents through NJ FamilyCare was unusually generous, compared to most other states. However, the program for adults rapidly filled up and had to be closed. In addition, the premium and co-payment structure serve to reduce participation among children, particularly in families that do not believe their children have an immediate need for health care services.

The State's hospital payment assistance program is a worthy innovation, targeting funds directly at needy patients, rather than at the hospitals themselves. Its financial structure seems rather wobbly, however. Funding comes from a variety of special taxes and assessments, funds siphoned from other programs, securitization of tobacco settlement funds, and other non-renewable sources.

The most broadly studied health policy innovations in New Jersey have been the individual and small group health plans. However, their success – or lack of success – is widely debated, and legislators continue to tinker with them, modifying regulations and changing premium practices from year to year. What is certain is that the individual health insurance program demands an overhaul, as it appears to be disintegrating rapidly. Although the potential market for individual insurance is almost certainly quite small, it would be indefensible to neglect this non-group market.

The high cost of care in the State places a substantial burden on both the government and the private sector. Rising Medicaid costs, particularly costs associated with seniors and with pharmaceutical coverage, continue to be a problem. The new Medicare Part D program may help alleviate this burden in the future, but it is likely to pose new problems in the short term. One potential area of cost-control innovation is the State's employee health benefit program, which does not seem to have been a focus of policy attention in the past.

The State's hospitals include a few stars that have worked hard to improve quality and implement new information technologies, but, as in most other states, there are many laggards as well. The State's hospital systems have been successful in negotiating with managed care plans. Now, they must turn to reducing costs and improving quality for those whom they serve.

The State's population has good – but not exceptionally good – health status. More could be expected of a prosperous, urban state. One problem may be the highly fragmented nature of health policy. Responsibility for health programs lies in several different state agencies and in a host of local public health departments.

Overall, there is considerable scope for improving the health care system of the State of New Jersey. Improvements could benefit both the economic and physical health of the State's citizens.

Table 1: Characteristics of Medicaid

	New Jersey	United States
Total Medicaid Enrollment (2003)	923,100	47,060,700
Total Medicaid Expenditure (2003)	$7,895,936,924	$266,817,101,410
Percent Expenditure on Acute Care	41.7	58.3
Percent Expenditure on Long- Term Care	44.2	36.4
Disproportionate Share Hospital Payments	14.1	5.3
Medicaid Payment per Enrollee (FY2001)	$5,437	$4,011
Medicaid Managed Care as a Percentage of Medicaid Enrollment (2004)	69.6	61.3
Federal Matching Rate Percentage 2005-2006	50	N/A
Payments By Enrollment Groups (Percentages) (2001)		
Children (Ages 0-18)	13.9	16.3
Adults (Ages 19-64)	13.6	10.6
Elderly (Ages 65+)	37.9	28.9
Blind and Disabled	33.5	39.5
Unknown	1.1	4.7

Source: Kaiser Family Foundation. (2005). State Health Facts.
www.statehealthfacts.kff.org [Accessed August 2005].

Figure 1:
Health Insurance Status in New Jersey and the USA as a whole.

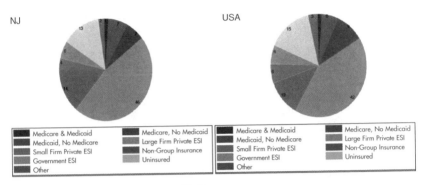

NJ   USA

Medicare & Medicaid	Medicare, No Medicaid
Medicaid, No Medicare	Large Firm Private ESI
Small Firm Private ESI	Non-Group Insurance
Government ESI	Uninsured
Other	

References

American Medical Association. 2005. *International Medical Graduates.*
  http://www.ama-assn.org/ama/pub/category/211.html [Accessed August 2005].
Bovbjerg, Randall R., Frank C. Ullman, Alison Evans Cuellar, Susan Flanagan. 1998.
  Health Policy for Low-Income People in New Jersey. May 1, 1998.
http://www.urban.org/url.cfm?ID=307466.
Cantor, Joel. 2005. "Small Business Health Insurance in New Jersey: Issues and
  Options." Presentation at New Jersey Appleseed Forum on Reforming the Small
  Business Health Insurance Market: Potential State Initiative. April 5, 2005;
  Monheit, Alan C., Joel C. Cantor, Piu Banerjee. *Assessing Policy Options for the
  Non-Group Health Insurance Market: Simulation of the Impact of Modified
  Community Rating on the New Jersey Individual Health Coverage Program.*
  March 2005. Rutgers University Center for State Health Policy.
Cantor, Joel, S. Brownlee, J. Sia, C. Huang. 2005. *Availability of Physicians in New
  Jersey.* Rutgers Center for State Health Policy.
Cantor, et al. 2005. *Availability of Physicians in New Jersey.* Rutgers Center for State
  Health Policy, Kaiser Family Foundation. 2005. S*tate Health Facts.*
  www.statehealthfacts.kff.org [Accessed August 2005].
Center for Disease Control. 2004. National Vital Statistics Reports. Vol. 53, No. 5,
  October 12, 2004. Table 29.
Center for the Evaluative Clinical Sciences. 2000. Dartmouth Medical School,
  Dartmouth Medical Atlas, 1999. http://www.dartmouthatlas.org/about.php.
  Figures based on Medicare data for 1996.
Center for Medicaid and Medicare Services. *2000. State Health Accounts 1980-2000.*
  http://www.cms.hhs.gov/tatistics/nhe/state-estimates-provider/2000/state.pdf
  [Accessed August 2005].
Center for Medicaid and Medicare Service. 2005. *National Health Care Expenditures
  Projections: 2004-2014.* http://www.cms.hhs.gov/statistics/nhe/projections-
  2004/proj2004.pdf [Accessed 2005].
Dickson, G. and L. Flynn. 2005. "New Jersey's Educational Capacity: Impact on
  Nursing Supply." New Jersey Collaborating Center for Nursing.
DeLia, D., M. Koller, C. Schneider, and L. J. Glickman. 2004. *The Medically
  Uninsured in New Jersey: A Chartbook.* Rutgers Center for State Health Policy.

Draper, Debra A., Linda R. Brewster, Lawrence D. Brown, Lance Heineccius, Carolyn A. Watts, Elizabeth Eagan, Leslie A. Jackson, Marie C. Reed. 2001 & 2005. "Financial Pressures Continue to Plague Hospitals. Northern New Jersey." *Center for Studying Health System Change. Community Report No. 12.* Summer 2001; Mays, Glen P., Robert A. Berenson, Thomas Bodenheimer, Laurie E. Felland, Anneliese M. Gerland, Lydia E. Regopoulos. "Urban-Suburban Hospital Disparities Grow in Northern New Jersey." *Center for Studying Health System Change. Community Report No. 4.* August 2005.

Draper, et al. 2001. "Financial Pressures Continue to Plague Hospitals. Northern New Jersey." *Center for Studying Health System Change. Community Report No. 12.* Summer 2001.

Draper, Debra A., John F. Hoadley, Jessica Mittler, Sylvia Kuo, Gloria J. Bazzoli, Peter J. Cunningham, Len M. Nichols. 2003. "Rising Costs Pressure Employers, Consumers in Northern New Jersey Health Care Market." *Center for Studying Health System Change, Community Report No. 4.* Winter 2003.

Forums Institute for Public Policy. 2005. *2005 Hot Health Policy Issues for State Policymakers.* Background Information for New Jersey Health Policy Forum. Wednesday, February 9, 2005. Thomas Edison State College, Trenton, New Jersey. www.foruminstitute.org

Forums Institute for Public Policy. 2005. *2005 Hot Health Policy Issues for State Policymakers.* Background Information for New Jersey Health Policy Forum. Wednesday, February 9, 2005. Thomas Edison State College, Trenton, New Jersey. www.foruminstitute.org [Accessed August 2005].

Fox, K., C. L. Cuite, Y. Diaz and J. C. Cantor. 2001. *Employer-Sponsored Health Insurance in New Jersey.* Rutgers Center for State Health Policy.

Fox, M. and D. Gaboda. 2002. *Health Insurance Coverage in New Jersey: Recent Trends and Policy Challenges.* Rutgers Center for State Health Policy.

Glied, Sherry. 2002-2004. Author's tabulations of the Current Population Survey, 2002-2004.

Greenwald, L. D. 2004. "Financing New Jersey's Hospitals." *New Jersey Medicine: 101(10): 35-36.*

Health Care Finance. 2003. *Monitoring Mergers in New Jersey: New Law Requires Scrutiny of Not-For-Profit Hospital Acquisitions.* http://hcfinance.com/dec/dec-con.htm [Accessed August 2005].

Kaiser Family Foundation. 2005. *State Health Facts.* www.statehealthfacts.kff.org [Accessed August 2005].

Keehan, Sean P., Helen C. Lazeby, Mark A. Zezza and Aaron C. Catlin. 2004. "Age Estimates in the National Health Accounts." *Health Care Financing Review.* Web Exclusive. December 2004. l, 1: 1-16.

Leapfrog Hospital Survey Results for New Jersey. 2005. The Leapfrog Group. Downloaded August 2005. www.leapfroggroup.org.

Mays, Glen P., Robert A. Berenson, Thomas Bodenheimer, Laurie E. Felland, Anneliese M. Gerland, Lydia E. Regopoulos. 2005. "Urban-Suburban Hospital Disparities Grow in Northern New Jersey." *Center for Studying Health System Change. Community Report No. 4.* August 2005; Draper, Debra A., John F. Hoadley, Jessica Mittler, Sylvia Kuo, Gloria J. Bazzoli, Peter J. Cunningham, Len M. Nichols. 2003. "Rising Costs Pressure Employers, Consumers in Northern New Jersey Health Care Market." *Center for Studying Health System Change. Community Report No. 4.* Winter 2003.

Mays, et al. 2005. "Urban-Suburban Hospital Disparities Grow in Northern New Jersey." Center for Studying Health System Change. Community Report No. 4. August 2005.

Medicare. 2005. *Medicare Personal Plan Finder.* http://medicare.gov/MPPF [Accessed August 2005].

Medicare+Choice Plan Withdraws effective January 1, 2002 from MCOL, Medicare HMO Summary Statistics. http://www.medicarehom.com/mrepnr02.htm. [Accessed August 2005].

Monheit, Alan C., Joel C. Cantor, Margaret Koller, Kimberley S. Fox. 2003. "Community Rating and Sustainable Individual Health Insurance Markets in New Jersey." *Health Affairs.* July/August 2004. Vol. 23, Issue 4; pg. 167.

Monheit, et al. 2003. "Community Rating and Sustainable Individual Health Insurance Markets in New Jersey." *Health Affairs.* July/August 2004. Vol. 23, Issue 4; pg. 167; LoSasso, Anthony T., Ithai Z. Lurie. *The Effect of State Policies on the Market for Private Nongroup Health Insurance.* Northwestern University Institute for Policy Research Working Papers 04-09. October 28, 2003.

Monheit, Alan C., Joel C. Cantor, Piu Banerjee. 2005. *Assessing Policy Options for the Non-Group Health Insurance Market: Simulation of the Impact of Modified Community Rating on the New Jersey Individual Health Coverage Program.* March 2005. Rutgers University Center for State Health Policy.

New Jersey Department of Banking and Insurance. 2005. *New Jersey Mandated Health Benefits Advisory Commission.* http://www.state.nj.us/dobi/insmnu.shtml [Accessed August 2005].

New Jersey Department of Banking and Insurance. 2005. *Health Insurance Programs.* http://www.state.nj.us/dobi/reform.htm [Accessed August 2005]

New Jersey Department of Human Services. 2005. Division of Medical Assistance & Health Services. http://www.state.nj.us/humanservices/dmahs/index.html [Accessed August 2005).

New Jersey Department of Health and Senior Services. 2002. *New Jersey Health Statistics.* http://www.state.nj.us/health/hcsa/subchapter_13pdf [Accessed August 2005].

New Jersey Department of Health and Senior Services. 2004. *New Jersey HIV/AIDS Semi-Annual Newsletter.* http://www.state.nj.us/health/aids/qtr1204.pdf [Accessed August 2005].

New Jersey Department of Health and Senior Services. 2005. *Eligibility For and Basis for Payment for Disproportional Share Hospitals.* http://www.state.nj.us/health/hesa/subchapter_13,odf [Access ed August 2005].

New Jersey Department of Health and Senior Services. 2005. *Information Sheet.* http://www.state.nj.us/health/seniorbenefits/paadapp.htm [Accessed August 2005].

New Jersey Department of Health and Senior Services. 2005. *Information Sheet.* http://www.state.nj.us/health/seniorbenefits/paadapp.htm [Accessed August 2005]. Kaiser Family Foundation. 2005. *State Health Facts.* www.statehealth-facts.kff.org [Accessed August 2005].

New Jersey Department of Health and Senior Services. 2005. *Inpatient Average Length of Stay (Days) By Primary Payer: UB-92 Data for 2003.* http://ww.state.nj.us/health/hcsa/avlos03.pdf [Accessed August 2005].

New Jersey Department of Health and Senior Services. 2005. *New Jersey Hospital Care Payment Assistance Fact Sheet.* http://www.state.nj.us/health/hcsa/ccfactsh.htm [Accessed August 2005].

New Jersey Department of the Treasury. *New Jersey Budget in Brief, 2006*.
    http://www.state.nj.us/treasury/omb/publications/06budget/index.shtml
New Jersey Department of the Treasury. 2005. *New Jersey Budget in Brief, 2006*.
    http://www.state.nj.us/treasury/omb/publications/06budget/index.shtml: Cantor,
    Joel. *Small Business Health Insurance in New Jersey: Issues and Options*.
    Presentation at New Jersey Appleseed Forum on Reforming the Small Business
    Health Insurance Market: Potential State Initiatives. April 5, 2006.
New Jersey Department of Treasury, Division of Pensions and Benefits. 2005. *State
    Health Benefit Program*. http://www.state.nj.us/treasury/pensions [Accessed
    August 2005].
New Jersey FamilyCare. http://www.njfamilycare.org [Accessed August 2005].
Princeton University Policy Research Institute. 2005. *Regional Update: Cigarette
    Taxes*. Summer 2005. http://region.princeton.edu/issue_53.html
Riki, Jacob and Paula Toynton. 2003. "Syringe Exchange." *New Jersey Medicine*.
    September 2003, 100(9)" 55-59.
See http://web.doh.state.nj.us/hpr/
Silow-Carroll, S., et al. 2002. "Assessing State Strategies for Health Coverage
    Expansion: Case Studies of Oregon, Rhode Island, New Jersey, and Georgia."
    The Commonwealth Fund.
Swartz, Katherine and Deborah W. Garnick. 1999. "State report: Hidden assets:
    Health insurance reform in New Jersey." *Health Affairs*. July/August 1999.
    Vol. 18, Issue 4; 180-188.
United States Census Bureau. *Health Insurance Coverage Status and Type of
    Coverage by State*. Table HI-4.
Volpp, K.G.M. S. V. Williams, M. V. Pauly, et al. 2003. *Market Reform in New Jersey
    and Quality of Care: A Cautionary Tale*. Leonard Davis Institute of Health
    Economics.

Special thanks to Emily Miller for her research assistance.

CHAPTER FOUR

Medicaid in New Jersey:
Options for Reform

By
Sherry Glied, Michael Sparer,
and Megan Vanneman

Introduction

New Jersey's Medicaid Program presents a policy paradox. Rising costs in an era of budget deficits prompt policymakers to consider a range of cost containment measures, including eligibility, benefit, and reimbursement cutbacks. At the same time, rising numbers of uninsured and underinsured people, along with the ongoing erosion of the employer-sponsored insurance system, stimulate state officials to consider strategies that will help these populations, such as liberalizing eligibility rules or expanding outreach in an effort to increase enrollment.

The goal of this paper is to summarize the various options for reforming Medicaid – by reducing costs, improving quality, or expanding access to services. There are tradeoffs to be made, and this paper will draw on the experience of other state Medicaid programs to suggest some of the pros and cons of the various strategies.

Medicaid in New Jersey: An Overview

New Jersey's Medicaid Program and its State Child Health Insurance Program (SCHIP), together, form one of the nation's most generous systems of public health insurance. These public insurance programs provide a wide array of medical services to roughly 912,000 state residents in four distinct populations: 498,000 children, 136,000 low-income adults, 134,000 blind and disabled persons, and 144,000 low income elderly. (Kaiser Family Foundation, 2005).

Child Eligibility

Children under 18 in New Jersey are eligible for public insurance if they live in families with incomes at or below 350% of the Federal Poverty Line (FPL), about $56,000 for a family of four. This is the highest eligibility limit for public health insurance for children in the nation. Formally, infants in families with incomes at or below 200% of the federal poverty level, pregnant women with incomes at or below 200% of the federal poverty level, and other children in families with incomes at or below 133% of the federal poverty level obtain coverage through Medicaid. Children in families with incomes above this level and at or below 350% FPL are covered through SCHIP.

From the beneficiary perspective, it makes little difference if enrollment is in Medicaid or SCHIP. There is a single application process for the two programs, a single provider delivery network, and even a single program name (KidCare). Family income level does, however, determine whether a premium is charged and, if so, how much. Beneficiaries in families with incomes at or above 150% of the federal poverty level are required to pay premiums. The premiums range from $17.50 per month for a family at 150% of the federal poverty level to $110 per month for families with incomes above 300% of the poverty level. (Kaiser Family Foundation, 2005).

From the State's perspective, the main difference between the two programs is that the federal match rate for Medicaid is 50%, while the rate for SCHIP is 65%.

Adult Eligibility

New Jersey in 2001 enacted public insurance coverage for parents with Medicaid/SCHIP-eligible children and incomes below 200% of the federal poverty level. Federal Medicaid dollars help finance this coverage for parents with income at or below 133% of the poverty level, while SCHIP dollars help finance coverage for parents between 134-200%. This parental coverage program is very generous by national standards. Facing a budget crisis in 2002, the State froze new enrollment in the program. Three years later, with an improving economy, the State re-opened enrollment to parents with incomes below 100% of the poverty level (with plans to increase the income level to 133% by 2007). (Smith et al., 2005).

New Jersey in 2001 also enacted public coverage for single adults with incomes at or below 100% of the federal poverty level. This coverage was funded exclusively with state dollars. Due to budget crunch, the State also froze new enrollment in this program in 2002, but, unlike parental coverage enrollment, this program remains closed today. State officials have, however, requested federal permission to convert the program into a Medicaid waiver initiative, thereby capturing federal dollars to pay half the cost. If the waiver request is approved, the State will again permit enrollment into this program. (Smith et al., 2005).

Benefits

The Federal government requires state Medicaid programs to cover a basic benefit package, but offers to contribute financially when states choose to cover a wide range of additional optional benefits. State programs may cover still other benefits (such as abortions), though they must do so without federal funding. The flexibility over the composition of benefit packages leads to significant interstate variation. Indeed, no two states offer the same benefit package.

New Jersey's Medicaid benefit package is quite generous, covering all but a handful of the optional benefits. New Jersey also is one of 19 states that use state funds to cover abortions. The State's most notable benefit exclusions are occupational and physical therapy services, both of which are covered by more than half of all states. Interestingly, Pennsylvania joins New Jersey in excluding coverage for these two services, while New York covers both. In contrast, both New Jersey and Pennsylvania cover podiatry and chiropractor services, while New York excludes both. (Kaiser Family Foundation, October 2004; Kaiser Family Foundation, 2005).

Beneficiary access to these benefits comes primarily through hospitals and outpatient clinics, rather than office-based physicians. In 2004, for example, the State spent only 1.8% of its acute care Medicaid bill on physician/lab/x-ray services, compared to the national average of 6.7%. That same year, the State spent 16.7% of its acute care Medicaid bill on outpatient clinic services, as opposed to the national average of 11.5%. The main reason for the institutional bias is that the State pays unusually low reimbursement rates to physicians, paying only 56% of the national average physician reimbursement level. (The Robert Wood Johnson Foundation, 2005).

In the mid-1990s, New Jersey, like many other states, turned to managed care as a strategy to stabilize program costs, increase beneficiary access, and improve overall quality. Today, more than 69% of the State's Medicaid beneficiaries are enrolled in one of five HMOs.

Finances

New Jersey in 2004 spent $8 billion on its Medicaid program, roughly half of which was financed with federal funds. The State (in 2001) spent roughly $5,437 per Medicaid enrollee, 10th highest among the states. The national average per enrollee spending was $4,011. New Jersey spends much less than New York, which operates the most costly Medicaid program in the nation ($7,817 per enrollee), and about 20% more than Pennsylvania, which spent $4,634 per enrollee. (Kaiser Family Foundation, 2005).

The Problem in a Nutshell

New Jersey's Medicaid program faces two conflicting and serious challenges. First, uninsurance rates in New Jersey, as nationally, have been climbing with health care costs. The overall uninsurance rate among those under 65 in New Jersey in 2002-2004 was 16%, placing New Jersey at the mid-point among US states. This moderate overall rate primarily reflects the relatively high average income of New Jersey residents. The uninsurance rate among lower income New Jerseyans – those with incomes below 200% FPL – however, was 36%. Only six states had higher low-income uninsurance rates. New Jersey has a much higher rate of uninsurance among low-income residents than does Connecticut (26%), Massachusetts (24%), New York (29%), or

Pennsylvania (26%) and about the same rate as Maryland (36%). (Authors' tabulations of the Current Population Survey 2002-2004).

These high low-income uninsured rates are particularly striking because low-income residents of New Jersey have relatively high rates of employer-sponsored insurance – comparable to those in other Northeast states and most other regions of the country. The pattern of relatively high low-income uninsured rates and high employer-sponsored insurance rates in New Jersey holds for both children and adults (though more strongly for adults). This relationship suggests that the high rates of uninsurance in New Jersey reflect primarily a failure of access to the public insurance system.

Counterbalancing the problem of limited access is the rising cost of Medicaid in New Jersey. Until recently, the State's Medicaid program was a national leader in cost containment. State Medicaid expenses grew only 2% between 1995 and 2000, compared with 5% nationally, and as a result the program's share of general fund revenue declined from 16% to 14%. (Gaboda et al., 2005). Beginning in 2000, however, Medicaid costs in New Jersey and around the nation began to rise dramatically (over 12% in 2002), leading the State to enact the enrollment freeze on adult coverage. While cost increases have moderated over the last couple of years, costs are still rising at more than 7%, leading to ongoing budgetary pressures.

Policymakers in New Jersey need to simultaneously expand access to coverage and contain the costs of that coverage. This dilemma, while challenging, is not unique to New Jersey. The experience of other states may help guide New Jersey to a better way out of the box. Below we discuss options for expanding coverage and reining in costs.

Increasing Access to Public Insurance for Low-Income Children and Adults

New Jersey has been a national leader in expanding eligibility to Medicaid and SCHIP. In the early and mid-1990s, New Jersey moved aggressively to expand the number of Medicaid beneficiaries. As a result, the number of Medicaid recipients grew 37% between 1990 and 1995. (Bovbjerg et al., 1998). Similarly, following Congressional enactment of SCHIP in 1997, New Jersey created one of the most generous SCHIP Programs in the nation, not only covering children up to 350% of the federal poverty level, but also becoming one of a handful of states to use SCHIP dollars to cover parents and state-only dollars to cover single adults.

However, even before the fiscal crisis in 2002 caused the State to cut back its enrollment efforts, policymakers in New Jersey recognized that there were still large numbers of uninsured children who could be enrolled in KidCare, but were not. This pattern replicated a national trend. Some families were unaware of the potential coverage. Others were unwilling to navigate needed administrative hurdles. Still others worried about jeopardizing their immigration status. Premiums deterred even more potential enrollees. For all of these reasons, about one-fifth of the State's children with incomes below 200% FPL and 12%

of children with incomes between 200-350% FPL are uninsured, notwithstanding their likely eligibility for public coverage.

As the State's economy declined during the early 2000s, state officials engaged in relatively few new efforts to find and enroll youngsters who were eligible but still uninsured. To be sure, the State did create a single Medicaid/SCHIP enrollment application, and blended the two programs together in a seamless structure that eased the administrative burden for applicant families. Nonetheless, the State's decision to freeze adult enrollment and to impose relatively high premiums on families with income at or above 150% of the poverty level kept overall enrollment low.

Unlike several other states, however, New Jersey resisted the political and economic lure of more draconian eligibility cutbacks. Missouri, for example, reduced the eligibility level for parents from 75% of the federal poverty level to 23%. Similarly, Oregon, Tennessee, and Mississippi have also cut significantly the number of persons receiving publicly funded health insurance.

In 2004-2005, as the State's economy began to recover, policymakers changed course and adopted a series of efforts designed to increase public insurance coverage (and thereby reduce the number of uninsured). Most obviously, the State lifted the freeze on adult enrollment for parents at or below 100% of the federal poverty level, the first step in a phased-in expansion that will cover parents at or below 133% of the poverty level by 2007. This change will not only increase the number of adult beneficiaries, it also will likely increase the number of child enrollees (studies clearly demonstrate increased take-up of coverage for children when parents are also eligible for coverage). (Thorpe and Florence, 1999; Feder, Uccello et al., 1999). State officials also requested federal permission to begin enrolling childless adults at or below 100% of the federal poverty level into a Medicaid-waiver program.

Equally important, state officials enacted a major initiative to encourage more of the eligible but unenrolled to sign up for coverage. In 2004, for example, the State conducted a pilot program in eight school districts in which Medicaid/SCHIP applications were distributed to all families eligible for federally subsidized school lunches. (Gaboda et al., 2005). The following year, the state legislature enacted the Family Health Coverage Act of 2005, which 1) reduced to one page the joint Medicaid/SCHIP application; 2) eased the verification requirements imposed on applicants (requiring, for example, only one pay stub to verify income); 3) expanded the State's program of presumptive eligibility under which safety net health care providers can directly enroll applicants even in advance of a final administrative determination; 4) reduced from six months to three the period in which a SCHIP applicant must be uninsured prior to enrollment; 5) established 12-month continuous eligibility, thereby minimizing dramatically the number of persons who will churn on and off the rolls due to failure to properly recertify; and 6) increased significantly the funding for outreach and education by community-based organizations. (Cohen Ross and Cox, 2005). Indeed, according to a recent survey, New Jersey has become a national leader in the effort to perform outreach and simplify administration. (Cohen Ross and Cox, 2005).

There are, of course, additional ways the State could ease the application process. The State could, for example, permit applicants to self-declare their income, as 18 other states already do. The State could eliminate the requirement that SCHIP beneficiaries be uninsured for any particular period of time prior to enrollment, as 18 other states (including New York and Pennsylvania) have done. Most significantly, the State could reduce the premium imposed upon families at or above 150% of the federal poverty level. There is little question, for example, that requiring families at or above 300% of the poverty level to pay a premium of $110 per month is a strong deterrent to enrollment.

Making it easier to enroll and maintain enrollment in the Medicaid program will likely reduce the number of low-income people who go without insurance in New Jersey. At the same time, easing enrollment burdens is likely to lead to increased displacement of private coverage. Some people who might have enrolled in private coverage are likely to remain on Medicaid if they can easily do so. Others offered the choice between costly employer-sponsored coverage and equally accessible, free Medicaid coverage may choose public coverage. Finally, employers, recognizing the reduced need for private coverage among their low-income enrollees (and especially the dependents of these enrollees), may raise required contribution rates for dependent coverage. (Buchmueller et al., 2005).

Although crowd-out and increased enrollment will generate higher costs, the magnitude of the funding burden generated by simplifying eligibility or by crowd-out may be smaller than one might predict. Administrative simplification and easier reenrollment is likely to attract people to Medicaid, who have relatively low need for health services. High users – and the providers who treated them – would likely have taken steps to gain and maintain eligibility even when doing so was difficult.

Controlling Costs by Cutting Benefits

One strategy to reduce the costs of the Medicaid program – either to expand coverage to more people or to reduce public costs – is to alter the Medicaid benefit package, either by increasing co-payments or by reducing benefits. One straightforward way that this could be accomplished is through reduction in optional Medicaid benefits (those not required by the federal program). According to a recent survey, for example, 16 states are planning benefit reductions in 2006, including Indiana (cutbacks in dental coverage), Maine (podiatry, durable medical equipment, and mental health), and Missouri (dental, podiatry, vision, and rehab services). (Smith, et. al., 2005). New Jersey has not cut benefits in recent years and has no plans to do so in the coming year.

Benefits may also be changed more systematically through a federal waiver. Several states have gone this route. In the 1990s, Oregon strove to balance an expansion in Medicaid eligibility with a reduction in Medicaid benefits, reshaping the Medicaid benefit package through a system of health service prioritization. More recently, Utah received federal permission to cut benefits to current adult beneficiaries and to use the savings to finance a Medicaid expansion that provides primary care services to an additional group of previously uninsured adults. (Kaiser Commission, 2005). The waiver is the first that permits states to develop varying benefit packages for different Medicaid populations.

While the logic of reducing benefits to expand coverage makes ample sense on paper, it appears more difficult to accomplish in practice. Oregon realized very limited savings from its elaborate prioritization process. Many of the low priority services that were cut had generated relatively low expenditures to begin with. More draconian limits, such as those in Utah, raise the risk of leaving the sickest beneficiaries without access to the care they need. Such limits are likely to generate provider and patient backlashes that effectively limit the potential savings. Limits on optional services (such as dental and mental health coverage) can have the same effect, and may even generate perverse cost increases if more costly mandatory services are substituted for de-covered optional services. Cutting mental health or dental services, for example, could well lead to higher overall costs if beneficiaries who go without needed preventive care end up suffering from (preventable) medical emergencies.

There is also an effort in some states to adopt a variety of tools to convert beneficiaries into "cost conscious consumers." One strategy is to increase co-payments for Medicaid services. In 2006, for example, 13 states are imposing new or higher co-payments (most commonly on prescription drugs and non-emergency use of hospital emergency rooms). (Smith et al., 2005). Moreover, the National Governors' Association has urged Congress to provide states with increased flexibility to impose still higher co-payments. New Jersey already imposes co-payments at or near the maximums currently allowed (as opposed to New York and Pennsylvania, neither of which imposes co-payments at all).

More ambitiously, South Carolina and Florida are seeking to restructure their Medicaid programs to encourage beneficiaries to become savvy health care consumers. South Carolina is seeking federal permission to provide Medicaid beneficiaries with risk-adjusted "personal health accounts" that would be used either to pay health plan premiums or to pay directly for health care services (other than in-patient hospital care). No longer would there be a mandated minimum Medicaid benefit package. Health plans and providers presumably would, instead, compete for beneficiaries' business. (Solomon, 2005). The Florida proposal is similar: health plans would offer a variety of benefit packages to beneficiaries (though the current minimum benefits would need to be included), and beneficiaries would choose either to join a plan or to opt out and use Medicaid subsidies to buy employer-sponsored coverage. (BNA Health Policy Reporter, 2005).

Controlling Costs by Cutting Reimbursement

Over the last two years, Medicaid programs in every state have either decreased or frozen provider payments as part of a cost containment initiative. (Smith et al., 2005). Compared to some states, New Jersey's efforts in this arena were rather mild, consisting of a one-year freeze on hospital outpatient rates that was expected to save the State $24 million and an ongoing freeze on fee-for-service physician fees. (Holahan et al., 2004).

State provider payment policy, however, is increasingly an ineffective cost-containment tool, since Medicaid managed care plans, which now control roughly 70% of the market, generally determine their own provider reimbursement rates. State policymakers could, of course, lower the rates paid to the managed care plans, thereby achieving far more significant cost savings for the program. Nonetheless, New Jersey's managed care initiative faces problems of its own which make rate cuts unlikely anytime soon. Over the last several years, eight of the thirteen HMOs that participated in the State's Medicaid managed care initiative have left the market. Several plans became insolvent due to fraud and abuse during the late 1980s. (Bovbjerg and Ullman, 2002). Only five HMOs continue to participate in the program. Lowering rates further would likely lead to a continued exodus of plans. Without a selection of plans available, the viability of the managed care model is likely to erode. As a result, state officials in 2004 actually increased health plan rates by 8.5%. (Holahan et al., 2004).

Controlling Costs by Cutting the Cost of Prescription Drugs

According to a recent study by the HHS Office of Inspector General, New Jersey's Medicaid program pays the highest rates in the nation for prescription drugs. (HHS Office of the Inspector General, 2004). New Jersey also spends a far higher percentage of its Medicaid dollar on prescription drugs than do most states. In 2004, for example, the State spent 22.6% of its acute care bill on drugs, compared to the national average of 17.9%. Pennsylvania, by contrast, spent only 10.5% on prescription drugs. Not surprisingly, New Jersey officials characterize rising pharmacy costs as the primary driver of Medicaid inflation. (Smith et al., 2005). Nonetheless, New Jersey has implemented far fewer pharmacy cost containment initiatives than other states. In 2004, the State did begin to require mandatory substitution of generic drugs for brand name drugs in its Medicaid and state-only pharmaceutical programs. The State also increased the discount it receives, from average wholesale price (AWP) minus 10% to the AWP less 12.5%. (Bovbjerg, 2004). Despite these incremental efforts, however, the State's overall record in this policy arena is not good.

State policymakers could, for example, achieve prescription drug price reductions through the development of a preferred drug list (PDL). Competition among companies to have their drugs on the Medicaid PDL could drive costs down. The VA and some state Medicaid programs have achieved significant savings through the use of such lists. Indeed, while New Jersey officials rejected a PDL proposal in 2004, 31 other states (including Pennsylvania) enacted or expanded such lists. (Smith et al., 2005). To be sure, unlike generic substitution (where the generic substitute is required to be chemically identical to its brand name counterpart.), PDLs impose real costs on consumers. Drugs on the list may not be identical to those that consumers are currently taking, and adverse health effects may result. For this reason, states typically establish appeals processes through which providers can request exemption from the PDL. As a result, the effectiveness of PDLs as a cost containment strategy is likely to vary in inverse proportion to the ease with which providers can appeal PDL decisions. Even with these caveats, however, New Jersey officials ought to consider again enacting a PDL.

State policymakers also could adopt a variety of other pharmacy cost containment measures, ranging from imposing co-payments on all drugs to requiring prior authorization on additional drugs, imposing limits on monthly prescription purchases, or entering into multi-state purchasing pools. In May 2005, for example, federal officials approved plans by Louisiana, Maryland, and West Virginia to form the second multi-state prescription drug purchasing pool. Eight other states (Alaska, Hawaii, Michigan, Minnesota, Montana, Nevada, New Hampshire, and Vermont) previously established a purchasing pool. (Centers for Medicare and Medicaid Services, 2005b). To date, New Jersey has been reluctant to move aggressively in this arena.

Controlling Costs – Long Term Care

New Jersey spends about 39% of its Medicaid dollars on long-term care, slightly more than the national average (35%) but less than either New York (41%) or Pennsylvania (44%). (Kaiser, 2005). Developing strategies to contain long-term care costs is likely to be essential as the State's population ages.

There are several possible directions to go to reduce long-term care costs. First, the State could try to cut the actual cost of long-term care services. Second, the State could seek to shift more of the cost of such services to other payers. Third, the State could encourage a reorganized (and presumably more efficient) long-term care system.

One way to cut the cost of long-term care is to make it more difficult for older persons to become Medicaid eligible. Both President Bush and the National Governors Association, for example, have recommended that Congress tighten transfer of asset rules, thereby minimizing the number of middle-class seniors who use financial gimmickry to become Medicaid eligible. (Centers for Medicare and Medicaid Services, 2005). Despite the ongoing rhetoric about this issue, however, it is unclear how many persons are actually engaged in such asset transfer activities, and how many dollars actually could be saved by tougher rules. The State also could make it more difficult for Medicaid beneficiaries to qualify for long-term care services. Arizona, for example, has enacted strict pre-admission screening rules. Another option would be to cut reimbursement for long-term care facilities, but this is difficult to enact politically and could encourage poorer quality care. Finally, the state could seek to cut the supply of long-term care facilities through certificate-of-need procedures, but here, too, there is little evidence that certificate-of-need changes actually reduce costs.

As an alternative to cutting the long-term care bill, the State could try, instead, to shift more of the cost of that bill to other payers. Over the last decade, for example, states have worked with the nursing home industry to maximize Medicare reimbursement (which is borne entirely by the federal government). These Medicare maximization efforts are a large part of the reason that the Medicare share of the nation's nursing home bill has risen from just under 4% to roughly 12% in less than a decade.

States also can seek to encourage greater use of private long-term care insurance. The market for this product has historically been quite small (roughly 5-6% of all seniors), mainly because it is very expensive, and because it often offers a poor benefit package (paying only a relatively small portion of an actual nursing home bill for the policyholder). There is much discussion of policy options that might make such high-quality long-term care insurance policies more affordable. Some suggest tax credits (though there is little likelihood that a credit would be generous enough to do more than subsidize those who already own policies).

More attractive is a public-private partnership now underway in four states (California, Connecticut, Indiana, and New York) under which Medicaid acts as a re-insurer for private coverage, even for persons with assets well above the Medicaid limits. In New York, for example, persons who buy three years worth of nursing home coverage become Medicaid eligible when they exhaust their private-coverage benefit, even if they have significant assets in the bank. Similarly, in Connecticut, persons who buy $100,000 in private coverage can enroll in Medicaid once they have exhausted their private coverage, even though they still have $100,000 in the bank. To be sure, enrollment in these programs remains below expectations, partly because relatively few people have heard of the initiative, and partly because the policies are still relatively expensive. Nonetheless, this sort of public-private partnership remains one of the more promising strategies for encouraging greater use of private long-term care insurance, and New Jersey officials might well seek federal permission to adopt their own version.

The final reform strategy is the effort to reorganize the long-term care delivery system, primarily by seeking to shift more of the long-term care dollar to home and community-based services. New Jersey now spends 31% of its long-term care dollar on home and community-based services (such as home health care, personal care, and even assisted living) compared to a national average of 37%. To be sure, home and community-based services are not necessarily cheaper (or better) than institutional care, mainly because of the so-called "woodwork effect," which suggests that government might end up financing home care currently provided informally (or not at all). Done right, however, home and community-based services can be cheaper and more appealing to the elderly than institutionalization, and, given demographic trends, it makes good sense to move in this direction.

Disease Management, Care Management, and Health Information Technology

In the early 1990s, nearly every state (including New Jersey) began encouraging (or requiring) large numbers of Medicaid beneficiaries to enroll in managed care delivery systems. The assumption was that managed care would provide improved access and quality at a reduced price. Over time, policymakers recognized that managed care is not a magic bullet; commercial HMOs have entered and left the Medicaid market, enrollees have continued to rely excessively on hospital emergency rooms, and beneficiary access has improved only marginally. One of the more interesting developments in recent years, however, is that many states are moving away from health plan contracting, substituting in its place state-administered primary care case management (PCCM) programs. North Carolina, for example, has received national recognition for its PCCM Program and its innovative disease and care management initiatives. As New Jersey struggles with declining health plan participation in its managed care initiative, the PCCM model could prove to be an attractive alternative.

State managed care initiatives also are increasingly focusing on new populations, especially those persons with more chronic and complicated medical conditions. This trend is in sharp contrast to the early days of Medicaid managed care, when states concentrated almost exclusively on healthy moms and young children. States now recognize that the high risk and high cost patients are perhaps most in need of care management, and that the potential rewards from working with these populations (both in reduced costs and improved care outcomes) are the most dramatic.

A recent survey of state Medicaid programs, however, suggests that New Jersey is not moving ahead aggressively with either disease or care management programs. (Smith et al., 2005).

Those states that are moving ahead with disease and care management initiatives are often assisted by advances in health information technologies that enable providers and payers to share patient data. Blue Cross Blue Shield of Tennessee, for example, is working with the Cerner Corporation and the State Medicaid agency to implement a program called Community Connection, under which providers around the state will have access over a secure website to the medical records of every Medicaid enrollee. (HealthCare IT News, May 2005). The Tennessee initiative represents a dramatically different way of using information technology in Medicaid programs. Instead of simply using information technology to collect payment data, states are now able to collect more informative patient and system data. (Milligan, 2005). New Jersey should be moving in this direction as well.

Reducing Fraud and Abuse

In 2005, 28 states reported new or enhanced efforts to reduce Medicaid fraud and abuse. (Smith et al., 2005). Most of these initiatives focused on provider fraud. Several states enhanced their ability to analyze provider claims and detect fraud. Other states increased reviews of pharmacy dispensing patterns in an effort to control pharmacy fraud. Still other states increased oversight of nursing home applications in an effort to uncover fraudulent asset transfers. New Jersey did not report any new efforts to reduce fraud and abuse. (Smith et al., 2005).

Medicaid in New Jersey: Options and Opportunities

Policymakers in New Jersey need to simultaneously expand access to public insurance coverage and contain the costs of that coverage. This past year, state officials took several steps that are likely to achieve the goal of expanded access. The decision to lift the freeze on parental enrollment, along with the request for federal permission to enroll single adults with incomes at or below 100% of the poverty level into a Medicaid waiver program, reflect the State's commitment to increased access. Even more important, the State enacted one of the nation's most comprehensive efforts to encourage more of the eligible but unenrolled to sign up for coverage, increasing outreach, simplifying the application process, and easing the renewal process. The State could undoubtedly do more (lowering the premiums on SCHIP enrollees would be a good start), but, on balance, state officials have moved aggressively on access in a still uncertain economic environment.

State officials have not, however, acted nearly as aggressively on efforts to contain the costs of public coverage. To be sure, these officials have wisely avoided traditional, and largely ineffectual, cost containment measures, such as cutting optional benefits or reducing provider reimbursement. The savings generated by cutting optional benefits (like dental coverage) are generally less than the costs imposed by the denial of such benefits (and the ill will generated in both the provider and beneficiary communities). State officials have also wisely held off on suggesting some of the more draconian reforms now underway in states like Florida, South Carolina, and Utah. There are, however, other options that could and should be on the Medicaid agenda.

Perhaps the most obvious (though politically difficult) target for cost containment is pharmacy costs. The State ranks first in the nation in the fees it pays for prescription drugs, and the rapidly rising pharmacy bill threatens the fiscal integrity of the program. Critics suggest that the State's relative inaction is due to the presence in the State of several large pharmaceutical companies. Joel Cantor, director of the Rutgers Center for State Health Policy, notes that, "New Jersey is the home of the pharma industry, and there is a fair amount of pressure to not mess with the goose that lays the golden egg (quoted in Ash, 2005). As difficult as the politics may be, state officials ought to push hard to use some of the pharmacy cost-containment tools that are in widespread use elsewhere.

The adequacy of the state's disease and care management programs, its efforts to encourage more home and community-based long-term care services, and its programs to combat provider fraud, are harder to gauge, but they all represent areas in which other states are moving ahead, and New Jersey ought to seek a leadership position.

On balance, however, state officials seem to be doing a good job of balancing the need for increased access with the need to keep costs under control. The New Jersey Medicaid program has generous eligibility criteria, offers comprehensive benefits, and keeps costs at a moderate level. The options for reform described in this report represents opportunities to make one of the nation's best programs of public health insurance even better.

References

Ash, Lorraine. 2005. "New Jersey Drug Costs Highest in US," DailyRecord.com, November 13.

BNA Health Policy Reporter. 2005. "Florida Medicaid Waiver Approved, October 24."

Bovbjerg, Randall and Frank Ullman. 2002. *Recent Changes in Health Policy for Low-Income People in New Jersey.* March. The Urban Institute.

Bovbjerg, Randall et al. 1998. *Health Policy for Low-Income People in New Jersey.* The Urban Institute. August.

Bovbjerg, Randall. 2004. *State Responses to Budget Crises in 2004: New Jersey.* February. The Urban Institute.

Buchmueller, Thomas, P. Cooper, K. Simon and J. Vistnes. 2005. "The Effect of SCHIP Expansions on Health Insurance Decisions by Employers." *Inquiry* 42; 3 (November): 218-231.

Centers for Medicare and Medicaid Services. 2005. *Transfers of Assets.* http://www.cms.hhs.gov/medicaid/eligibility/assets.asp [Accessed November 2005].

Centers for Medicare and Medicaid Services. 2005b. Press Release, "HHS Approves Second Multi-State Purchasing Pool to Lower Medicaid Drug Prices, May 27."

Cohen, Ross and Donna and L. Cox. 2005. "In a Time of Growing Need: State Choices Influence Health Care Coverage Access for Children and Families: A 50-State Update on Eligibility Rules, Enrollment and Renewal Procedures, and Cost-Sharing Practices in Medicaid and SCHIP for Children and Families. October 2005," Kaiser Commission on Medicaid and the Uninsured.

Feder, J. and C. Uccello, et al. 1999. "The difference different approaches make: Comparing proposals to expand health insurance." *Expert Proposals to Expand Health Insurance Coverage for Children and Families.* Kaiser Family Foundation. Washington, DC. 2.

Gaboda, Dorothy, S. Chase, S. Williams and C. Schneider. 2005. *NJ FamilyCare Express Enrollment: Report on Pilot Program, 2005.* Rutgers Center for State Health Policy, April.

Healthcare IT News. 2005. "Tennessee Blues, Cerner View Shared Project as Unique," Daily News, May 23.

HHS Office of Inspector General. 2004. *Variation in State Medicaid Drug Prices.* September, OEI-05-00681

Holahan, John, R. Bovbjerg, T. Coughlin, I. Hill, B. Ormond and S. Zuckerman. 2004. State Responses to Budget Crisis in 2004: Case Study – New Jersey, Kaiser Commission on Medicaid and the Uninsured.

Kaiser Commission on Medicaid and the Uninsured. 2005. Overview of Utah Section 1115 Waiver.

Kaiser Family Foundation. 2005. *State Health Facts.* www.statehealthfacts.kff.org [Accessed September 2005].

Milligan, Charles. 2005. [October 26-27th, 2005]. *Presentation for the Medicaid Commission Meeting:* "Program Administration: Financing IT and Fraud & Abuse." Center for Health Program Development and Management. http://www.cms.gov/faca/mc/milligan_module5.pdf [Accessed November 2005].

Smith, Vernon, K. Gifford, E. Ellis, A. Wiles, R. Rudowitz and M. O'Malley. 2005. "Medicaid Budgets, Spending and Policy Initiatives in State Fiscal Years 2005 and 2006: Results from a 50-State Survey. October 2005," Kaiser Commission on Medicaid and the Uninsured.

Solomon, Judith. 2005. "Risky Business: South Carolina's Medicaid Waiver Proposal." Center on Budget and Policy Priorities, August 10.

The Robert Wood Johnson Foundation. 2005. *Changes in Medicaid Physician Fees, 1998-2003: Implications for Physician Participation.* http://www.rwjf.org/newsroom/featureDetail.jsp?featureID=550&pageNum=1&ty pe=3 [Accessed October 2005].

Thorpe, K. and C. Florence. 1999. "Covering uninsured children and their parents: Estimated costs and number of newly insured." *Medical Care Research and Review* 56(2): 197-214.

CHAPTER FIVE

Homeless In New Jersey:
Why Does It Happen?

By
Glenda Kirkland

Is a homeless person the victim of prevailing economic conditions or someone who brings his situation on himself? Public policies are developed to solve social problems. The appropriateness of a policy choice depends upon one's understanding of the problem being addressed. In the United States, we debate whether individual-level pathologies cause social problem, or whether the causes lie in deficiencies or disruptions in social, political, or economic systems. In New Jersey and other locales, homelessness presented a burgeoning social crisis beginning in the early 1980s. Amidst a barrage of media attention and public pressure, policy makers were called upon to respond. Policy responses are developed in context and, in the case of homelessness, the context was ambiguous. This paper examines the contextual frame within which homelessness evolved in New Jersey from 1980-2000.

The Historical Background of
U. S. Social Welfare and Housing Policies

Social Welfare Policy

Our institutions organize meaning and reflect what we value in society (van Til 1994). Traditionally in the United States, the two institutions responsible for the indigent, disabled, and infirm were the family and religious groups. The family was the institutional unit of economic production, education, and social welfare, caring for the poor and the ill. The early government raised taxes for public works projects and the military. Under Elizabethan poor laws, localities cared for their own destitute. With the growth of the federal government, there was created a national arena for airing both public and private concerns. The emergence of the political party structure, and activities evolved from their early aristocratic composition to a more democratic membership. During the Pierce presidency, there was pressure to create public institutions for the care of the insane. Pierce vetoed the federal legislation, but care was provided by the states. Except for post-Civil War veterans programs, the trend for government to stay out of social welfare efforts lasted until the 1930s. In the 1880s, wealthy individuals attempted to redress the social evils wrought by the industrial revolution and to assist in the pursuit of common social goals, including support of the arts. Private efforts, such as the Red Cross, predominated until after World War I. The catastrophe of the Great Depression overwhelmed private efforts to ameliorate social despair, and New Deal policies of the federal government continued to grow, funded in part by universal income tax revenue (van Til 1994).

Throughout much of the 1800s, a positivist approach was employed in understanding and solving social welfare problems. The positivist approach involved the application of knowledge and the scientific method to solve problems, including the gathering of empirical data. In Germany's Bismark era, social welfare legislation was drafted based on "fact-finding reports." The social survey tradition was used by Charles Booth in London at the end of the 1800s to try to find the causes and ramifications of poverty. Booth was studied by American social welfare advocates and his techniques copied in early Chicago and Pittsburgh social welfare research (Parsons 1995). Given problems to solve, there are four broad policy vehicles the government can employ: distributive, distributing new resources; redistributive, changing the distribution of existing resources; regulatory, regulating and controlling activities; and "constituent," setting up or reorganizing institutions (Lowi 1964; 1972). Debates ensue concerning the nature and definition of social problems and the correct government tools for addressing them. Yet social welfare policy in the United States can often be reduced to simple questions of where society's institutions are willing to locate the "safety net." Social, economic, and political institutions form "a system of rewards and penalties that is intended to encourage effort and channel it into socially productive activity" (Okun 1975:1). The U. S. tradition in social welfare has been a focus on "curing the ills" of the poor and dependent people as individuals, remaking them into "worthy, independent people" (Skocpol 1992).

Rueschemeyer and Skocpol in *States, Social Knowledge and the Origins of Modern Social Policy* trace the historical development of U.S. and U.K. government services for children and the poor. In the English tradition, social welfare issues were viewed as structural problems of inefficiency in the capitalist market system. While England developed programs to "smooth" the imperfect adjustments in the economy that resulted in unemployment and poverty, social welfare experts in the United States followed a different path, looking to individual pathologies that were diagnosed and treated via the case method. Aggregates of individual pathologies were analyzed via survey methods, as if the nation's poverty was an epidemic constructed by multitudes of "infected" persons. England's nonjudgmental distribution of material aid was substituted in this country by moral support and advice by social workers to assist the "victim" in his or her "moral struggle" (Foucault 1972) against poverty. This approach is consistent with traditional American emphasis on individual initiative and hard work (Chelf 1992). High infant mortality rates directly linked to conditions of poverty were the focus of women's civic action groups pressing for protective legislation in the 1920s. Rather than address the underlying causes of poverty, the American Medical Association entered the discussion and framed infant mortality risk as a medical problem of pregnancy that needed to be addressed one patient at a time (by physicians) rather than systemically (Rueschemeyer & Skocpol 1996). Social stigmas and inequalities are often translated into problem statements to be addressed by social programs (Rueschemeyer & Skocpol 1996).

Defining the condition to be cured by government predetermines the appropriate solutions. Is the condition to be cured an individual-level ailment or a structural-level failure? An addict needs rehabilitation, an undereducated person needs job skills training. Systemic failures are frequently translated into individual failures, as it is difficult for the public sector to envision curing something wrong with itself, due to failures in the economic system or previously misguided policies that have produced unintended consequences.

Values that are socially constructed based on power relations result in multiple ways of knowing, experiencing, and interpreting programmatic outcomes. "The traditional values of human life focus on justice and freedom, violence and oppression, happiness and gratification, poverty, illness and death, victory and defeat, love and hate, salvation and damnation…they are ultimate values: they define what Life is all about" (Habermas 1971:96). Values influence policy and programs. The political dynamics in operation in society influence problem statements, how they are to be addressed, who defines it, and who measures progress (Parsons 1995)?

Values are social constructions. Most post-modern theorists agree that the way we know and perceive value and meaning is socially constructed and relative to the individual (Schneider & Ingram 1993). Historically in the United States, the "knowledge-bearing" elite power groups devise programs in response to political challenges to dominant class interests by subordinate classes. Threats to the established order are addressed by programs designed by dominant classes. Those programs serve the interests of subordinate classes according to the understanding and interpretation of those interests by the dominant classes. State knowledge is not neutral or scientific; many social policies effectively "neutralize" the voice of the poor, while elite groups continue to enjoy "the sorts of relationships and resources it takes to achieve intellectual authority" (Rueschemeyer & Skocpol 1996). An official knowledge based on power relations (Foucault 1972; Rueschemeyer & Skocpol 1996) can be part of a social construction that defines unwanted behavior in pathological terms. This construction can establish ideological statements about the way the world is, the legitimate methods of inquiry, and credentials of expert voices.

Social norms specify what actions are regarded by a set of persons as proper or correct, or improper or incorrect; norms can be internalized. "Norms are macro level constructs based on purposive actions at the micro level but coming into existence under certain conditions through a micro-to-macro transition. Once in existence, they lead, under certain conditions to actions of individuals (that is sanctions or threats of sanctions) which affect the utilities and thus the actions of the individuals to whom the sanctions have been or might be applied. Thus norms constitute a social construction which is a part of a feedback process…;" norm violation and sanctioning capabilities are positively associated with power in the system (Coleman 1990:242).

"Human knowledge consists of a series of constructions, which, precisely because they are humanly generated, are problematic, that is, indeterminate, unsettled and ambiguous" (Guba & Lincoln 1989). With increased record keeping and data gathering, the state in many cases has become the collector and keeper of "official knowledge" (Rueschemeyer & Skocpol 1996). Public agencies are established and charged with "monitoring the conditions of various segments of the population, recommending preventative or protective legislation and then eventually administering social welfare legislation" (Rueschemeyer & Skocpol 1996:287). This knowledge includes both cognitive ideas about "what is the case" and "prescriptive," normative ideas about what should be the case" and "what should be done" (Rueschemeyer & Skocpol 1996).

Power relationships influence behavior in programs and judgments about which information is worth gathering (Schmidt 1994). Interpretation and knowledge of program impacts can be politically imposed and effectively manipulated by powerful language and symbols. Policies are communicated and understood in social contexts, through the use of objects, language, rituals, and symbols that represent social values and meanings. The role of authority in hierarchical relationships should not be overlooked (Balk 1992). It should always be asked "what rules of right are implemented by the relations of power in the discourses of truth" (Foucault 1976)? Faith in authority relationships is a guiding myth in U. S. society (Campbell 1980). Full information is not always available to actors, power is not distributed evenly, people get heard from unequally, and everyone's options are not considered (Etzioni 1967). Nor do legislators or program employees "leave their contexts at home" (Yanow 1996). Lindblom proposes that ordinary people using ordinary knowledge be included in the discourse, that program impacts be probed for the perspectives of ordinary people and discussed by a wide audience, thus disrobing the political construction of technical expertise and exposing it as an inferior cognitive approach (Lindblom 1990).

For some theorists, the issue is deviance, that is, those who depart from our shared expectation of what is "normal" serve to define what normal behavior is. Highlighting and recognizing the deviant behavior cannot only promote change on the part of the deviants themselves, but it can also reinforce the dominant notion of acceptable behavior. Structural functionalists, such as the anthropologist Margaret Mead, held that people are a product of their culture and society. Problems in society were by-products of how these social systems operated as well as how the culture framed and defined reality for the individual. A social problem can be seen as a condition of deviance from the generally held norms. Society first becomes aware of this condition as a problem when its values are threatened. It is then that public administrators are called upon to address the emerging threat to the status quo (Fuller and Myers 1941).

Housing Policy

In the 1980s and early 1990s, it became politically unfeasible to continue to provide income support to low income families who failed to thrive in the economic environment. Their failure was due to individual behavior, which was deemed contrary to the norm. At the same time, behavior that was favored continued to receive public support in the form of tax exemptions for single family home ownership, preferential tax treatment for unearned income, and capital gains exemptions on investment earnings from the sale of primary residences. "Housing, like so many other areas of social policy, became, after an initial surge of interest, a field for experts, with the incursions of general public opinion becoming less and less informed and less and less useful"(Glazer 1988:7). Both preceding and during the debate on welfare reform and in the midst of its implementation, many communities were seeking solutions to the problem of family homelessness. Most homeless families were also poor families; the two policy arenas concerned a large, shared clientele. Were homelessness policies motivated by media pressures to take action yet limited by political pressures to keep costs to a minimum? Were policy alternatives, which were redistributive in nature, discarded in favor of policy approaches built on regulating participant behavior? Was policy a direct response to the values of the majority of voters? Did the policy simply reflect the fact that society's sense of responsibility to care for the indigent was slipping down in priority in our national consciousness? Since clientele of the programs are poor and not very well organized, they were not included in the decision making process; they did not present the feared backlash that, for instance, the AARP can muster (Pear 1996).

Housing is a critical, psychological, survival need for an individual, and, as such, constitutes a major concern (interest, as defined by Coleman 1990) over which an individual would want control. The literature establishes housing as a fundamental determinant of social well-being for both the individual, the family, and the community (Hayden 1984). With passage of the Housing Act of 1949, housing was affirmed as a national goal to provide a "decent home and suitable environment for every American family" (Fisher 1975). Housing is especially critical to child development (Schorr 1988; Solnit 1992), family stability (Hasci 1997), mental health (Wilner 1962), and personal happiness (Hayden 1981). From such seminal thinkers as Carl Sauer of Berkeley came studies of the influence of man on his habitat and the effects of habitat on human behavior. In *The Agency of Man on Earth*, Sauer developed the psychologically-based rationale for the importance of the infant-mother bond, which mushrooms and amplifies to generate kinship bonds, then systems of kinship bonds and then into wider social systems. Since antiquity (Glacken 1956), scholars have examined the influence of the physical environment on human culture. Housing issues constitute a major sub-field in psychology and mental health, economics, population and demographics, social sciences and human behavior, and urban studies. Carl Jung theorized the home as a symbol of self. Economic resources spent on shelter needs constitute a substantial portion of both government and private budgets. The federal benchmark established for household income allocated for housing is 30%; at the end of the 1980s, 63% of low-income renters spent at least half their incomes on rent. In 1995, the federal government spent $25 billion on housing programs (Chelf 1992).

Maslow's classic "Theory of Human Motivation" published in 1943 establishes a generally-accepted framework of the hierarchy of human needs and subsequent behavior based on motivation designed to fulfill those needs. According to Maslow's theory, basic needs must be satisfied before an individual can address higher order requirements that a complex society demands of her. If a person is hungry or homeless, in addition to the insurmountable technical difficulties of holding a job, such as physical energy, no place to shower or change, and inadequate sleep, Maslow theorizes that the individual will be unable to focus on anything at all until the most basic of her needs are met. Shelter is one of the most basic needs. More modern studies continue to measure the impact of poor housing on human well-being, such as the likelihood that children will be underweight (DeParle 1996). "A sense of place" or the "chronological connectivity to one's habitat can bring meaning and dignity to life" (Kunstler 1996). The international United Nations HABITAT Conference held in 1996 with over 16,000 participants declared shelter a "basic human right" (Johnson 1996).

Perhaps due to the scale and complicity of housing needs in human existence, the approach to the subject must be multidisciplinary in scope. The historical and anthropological framework is eloquently established by Carl Sauer. Jacob Riis in *How the Other Half Lives* documented the health and social dysfunction ramifications of poor urban housing. "By far the largest part, 80% at least, of crimes against property and against the person are perpetrated by individuals who have either lost connection with home life, or never had any, or whose homes have ceased to be sufficiently separate, decent and desirable to afford what are regarded as ordinary wholesome influences of home and family" (Riis 1890). Riis saw tenement housing reform as the key to ending poverty. Twenty-four years later, Lawrence Veiller in *A Model Housing Law* joined Riis in defining the social ills resulting from a lack of proper, affordable housing for decent families who wished to raise their children properly. Veiller proposed looking at every facet of this complicated area, which encompassed economics, education, and changes in building codes through legislation and enforcement of laws (Veiller 1914). Housing is essential to family life for the "associated privacy, intimacy and readiness of emotional exchange" it provides (Solnit 1992:5).

Economists have offered substantial evidence of the strong link between poverty and housing quality (Nevitt 1967; Stegman 1970; Pugh 1980; Ball 1988; Kemeny 1981 and 1992; O'Flagherty 1996). However, economists do not always agree on the most effective method for upgrading housing conditions in a capitalistic market. The decades of federal programs to promote home ownership, taking the form of mortgage guarantees, tax credits and direct rent subsidies to private developers are viewed by many as government intervention to support private housing, industrial producers, and financiers rather than the inhabitants of inferior housing (Stegman 1970; Pugh 1980; Ball 1988; Kemeny 1981 and 1992). Three other theorists, Ernest Fisher in *Housing Markets and Congressional Goals*, Enid Gauldie in *Cruel Habitations: A History of Working-Class Housing 1780-1918*, and Jim Kemeny in *Housing and Social Theory,* concur that housing availability and quality reflect the power structure, inequalities, and racism in the overall society. Housing in the U.S. is inextricably tied to capitalist economic values: the central issue is who will control the economic structures of housing provision, and in whose interests (Ball 1988)?

A catalog of housing policies and expenditure levels requires a look at more agencies than the U.S. Department of Housing and Urban Development. Housing has been seen as a major area of government activity and public responsibility since the 1930s (Wheaton 1947), yet addressing housing has been fragmented and uncoordinated. Prior to 1930s, housing was seen as a public health, social reform, or building code issue. Government data gathering and reporting focused on specific conditions or aspects of the housing market, with no comprehensive picture. In 1932, the Federal Home Loan Bank was created to prop up mortgage lending institutions. Other New Deal era agencies, The HOLC and FSLIC were similarly established to reduce mortgage foreclosures and instill bank depositor confidence in the home mortgage system. The FHA sought to reform mortgage lending practices, while the PWA worked to provide employment through the construction of housing. In 1937, the USHA was created to provide federal subsidies to local agencies for slum clearance and building of low income housing. During World War II, the Defense Housing Coordinator in the then National Housing Agency provided oversight of wartime demand for housing, and began planning for a post-war housing shortage. In 1944-45, the Senate Committee on Housing and Urban Development held hearings to investigate national housing priorities and inadequacies.

Government policies intervened in the housing market by building housing, providing housing subsidies, and extending support through the Internal Revenue Service for preferred consumer behavior, such as single family home ownership. Policy approaches come in and out of favor. The Housing Act of 1949 funded 800,000 units of public housing over six years. Five years later, the Housing Act of 1954, funded only 10,000 units per year. In 1974 federal legislation created a private market housing program known as Section 8, an income-based, means-tested program, which, rather than building housing units, subsidized the leasing of private market units. By 1995, the federal government was spending $25 billion on various housing programs (Chelf 1992).

The Causal Theories of Homelessness

Defining the Problem

There was at the time and continues to be, no agreement about what causes homelessness, about how many people are homeless, how to define who is homeless or how to remedy the situation. This lack of agreement raged in the 1980s and 1990s, in the public press and in peer-reviewed journals in economics, social sciences, and health sciences. Despite such a muddled context, government from the federal to the local levels responded to what was labeled by many as a homelessness "crisis." Until the passage of the HUD, Stewart B. McKinney Homeless Assistance Act in 1987, the federal authority primarily responsible for homeless services was The Federal Emergency Management Agency (FEMA), which offers temporary help following natural disasters, not cures for individuals. The HUD definition of "homeless" evolved from the concept of homeless persons living on the streets or in abandoned buildings, or lacking regular and customary access to conventional housing (Rossi 1989), to include those persons who were temporarily in shelters or housing intended for the homeless. (US Code: Title 42, Sec. 11302).

Artist, Misha Richter, *The New Yorker,* November 20, 1995

By 1992, HUD annual spending on homeless assistance programs had reached $404 million, serving about 20,000 persons. By 1996, 280,000 persons were receiving services under HUD funding, a 14-fold increase in four years (HUD 1996a). By 1996, attention to homelessness had subsided in the media. Using HUD's definition of who is homeless, the 2000 census revealed a 26.4% decrease in homeless persons in New Jersey from 1990 to 2000. HUD reported a 12% increase in the number of low-income families who were paying more than half their incomes for housing over the 1991 level preceding the economic expansion of the 1990s; the robust economy was causing rents to rise, squeezing the working poor out of the housing market (Molotsky 2000). By the summer of 2001, the number of homeless families in the New York City shelter system was at its highest level since 1986, mirroring the situation in other U.S. cities and attributed by "officials" to the high cost of housing in the economic boom. Similar to the height of the homeless crisis, this story received front page emphasis from *The New York Times* (Bernstein 2001). In the summer of 2002, *The New York Times* editorial page was urging the government to stimulate the production of affordable housing and realize the goal of "a decent home and suitable living environment for every American family," which was still unrealized since first promised in The Federal Housing Act of 1949 (*The New York Times*, July 5, 2002).

"Social problems are definitional activities of people around conditions and conduct they find troublesome" (Schneider 1985:209). Some adverse conditions are defined and addressed by government and some are not, often depending on the amount of pressure from the public or the media. Problem definitions are not devoid of politics. After problems are defined, people follow a process for "claiming" to have these problems, or documenting these problems and then there are "responding activities" on the part of the government or authorities...demand for services, the filing of lawsuits...to alleviate the problem situation (Schneider 1985:212). Thus, government must create categories and terminology for these problems, the causal factors, and possible solutions, if, in the political realm, it has been deemed the government's responsibility to address them. "The appropriate role of government depends on the nature of the imperfections" (Arnott 1987:965). Concerning homelessness in the mid-1980s, there was no agreement among experts on the nature of this social imperfection.

An undesirable condition or social "sickness" can be addressed as an array established by degrees of displaying or possessing the attributes of the condition. A small amount or some measure of the condition may be admissible, while what is considered excessive amounts to a social or legal transgression. For example, drinking and driving to a limited extent, is allowed by law; having a blood alcohol content in excess of the established limit is illegal. There are distinctions in law between acts of theft involving small amounts of value or money (petty larceny) and larger amounts of value or money (grand larceny). The law can become a "set of official symbolic categories for making claims to effect social change" (Gusfield 1981:218). For example, "to define rape as a crime makes the conflict one between the state and the accused" not between the accused and the rape victim (Schneider 1985:218). When public discussion and media attention focus on situations where groups of persons are "undervalued" by official behavior, these groups often "come out to demand their civil rights and integrity with demands on the government for entitlements" (Spector 1981). Many social and individual problems are medicalized when policy experts and government officials frame causal factors that need to be addressed to alleviate problems. Physical abuse of children by parents and others became known as "battered child syndrome" (Prohl 1977), naturally occurring menopause as the "deficiency disease" of women lacking in the hormones of their youth. It fell to public administration to determine what homelessness was, what was causing it, and what would fix it in the mix of mounting public attention and muddled advice from experts.

The 1980s were not the first time in United States history that the country looked at the situation and causes of homelessness. The nation had periodically seen the ranks of the homeless swell due to economic depressions and wars. An exposé of dire tenement conditions by Jacob Riis in 1890 blamed economic conditions for miserable and unhealthy housing. The first published study of homeless men, a "tramp census," conducted by J. J. McCook in 1892, explored characteristics of the homeless themselves. Seeing themselves as excluded from the capitalist dream, the unemployed homeless or "tramping armies" organized protest marches on Washington in 1894. During the Progressive movement, many sought a "scientific" understanding of the causes of homelessness. During the same period, a medical diagnosis of "dromomania" emerged to describe the homeless lifestyle as a form of mental illness, the individuals as pathological. Others, such as Robert Hunter (1910), found homelessness was due to structural faults in society, such as low wages and economic downturns, not individual pathology. Similar to the government's response at the end of the 20th century, until the time of the Great Depression laws were passed and programs started that addressed both macro-level structural causes and micro-level individual causes of homelessness. States adopted laws to compensate injured workers, provide foster care for children, widows' pensions for women to care for children in the home (the precursor to AFDC), as well as asylums for the insane and public hospitals to serve the ill. It was not until 1912, that the federal government established the Federal Children's Bureau to oversee the welfare of children, and not until 1917 that it enacted the Smith-Hughes Vocational Education Law for retraining the unemployed. Despite addressing structural problems that contributed to homelessness, the homeless population was still generally referred to as dope addicts and drunks (characteristics of individual pathology) through the mid 1930s.

The overwhelming economic catastrophe of the Great Depression caused homelessness to soar; by 1933, 1.5 million people were without shelter, and many descended on police stations for overnight accommodations. The Depression jolted the public with the realization that individual economic prosperity or failure did not occur outside the prevailing economic conditions. In 1932, Congress established the Committee on the Care of the Transient and Homeless, and on July 26, 1933 created FEMA, the Federal Emergency Relief Administration, which by 1935 was assisting over 373,600 homeless people a month (Erickson & Wilhelm 1986). The Works Progress Administration surveyed the homeless population in 12 American cities during 1933-1935 (Erickson & Wilhelm 1986). The New Deal programs enacted from 1933-1937 sought to address macro-level factors of unemployment and home ownership. The legislation that produced Aid for Families with Dependent Children remained, for the most part, in place until modified in 1988 by the Family Support Act, and later in 1996 when it was substantially changed by the Personal Responsibility and Work Opportunity Reconciliation Act, commonly known as "welfare reform." Once again, the dislocations in employment and housing seen after World War II were addressed by the federal government through legislation that alleviated stress at the individual level due to problems created at the structural or macro-level by supporting returning veterans. This action took the form of unemployment compensation, tuition assistance, below-market rate mortgages, and federal assistance to local governments for the redevelopment of blighted areas. Great Society legislation during the period 1964-1974, as well, sought to address macro-level factors rather than individual factors contributing to poverty, poor nutrition, poor education, and poor housing.

Homelessness reappeared on the public agenda in the mid-1980s (Bassuk 1984, Burt 1992, Jencks 1994, Piliavin, et. al. 1994, O'Flaherty 1995). In 1983, *The New York Times* indexing scheme segregated by the term "homeless;" prior to that time, the category was labeled, "vagrants" or "vagrancy" (O'Flaherty 1996). As shown in the chart below, the number of articles with the word "homeless" in the headline or lead paragraph more than doubled from 1979 to 1980. By 1983 the number had doubled again, and by 1985 the number of articles was three times the 1983 level. By the end of the decade, in 1990, there were 35 times as many articles concerning homelessness than in 1980. The significance of homelessness is reflected by the cover story positioning in leading newspapers and newsmagazines. Homelessness became less prominent in 1995-1996, which is especially evident in coverage by a major newspaper of record, *The New York Times*. Although over 6,000 articles appeared in 1998, they were not receiving the prominent display of previous years.

Number of Articles with "Homeless" in Headline or Lead Paragraph 1972-1998

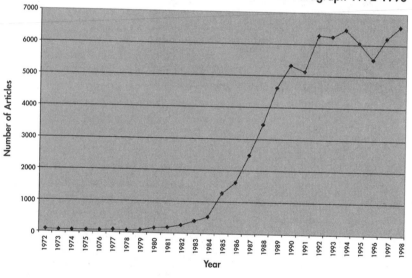

Source: Lexis Nexis Index of Top 50 U. S. Newspapers and International English Language National Newspapers.

Discussions about homelessness rose dramatically in the social and health sciences and economics peer-reviewed journals during and preceding the rise in homelessness. After the Progressive Era, sociologists and psychologists held some interest in unsheltered people. A 1923 paper estimated a "tramp problem" of 2 million unemployed men, described as having "inadequate personalities, defective mentalities and physical defects," and from whom young boys should be kept away (Anderson 1923). The American Journal of Sociology discussed relief efforts and expenditures in 124 American cities in 1932 (Abbott 1933),

Eric Drooker, Artist.
Originally appeared on the cover of
The New Yorker. Copyright © 1995
The New Yorker Magazine, Inc.
Used by Permission.

Artist, Ronald Searle.
This illustration originally appeared
in *The New Yorker.*

Number of Citations with Key Word "Homeless"   1972-1998

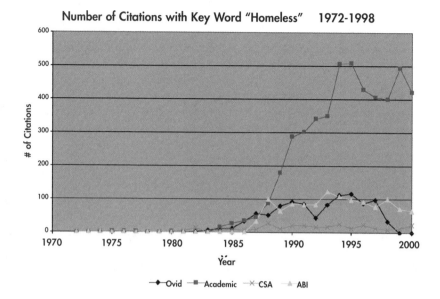

Source: Ovid – Wilson Social Science Abstracts Academic
Search Premier database of 3,430 publications
CSA = Cambridge Science Abstracts: Worldwide Political Science Abstracts
ABI Inform = ProQuest Index

others the situation and later-life adjustment of homeless youth (Levy 1933, Morgan 1941, Knight 1943, Brockington 1946, Borderia 1965), the efficacy of social policy (Titmuss 1951, Pringle 1960), the role of mental illness (Cohen 1951, Weinberg 1952, Bergler 1955, Levinson 1955, 1957, 1960, 1965, 1966, 1967, 1970, 1971, Himelstein 1957), and problems of the aged homeless (Lovald 1961).

The annals of alcoholism research abound with papers concerned with homelessness and addiction (Straus 1946, 1948, Straus & McCarthy 1952, Jackson & Connor 1954, Wattenberg & Moir 1954, Katz 1966). Howard Bahr in a 1967 study attributed the declining populations on "skid rows" in urban environments not to the declining numbers of homeless residents but to their dispersion to other settings (Bahr 1967). Matthew Dumont in 1968 suggested bartenders in taverns as outreach points for homeless men who were not being reach by traditional welfare agency providers (Dumont 1968). The "road to skid row" was reached through four phases, beginning with disassociation from mainstream society (Wallace 1968). Theorists struggled with questions of how to define the homeless, who the homeless were, how many there were, what methodology to use to answer these questions, and whether causes were at the macro-level or the individual level. With a view to prevention, they wanted to know what factors, macro or micro or a combination of the two, could be predicted to result in homelessness.

The debate about causes of homelessness as discussed in the peer-reviewed journals was organized around two different philosophies for understanding and addressing social needs in the United States. One philosophical camp contended that deficiencies and aberrations in social, political, and economic systems are prime factors for homelessness. The contrasting group focused on the characteristics and defects observed in many homeless individuals as personal causal factors, i.e., individual pathologies resulting in their inability to provide and maintain a roof over their heads. The government responded with programs reflecting both points of view, with no clear idea of how many persons needed services or how to define those in need of services.

Macro-Level Causal Theories

In general, macro-level causal theories reflect the philosophy prevalent in European countries, that homelessness is the result of lack of housing at prices the poor can pay. This situation is caused by "structural failures of three major economic sectors – the labor market, the housing market, and public welfare programs" (Rossi 1989:200). Structural theory arguments contend that individuals are not to blame for finding themselves without homes. Cutbacks in social-welfare programs, the feminization of poverty (the rise in low-income, single-parent, female-headed families), the deinstitutionalization of the mentally ill starting in the 1950s, reduced public housing stock, gentrification, high rents, high unemployment, increased domestic violence, disintegration of the traditional family, and an alienating social climate all have been cited as causing homelessness for people through no fault of their own (Bassuk 1984, Jencks 1994). Supportive of economic causes were, it is no surprise, the economists (Henderson 1977, Braid 1981, Arnott et al 1983, Adams 1986, Marin 1987, Dreier 1987, Calsyn 1991, Doling 1997). Supportive of systemic social ills as the causes of homelessness were theorists encouraging government action to cure social inequality, especially poverty (Harrington 1962, Lukes 1974, Sexton 1983, Stern 1984, Wilson 1987, Freeman & Hall 1987, Rossi 1989, Fox & Roth 1989, Welfeld 1989, Colwell 1990, Shane 1991, Chelf 1992, Wright 1993, Bassuk 1996). Others blamed inept social policies (Weisbrod 1965, McGuire & Weisbrod 1981, Stoner 1983, Robbins 1986, Fabricant et al 1986, Hope & Young 1986, Robbins 1986, Hatchett 1987, Belcher 1988, Hayes 1989, Filer 1990, 1992, Tucker 1991, Shane 1991, Burt (a) 1992, Shlay & Rossi 1992, Honig & Filer 1993, DeParle 1996). Some theorists were convinced that the deinstitutionalization of the mentally ill, which began in the 1950s was a leading cause of the rise in homelessness some thirty years later (Hope & Young 1984, Jencks 1994). A great debate ensued over the impact of rent control laws (Tucker 1987, Quigley 1990, Applebaum 1991, Tucker 1992, Grimes & Chressanthis 1997, Gissy 1997, Early & Olsen 1998) and gentrification (Kasinitz 1986). Many theorists held that the causes of homelessness were complex and a blend of both macro-level disruptions in the economy, which were more difficult to overcome by the most vulnerable citizens (Main 1986, Erickson & Wilhelm 1986, Bingham et al 1987, Marcuse 1988, Wolch et al 1988, Wright & Rubin 1991, Sen 1992, Culhane et al 1996). A handful of theorists, primarily economists, acknowledged that, due to lack of information and solid evidence of causal relationships, more empirical research and better methodology were needed to fully understand the phenomenon of homelessness (Bingham et al 1987, Turner et al 1987, Moore et al 1988, Friedrichs 1988, Cragg & O'Flaherty 1990, O'Flaherty 1991, 1995, 1996, Cordray 1991, Cowan 1991, Anderson 1991, Culhane 1994).

Micro-Level Causal Theories

The condition of homelessness is frequently medicalized by government programs in keeping with expert opinions held by micro-level causal theorists. Government and private housing programs were developed to address drug addiction, mental illness, developmental disabilities, and lack of education and job skills, and to provide temporary housing until these pathologies were "cured." Some HUD programs provide permanent subsidized housing with services, such as Shelter + Care and Housing Opportunities for Persons With Aids (HOPWA), an acknowledgement that some individuals' deficiencies are permanent. Some theorists maintain the underlying causal factors are a "sickness" of the society or economy, causing this dysfunction of the individual, which is the approach in European social democracies. The individual is nonetheless dysfunctional and should therefore be provided housing and services without blame. "Professionals create the problems they own and treat (Freidson 1970) and in so doing make moral judgments." People who live outside the circle of acceptable behavior are seen as not in control of their lives or in need of counseling to behave more normally. The social construction of these acceptable behavior sets are not built with equal participation by individuals outside the set, as the set definers have a higher level of power. The construction and definition of target populations influence government policy agendas, funding choices, and funding levels (Schneider and Ingram 1993). There is no agreement about whether macro-level disruptions of the housing market propel families into homelessness, or whether it is caused at the micro-level by the personal failure of the homeless themselves (Quigley 1996). Despite billions of dollars in public spending to alleviate the situation, there is no unified strategic approach and no agreement on the effectiveness of these programs (Ellickson 1990).

In the macro-level causal scenario, the poor are not responsible for having insufficient funds to pay for housing, whether due to low or no income or lack of housing at prices they can afford, the society is. The mentally ill and substance abusing homeless need housing and services. The poor need only meet eligibility standards based on a formula comprised of income, family size, and local market rental prices. If the family meets the eligibility standards, the government covers the difference in rent between some percentage of income and the defined level of fair market rents. Micro-level housing programs are based on a philosophical approach rooted in the U.S. traditions of social welfare, that is, a focus on "curing the ills" of the poor (Skocpol 1992). Under these programs, participants are provided income and housing supports contingent on their obligatory participation in supportive services, such as substance abuse treatment, job training, job readiness programs, and community work assignments. As documented in the legislation and program guidelines, it is successful completion of these services that determines program outcomes and not the provision of income or housing assistance per se. These programs did not measure "success" by the numbers of persons the government succeeded in rescuing from homelessness. Rather, programs reflecting the "fix the person" agenda measured success by the number of clients who participated in and completed the supportive services regimen.

Christopher Jencks' *The Homeless*, published in 1994, thoroughly examined the reasons for the increase in homelessness in the 1980s and proposed causes and remedies. He did not find homelessness to be a housing market phenomenon, but rather a situation caused by political and social changes, including the reduction in involuntary commitment of the mentally ill without adequate provision for alternative housing, the crack epidemic, an increase in long-term joblessness, a decline in the frequency of marriage, reductions in cash welfare benefits, the destruction of skid-row neighborhoods, the cutbacks in federal spending for low income housing, and local rental control ordinances. He examined the effect of emergency shelters as a mechanism for people to "self-define" as homeless in order to "jump the queues" for subsidized housing, thus artificially swelling the ranks of those defined as homeless. Jencks described the "cumulative effect of disadvantages" creating "personal vulnerabilities," which contributed to a slide into homelessness.

Despite his research showing that during the late 1980s the proportion of the population that was "merely" economically vulnerable shrank, he determined the odds of becoming homeless rose. The reasons for this dichotomy were the crack epidemic, rising rents, the decline of marriage, and the creation of new shelters for poorly housed persons to move to, thus entering into the count of homeless persons, which included those in shelters but did not include those who were poorly housed. Jencks reported that rents rose in the 1970-1980s, faster than the growth of poor incomes. Despite this development, there was a high vacancy rate in low rent units. Jencks explained that tenants chose higher priced rental units than their reported incomes, which would possibly suggest their real income was more than their reported income. Most cheap housing was also undesirable housing where no one wanted to live, which also partially explained the high vacancy rate. Jencks was also concerned with why, when the economy started to recover, homelessness did not decline. He attributes the crack epidemic and the rise of shelter services to explain this counter-intuitive scenario. Since federally subsidized housing units were insufficient to meet the number of persons who were eligible, and since voluntarily applying for homeless shelter services gave a family priority on the waiting list for subsidized housing, Jencks saw the expansion of shelter services for the homeless as another reason for the rise in homelessness in the 1980s.

Concerning the potential impact of welfare reform on poor family incomes, Jencks advised against disconnecting homelessness reduction policies from welfare policies. He did predict that a needed increase, not decrease, in welfare benefits for families would have no political support. One solution offered by Jencks, surprising in light of his micro-level causal theories, favored a macro-level government intervention to increase rent subsidies available to mothers with children at home rather than providing costly homelessness services. Thus HUD could assist more families without increasing its budget. If families chose to take advantage of "pathology-fixing" and expensive social services, they could do so via a voucher system that did not cover the provision of housing (Jencks 1994).

The dilemma of what causes homelessness has not been resolved (O'Flaherty 1995). Homelessness rose between 1990 and 2000 by 22% . New York City shelters in the summer of 2001 were at their highest levels of occupancy since 1986 (Bernstein 2002). Clarifying whether or not homelessness is a housing market issue would guide the government on how the problem could be ameliorated, especially in light of the reality that 15 years of government programs had not eliminated the problem.

An Analysis of Macro- and Micro-Level Conditions in New Jersey

This paper now looks at the context of homelessness in New Jersey during the twenty-year period 1980-2000. Both structural causal factors and individual-level causal factors are examined. The three major theories of individual-level pathology that are examined are substance abuse, mental illness, and involvement with the criminal justice system. The macro-level explanatory model examined is *An Economic Theory of Homelessness and Housing,* published in the *Journal of Housing Economics (4: 13-49, 1995).*

Macro-Level Conditions – Housing

Brendan O'Flaherty sets forth a "theory of the housing market that includes homelessness and relates it with other measurable phenomena." In his model what is important in the housing market is "quality differentiation on the supply side and income differentiation on the demand side" (O'Flaherty 1996:97). Stated another way, the essential question is, do people become homeless because there are more people than housing units or because certain people cannot afford or choose not to live in the housing units which are available.

The O'Flaherty (1995) theory sets forth a model of the housing market in which possibility of homelessness is one housing choice, the "demand side" of the model, along a continuum of housing qualities choices available, as well as the determinants of the price and quantities of housing offered on the "supply side" of the model. The model assumes perfect competition, free entry, and conditions of equilibrium. "Houses differ only in quality; people differ only in income." It has six features:
1.   The rent function is determined by market-clearing, given a distribution of consumers by income and a distribution of housing by quality."
2.   "Higher income households consume higher quality housing and the consumers who are homeless are the ones with the least income."

3. "How fast a house deteriorates depends on maintenance, and how much is spent on maintenance depends on the steepness of the value function."
4. "The value of a housing unit is the present value of net rent (rent net of profit-maximizing maintenance expenditures and...rent collection costs."
5. "A house is abandoned when its net rent (and hence its value) falls to zero."
6. "Construction occurs at those quality levels at which value equals construction cost; these qualities are typically higher qualities. Value of housing in the construction interval is supply-determined; below the construction interval demand matters in some equilibria, but not in all."

In this model, the homeless are a "kind of consumer" on the demand side. Consumers choose between two "goods" in this model, housing and nonhousing, which are used in this model as numeraires. The consumers have various income levels, including zero. On the supply side of this model, there is a continuum of housing qualities with "quality zero corresponding to homelessness." Housing suppliers can increase the supply of housing by building new units, renovating abandoned units, or maintaining and not abandoning existing units. However, there can be situations where there is an insufficient supply of housing at a given price/quality level. Better quality housing is more expensive and desirable. Although consumers have differing incomes, "each has the same utility function" for housing:

$$u(q, x)$$

where: $q \in R^+$ denotes the quality of housing (or lack thereof) consumed

$x \in R^+$ denotes the amount of the numeraire good

let: $p(q)$ be a function giving the price for eachquality level of housing

assume: $p(0) = 0$

$p(.)$ is strictly increasing the price function need not be continuous

let: $W(q \mid p, y) = u(q, y - p(q))$

denote the semidirect utility of quality q for a consumer with income y

and: $W^*(y \mid p) = \{q^* \mid p, y) \geq W(q \mid p, y) \text{ for all } q\}$

denote the demand quality set for income y.

Therefore, $W^*(y \mid p)$ is an increasing function of y.

"Richer people demand higher quality housing. A person is homeless if zero (0), is the only element in her demand quality set."

let: $b(q \mid y)$ be the "homeless bid-rent curve" for a consumer with income y,

meaning for each quality q, a consumer with income y, is indifferent between being homeless and consuming quality q housing at price b(q | y):

$$u(0, y) = u(q, y - b(q | y)).$$

then: b(0 | y) = 0 for all y

b is continuous and twice differentiable in both its arguments.

"Homeless bid-rent curves are always higher for higher incomes, except at zero (0).

Richer people are always willing to spend more for a given quality of housing rather than be homeless." A person can also find herself homeless if her bid-rent curve is below the price-quality schedule for all values above zero. Using this model, all persons below a specified income level are homeless, and one can look at the percentage in the population that has this income level at a given point in time compared to the percentage in the population that has this income level at various other points in time.

On the supply side, housing of a certain quality and price can be produced through construction or through "filtering," however once existing, it is either maintained or not. [Note: Housing built as higher quality housing is usually maintained; housing that filters down, or deteriorates, is generally built in the low quality range for the middle and lower middle classes and is not maintained and is allowed to deteriorate. It then becomes the lowest quality housing at the lowest prices, inhabited by the poor, until it is abandoned (O'Flaherty 1996).]

let: c(q)   be the construction cost schedule: it costs c(q) To construct a unit of quality q housing;

assume: c   is twice continuously differentiable on R++ with c'> 0 and c" > 0 , with c(0) = 0 and c(q) > 0 for all q > 0

if: m > 0   m maintenance dollars are being spent on the u unit, quality stays constant

if: m = 0   nothing is being spent on maintenance, quality deteriorates

There are at least five other costs of maintaining a house as long as rent is being collected on the property: bookkeeping costs, utility costs, liability costs, real estate taxes, and opportunity costs. In the model, these costs are referred to in sum as rent-collection costs H, and H = 0, simplify the analysis. "Prices are determined by supply cost for sufficiently high quality houses. Let q*satisfy"

$$c'(q^*) = m$$

for qualities higher than q*, the marginal cost to construct quality housing is greater than the cost of maintaining existing housing, so housing is maintained. In order for housing to be built and maintained forever, the present value of net rent, or the amount the owner earns for the property, less expenses, must equal or exceed the construction costs for a new unit. If present values for net rent falls below the construction costs for a new unit when maintenance is expen-

sive, the unit is eventually abandoned. New construction is better than maintenance for producing housing. O'Flaherty calls this scenario the "cheap construction" case.

let: $p(q) = c(q) - mq$
if: $p(q^*) > 0$ and $q^* > 0$ then a cheap maintenance equilibrium
if: $p(q^*) < 0$ then a cheap construction equilibrium.

"Which case applies is independent of the rate of interest or the distribution of income or demand; it depends only on the construction cost schedule
and the cost of maintenance." When the price of a house falls because it is not
maintained, the owner can put money into maintenance or money into the bank
rather than maintain the house. Economically, the owner should be indifferent.
In a cheap maintenance case, equilibrium means that "no construction occurs
below q^*, and all qualities that are supplied are maintained, but the lowest quality units are neither supplied or demanded." When maintenance costs, such as
interest rates or rent-collection costs, rise, this causes the prices of all housing
along the continuum to rise. From the point of view of the homeless "consumer," homelessness is free. Some low quality housing disappears from the
market, since cheap maintenance induces owners to maintain their property,
thus pricing it out of the reach of the homeless. The very lowest quality housing is not desired by homeless people since it costs more than "free." In this situation of equilibrium, prices are determined by supply-side factors.

In order for homelessness to increase in this equilibrium, the <u>percentage</u> of
persons in the population whose bid-rent curve is below the price-quality
schedule for all values > 0 must increase. In other words, more people relative
to the size of the population are poor. This is a situation of increasing income
inequality. Increased income inequality can also occur when the numbers of
high income and low income persons rise, and the middle income segment
decreases. If the prices of all quality levels of housing increase, then housing
costs more for everyone. Persons secure a lower quality of housing for the
money they have to spend on housing, or forego other types of consumption to
continue to pay for the same quality of housing that is now at a higher price. In
this scenario, the lowest quality housing is secured by those with less (but still
some) purchasing power, and homelessness increases for those with even less
or zero purchasing power.

This same situation can occur if the <u>percentage</u> of the population demanding housing at a certain price/quality level decreases. If the lower middle class
shrinks, demand falls for that price/quality level of housing. Supplying public
housing to the lower middle class has the same effect. "Housing for the poor is
a by-product of housing for the lower middle class." Less housing filters down
to the very poorest. Homelessness under this scenario will rise, just as it does
with an increase in the percentage of poor persons. Public housing programs
offering housing or vouchers to the very poorest, where supply of housing at
the low prices they can afford is not met, will reduce homelessness. The provi-

sion of free housing in homeless shelters might attract persons who would otherwise not be defined as "homeless," especially if the shelters are attractive, safe, and habitable. Since one of the easiest ways to count the homeless is to count the persons in shelters, this may be a partial explanation for the rapid increase in the "numbers" of persons who are homeless. The provision of housing in free shelters for the homeless also reduces the demand for the very worst housing, thus causing some of it to disappear from the market, hastening the slide from deteriorated housing to housing abandonment, and causing higher prices for the remaining units that still exist

Past homelessness is a factor in duration of the homeless experience. Without assistance with such things as security deposits, it is more difficult to get back on one's feet and easier to descend into homelessness. High rates of homelessness result in the establishment of shelters, which in turn attract some people who would otherwise have avoided homelessness somehow. Once opened, shelters tend to remain in operation, thus drawing some into the homelessness cycle, from which it is difficult to extricate oneself.

O'Flaherty used his model to determine the reasons homelessness rose in certain major cities over a time period when the economy was relatively strong and the vacancy rate, between 2 and 10%, exceeded the estimated homelessness rate of about 1% (O'Flaherty 1996). In his study, income inequality rose, creating a smaller middle class and changing housing prices, which in turn caused bad housing to be more expensive and fewer housing units to filter down to the poor. The resulting rise in homelessness triggered the growth of homeless services, which made the number of homeless rise even more (since they were in shelters and easier to count) and enabled more people to "self-define" as homeless and receive services, rather than being badly housed or entering a shelter system from which is it very difficult to exit. The economic factors important to the model are demand side variables, including such as income distribution, and supply side variables, the number and price of housing units and the provision of housing and housing assistance specifically for the homeless. The model demonstrated that "a set of opportunities available to people changed, and they changed their behavior accordingly" (O'Flaherty 1996:3).

What were the general conditions in the housing market in New Jersey for the period 1980-2000, the private housing market, government assisted housing and housing programs designed to serve the homeless population? These factors define the situation in which people made housing choices and the factors influencing the price and quantities of available housing. Income levels and distribution influence an individual's ability and/or willingness to pay for housing. Thirteen independent factors were constructed to represent the major factors in the O'Flaherty explanatory model: the housing market, income distribution, the size of the middle class, the number of poor people, and interest rates on investment alternatives available to real estate investors.

Housing Market and Income Distribution Factors

Factor	Definition
Middle Class	
Proportion	The percent of aggregate income earned by the middle 60% of the population of New Jersey
Poor People	
Rent ratio	Average rent as a percent of average poor income
State poverty	Percent of persons below poverty, entire state
City poverty	Percent of persons below poverty, in the six cities of: Atlantic City, Camden, Jersey City, Newark, Paterson, and Trenton
Housing Market	
Real Estate Taxes	The rate of annual change in a blended tax rate computed from general tax rate and tax levy per capita
Mortgage Rate	Mortgage interest blended rate: FHFB monthly effective rate with points amortized over 10 years, combination of fixed rate and adjustable rate loans
Rents in State	Average monthly rent for entire state
Rents in Cities	Average monthly rent for the six cities of: Atlantic City, Camden, Jersey City, Newark, Paterson, Trenton
Affordability Index	HUD housing market indicator, a ratio of median family income required to qualify for mortgagepayments
Shelter Price Index	Annual change in the Shelter Price Index, from the U.S.Bureau of Labor Statistics
Vacancy NJ	Rental vacancy rate inclusive of public housing
Vacancy Cities	Rental vacancy rate, inclusive of public housing, in the six cities of: Atlantic City, Camden, Jersey City, Newark, Paterson and Trenton
Interest Rates	
"Expected" Investment Interest	Blended rate of interest earned by long-term U.S. government securities and 30-year U. S. treasuries adjusted by the existing rate of inflation

Median household gross rent (in 1999 dollars) in New Jersey rose over the 30-year period 1970-2000. However, taken by itself, rent level does not indicate that rental housing is relatively more or less affordable. Any rent analysis must be viewed in light of overall household income levels and distribution.

Over the period in question, six New Jersey cities saw significant levels of homelessness: Atlantic City, Camden, Jersey City, Newark, Paterson, and Trenton. Characteristics of these cities are highlighted as "six major cities." They are not necessarily the cities with the highest populations overall. Average rent levels in the six major cities followed the same trend as New Jersey overall, except during the decade 1970-1980, when rents actually fell by 3%. For the 30 year period, New Jersey experienced a 36.6% increase in average rent levels, compared to a 29.9% increase for the cities. The steep rise in rent levels from 1980 to 1990 was 36.6% for New Jersey overall and slightly lower at 35.4% for the cities. City rents on average were consistently lower than New Jersey as a whole, ranging from 14.5% lower in 1970 to 24.4% lower in 1990.

New Jersey Rent Levels 1970-2000 (in 1999 Dollars) Inclusive of Public Housing Units

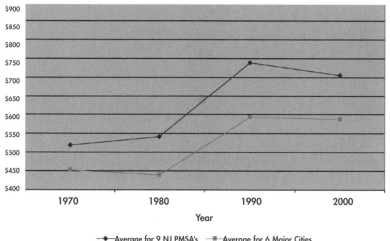

Source: U. S. Bureau of the Census, HUD SOCDS Dataset, Median Household Gross Rent, from Census Data 1970, 1980, 1990, 2000
* Six major cities: Atlantic City, Paterson, Jersey City, Newark, Camden, Trenton

Despite New Jersey's higher proportion of multiple dwelling units, housing has consistently been less crowded than for the United States overall. Both crowded housing, defined by the U. S. Bureau of the Census as 1.01 or more persons per room, and severely crowded housing, defined as 1.51 or more persons per room, declined in this country overall from 1940 to 1980. From 1980 through 2000, crowding has increased both in New Jersey and the country as a whole.

Taken by itself, the number of housing units is not indicative of crowded conditions. Housing stock must be viewed in light of population trends. During the period of increasingly crowded conditions, both New Jersey and the country as a whole saw a substantial growth in the number of year-round housing

US and New Jersey Crowded and Severely Crowded Housing Units 1940-2000, Inclusive of Public Housing Units

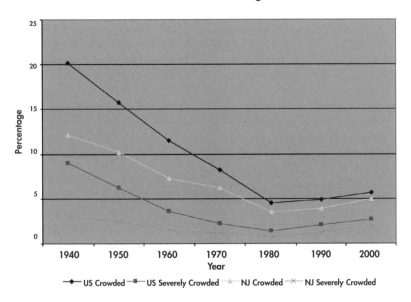

Source: U. S. Bureau of the Census, Historical Census of Housing Tables – Crowding
Crowded = 1.01 or more persons per room (includes severely crowded units)
Severely crowded = 1.51 or more persons per room

units, a 66% increase for the United States and a 39% increase for New Jersey from 1970 to 2000.While New Jersey overall experienced a 39% increase in housing units, the major cities in New Jersey saw a 10.8% <u>loss</u> of housing units from 1970 to 2000. This loss was acute for the city of Newark from 1980 to 1990, when it realized a loss of almost 19,000 housing units or 15.6%. Viewed in isolation, one could expect that such a loss in housing stock might contribute to the rise in homelessness during the 1980s. However, during the decade 1980-1990, Newark lost 16.4% of its population, while New Jersey's six major cities lost 5.4% of their population from 1980-1990.

Two important factors in the housing market are the number of people seeking housing and the number of units offered in the market. If supply is short, the price of housing will increase, and housing will become more crowded, and if the market is flooded with units, the prices will go down. In both New Jersey overall and in four of the six major cities, the number of persons seeking each unit of housing declined over the 30-year period.

The rise in vacancy rates is seen by some homeless experts as a cause of homelessness (Jencks 1994). [For a critical analysis of this theory, see Park 2000.] The vacancy rate is caused by the interaction between landlords who set rents and tenants who pay rents. If apartments are priced too high for the market, landlords have to wait longer to fill them or lower the rent to fill them. A "natural vacancy rate" generally exists in a housing market, that is, a vacancy rate at which rents are neither rising nor falling. Rents rise when the actual

Person Per Housing Unit for Six Major New Jersey Cities
1970 – 1990

City	Total in 1970	Total in 1980	Total in 1990	Total in 2000	Total Lost/Gained	
Atlantic City	2.09	1.92	1.97	2.22	.13	6.2%
Paterson	2.94	2.87	3.06	3.17	.23	7.8%
Jersey City	2.83	2.54	2.52	2.57	(.26)	9.2%
Newark	3.0	2.71	2.69	2.73	(.27)	9%
Camden	2.97	2.60	2.90	2.69	(.28)	9.4%
Trenton	2.97	2.57	2.64	2.53	(.44)	15%
Average	2.80	2.54	2.63	2.65	(.15)	5.4%

	Total in 1970	Total in 1980	Total in 1990	Total in 2000	Total Lost/Gained	
New Jersey	3.11	2.74	2.60	2.63	(.48)	15.4%

Source: U. S. Bureau of the Census, HUD SOCDS Dataset, Total Population,
from Census Data 1970, 1980, 1990, 2000

US and New Jersey Rental Vacancy Rates 1986-2000,
Inclusive of Public Housing

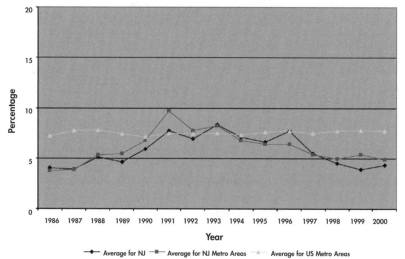

Source: US and NJ Metropolitan Areas: U.S. Bureau of the Census,
Housing Vacancies and Homeownership Annual Statistics: 2001, Table 5. Rental
Vacancy Rates for the 75 Largest Metropolitan Areas: 1986-2001.
Average for NJ: U.S. Bureau of the Census, Housing Vacancies and Homeownership
Annual Statistics: 2001, Table 3. Rental Vacancy Rates by State: 1986-2001.

vacancy rate is below the natural vacancy rate, and rents fall when the vacancy rate is above the natural vacancy rate (O'Flaherty 1996). As illustrated below, the natural vacancy rate for U.S. metropolitan areas appears to be around 7%. As discussed earlier, rents were rising sharply in the decade 1980-1990 in New Jersey overall and in major cities. The actual vacancy rate for both New Jersey and most major cities was below the natural vacancy rate until 1990, when rents began to fall again. Since 1991, rents have fallen and so have vacancy rates, except for the city of Newark.

For the city of Newark, vacancy rates stayed well below the natural vacancy rate until 1992, despite the fact that Newark rents rose by 30.9% over the decade 1980-1990. Rents remained level in Newark from 1990-2000, vacancy rates remained high, over the natural vacancy rate until 1997. From 1990 to 2000, Newark saw its population increase relative to available housing units.

New Jersey Rental Vacancy Rates in Newark Metropolitan Area 1986-2000, Inclusive of Public Housing Units

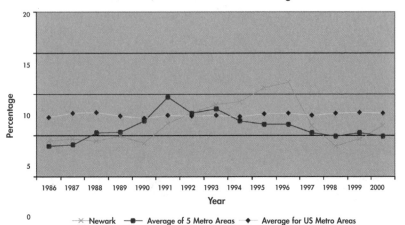

Source: U.S. Bureau of the Census, Housing Vacancies and Homeownership
Annual Statistics: 2001, Table 5. Rental Vacancy Rates
for the 75 Largest Metropolitan Areas: 1986-2001

During the decade 1980-1990, when homelessness rose in New Jersey, rents also rose, with owner occupancy levels remaining flat in major cities, except for Newark, and increasing owner occupancy in New Jersey overall. Reversing a 40-year decline in the number of crowded units, 1980 saw an increase in crowding continuing through 2000.

From 1980-1990, New Jersey overall saw a 10.6% increase in housing units, a less rapid growth rate than the previous decade at 16.8%. Major cities, however, experienced their greatest loss of housing units – 63.4% of their 30-year loss – in the 1980-1990 decade. Newark experienced 69% of its 30-year loss during the 1980-1990 period. The 30-year trend of fewer persons seeking each unit of housing also did not hold for the 1980-1990 period in the major New Jersey cities. The vacancy rate remained below the "natural vacancy rate" until 1990, when rent levels began to fall.

The decade 1980-1990 also saw a dramatic change in the affordability of housing, driven by historically high mortgage interest rates. This trend is shown using a monthly "effective" rate, which combines the fixed rate and adjustable rate and amortizes points. A Composite Affordability Index is created, which compares the ratio of median family income to income required to qualify for mortgage payments. A 1.00 ratio indicates housing is affordable to a consumer, a higher than 1.00 ratio means the consumer can more than afford the housing, and less than 1.00 means consumers cannot carry the required payments. The following chart illustrates the impact of high mortgage interest rates on housing affordability. Persons looking to buy a single family home might need to delay the purchase until mortgage rates come down, or buy a lower priced house. Owner occupancy rates in New Jersey overall, however, continued to rise during this time of high mortgage interest rates.

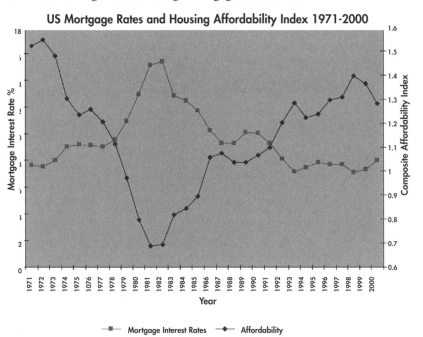

US Mortgage Rates and Housing Affordability Index 1971-2000

Source: US Department of Housing and Urban Development, PDR, US Housing Market Conditions, Historical Data, May 2002

Note: Interest rates are Federal Housing Finance Board's monthly effective rates (points are amortized over 10 years), combining fixed rate and adjustable rate loans.

Composite Affordability Index is the ratio of median family income to qualifying income. Values at 1.00 mean house is affordable, over 1.0, house is very affordable, less than 1, house is not affordable.

Landlords facing such a scenario must charge higher rents to cover the cost of higher interest payments, or reduce the debt/equity ratio for the property. Although the "real" long-term interest rate is used for decision making, the opportunity cost of equity must be factored into the landlord's operating costs, which, unless covered by the revenue stream, will cause the landlord to lose money on the property. Estimated long-term interest rates are interest rates earned by the security adjusted by the rate of inflation existing at the time an investor was making a decision whether to invest money in real estate or the securities market. Both alternative investments are long-term to reflect the long-term nature of a real estate investment. The combined bond and treasury yield, a simple average of the two interest rates, earned less than inflation until 1982 when it became a more attractive investment, continuing through 1989. Similar to the relationship between the mortgage interest rate and housing affordability, long-term rates are affected by the rate of inflation when an investor accounts for inflation in making a choice between securities and real estate. Higher real long-term interest rates, therefore, mean higher rents. From 1982 to 1989, government securities showed high yields while housing affordability dipped.

An increase in local real estate taxes was a contributing factor in the increased cost of property ownership. Using a blend of property tax rates and per capita tax levied for the six major New Jersey cities from 1984 to 1989, property tax rate increases exceeded both the percentage increase in the urban Consumer Price Index and the change in the rate of inflation. This trend partially explains the 35% rent increase in urban areas during the 1980s, at the same time the six major cities experienced a 7% loss in overall housing units and a 5% drop in population. The number of multiple dwelling units as a proportion of all dwelling units declined from 1980-1990 by 5%, as did the number of owner occupied units in the major New Jersey cities, except for Newark, and crowding got worse all over New Jersey. Housing became more expensive and rents rose. Several homelessness theories point to a pull-back in public assisted housing as contributing to the rise of homelessness in the 1980s (Hayes 1989, Wolch et al, Burt 1992(a), Shlay & Rossi 1992). The trend of public assisted housing as a percent of all rental housing from 1978 to 1999 was increasing, not decreasing.

Documenting provision of housing for the homeless is complicated by the inconsistency and vagueness in defining who the homeless are and what constitutes housing for them. The New Jersey Department of Human Services conducted two surveys, one in October 1985 and one in January 1986 (NJ Department of Human Services 1986), to determine the extent of the homeless problem in the state. Neither survey attempted to count "homeless visible on the street" or persons who have a regular sleeping accommodation not designed for human beings. The two surveys counted those in both public and private shelters and those persons temporarily or permanently receiving assistance to avoid being homeless. In other words, subjects included those receiving financial assistance to maintain their current housing, those "placed" (meaning cost was paid by a third party) in hotels and boarding homes, and children in the state foster care system due to inadequacy of housing. The combined caseloads of New Jersey Division of Youth and Family Services, county social service boards, municipal welfare providers, and private providers totaled 14,447 "homeless" persons. Only about 8% of these individuals were actually in the state's 45 "shelters" for the homeless, which had a nightly capacity of 1,472 beds. In fact a year-long count revealed that shelters served on average 200 persons per night and less than two-fifths of the shelters operated at capacity for 200 or more days of the previous year. Government social service boards reported that only 14% of families seeking assistance were referred to the shelter system, the remaining 86% being provided with some sort of financial assistance to maintain current housing and avoid homelessness. Sixty percent of shelter residents reported some sort of government income assistance. At the time of the surveys, an AFDC grant for a family of three was $385 per month, and the fair market rent of a one bedroom apartment was $450 per month.

Some 20% of the shelter residents were also clients of the New Jersey Division of Mental Health and Hospitals; an overall 29% of shelter residents responded that mental health issues affected someone in their immediate family. Most shelter residents reported that eviction by the landlord was the primary cause of homelessness; only 5% cited substance abuse as the cause. Fifty-eight percent of this 14,447 caseload, about 8,400, were children, and one-third of these children, about 2,800, were in DFYS-mandated foster care due to inadequate provision of housing by parents or guardians. These foster care children accounted for 18% of the DYFS caseload of children in placement outside the home (New Jersey Department of Human Services, 1986). The primary conclusion of the research was that inadequate income was the cause of homelessness.

The National Affordable Housing Act in 1990 began requiring that state and local governments applying for direct federal housing funding develop annual and five-year consolidated plans for addressing housing, including homelessness and economic development needs. In June 1993, the State of New Jersey conducted another statewide homeless survey to document the characteristics of the homeless population; it was not a "count." This survey's respondents numbered 4,261. They included those residing in shelters, as well as those frequenting soup kitchens and day-time drop-in centers who indicated they were "without shelter" or "living nowhere," considered "proxies for the unsheltered homeless" by the State (New Jersey Department of Community Affairs, 1999). At the time of this survey, the AFDC grant for a family of four was $424 per month, and the state's lowest fair market rent was $697 per month in the region near Camden. Only 11% of the respondents were employed. Over 75% indicated they were homeless for financial reasons or due to eviction for non-payment of rent. Sixteen percent indicated that substance abuse was the direct cause of homelessness; only 8% indicated mental or emotional problems as a cause. At the time of the survey, state-wide recipients of rental assistance through welfare to avoid homelessness totaled 4,600 families and 3,800 individuals. Again the primary conclusion of the research was that inadequate income was the cause of homelessness (New Jersey Department of Community Affairs, 1999).

The State of New Jersey's FY 2000 Five Year Consolidated Plan submitted to HUD continued to emphasize the widening income disparities in the state and the inability of those on the lower end of the economic scale to afford the state's housing. New Jersey was the "second most expensive place in the nation to rent a 2-bedroom apartment," 45% of the state's renters did not earn enough to rent a 2-bedroom apartment; "a minimum wage worker in New Jersey would have to work the equivalent of three full-time jobs to afford the typical 2-bedroom apartment" (NJ Department of Community Affairs 2000, p. 21). The current inventory of beds for homeless individuals totaled 9,117 with an additional 23,470 in need of services. For individuals in families, 10,040 were receiving services with an additional 17,290 in need of services (NJ Department of Community Affairs 2000).

One consistent historical yardstick for enumerating individuals fitting HUD's definition of "homeless" has been the accounting by the U. S. Bureau of the Census for persons <u>not</u> residing in households, defined by the Census as those residing in "group quarters." Group quarters are split into two major categories: institutional, generally defined as places where persons live in an institutional setting, and non-institutional, where persons reside more or less voluntarily in smaller or community settings, but not in traditional households with family members residing together. Institutional refers to: correctional institutions; homes for the aged/nursing homes; beds in wards for mentally ill, chronically ill, mentally retarded, physically handicapped, and drug and alcohol dependent; and patients in regular hospitals with nowhere to return to. Non-institutional refers to college dormitories, military quarters, rooming and boarding homes, various group homes, religious group quarters, agricultural worker dorms, maritime vessels, and, as variously defined by the U.S. Census Bureau, facilities for homeless individuals. Many homeless facilities served the family or household as a unit, although over the decades the U.S. Census counted all non-household residing persons, including the homeless, in group quarters. One way of examining the phenomenon of homelessness is to look at group quarters trends in New Jersey. This examination also reveals the heightened awareness of homeless persons by the U.S. Census Bureau, which in the 1990 Census expanded its definitional categories in an attempt to more accurately identify and count them.

Consistently over the 60-year period from 1940 to 2000, persons residing in group quarters in New Jersey accounted for about 2% of the overall population. The 1950 census for group quarters was abnormally high due to residents of military quarters.

Institutional facilities, which include correctional facilities, constituted less than 50% of all group quarters until 1990, when numbers in correctional institutions nearly tripled over 1980, and again by 2000, when there was a 150% increase in inmates. Another major category of the institutional population, homes for the aged and nursing homes, more than doubled from 1970 to 2000. Residents in mental or psychiatric hospitals declined by 39%, from 14,554 persons in 1970 to 8,807 persons in 1980, and by another 46% from 1980 to 1990, when only 4,725 persons were counted in these hospitals in New Jersey. However, a commensurate increase in residents of group homes for the mentally disabled is observed in the non-institutional category (see further

NJ Group Quarters Population 1940-2000

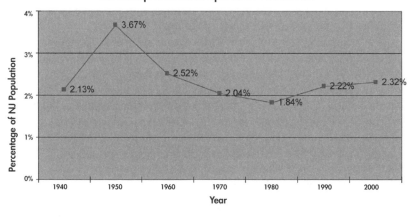

Group Quarters Population

Source: For 1940, 1950, 1960:
          General Population Characteristics, Table 19 – Household
          Relationship, By Color, for the State, by Size of Place, 1960, and for the
          State 1950, 1940, Page 32-45.
          For 1970:
          Characteristics of the Population, Part 32, NJ, Vol. 2, Table 154,
          Persons in Group Quarters by Type of Quarters, Sex, Race and Age,
          Page 32-713.
          For 1980:
          Detailed Population Characteristics, NJ, Table 207. Persons in Group
          Quarters by Type of Group Quarters, Age, Sex, Race and Spanish
          Origin. Page 32-175.
          For 1990:General Population Characteristics, NJ, Table 38. Persons in
          Group Quarters by Type of Group Quarters, Sex, Race and Hispanic
          Origin. Page 168 New Jersey.
          For 2000:
          PCT16: Group Quarters Population by Group Quarters Type [52], from
          the American Fact Finder website and the Emergency Transitional
          Shelter Population 2000, Special Report.

discussion of the mentally ill.) Rooming and boarding homes, included in the Non-Institutional category, declined from 26,951 persons in 1960 to 5,349 persons by 1990.

The homeless as a separate group was not broken out in the non-institutional category until the 1990 census. At that time 7,470 persons were counted as living in facilities for the homeless with an additional 1,639 counted as "visible homeless on the street." Based on a different methodology for counting the homeless, the 2000 census counted 5,500 persons homeless in New Jersey. Starting with the 2000 Census, rooming and boarding homes were no longer tabulated under group quarters at all. Staff in residence in 1960 and 1970 was classified under "other" for both institutional and non-institutional classifications. In the 2000 Census, "other" also included those in battered women's shelters and homeless visible in outdoor locations.

In looking at 60 years of census data, despite numerous changes in classifications and definitions, the percentage of persons in New Jersey residing in a non-household settings has remained stable at around 2%. Homeless persons could conceivably be residents of rooming and board homes in one census, on a mental ward in another census, and locked up in a correctional facility by the next census. The reverse route is just as conceivable: starting out in a correctional facility, spending time on a mental ward, and drifting out to a boarding home or the streets. The seemingly insignificant percentage shift from 1980 to 1990, .14%, amounts, however, to an increase of over 10,000 persons, after a steady decline from 1960-1980. From 1980-1990, residents of rooming and boarding homes decreased by 1,041, but the numbers of homeless visible on the street and in shelters and facilities for the homeless enumerated as a discrete classification totaled 9,109, accounting for most of the 10,000-person increase in the two census counts. According to the census bureau staff specialist for the group quarters count, for Census 2000, homeless visible in outdoor locations and families in battered women's shelters are included in the 8,743 total "other."

Macro-Level Conditions – Income Levels and Distribution

According to the causal theory being tested, homelessness can be predicted to rise if the middle class shrinks relative to other economic classes, since housing built for the middle class "filters down" to become housing for the lower classes, and if the proportionate number of persons whose incomes are below the price-quality schedule for housing increases.

Changes in the size of the middle class in New Jersey were measured as a change in the ratio of the middle class to the lower class. A rising percentage of poor to middle class will indicate higher rents for the poor and more homelessness. Following the methodology used by O'Flaherty to determine changes in the relative size of the middle class (O'Flaherty 1996, p. 128-132), income distribution histograms were constructed for the years 1969, 1979, 1989, and 1999, plotting the frequency distribution of family income in each income bracket using U.S. Census Bureau data for families in constant dollars. A midpoint was calculated for each income bracket. A regression line was fitted to the data in the lower income brackets, determining the slope of the line below median family income. A big variation, or steep slope, indicates a high ratio of middle class to poor. A small variation, or flat slope, indicates fewer middle class families to poor. Any change in this relationship was plotted for the 30-year period. The results of this analysis are shown in the table below. The slope flattened from 1969 onward, indicating that the size of the middle class was shrinking relative to the lower class, during the time that homelessness was rising.

New Jersey Income-Distribution Histogram Slopes
1969 – 1999

	1969	1979	1989	1999
Slopes of Incomes				
≤ median	.0009	.0003	.0003	.0002
t-value	4.4	1.25	4.8	3.9

Source of Income Data: U. S. Bureau of the Census, Characteristics for New Jersey,1970, 1980, 1990, 2000.

In any housing market, there is a minimum income needed in order for people to avoid homelessness. If the number of people below that minimum increases, homelessness will also increase. Again, following the methodology used by O'Flaherty (1996), various indicators of poverty were examined for the 30-year period 1969-1999.

Poverty in New Jersey 1969 – 1999

Year	1969	1979	1989	1999
Poverty rate		8.1 %	9.5%	7.6%	8.3%
Families below poverty level	6.4	7.6	5.6	6.3
Unrelated individuals				
below poverty level	31.3	20.6	17.4	18.4
Unrelated individuals				
< 65 below poverty level	23.4	19.4	16.3	16.2
Unrelated individuals < 65				
below 75% of poverty level	19.1	6.7 *	na	na

Source: U. S. Bureau of the Census, Characteristics for New Jersey, 1970, 1980, 1990, 2000.

In New Jersey overall, the poverty rate and number of families below the poverty level rose between 1969 and 1979, but fell between 1979 and 1989. It cannot be determined by these census reports just when in the 1980s poverty began to fall, but going into the 1980s it was rising. Unrelated individuals did not see an increase in poverty during the 30-year period for the state overall. For New Jersey's six major cities, however, the poverty picture is much worse. Not only is the rate of poverty double or triple the overall state rate, but the increase from 1969 to 1979, heading into the 1980 decade of rising homelessness, was over 8% compared to the 1.4% increase for the state overall.

Persons in Poverty in New Jersey Six Major Cities
1969 – 1999

% In Poverty

Year	NJ	Avg. 6 Cities	Atlantic City	Paterson	Jersey City	Newark	Camden	Trenton
1969	8.1%	18.6%	22%	16.5%	13.5%	22.3%	20.7%	16.3%
1979	9.5	27.0	24.9	25.2	21.2	32.8	36.9	21.2
1989	7.6	23.9	25	18.5	18.9	26.3	36.6	18.1
1999	8.3	24.9	23.6	22.2	18.6	28.4	35.5	21.1

Source: U. S. Bureau of the Census, HUD SOCDS Dataset,
Census Data 1970, 1980, 1990, 2000

A more detailed look at the housing purchasing power of those in poverty reveals the impact on homelessness with more clarity. The actual annual income levels are compared to the average annual urban rent prevailing at the time. Poor family purchasing power relative to housing actually increased from 1969 to 1979, although the poverty rate was rising. In the decade of the 1980s, families went from needing 63% of their incomes for rent to needing in excess of 100% of their incomes for rent.

Effect of Poverty on Rental Affordability
New Jersey 1969 – 1999

Year	1969	1979	1989	1999
Families below poverty level	6.4%	7.6%	5.6%	6.3%
Weighted average annual income of families in poverty	$1763	$3349	$5161	$7619
Average annual urban rent	$1165	$2119	$5214	$7050
Average rent as % of average poor income	66%	63%	100.1%	92.5%

Source: U. S. Bureau of the Census, Characteristics for New Jersey , 1970, 1980, 1990,
2000; HUD SOCDS Dataset, Census Data 1970, 1980, 1990, 2000

An additional comparison of changes in the price of shelter compared to changes in the overall consumer price index reveals that shelter prices rose sharply relative to other prices in the mid-1980s, and the annual increase in prices has remained higher than the CPI throughout the end of the century.

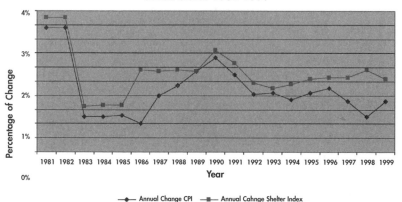

**Change in CPI and Shelter Price Indexes
United States 1981-1999**

*Source: U. S. Bureau of Labor Statistics, Monthly Labor Review
and Handbook of Labor Statistics*

The Micro-Level Conditions

The evaluation of the causes of homelessness due to personal characteristics or pathologies is done by examining the incidence of these pathologies as a proportion of the general population. Certain pathologies, such as substance abuse (including alcoholism), mental illness, and involvement with the criminal justice system have rates of occurrence in the population. This research looks at the pathological causes factors of homelessness by tracking the changes in rates of occurrence in the overall population for the time period under study.

Mental Illness

What, if anything, changed concerning the mentally ill population during the time period being examined? A mentally ill person's vulnerability to homelessness, or the probability that he or she will be homeless, will increase if the number of mentally ill people increases relative to the number of residential spots available to serve them, or, conversely, if the number of residential spots available for the mentally ill decreases relative to the number of mentally ill. The less severely mentally ill and the undiagnosed mentally ill seek housing in the same housing market as the rest of the population. Therefore, an increased probability of homelessness due to housing market conditions will increase the probability of homelessness for the mentally ill along with the rest of the population. For purposes of simplicity, this section will not examine the possibility that the situation of being homeless can cause the symptoms or appearance of mental illness, which is arguably the case (Snow et al. 1986; Wright 1989). The mentally ill were discovered in surveys of the homeless population in the 1980s, but this has historically been true in this country (Bahr 1973; Bahr & Caplow 1974).

Many theorists believe that mental illness causes homeless (Main 1983; Bassuk 1984; Lamb 1986; Levine & Stockdell 1986), and, further, that the deinstitutionalization of the mentally ill "onto the streets" contributed to the rise of homelessness in the 1980s (Sexton 1983; Hope & Young 1984; Lamb 1984; Warner 1989; Jencks 1994). Jencks especially saw the reduction in involuntary commitment of the mentally ill without appropriate and sufficient alternative housing as a major reason for the increase in homelessness during the 1980s. It is fair to assume that some severely mentally ill persons need assistance in obtaining shelter if they do not reside in family settings and are so incapacitated that they cannot provide for themselves. Deinstitutionalization concerns a policy shift in the nature of residential services provided for the severely mentally ill.

Since the mid-18th century, municipal and state governments have offered out-of-home residences to the severely mentally ill. The mentally infirm not living at home and in need of long-term custodial care were moved from acute and crisis care wards of general hospitals, jails, almshouses, and the streets to asylums established to serve them. Medical science offered little more in the way of cures or services than a hygienic environment and prevention of harm to themselves or others. It was not until after World War II that mental health professionals and patient advocates, equipped with an array of symptom-reducing and behavior-stabilizing drugs and an enlightened understanding of mental illness, developed preferable treatments based on social integration of patients in community based settings, which provided needed services in home-like, non-institutional environments. Beginning in earnest in 1955, the migration of the mentally ill from institutions to community settings continued through the early 1970s. By the mid-1970s, there was mounting criticism of the new treatment model, including a report from the GAO that the services were inadequate to address the chronic needs of these patients (US GAO 1977). Most felt that increased supportive services were required, including housing (US DHHS 1999; Grob 1983, 1991, 1994; Goldman & Morrissey 1985).

For the deinstitutionalized patient, there is a greater possibility of homelessness when homelessness is defined as "wandering" or "living on the streets." This holds for two reasons, physical freedom and freedom to self-medicate. The residential setting has changed from a "lock up" institution where patients could not wander off the grounds to a community or group home setting, where they are free to come and go. They could, by choice or due to mental incapacity, find themselves living on the street, even though a residential spot had been provided for them. They could be perceived as being "homeless" and included in studies and "counts" of the homeless population, due to atypical behavior often attributed to the homeless, such as sleeping on subway grates for heat, defecating on the sidewalk, and taking their meals at soup kitchens, when in fact they had a residence, but chose not to dwell in it. Psychotropic medications administered for moderate symptoms are dispensed in an institutional fashion in residential institutions. Staff dispense meds according to preset schedules, observe patients swallowing or injecting the meds, and keep detailed records. The dispensing routine is not as rigorously adhered to in the community-based or group home setting, which promotes self-help doctrines (NJ DHHS 2001). Insufficient medication could contribute to a deterioration in the capacity of the individual to function and allow atypical behaviors to emerge, which can mimic those of the homeless.

The proportion of mentally ill in the population over time by most accounts has not changed (Goldman 1984; Burt 1992; Jencks 1994). A recent Surgeon General's study reported 28% of the population suffering from mental or addictive disorders, ranging from simple phobias and anxiety disorders to severe incapacitation, in any given year in this country. Only 8% of the population receives treatment for their diagnosed illnesses. The severely mentally ill requiring residential placements outside the home are tabulated under the group quarters population by the U.S. Census Bureau. They constitute a portion of both institutional and non-institutional residents, whose combined populations have consistently been about 2% of the New Jersey population from 1940 to 2000.

The mentally ill can be included among populations in homes for the elderly, correctional institutions, rooming and boarding homes, shelters, and among the homeless visible on the streets. Starting with the 1960 census, rooming and boarding homes were segregated as a category, but it was not until the 1970 census that mental and psychiatric hospital patients were separately tabulated. These two categories, rooming and boarding homes and the institutionalized mentally ill, saw dramatic drops in census from 1960 to 2000. The number of homeless both in shelters and living on the streets according to the 1990 census for New Jersey was 9,109 persons. One simple explanation for homelessness could, therefore, be the diaspora of the previously institutionalized mentally ill, who decreased in numbers by 9,829 for the same period 1970-1990, about the same number as were homeless. They were not absorbed into the rooming and boarding house population, which also lost residents, over 40% during the same time period. It is not known what proportion of the deinstitutionalized mentally ill were or became elderly, but federal healthcare changes, which reimbursed states for elderly patients in nursing homes but not in state mental hospitals, could account for at least some part of the population of nursing home residents, which increased by nearly 24,000 from 1970 to 1990. An equally plausible explanation could be incarceration of the formerly institutionalized mentally ill, as correctional institution inmates nearly tripled from 1980 to 1990, and was nearly 5 times higher by the 2000 census. Since the overall proportion of New Jersey population remains unchanged at about 20% for the 60-year period 1940-2000, and the prevalence of mental illness in the population also remained unchanged, it is likely the deinstitutionalized mental ill remained part of the group quarters population. Unfortunately, the group quarters count did not segregate residents of group homes until the 1990 census, when there were 3,332 persons in group homes, compared to 12,252 in 2000. The provision of home-based support services and stabilized behavior due to improved medications also induced more families to provide care in the home (US DHHS 1999; Freeman & Smith 1963). Were deinstitutionalization to be a major causal factor of homelessness, however, it should have caused homelessness to rise in the late 1950's through 1970, when most patients were released (NY DMH 2000). By 1970, when most patients with 24-hour residential treatment services actually started to rise, increasing 31% between 1970 and 1976, and 75% between 1970 and 1986 when homelessness was rising dramatically (US CMHS 1999). SSI benefits, which started in the early 1970s, made it easier for the mentally ill to live in a community setting. Housing provision may have shifted away from the institutional setting into the community setting, but housing services for the mentally ill were being supplied during the time that homelessness was rising.

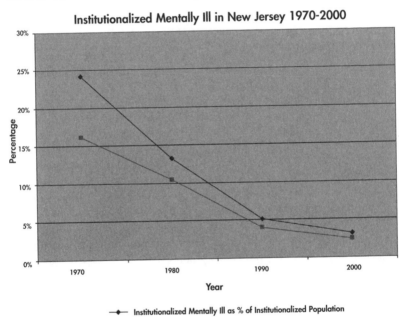

Institutionalized Mentally Ill in New Jersey 1970-2000

—◆— Institutionalized Mentally Ill as % of Institutionalized Population
—■— Institutionalized Mentally Ill as % of Selected Group Quarters

Selected Group Quarters = Group Quarters less college dormitories and military quarters

Source:
For 1970:   *Characteristics of the Population, Part 32, NJ, Vol. 2, Table 154, Persons in Group Quarters by Type of Quarters, Sex, Race and Age, Page 32-713.*
For 1980:   *Detailed Population Characteristics, NJ, Table 207. Persons in Group Quarters by Type of Group Quarters, Age, Sex, Race and Spanish Origin. Page 32-175.*
For 1990:   *General Population Characteristics, NJ, Table 38. Persons in Group Quarters by Type of Group Quarters, Sex, Race and Hispanic Origin. Page 168 New Jersey.*
For 2000:   *PCT16: Group Quarters Population by Group Quarters Type [52], from the American Fact Finder website and the Emergency Transitional Shelter Population 2000, Special Report.*

Substance Abuse

Similar to mental illness, numerous theorists point to substance abuse as a causal factor in homelessness (Freeman & Hall 1989; Ellickson 1990; Grisby et al. 1990; Welfeld 1990; Jencks 1994). Early writings on "tramps" and skid row inhabitants highlighted the incidence of alcoholism (Garrett & Bahr 1973; Main 1983) among this population historically. Public and government awareness and concern about fighting drug abuse coincided with attention to homelessness during the mid-1980s. A Gallup Poll in January 1985 indicated that 2% of the population surveyed felt drugs and drug abuses were the most important problems facing the country; by 1989, 38% of respondents felt drugs and drug abuse were our most important problem (The Gallup Poll Monthly, Report No. 235). Concern about the growing AIDS epidemic caused in part by the spread of HIV infection due to needle sharing by intravenous drug users contributed to the heightened alarm. The National Drug Enforcement Board was created in 1984, and the National Drug Policy Board in 1987. Congress enacted sweeping anti-drug measures in 1986 and again in 1988 (Kovan 1989).

Surveys of the homeless during the 1980s and 1990s found substantial numbers of the homeless presenting with drug abuse histories and addictions, leading some to conclude that substance abuse caused homelessness. As is the case with mental illness, simply being a substance user and homeless does not mean that substance abuse was the cause of homelessness. Asking someone about substance abuse does not always yield a truthful answer. Although urinalysis of shelter residents may provide an objective basis for determining recent substance use, "dirty urine" does not prove substance dependence, chronic incapacitation due to substance usage, preference for drugs over housing, or that substance abuse is the cause of one's being in the homeless shelter. One survey of the homeless themselves indicated that only 9% blamed alcohol or substance abuse for their inability to obtain housing (HUD 1999).

Drug use is often the result of high stress situations and the availability of drugs, such as was the case for the U.S. military during the Vietnam War. Drug availability in shelters has been well documented, and homelessness is understandably a stressful personal situation. Drug users become more vulnerable to homelessness if they become incapacitated due to drug addiction and cannot hold jobs, or do hold jobs but spend all their money on drugs instead of rent. These situations result in no income available for housing. No income puts them out of the housing market. If drug users available funds for housing are reduced due to their preference for drugs over other goods, depending on where they were on the housing demand curve, they would have reduced demand for housing in their former price/quality range and increased demand for housing in a lower price/quality range. Some addicts resort to crime for funds to support their habit and may not fall into the no income or lowered income scenarios. Those who are not very good at crime and get caught, secure no-cost housing in jails and prison, thus avoiding homelessness and putting themselves out of the housing market altogether. As will be discussed later, New Jersey correctional institutions saw a dramatic rise in drug abusing inmates during the time homelessness was rising.

Trying to understand the influence of substance abuse on homelessness is complicated by the source and type of information and the ability to differentiate between causality and coexistence. Using multiple indicators of drug use, this section will examine the number of substance users and the pattern of consumption from the 1970s through the 1990s. The analysis will focus on what, if anything, changed concerning substance abuse during the time homelessness was rising.

Alcohol

Regarding alcohol, the abuse of which is considered to be a predicating factor for homelessness, the chart below shows that the proportion of drinkers declined from 1979-1990, a time of increasing homelessness. Persons over the age of 18 indicating they were a "current drinkers" declined from 65.6% in 1985 to 60.7% by 1990, "heavy drinkers" from 11.8% to 9.1% for the same period. (Alcohol Epidemiologic Data System, National Institute on Alcohol Abuse and Alcoholism Survey). New Jersey alcohol-related fatalities declined from 56% in 1982 to 40% by 1999. The percent of drivers with high blood alcohol levels (equal to or above 0.10 g/dl) dropped from 26% in 1982 to 15% in 1999 (National Highway Safety Administration, 2000, Traffic Safety Facts).

Percent of US Population, age 12 and over, Reporting Previous Month Use 1979-1998

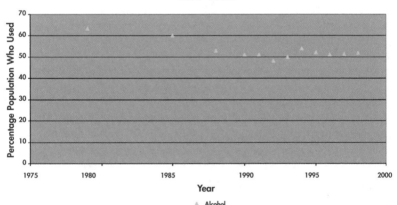

Source: US DHHS 1998 National Household Survey on Drug Abuse

Medical experts associate liver disease and cirrhosis with abusive alcohol use (Noble 1978). Rates of hospitalization due to chronic liver disease declined steadily from 1977-1989, according to the CDC's Behavioral Risk Factor Surveillance System, indicating a decline in per capital alcohol consumption. Age-adjusted rates of death due to chronic liver disease decreased by 23% from 1980-1989. Death rates per 100,000 population for alcohol-induced causes dropped from 8.4 to 6.8 from 1980 to 1991 (U. S. Centers for Disease Control 1993) during the time when homelessness was rising.

Heroin, Cocaine, and Crack

It is necessary to look at heroin, cocaine, and crack in tandem when examining the consumption patterns of substance abusers in the 1980s. The reason is that several leading measures of drug use during the 1980s do not isolate crack from cocaine and some indicators, such as vital statistics rates for drug-induced deaths, combine all drugs, except for alcohol, during most of that period. Trends in total use for the same time period for heroin, cocaine, and crack are shown in the following chart. Crack was differentiated from cocaine only after 1991 in the DHHS National Household Survey.

Percent of US Population, age 12 and over, Reporting Previous Month Drug Use 1979-1998

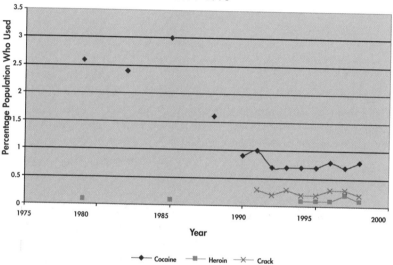

Source: US DHHS 1998 National Household Survey on Drug Abuse

The popularity of heroin, as measured by the number of new heroin users, peaked in 1972, then came down during the years when homelessness was rising, with year-to-year fluctuations in numbers of new users. Measuring usage as a percentage of the population who are "lifetime" heroin users indicates a steady, downward trend, from 1.3% of the population in 1979 to less that 1% through the 1980s (National Household Survey on Drug Abuse 1979-1991).

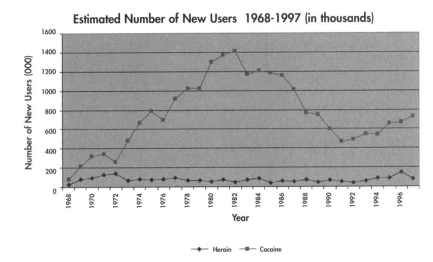

Source: US DHHS 1998 National Household Survey on Drug Abuse

The trend over 20 years for users of heroin is very different from the cocaine trend in actual numbers of new users and overall users of cocaine. During its peak year, 1985, there were 40 times more current cocaine users, 5.7 million, than current heroin users, 137,000.

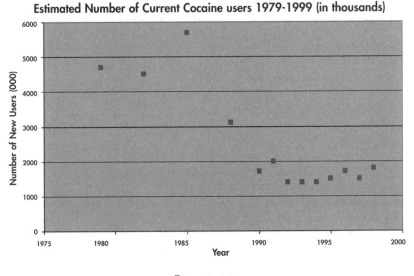

Source: US DHHS National Household Survey on Drug Abuse, 1979-1991; 1998 and Substance Abuse and Mental Health Services Administration 1992-1999.

Services to individuals in drug treatment facilities reflect the overall rise in drug use as well as funding for treatment services.

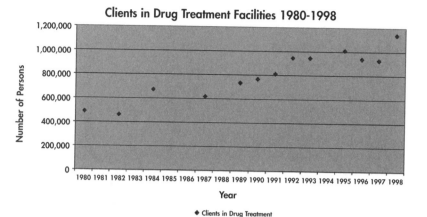

Clients in Drug Treatment Facilities 1980-1998

Source: SAMHSA, Office of Applied Studies, National Drug and Alcoholism Treatment Unit Survey (NDATUS) 1980-1993; 1995-1998.

Those who attribute the rise in homelessness, in part, due to substance abuse maintain that it was specifically the crack epidemic that contributed significantly to homelessness during the time period under consideration. It could be said that the availability of crack at low prices would entice the "rational actor" to purchase the cheaper substance to abuse, hence freeing more money for rent. Anecdotal evidence suggests that the lowered prices for crack, a smokeable form of the more expensive cocaine, was a deliberate marketing ploy to create more addicts by making a very inexpensive, highly psychologically addicting drug readily available in the inner cities. Despite the low prices for crack, crack addiction can have the reverse effect on money available for rent. For $10 a hit, a heroin addict can stay high and/or not sick for about 12 hours. Due to the unique pathology of crack addiction, people in active abuse will be unable to stop purchasing crack until their last dime is spent or until they die. For a $5 hit of crack, the effect last for only two to four minutes. "…The more you have the more you want, until your money is gone. It's not a physical craving, so there is no 'cure', but a powerful psychological craving. You want the feeling…you CHASE it" (Abdur-Razzaq 2000). Crack is cheaper now than when it was first introduced. The insidious consequence of the low street price of crack was to entice more first time buyers (Wells and Triplett 1992).

Both new users of cocaine and overall use dropped dramatically from 1985 to 1990. Based on their National Household Survey on Drug Abuse, the U.S. DHHS reports that cocaine use nationwide peaked in 1985 (5.7 million people or 3% of the population) dropped to 1.4 million people (0.7% of the population) by 1992, with little change thereafter. The estimated number of crack users was approximately 437,000 (one-third of cocaine users) for the ten year period 1988-1998. The number of <u>new</u> users of any form of cocaine stood at 470,000 in 1991, and decreased by 55% by 1997; at the peak period, 1980–1986, new users were double the 1990s number. Specifically for new users of crack, DHHS reports there has been little change since 1985, however the age of first time use has crept into the 18-25 year-old range.

Data from the federal Drug Abuse Warning Network (DAWN) for the time period provides mixed initial impressions for cocaine-involved drug deaths and emergency room treatment with no consistent breakout for "crack," the cheap, smokeable form of cocaine. Rates for drug-induced deaths (heroin and other drugs, but not alcohol) increased from 3.0 deaths per 100,000 population in 1980 to 3.5 by 1985 and 4.1 by 1991. Purity and price could arguably provide as much of the explanation as prevalence.

Prices dropped about in half between 1981 and 1986 for cocaine (not crack cocaine). Dramatic increases in purity are a primary cause of unintentional drug overdoses leading to hospital admissions and deaths (Wells & Triplett 1992). Street prices for heroin followed an almost identical pattern during the time period. New users and addicts could increasingly obtain purer drugs for less money, which, in the economics of the drug market, reflects a predictable dealer response to the decrease in drug use, at least for heroin.

Heroin "Street" Price Purity Trend 1981-1998

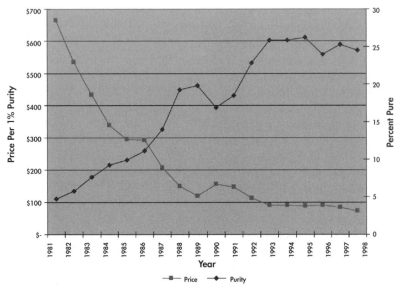

Source: System to Retrieve Information from Drug Evidence (STRIDE), Drug Enforcement Administration, 1981-1997.

For heroin, the price/purity ratio became so "favorable" by 1992 that smoking and sniffing, rather than intravenous injection and "skin popping," forbidding deterrents to the uninitiated, became attractive recreational drug activities, which some see as the reason for the rise in heroin use in the mid-1990s (Epstein and Gfroerer 1997). Despite the plethora of data and coincidental evidence, homelessness cannot be conclusively attributed to the increase in cocaine use, although anecdotal evidence observed by the author in over 10 years of work with the homeless population suggests that drug use, especially given the insidious nature of crack cocaine addiction (Wells & Triplett 1992), accounts for homelessness for some.

Criminal Justice

This section will examine factors in criminal justice as possible causes of the rise of homelessness in New Jersey in the 1980s. Surveys of the homeless frequently document incarceration history as a characteristic personal "vulnerability" (Shlay and Rossi 1992; Wright 1989; Burt and Cohen 1989). Similar to the examination of other possible causal factors, the analysis will focus on what, if anything, changed concerning the incarcerated population during the time period under review, including proportionate numbers incarcerated and proportionate numbers being released from jails and prisons back into the community and the housing market.

Incarcerated individuals are consumers of housing but many also contribute to the income levels of households with which they are involved either as partners, family members, or parents. Previous incarceration is generally seen as a contributing factor to homelessness among single men and women when they are released (O'Flaherty 1996), due to difficulty finding employment and being prohibited from residing on their own or with family members in federally-subsidized public housing projects. Some view incarceration of breadwinners and parents as a compelling factor in family homelessness (Baum and Burnes 1993). A recent study found that 44% of the fathers of homeless children had a history of incarceration. More than half of the fathers of homeless children are likely to spend time with their children and provide financial support for the children, if they are allowed parental contact while incarcerated. (Institute for Children and Poverty 2000). A majority of both men and women in state institutions do not see their children while they are incarcerated (U. S. Department of Justice 2000). Providing income assistance, of course, is not possible if they are in jail. Forty-five percent of men in state facilities and 36% of men in federal facilities had minor children under 18 years of age (U.S. Department of Justice 2000).

Incarceration is one type of institutional housing as enumerated by the U.S. Bureau of the Census for persons residing in group quarters or not residing in households. The "homeless," when designated as such in the 1990 census and 2000 census, were enumerated as persons residing in non-institutional settings, but not households. Consistently over the 60-year period, 1940 to 2000, persons residing in non-household settings accounted for about 2% of New Jersey's population. As shown in the table below, the institutionally-housed accounted for less than 50% of all group quarters in New Jersey until 1990, when numbers in correctional institutions nearly tripled over 1980 and rose from .14% of the population to .38% of the population in New Jersey. The institutionally-housed included those in mental and psychiatric facilities (not community group homes), wards and hospitals for drug and alcohol treatment, and nursing homes. The proportion of correctional inmates in these types of facilities doubled from 1980 to 1990, and accounted for over 40% of this population by 2000.

A recent study of homelessness in California examined the relationship between rates of institutionalized mental patients and incarceration. Regressing the population rates of in-patient mental hospitals jails/prisons, per 100,000 in the population revealed a negative and significant relationship. While the census in mental hospitals had gone down, community group homes, nursing homes, and correctional institution populations had gone up (Quigley, Raphael and Smolensky 2001).

Trends in Correctional Institution Population in New Jersey 1940-2000

Year	1940	1950	1960	1970	1980	1990	2000
NJ Population	4,160,165	4,816,435	6,066,782	7,168,143	7,364,823	7,730,188	8,414,350
Institutional Group Quarters	41,833	50,479	63,286	60,013	66,503	92,670	110,169
% of Total Group Quarters	47.27%	28.53%*	41.44%	40.97%	49.08%	54.08%	56.55%
% of NJ Population	1.01%	1.05%	1.04%	0.84%	0.90%	1.20%	1.25%
Correctional Institutions	n/a	6,193	7,829	8,872	10,261	29,093	47,941
% of Total Group Quarters		3.50%	5.13%	6.06%	7.57%	16.98%	24.61%
% of Inst. Group Quarters		12.27%	12.37%	14.78%	15.43%	31.39%	43.52%
% of NJ Population		0.13%	0.13%	0.12%	0.14%	0.38%	0.56%

This percentage shift is due to increased number of military in non-institutional quarters.

Source:
For 1940,
1950, 1960:   *General Population Characteristics, Table 19 – Household Relationship, By Color, for the State, by Size of Place, 1960, and for the State 1950, 1940, Page 32-45.*
For 1970:   *Characteristics of the Population, Part 32, NJ, Vol. 2, Table 154, Persons in Group Quarters by Type of Quarters, Sex, Race and Age, Page 32-713.*

For 1980:   *Detailed Population Characteristics, NJ, Table 207. Persons in Group Quarters by Type of Group Quarters, Age, Sex, Race and Spanish Origin. Page 32-175.*

For 1990:   *General Population Characteristics, NJ, Table 38. Persons in Group Quarters by Type of Group Quarters, Sex, Race and Hispanic Origin. Page 168 New Jersey.*

For 2000:   *PCT16: Group Quarters Population by Group Quarters Type [52], from the American Fact Finder website and the Emergency Transitional Shelter Population 2000, Special Report.*

The number of sentenced persons in New Jersey and their proportion of the overall population climbed dramatically in the 1980s and 1990s. There were 76 sentenced prisoners per 100,000 population in 1980, and by 1990 the rate had increased 3.5 times to 271 per 100,000 residents, with a much less dramatic increase in the 1990s. A simple result of this trend would be a decrease in the number of persons seeking housing during the period when homelessness rose in the 1980s, thus not contributing to it. Another more plausible explanation, which supports a positive correlation between incarceration rates and homelessness, would be that the increase in incarceration of persons contributing to household income, despite the fact that their incomes were gained through illegal means, reduces the income available for rent.

**Number of Sentenced Prisoners Per 100,000 Residents
New Jersey 1980-2000**

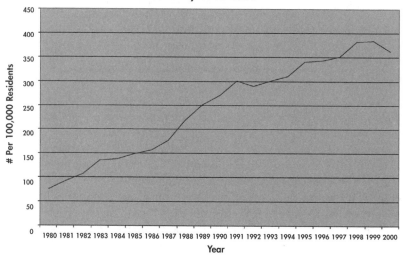

Source: U. S. Department of Justice, Bureau of Justice Statistics, Prisoners in State and Federal Institutions, SD-NPS-PSF-B, NCJ-80520, p. 16.

Anecdotal evidence gathered during the author's ten years of experience in the distribution of personal mail to residents of homeless facilities for women and families points to a significant number of homeless women who regularly receive correspondence from incarcerated male partners.

The increase in the total number of prisoners is reflected in an increase in the numbers of persons being released from jails and prisons, and, over time, in the total stock of ex-offenders in the community seeking housing (O'Flaherty 1996). As shown in the chart below, the numbers of inmates being released also rose during the period when homelessness was rising.

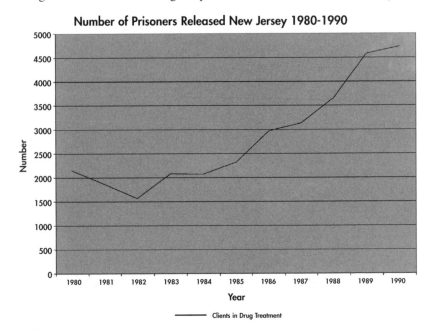

Number of Prisoners Released New Jersey 1980-1990

Source: New Jersey Department of Corrections, Annual Reports.

Some theorists have examined the phenomenon of a rising prison population and suggest causes other than simply an increase in crime (Wilson 1987; Schneider and Ingram 1993; Hacker 1992). "Patterns of income and wealth in the United States are strongly skewed along racial lines" (Burnham 2001). Prisons and their populations grew during a time of welfare reform and contraction in government supports for social and economic programs (Gottschalk 2002), which were benefiting primarily black Americans (Slessarev 1988) and unmarried women (Bane 1988).

The rate of 110 prisoners per 100,000 people remained fairly constant in the United States from the 1920s through the 1970s (Blumstein and Beck 1999), and was only slightly higher than other Western industrialized countries. By the end of the century, the U.S. incarceration rate was six to 10 times Western European countries (Beck and Harrison 2001). African Americans accounted for 8.7% of New Jersey's population in 1960, but 16.6% of prison inmates, twice the black rate in the population. By 1970, blacks were represented in prisons in New Jersey at 3.5 times the rate in the population, at 4.5 times in 1980 and 4.7 times in 1990. Black youth accounted for an alarming 64% of the residents in juvenile institutions in 1990, 4.8 times their rate in the state population (U.S. Census Bureau 1960-1990). In the 1990 census, the first to provide a detailed breakout of the location of the homeless, New Jersey blacks accounted for 64.1% of the homeless in shelters and 71.7% of the homeless visible on the street, when their overall percentage of the state population was 13.4%.

Incarceration, racism, poverty, drug addiction, and homelessness intertwine to create a tangle of consequences in the "economic underworld" (Harrington 1962), the solutions to which have no consensus of opinion, the victims of which are perceived as deviant (Schneider and Ingram 1993), and the government response to which is "unusually underdeveloped" compared to European welfare states (Orloff 1988). One theorist of public welfare policy argues "welfare policy....is not addressed to the poor – it is addressed to us. It is an affirmation of majoritarian values through the creation of deviants. The poor are held hostage to make sure that the rest of us behave" (Handler 1995). Considering the phenomenal rise in the prison population, "held hostage" has become more real than symbolic.

Summary of Findings

This paper sets forth a systematic analysis of the context in which homelessness was rising in New Jersey during the years 1980-2000. The O'Flaherty explanatory model, which proposes an economic theory of the housing market that includes homelessness, was also examined. Data was collected, for a 20-year period, from 1980–2000. Data that were published, collected or commonly relied upon by public officials and decision makers were selected for the data sets. Three individual-level pathologies were examined: substance abuse, mental illness, and involvement with the criminal justice system.

The Housing Market and Income Distribution

The middle class, defined by the proportion of aggregate income earned by the middle class, was shrinking in New Jersey from 1969-1999. The shrinking middle class corresponds to the rise in homelessness, especially in the major cities in New Jersey. The trend of a shrinking middle class purports tighter and tighter markets for lower cost units, as the number of units becomes fewer and more expensive. Average rent as a percent of average poor income rose dramatically, from rent using 63% of poor income in 1980 to over 100% by 1990 and remaining over 90% throughout the rest of the decade. This was also found to be true in the California study (Quigley, Raphael and Smolensky 2001). New Jersey's percent of dwelling units with two or more units was considerably higher than the national average, especially in the six cities. Crowding and severe crowding increased in New Jersey from 1980 onward. The six cities in New Jersey lost 7% of their housing units from 1980-2000, with average occupancy per unit rising from 2.54 persons per unit in 1980 to 2.65 persons per unit by 2000.

A negative correlation with poverty rates confirms the phenomenon of rising homelessness during times of economic prosperity (O'Flaherty 1996). Applying the O'Flaherty economic theory of homelessness and housing model, those at the lowest level of income were becoming perilously close to the point on the bid-rent curve where they were below the price-quality schedule for all values above zero.

Tax rates, as the indicator was constructed, showed no consistent trend during the 20-year period.

Mortgage rates were at their highest when homelessness was rising. Rising mortgage rates depressed the affordability index below 1.0, or "affordable," for all years that rates exceeded 8%. The change in the shelter price index exceeded that of the consumer price index in all but one of the 20 years from 1980-2000.

The negative correlation of vacancy rates in cities supports the theory that a shrinking middle class results in a decline in low cost units which filter down to the poor, and that homelessness rises when the poor housing market gets tighter and vacancy rates fall for these lower cost units. This was also found to be true in the recent study of homelessness in California (Quigley, Raphael & Smolensky 2001).

A negative, "estimated," long-term interest rate prevailed for the first two years of the 1980s, then rose dramatically. During the time when homelessness was becoming a crisis in New Jersey, even "safe" long-term government securities presented an attractive investment alternative to real estate. Existing home sale prices rose dramatically, nearly doubling during the 1980's. Through the period until 1995, the increasing supply of subsidized housing did not alleviate the housing crisis for the lowest income levels.

Individual-Level Pathologies

Mental Illness

The proportion of mentally ill in the population over time by most accounts has not changed (Goldman 1984; Burt 1992; Jencks 1994). The institutionalized mentally ill in New Jersey, that is those residing in institutional, non-community settings, declined from 1980–2000, from 8,807 persons to 3,541 persons, a decrease of 5,266 persons over 20 years. In the decade preceding the rise of homelessness, the 1970s, the decrease was 5,927 persons over the 10-year period. The deinstitutionalized mentally ill were not likely to have been absorbed into the rooming and boarding house population since those facilities lost about 40% of their residents over this time period. A recent study of homelessness in California revealed a negative and significant relationship between the census in mental institutions and community group homes, nursing homes and correctional institutions (Quigley, Raphael and Smolensky 2001). Due in part to the changes in federal health care regulations, which reimbursed states for elderly patients in nursing homes but <u>not</u> in state mental hospitals, the elderly mentally ill could easily have been absorbed into nursing homes, whose residents increased by 28,352 from 1970-2000. Community group homes, not an isolated category until the 1990 census when 3,332 residents were counted in New Jersey, were seen as more suitable living arrangements than institutions. Both SSI benefits and improved medications made it easier to care for the mentally ill in a home setting. By 2000, group homes held 12,252 residents. A third plausible explanation could be incarceration of the deinstitutionalized mentally ill, as correctional inmates grew by 37,680 persons over the 20-year period.

Substance Abuse

Alcohol abuse has long been associated with the vagrant, hobo, and Skid Row inhabitant. The major indicators of alcohol abuse declined during the time that homelessness was rising. Alcohol consumption overall, "heavy drinking," alcohol-related fatalities, and persons driving under the influence of alcohol declined during the 20-year period. Medical problems associated with heavy alcohol consumption and death rates due to alcohol-induced causes also dropped during the period.

Usage trends for heroin were flat during the time homelessness was rising in New Jersey. The numbers of current users, new users, and number of "lifetime" users all showed flat or declining trends. Due to lack of data, the widely held theory that crack, the smokeable and highly-addictive form of cocaine, contributed to rising homelessness could not be supported or refuted. By most measures, crack was not isolated from cocaine as a distinct substance until 1991. Cocaine indicators, meaning both cocaine and crack combined, showed a dramatically rising trend in the early eighties, peaking from 1984-1986, then slowly declining by the mid-1990s. During its peak, there were 40 times more cocaine users than heroin users. Powder-cocaine became a highly fashionable recreational drug among the affluent and the trend-setting populations which makes it difficult before 1991, to control for crack, an inexpensive inner-city drug of choice, and its causal relationship to homelessness.

Criminal Justice

Surveys of shelters and soup lines frequently document incarceration history as a "personal vulnerability" to homelessness. Incarceration has increased dramatically both as a percentage of persons living in non-household settings and as a percentage of the population overall. Although these individuals were not seeking housing while incarcerated, thus reducing demand in the market, they were also not contributing to the household incomes of their families, thus reducing the funds available for rent. Unless those incarcerated remain incarcerated, the overall size of the released prisoner population will rise. Those with incarceration histories will find it harder to get jobs and impossible to qualify for or live in federally subsidized housing. No available measure exists to retroactively determine whether rising incarceration rates contributed to rising homelessness from the 1980s on. Improved survey data would be of tremendous help with this question. While the effects of the rise in incarceration rates may or may not have been a factor in the rising homelessness in New

Jersey during the 1980s, the "time bomb" effect may trigger future waves of homelessness.

Policy Recommendations

The purpose of this research was to demonstrate the utility of constructing a well-grounded model that allows public administrators to interpret, track, predict, and make credible decisions about homelessness in New Jersey. This research examines the dimensions of homelessness in New Jersey which grew into a burgeoning social crisis in the early 1980s. It also illustrates a broader issue in public administration – amidst a barrage of media attention and public pressure, the government can be urged to ameliorate situations that are ill-defined. Two other recent studies applied this O'Flaherty economic model to assist public administrators in their understanding of homelessness. In a study of homelessness in California, Quigley, Raphael, and Smolensky constructed the model using state-specific indicators of the dependent variable, homelessness, and arrived at findings that supported the O'Flaherty theory. Another application of the O'Flaherty model looked at national-level data for the relationship between homelessness and vacancy rates (Park 2000). This study, which was based on an exhaustive investigation supports the theoretical assumptions about vacancy rates in the O'Flaherty model.

In *Frame Reflection: Toward the Resolution of Intractable Policy Controversies*, Donald Schon and Martin Rein discuss the case history of policy makers grappling with the homelessness dilemma during this same time period in Massachusetts. There "a crisis of homelessness broke into public consciousness in the Commonwealth of Massachusetts, triggering an unfolding policy drama" (Schon & Rein 1994:129). As they tried to develop an appropriate policy approach, public officials were confronted with multiple definitions, conflicting interpretations, and gaps and contradictions in the available data. The need for developing an explanatory model is especially great when, as was true in Massachusetts, a policy controversy occurs in a politically-charged and "muddled" atmosphere. The more that controversial problems seem immune to resolution by "facts," the greater the need for public administrators to garner agreement around a neutral explanatory model. One way of accomplishing this would be to require that any entity receiving public funding employ standardized definitions and methodologies.

Estimating the Number of Homeless Persons

During the 20-year period, 1980-2000, there were only five state-wide observations of the number of homeless persons, three surveys conducted by the New Jersey Department of Community Affairs, the 1990 census and 2000 census. Additionally, the definitions of the homeless and the survey or count methodology used in the five New Jersey surveys were not consistent. When localities computed homeless estimates for the purpose of documenting the need for funding for homeless services, as in the three New Jersey government agency reports, their estimates were somewhat higher than more objective observers. [see Table following] The homeless, per se, were not tabulated in the 1980 Census. The 1990 census, although heavily criticized for its methodology, counted and reported the homeless in facilities serving the homeless as well as "homeless visible on the street." The 2000 Census count on the homeless was based on a Service-Based Enumeration on March 27, 2000 [but does not include a complete tabulation of service users at canvassed sites], a soup and mobile food van count on March 28, 2000, and a count at targeted, non-sheltered outdoor locations on March 29, 2000. Those at soup kitchens, mobile food vans, and outdoor locations were not reported on a separate line as in the 1990 count, but were included in "Other." In 2000, these counts were only conducted for places of 100,000 or more and reported only for those with 100 or more in emergency and transitional shelters. The 2000 Census Bureau Special Report on the homeless admits that, before more accurate numbers can be known, "a generally agreed upon definition of which population groups to include in the total would need to be established (U.S. Bureau of Census 2000). [For a comprehensive discussion of the strengths and weaknesses of studies to estimate homelessness see Garfinkel and Piliavin 1994; Burt 1995, Shlay and Rossi 1992, Quigley, Raphael & Smolensky 2001].

A comparison of the rate of homelessness reported in the five New Jersey surveys and other widely-used studies is shown in the Table below.

Comparison of New Jersey Surveys with Other Surveys

Source	Rate of Homeless in the Population	
New Jersey Surveys		
NJ DCA – 1986 Study	.001905	
NJ DCA – 1993 Study	.001789	
NJ DCA – 2000 Plan	.002205	
U. S. Census 1990	.001178	
U. S. Census 2000	.000624	
Other Surveys		
Freeman & Hall (1987)	2.23 street/shelter ratio	
Quigley, Raphael & Smolensky (2001)	.001-.003	
Burt (1989, 1992)	City	Suburbs
	.00042	.00007
	.00088	.00010
	.00153	.00020
	.00205	.00045
Tucker (1987)	.00031	(cities only)
Jencks (1994)	.000552	
HUD (1984)	.0005 – .005 (cities only)	

There are limitations to public administrators' reliance on rational, positivist models alone, particularly amidst political controversy. As Lindblom warns, "some expressed attitudes, beliefs or values become influential because they are regarded as commanding wide agreement....persons well situated to reach audiences can circulate expressions of attitude, belief and value that may be influential even if no one, not even the source of the messages, ever comes to believe them" (Lindblom 1990:75). "Expert" knowledge is split about causes of homelessness and the appropriate government remedies. Many see homelessness as a condition resulting from disturbances and inequalities in the housing and income sectors of our economy. Others approach the problem as one brought on by individual level pathologies. Our understanding of homelessness reflects the approach to social welfare problems in the United States as aggregates of individual level pathologies (Skocpol 1992; Rueschemeyer and Skocpol 1996). There has been no consensus about who is defined as homeless and how they should be enumerated.

Despite this lack of clarity, government was called upon to address this crisis in the 1980s. Short-term remedies may or may not have been effective then, however long-term solutions and preventative policies, clearly have not worked. By autumn of 2002, homelessness was back on the front page of *The New York Times*, which reported "crowds not seen since the 1980s" at shelters, soup kitchens and feeding vans" (Kaufman and Flynn 2002).

This research encountered numerous difficulties due to the "organized anarchy" of imperfect information (Kingdon 1995) surrounding homelessness, or, as Ellickson so aptly described the situation in 1990, The Homeless Muddle. Prominent among these difficulties are:

1. lack of an agreed-upon theoretical model of the causal factors of homelessness;
2. lack of consistently applied definitions of what is meant by the homeless;
3. lack of consistently applied survey and enumeration methodology, especially with U. S. Census Bureau information;
4. lack of sufficient data for many of the critical factors, including difficulties encountered obtaining data through The Freedom of Information Act.

There are similar social problems that are surrounded by controversial and muddled aura: poverty, affirmative action, and welfare reform are good examples. Taking a positivist, rational approach, we can discover what things we can "properly and successfully do" (Wilson 1887; Bobrow & Dryzek 1987). One theoretical model of homelessness was the subject of this research. This model puts forth an economic theory of homelessness as a housing market resultant (O'Flaherty 1996). This theory regards homelessness as a type of housing for which supply and demand are influenced by measurable factors. One measurable influencing factor is the distribution of income, quantified by the proportionate size of the middle class. According to this theory, housing for the poorer classes is a by-product of housing originally built for the middle class which filters down. Increasing income inequality, caused by a shrinking middle class and more poor people, both decreases the supply of housing at the lowest prices and increases the demand for it. Data to test this theory were gathered over a 20-year period, 1980 to 2000, a time when homelessness was rising in the state of New Jersey. Thirteen income and housing indicators were constructed to test the theory, but there were only five observations of the number of persons homeless in New Jersey during the 20-year period against which to compare those indicators. The homeless could be estimated as a likely percentage of the population, but they had rarely been counted.

Despite this limitation, the research found empirical evidence to support the theory that the middle class was shrinking when homelessness was rising and fewer low-cost units filtered down to the lower classes, resulting in stronger demand for those units as evidenced by lowered vacancy rates and crowded occupancy. In addition, more families at the lowest income level slipped to the point on the bid-rent curve where they were below the price-quality schedule for all values above zero, and they became homeless. At the beginning of the 1980s, New Jersey's middle class earned less than its proportionate share of aggregate income, 57% of the income for 60% of the population. Over the 20-year period, the middle class lost an additional 3.3% of the state's aggregate income. Monthly rents rose by 34% in the six major cities and by 30% for the state overall. In 1980, rent consumed 63% of the average poor family's income. When homelessness was at its peak, even 100% of a poor family's income could not cover the rent. By the year 2000, 92.5% of income was required by poor families to pay the rent. Housing in the cities became more scarce as it became more expensive.

Homelessness is a complex reality. Public administrators are relied upon to address this and other vexing social problems, which are not simple to explain. Public administrators often operate with limited knowledge and understanding, and solutions are often developed independent of the problem stream (Kingdon 1995). An issue need not be simple in order to be understandable. An issue need not be simple in order for an agreement to be reached on the parameters of the problem. Solutions to public problems should be created with models that help us understand causation, evaluate alternatives, and anticipate how different interventions would correct the problem. Theories involving large numbers of causal variables can increase the possible interventions (Linder and Peters 1985). By adopting a mixed-scanning approach (Etzioni 1967), despite complete understanding of causes, a direction could be established with built-in feedback strategies for program evaluation.

Public officials could improve information by involving stakeholders in program design and implementation as a condition of public funding. "One role of policy research is to produce information which increases the rational capacity of the system" (Schneider 1986:358). Surveys of the formerly homeless themselves would illuminate the relationship between homelessness and substance abuse and incarceration history. More frequent and anonymous surveys and enumerations of service providers, not tied to funding decisions, would be another useful methodology for gathering objective information. A systematic process to gather information needed for such a causal model could be further improved by internal consistency on definitions of the homeless and the methodology for enumeration. An agency such as HUD could standardize usage in these areas. HUD could suggest that children in foster care whose parents are homeless should always or should never be included in an enumeration. Better information could be gathered if the government knew what it should track, measured it consistently, and set the standard for others. Regarding homelessness, the state could be the collector and keeper of "official knowledge" (Rueschemeyer and Skocpol 1996).

An example of the value of meaningful definitions and internal consistency in structuring a complex issue is our understanding of money. Although there are differences, for instance, between monetarists and post-Keynsians over how the theoretical economic model works and how the government should tweak it and when, there is consensus that the model is complex and government intervention in one segment impacts other segments of the model. There is an understanding that "money" means different things. There are different kinds of money designations, and they are different in how they are calculated. The most ordinary definition of money is currency, paper bills and coins, money in one's bank account. This is defined as M_s, money supply held by the public, by all those who refer to it and track it. There are other categories of money, as well. M_d is money demanded, M_t is transaction demand for money, M_{sp} is speculative demand for money. M_d and M_{sp} are not analogous. Although these theoretical notations are not used by people trying to measure the money supply, they help explain that pressure on one category of money can cause a shift in another category of money.

One reason for conflicting theories about what causes homelessness derives from multiple definitions of the homeless. There are in fact several valid definitions that describe the condition of being homeless. Similar to the ordinary definition of money, the ordinary definition of the homeless could be someone sleeping on the street or in an abandoned building without heat and electricity. One could assign H_1 to this type of homeless person. There are persons in shelters or receiving homelessness prevention assistance in the form of rent subsidies who are also defined as homeless. One could assign H_2 to this type of homeless person. There are persons who drift on and off the streets and in and out of shelters and even prisons, who are receiving services from community group homes for the mentally ill and from addiction programs. They may be handicapped by individual level pathologies or unable to get jobs due to felony convictions; they may keep a roof over their heads part of the time, and other times, not. One could assign H_3 to this type of homeless person. There is also a segment of the population living in tenuous financial or housing circumstances that could slide into H_1 or H_2 status with the slightest push. One could assign H_4 to this segment of the population. Just as is true in the monetary model, theoretically there is an equilibrium for the four categories of homelessness. As this research demonstrates, measurable factors in the economy and housing market can be used as predictors for changes in any one of the four categories of homelessness, which could ripple through other categories.

Ideally, public administrators should advocate for the provision of housing and services for the homeless, but, at the very least, they need to put the public funding allocated for this purpose to the most effective use. Under conditions of uncertainty and imperfect information, it is correct to approach a social problem such as homelessness as a complex issue with "bounded conditions that limit rationality" (Forester 1984). It may not be politically or otherwise feasible at this time to correct the causes of growing income inequality in the United States, which contribute to rising homelessness, win the war on drugs, and prevent social pathologies that lead to crime or cure mental illness. Public administrators could, however, establish standardized definitions, methodologies, and categories for the various conditions of homelessness, which would assist in research, policy design, and program effectiveness. Standardized terminology should reflect the complexities and interrelationships of the homeless condition. It would provide a uniform structure for cost-benefit analysis, advance the tenets of public productivity, and enable government to more effectively predict the number and design responses to the human casualties of homelessness.

References

Abbott, G. 1933. The Child. *American Journal of Sociology. 38:880-888.*

Abdur-Razzaq, D. 2000. Substance abuse counselor, East Orange, N.J., *interview*, February, 2000.

Adams, C. T. 1986. Homelessness in the post-industrial city. *Urban Affairs Quarterly 21, 527-49.*

Adorno, T. W., Frenkel-Brunswik, Else, Levinson, Daniel J. and R. Nevitt Sanford. 1950. *The Authoritarian Personality.* Harper & Row, N. Y.

Adorno, T. W., Frenkel-Brunswik, Else, Levinson, Daniel J. and R. Nevitt Sanford (1973). *The Jargon of Authenticity.* Northwestern University Press, Evanston, Ill.

Adorno, T. W., Frenkel-Brunswik, Else, Levinson, Daniel J. and R. Nevitt Sanford (1983). *Against Epistemology: A Metacritique.* The MIT Press, Cambridge.

Allison, G. 1971. *Essence of Decision: Explaining the Cuban Missile Crisis.* Little, Brown, Boston.

Ammons, David N. 1992. Productivity Barriers in the Public Sector. *Public Productivity Handbook*, Marc Holzer, Ed. Marcel Dekker, Inc., New York.

Anderson, D. L. 1991. Using longitudinal records to estimate transient and resident homeless populations. *Housing Policy Debate 2(3) 883-900.*

Anderson, N. 1923. The Juvenile and the Tramp. *Journal of Criminal Law & Criminology 14:290-312.*

Angell, Robert C. 1936. *The Family Encounters the Depression.* Peter Smith, Gloucester, MA.

Applebaum, R., et al. 1991. Scapegoating Rent Control: Masking the Causes of Homelessness. *Journal of the American Planning Association 57 (Sp) 153-164.*

Appleby, P. 1949. *Policy and Administration.* The University of Alabama Press, Alabama.

Arendt, Hanna. 1958. *The Human Condition.* The University of Chicago Press, Chicago.

Arnott, Richard. 1987. Economic Theory and Housing. *Handbook of Regional and Urban Economics*, Vol. II, Edited by E.S. Mills, Elsevier Science Publishers, B.V.

Arnott, Richard,. et al. 1983. Housing quality, maintenance and rehabilitation. *Review of Economic Studies. 50, 467-494.*

Association for Children NJ. 1997. *In Their Own Words: An Inside View of New Jersey's Child Protection System,* Newark, NJ.

Bahr, Howard M. 1973. *Skid Row: An Introduction to Disaffiliation.* Oxford Univ. Press, NY.

Bahr, Howard M. 1967. The gradual disappearance of skid row. *Social Problems 15(1), 41-45.*

Bahr, Howard M. and Caplow, Theodore. 1974. *Old Men Drunk and Sober.* New York University Press, NY.

Bahr, Howard M. & Garrett, G. R. 1976. *Women Alone.* Lexington Books, Lexington, MA.

Balk, Walter L. 1992. Organization Theories as Instigators of Public Productivity Improvement Action. *Public Productivity Handbook,* Marc Holzer, ed., Marcel Dekker, Inc. New York.

Ball, Michael, Michael Harloe, and Marrtje Martens. 1988. *Housing and Social Change in Europe and the USA.* Routledge, London.

Bane, Mary Jo. 1988. Politics and Policies of the Feminization of Poverty. In *The Politics of Social Policy in the United States,* Ed. Weir, M, Orloff, A.S. and Skocpol, T., Princeton University Press, Princeton, NJ.

Barclay, George W. 1958. *Techniques of Population Analysis.* John Wiley and Sons, Inc., NY.

Barnard-Columbia Center for Urban Policy. 1996. *The Continuum of Care: A Report on the New Federal Policy to Address Homelessness.* Government Printing Office, Washington D.C.

Bassuk, Ellen L. et al. 1997. Homelessness in Female-Headed Families: Childhood and Adult Risk and Protective Factors. *American Journal of Public Health.* Vol. 87, No. 2.

Bassuk, Ellen L. et al. 1996a. Single Mothers and Welfare. *Scientific American,* October.

Bassuk, Ellen L. et al. 1996b. The Characteristics and Needs of Sheltered Homeless and Low-Income Housed Mothers. *Journal of the American Medical Association.* Vol. 276, No. 8.

Bassuk, Ellen L. et al. 1984. The Homelessness Problem. *Scientific American.* Vol. 251.

Baum, A. and Burnes, D. 1993. *A Nation in Denial: The Truth About Homelessness. Westview Press,* Boulder, Colo.

Beck, Allen J. and Harrison, Paige, M. 2001. Prisoners in 2000. *Bureau of Justice Statistics Bulletin,* no. NCJ 188207, August: 1-15.

Belcher, J. R. and Singer, J. (1988) Homelessness: a cost of capitalism. *Social Policy 18, 44-48.*

Bergler, E. 1955. To kill with kindness. *International Journal of Sexology 7, 148-149.*

Bernstein, Jared, et al. 2000. Pulling Apart: *A State-by-State Analysis of Income Trends.* Center on Budget and Policy Priorities, Economic Policy Institute, Washington, D.C.

Bernstein, Nina. 2002. A Homeless Problem is Back: Overnight in a City Office. *The New York Times,* August 7, 2002, page B1.

Beshers, James M., ed. 1965. *Computer Methods in the Analysis of Large-scale Social Systems.* The MIT Press, Cambridge.

Bingham, R. D., et al. 1987. *The Homeless in Contemporary Society.* Sage, Beverly Hills.

Blalock, Herbert M, Jr. 1960. *Social Statistics*. McGraw-Hill Book Co., New York.

Blasi, Gary L. 1990. Social Policy and Social Science Research on Homelessness. *Journal of Social Issues. Vol. 46, No. 4.*

Blumstein, Alfred and Beck, Allen J. 1999. Population growth in U.S. prisons, 1980-1996. In Prisons: *Crime and Justice – A Review of Research*, vol. 26, ed. Michael Tonry and Joan Petersilia. The University of Chicago Press, Chicago.

Bobrow, Davis B. and Dryzek, John S. 1987. *Policy Analysis by Design*. University of Pittsburgh Press, Pittsburgh.

Bohanon, Cecil. 1991. The Economic Correlates of Homelessness in Sixty Cities. *Social Science Quarterly 72:4.*

Borderia, H. 1965. Preliminary report of a study of institutionalized children. *Psicologia y Educacion 1(1), 45-57.*

Bouckaert, Geert. 1992. Public Productivity in Retrospective. *Public Productivity Handbook, Marc* Holzer, ed., Marcel Dekker, Inc., New York.

Braid, R. 1981. The short-run comparative statistics of a rental housing market. *Journal Urban Economics. 10, 286-310.*

Breakey, William R. and Fischer, Pamela J. 1990. Homelessness: The Extent of the Problem. *Journal of Social Issues. Vol. 46, No. 4.*

Brockington, C. F. 1946. Homelessness in children; causes and prevention. *Lancet 250, 933-936.*

Brownlow Committee. 1937. President's Committee on Administrative Management – Report with Special Studies. U.S. Government Printing Office, Washington, DC.

Bruner, Jerome. 1990. *Acts of Meaning*. Harvard University Press, Cambridge.

Brazelton, T. B. 1991. Is America Failing Its Children? *The New York Times Magazine*, January 13, 1991.

Burnham, Linda. 2001. Welfare Reform, Family Hardship, and Women of Color. *The Annals of the American Academy of Political and Social Science*, Vol. 577, September.

Burt, Martha R. 1995. Critical Factors in Counting the Homeless. *American Journal of Orthopsychiatry, 65:3, July.*

Burt, Martha R. 1992. *Over the Edge: The Growth of Homelessness in the 1980's*. Russell Sage Foundation, NY.

Burt, Martha R. and Cohen, Barbara E. 1989. *America's Homeless: Numbers, Characteristics, and the Programs that Serve Them*. The Urban Institute Press, Washington, D.C.

Cameron, Stephen V. and Heckman, James J. 1998. "Life cycle schooling and dynamic selection bias: models and evidence for five cohorts of American males." *Journal of Political Economy, Vol 106, No. 2.*

Campbell, Donald T. and Stanley, Julian C. 1963. *Experimental and Quasi-Experimental Designs for Research*. Houghton Mifflin, Co., Boston.

Campbell, J. 1980. *The Masks of Gods*. Penguin Books, New York.

Caslyn, R. J. and Morse, G. A. 1991. Predicting chronic homelessness. *Urban Affairs Quarterly 27(1), 155.*

Chelf, Carl P. 1992. *Controversial Issues in Social Welfare Policy: Government and the Pursuit of Happiness*. Sage Publications, Newbury Park.

Cohen, J. 1951. Mental health of homeless and transplanted persons. *Bulletin of the World Federation for Mental Health. 2(4), 32-37.*

Coleman, James S. 1990. *Foundations of Social Theory*. Belnap Press of Harvard University Press, Cambridge.

Collins, Randall. 1981. *Sociology Since Midcentury: Essays in Theory Cumulation.* Academic Press, NY.

Collins, Randall. 1982. *Sociological Insight: An Introduction to Nonobvious Sociology.* Oxford University Press, NY.

Colwell, P. F. and Mottlowitz, K. B. 1990. Explaining homelessness rates. *Office of Real Estate Research ORER Paper No. 77, April.*

Colwell, William Lee and Koletar, Joseph W. 1984. Performance Measurement for Criminal Justice: The Federal Bureau of Investigation (FBI) Case. *Public Productivity and Management Review Vol. 8, No. 3.*

Conan, Michel. 1995. "Making Connections with IT." *Urban Studies. 32:10, 1645-1653, Dec.*

Conrad, Peter. 1992. Medicalization and Social Control. *Annual Review of Sociology. Vol 18.*

Cordray, D. S. and Pion, G. M. 1991. What's behind the numbers? Definitional issues in counting the homeless. *Housing Policy Debate 2(3) 587-616.*

Cowan, C. D. 1991. Estimating census survey undercounts through multiple service contacts. *Housing Policy Debate 2(3) 869-82.*

Cragg, Michael and O'Flaherty, Brendan. 1999. Do Homeless Shelter Conditions Determine Shelter Population? The Case of the Dinkins Deluge. *Journal of Urban Economics. 46, 377-415.*

Culhane, Dennis P. 1994. Public shelter admission rates in Philadelphia and New York City: the implications of turnover for sheltered population counts. *Housing Policy Debate 5(2) 107-40.*

Culhane, Dennis P. and Kuhn, Randall. 1998. Patterns and Determinants of Public Shelter Utilization among Homeless Adults in New York City and Philadelphia. *Journal of Policy Analysis and Management, Vol. 17, No. 1, 23-43.*

Culhane, Dennis P. et al. 1996. Where do the homeless come from: a study of the prior address distribution of families admitted to public shelters in New York City and Philadelphia. *Housing Policy Debate 7(2) 327-65.*

de Lange, D. 1984. The Gender Comment: Gender Implications of Reports to the Housing Committee. British Library, Document Supply Center.

de Leon, Peter. 1988. The Contextual Burdens of Policy Design. *Policy Studies Journal 17:2.*

Denhardt, R. B. 1984. *Theories of Public Organizations.* Brooks-Cole, Monterey, CA.

DeParle, Jason. 1996. Slamming the Door, *The New York Times Magazine, October 20.*

Doling, J. F. 1997. *Comparative Housing Policy: Government & Housing in Advanced Industrial Countries.* St. Martin's Press, New York.

Downs, A. 1967. *Inside Bureaucracy.* Little, Brown, Boston

Downs, A. 1972. Up and Down with Ecology: the Issue Attention Cycle. *The Public Interest 28, Summer.*

Dreier, Peter. 1987. Community-based housing: a progressive approach to a new federal policy. *Social Policy 18(2), 18-22.*

Dumont, M.P. 1968. Tavern culture: the sustenance of homeless men. *American Journal of Orthopsychiatry 37(5) 938-945.*

Early, Dirk W. and Olsen, Edgar O. 1999. Rent control and homelessness. *Regional Science and Urban Economics 29(1), 797.*

Ellickson, Phyllis L. 1978. *Public Perceptions of Housing Allowances: The First Two Years.* (Housing Assistance Supply Experiment, Green Bay, Wisc.) Rand Corporation, Santa Monica, CA.

Ellickson, Phyllis L. 1978. *Public Knowledge and Evaluation of Housing Allowances: The First Two Years.* (Housing Assistance Supply Experiment, St. Joseph County, Ind.) Rand Corporation, Santa Monica, CA.

Ellickson, Robert C. 1990. The Homeless Muddle. *The Public Interest*, Vol. 99.

Elliott, Marta and Lauren J. Krivo. 1991. "Structural determinants of homelessness in the United States." *Social Problems, 38(1): 113-131.*

Epstein, Paul D. 1992. Measuring the Performance of Public Services. *Public Productivity Handbook*, Marc Holzer, ed., Marcel Dekker, Inc. New York.

Epstein, Joan F. and Gfroerer, Joseph C. 1997. *Heroin Abuse in the United States.* OAS Working Paper, August. Office of Applied Studies, U.S. Substance Abuse and Mental Health Services Administration.

Erickson, Jon and Wilhelm, Charles, eds. 1986. *Housing the Homeless.* Rutgers University Press, New Brunswick, NJ.

Etzioni, Amitai. 1967. Mixed Scanning: A "Third " Approach to Decision Making. *Public Administration Review*, December 1967.

Fabricant, M. et al. 1986. No haven for the homeless in a heartless economy. *Radical America 20(2-3) 23-34.*

Fainstein, Susan and Campbell, Scott, eds. 1996. *Readings in Urban Theory.* Blackwell Publishers, Malden, MA.

Felbinger, Claire L., Holzer, Marc and White, Jay D. 1999. The Doctorate in Public Administration: Some Unresolved Questions and Recommendations. *Public Administration Review 59:5.*

Filer, R. 1992. Opening the door to low cost housing. *City Journal*, Summer: 37-46.

Filer, R. 1990. What really causes family homelessness? *City Journal*, Fall, 22-31.

Fisher, Ernest M. 1975. *Housing Markets and Congressional Goals.* Praeger Publishers, NY.

Fischer, Frank. 1995. *Evaluating Public Policy.* Nelson Hall Publishers, Chicago.

Fischer, Frank and John Forester. 1993. *The Argumentative Turn in Policy Analysis and Planning.* Duke University Press, Durham.

Fogel, Robert William. 1989. *Without Consent or Contract: The Rise and Fall of American Slavery.* W. W. Norton & Co., N. Y.

Forester, John. 1984. Bounded Rationality and the Politics of Muddling Through. *Public Administration Review*. Vol. 44, No. 1, Jan/Feb.

Foucault, Michel. 1965. *Madness and Civilization: A History of Insanity in the Age of Reason.* Random House, NY.

Foucault, Michael 1976. *Power/Knowledge: Selected Interviews & Other Writings.* Colin Gordon, Ed., Pantheon Books, NY.

Foucault, Michael. 1977. *Discipline & Punish: The Birth of the Prison.* Random House, NY.

Foucault, Michael. 1978. *The History of Sexuality: Vol. 1: An Introduction.* Random House, NY.

Foucault, Michael. 1985. *The Use of Pleasure: The History of Sexuality, Vol.2.* Random House, NY.

Foucault, Michael. 1986. *The Care of the Self: The History of Sexuality, Vol. 3.* Random House, NY.

Foucault, Michael. 1994. *Ethics: Subjectivity and Truth.* Paul Rabinow, ed. The Essential Works of Michel Foucault, 1954-1984, Volume One, The New Press, NY.

Foucault, Michael. 1998. *Aesthetics, Method and Epistemology.* Paul Rabinow, ed. The Essential Works of Michel Foucault, 1954-1984, Volume Two, The New Press, NY.

Fox, Kenneth. 1990. *Metropolitan America: Urban Life and Urban Policy in the United States*, Rutgers University Press, New Brunswick.

Fox, E. R. and Roth, L. 1989. Homeless children: Philadelphia as a case study. *Annals of the American Academy of Political and Social Sciences 506, NW, 141-151.*

Frederickson, H. G. 1976. The Lineage of Public Administration. *Administration and Society 8:144-174.*

Freeman, Richard B. and Brian Hall. 1987. "Permanent Homelessness in America?" *Population Research and Policy Review, 6:3-27.*

Freeman, Richard B. and Smith, Ozzie G. 1963. *The Mental Patient Comes Home.* Wiley, N. Y.

Freidson, E. 1970. *Profession of Medicine.* Dodd Mead, N.Y.

Friedrichs, J. 1988. *Affordable Housing and the Homeless.* Walter de Gruyter, N.Y.

Fuller, R. and Myers, R. 1941. Some aspects of a theory of social problems. *American Sociol. Review 6, 24-32.*

Gallup Poll (1999) Report No. 235. The Gallup Poll Organization, Princeton, N.J.

GAO. 1977. *Returning the Mentally Disturbed to the Community: Government Needs to Do More.* General Accounting Office, Washington, D.C.

Garfinkel, Irwin and Piliavin, Irving. 1994. *Trends in the Size of the Nation's Homeless Population during the 1980's: A Surprising Result.* Institute for Research on Poverty Discussion Paper no. 1034-94, University of Wisconsin-Madison.

Garrett, G. R. and Bahr, H. M. 1973. Women on skid row. *Quarterly Journal of Studies on Alcohol 34(4) 1228-1243.*

Garrett, Bowen and Glied, Sherry. 2000. Does State AFDC Generosity Affect Child SSI Participation? *Journal of Policy Analysis and Management. Vol 19, No. 2.*

Gauldie, Enid. 1974. Cruel Habitations: *A History of Working-Class Housing 1780-1918.* Allen and Unwin, London

Gergen, Kenneth J. 1994. *Realities and Relationships: Soundings in Social Construction.* Harvard University Press, Cambridge.

Gissy, W. G. 1997. Rent controls and homeless rates. *International Advances in Economic Research 3(1), 113-21.*

Glacken, Clarence. 1956. Changing Ideas of the Habitable World. *Man's Role in Changing the Face of the Earth.* The University of Chicago Press, Chicago.

Glaser, Barney G. 1992. *Basics of Grounded Theory Analysis: Strategies for Qualitative Research.* Aldine Press, Chicago.

Glaser, Barney G. and Strauss, Anselm, L. 1967. *The Discovery of Grounded Theory: strategies for qualitative research.* Aldine de Gruyter, N. Y.

Glazer, Nathan. 1988. *The Limits of Social Policy.* Harvard University Press, Cambridge.

Goffman, Erving. 1967. *Interaction Ritual: Essays on Face-to-Face Behavior.* Pantheon Books, N.Y.

Goffman, Erving. 1961. *Asylums.* Anchor Books, Garden City.

Goffman, Erving. 1959. *The Presentation of Self in Everyday Life.* Anchor Press, N.Y.

Gold, Martin. 1999. *The Complete Social Scientist: A Kurt Lewin Reader.* American Psychological Association, Washington, D. C.

Goldman, H. H. 1984. *Review of General Psychiatry.* Lange Medical Publications, Los Altos.

Goldman, H. H. and Morrissey, J. P. 1985. *The alchemy of mental health policy: homelessness and the fourth cycle of reform.* American Journal of Public Health 75(7) 727-31.

Gottlieb, Manuel. 1964. *Estimates of Residential Building, United States 1840-1939.* National Bureau of Economic Research, N.Y.

Gottschalk, Marie. 2002. Black Flower: Prisons and the Future of Incarceration. *The Annals of The American Academy of Political and Social Science, Vol. 582,* July.

Gowlembiewski, R. T. 1977. A critique of "democratic administration" and its supporting ideation. *American Political Science Review 71:1488-1507.*

Grimes, Paul W. and Chressanthis, George A. 1997. Assessing the Effect of Rent Control on Homelessness. *Journal of Urban Economics 41.*

Grisby, C. et. al. 1990. Disaffiliation to entrenchment: a model for understanding homelessness. *Journal of Social Issues 46:4, 141-156.*

Grob, Gerald N. 1994. *The Mad Among Us: a History of the Care of America's Mentally Ill.* Free Press, NY.

Grob, Gerald N. 1991. *From Asylum to Community: Mental Health Policy in America.* Princeton University Press, Princeton.

Grob, Gerald N. 1983. *Mental Illness and American Society.* Princeton University Press, Princeton.

Guba, Egon G. and Lincoln, Yvonne S. 1989. *Fourth Generation Evaluation.* Sage Publications, Newbury Park.

Gulick, L. H. and Urwick, L., eds. 1937. *Papers on the Science of Administration.* Institute of Public Administration, New York.

Gusfield, Joseph. 1981. *The Culture of Public Problems.* The University of Chicago Press, Chicago.

Habermas, Jurgen. 1986. *Autonomy & Solidarity: Interviews with Jurgen Habermas.* Peter Dews, ed. Verso, New York.

Habermas, Jergen. 1970. *On the Logic of the Social Sciences.* The MIT Press, Cambridge.

Hacker, Andrew. 1992. *Two Nations: Black and White, Separate, Hostile, Unequal.* Charles Scribner's Sons, N. Y.

Handler, Joel F. 1995. *The Poverty of Welfare Reform.* Yale University Press, New Haven.

Halachmi, Arie. 1992. Evaluation Research: Purpose and Perspective. *Public Productivity Handbook,* Marc Holzer, Ed. Marcel Dekker, Inc., New York.

Haltry, Harry P. and Donald M. Fisk. 1992. Measuring Productivity in the Public Sector. *Public Productivity Handbook,* Marc Holzer, ed. Marcel Dekker, Inc. New York.

Handler, Joel F. 1995. *The Poverty of Welfare Reform.* Yale University Press, New Haven.

Harrington, Michael. 1962. *The Other America: Poverty in the United States.* The Macmillan Company, N.Y.

Harvey, David. 1996. "Social Justice, Postmodernism, and the City." in *Readings in Urban Theory,* Susan Fainstein and Scott Campbell, eds., Blackwell Publishers, Malden, Mass.

Hasci, Timothy A. 1997. *Second Home: Orphan Asylums and Poor Families In America.* Harvard University Press, Cambridge.

Hatchett, D. 1987. The homeless. *Crisis* (Aug-Sep) 14-19.

Hawley, Amos H. and Rock, Vincent P. 1973. *Segregation in Residential Areas: Papers on Racial and Socioeconomic Factors in Choice of Housing.* National Academy of Sciences, Washington, D.C.

Hayden, Dolores. 1981. *The Grand Domestic Revolution: A History of Feminist Designs for American Homes, Neighborhoods and Cities.* The MIT Press, Cambridge.

Hayden, Delores. 1984. *Redesigning the American Dream: the Future of Housing, Work and Family Life.* W. W. Norton, New York.

Hays, R. Allen. 1985. *The Federal Government and Urban Housing: Ideology and Change in Public Policy.* State University of New York Press, Albany.

Hayes, R. M. 1989. Caring for America's Children. *Proceedings of the Academy of Political Science 37(2), p. 58.*

Heckman, James J. and Willis, Robert J. 1977. "A Beta-logistic model for the analysis of sequential labor force participation by married women." *Journal of Political Economy, Vol 85 (1).*

Heckman, James J. and Willis, Robert J. 1988. "The microeconomic evaluation of social programs and economic institutions: the value of longitudinal data for solving the problem of selection bias in evaluating the impact of treatments on outcomes." *Institute of Economics,* Academia Sinica, Nankang, Taipai, Taiwan.

Hempel, Carl G. 1952. *Fundamentals of Concept Formation in Empirical Science.* The University of Chicago Press, Chicago.

Hempel, Carl G. 1965. *Aspects of Scientific Explanation.* The Free Press, N.Y.

Henderson, J. V. 1977. *Economic Theory and the Cities.* Academic Press, N.Y.

Henry, Louis. 1976. *Population: Analysis and Models.* Academic Press, N.Y.

Himelstein, P. 1957. A comment on the use of the abbreviated WAIS with homeless men. *Psychological Report.* 3, 440.

Hobbes, Thomas. 1651. In *Leviathan, Parts 1 and 2.* Liberal Arts Press, Indianapolis.

Holzer, Marc. 1991. Building Capacity for Productivity Improvement. *Competent Government: Theory and Practice*, Halachmi, Arie and Holzer, Marc, eds., Chatelaine Press, Burke, VA.

Holzer, Marc and Callahan, Kathe. 1993. Fiscal Pressures and Productive Solutions. *Competent Government: Theory and Practice*, Halachmi, Arie and Holzer, Marc, eds., Chatelaine Press, Burke, VA.

Honig, Marjorie and Filer, Randall K. 1993. Causes of Intercity Variation in Homelessness. *The American Economic Review*, Vol 83, No. 1.

Hope, M. and Young, J. 1988. *The Faces of Homelessness.* Heath Co., Lexington, MA.

Hope, M. and Young, J. 1984. From back wards to back alleys: deinstitutionalization and the homeless. *Urban and Social Change Review 17(2), p. 7.*

Hopper, Kim. 1991. Monitoring and evaluating the 1990 S-night count in New York City. *Final Report for Joint Statistical Agreement 90.18.* Center for Survey Methods Research, U. S. Bureau of the Census, Washington, D. C.

HUD. 1995a. *National Evaluation of the Supportive Housing Demonstration Program: Final Report.* Office of Policy Development and Research, Washington, D. C.

HUD. 1995b. *Review of Stewart B. McKinney Homeless Programs Administered by HUD: Report to Congress.* Office of Policy Development and Research, Washington, D. C.

HUD. 1996a. *The Continuum of Care: A Report on the New Federal Policy to Address Homelessness.* Office of Community Planning and Development, Washington, D.C.

HUD. 1996b. *Learning from Each Other: New Ideas for Managing the Section 8 Certificate and Voucher Programs.* Office of Policy Development and Research, Washington, DC.

HUD. 1997a. *Rental Housing Assistance – The Crisis Continues: The 1997 Report to Congress on Worst Case Housing Needs.* Office of Policy Development and Research, Washington, D. C.

HUD. 1997b. *The Impact of Federal Welfare Reform on HUD Public and Assisted Housing: An Initial Assessment.* Office of Policy Development and Research, Washington, D.C.

HUD. 1999a. *Waiting in Vain: an update on America's rental housing crisis.* HUD USER, Rockville, MD.

HUD. 1999b. *Homelessness: Programs and the People They Serve.* Findings of the National Survey of Homeless Assistance Providers and Clients. Office of Policy Development and Research, Washington, D.C.

HUD. 1984. *A Report to the Secretary on the Homeless and Emergency Shelters.* Office of Policy Development and Research, Washington, D.C.

Hummel, Ralph P. 1994. *The Bureaucratic Experience.* St. Martin's Press, N.Y.

Hunter, Robert. 1910. *Poverty.* New York

Huttman, Elizabeth D. 1969. *Stigma and Public Housing: a Comparison of British and American Policies and Experience.* University of California, Berkeley.

Huttman, Elizabeth D. 1985. *Housing Needs and Policy Approaches: Trends in Thirteen Countries.* Duke University Press, Durham.

Hutchens, Robert, George Jakubson and Saul Schwartz. 1989. "AFDC and the formation of subfamilies." *Journal of Human Resources, 24:600-627.*

Institute for Children and Poverty. 1999. *Today's typical homeless parent...*, NY, NY.

Institute for Children and Poverty. 2000. *Multiple Families: Multiplying Problems,* NY, NY.

Jackson, J.K. and Connor, R. 1954. The skid road alcoholic. *Quarterly Journal of Studies on Alcohol 14, 468-486.*

Jacobs, Jane. 1961. *The Death and Life of Great American Cities*, Vintage Books, N.Y.

Jacobs, Keith. 1996. "Discourse and Policy Change: The Significance of Language for Housing Research." *Housing Studies 11:4, Oct, 543-560.*

Jencks, Christopher. 1994. *The Homeless.* Harvard University Press, Cambridge.

Jennings, Edward T. Jr. and Zank, Neal S. 1993. *Welfare System Reform: Coordinating Federal, State and Local Public Assistance Programs.* Greenwood Press, Westport, CT.

Jennings, Edward T. Jr. 1996. Reforming Welfare in America. *Public Administration Review 56:3.*

Johnson, Martin. 1996. *United Nations Habitat II Conference in Istanbul, Turkey.* in The Housing and Community Advocate, N. J. Department of Community Affairs, Trenton.

Jones, James A. 1971. Federal efforts to solve contemporary social problems. In E. O. Smigel, ed., *Handbook on the Study of Social Problems.* Rand McNally, Chicago.

Kaplan, Abraham. 1993. Reading Policy Narratives: Beginnings, Middles and Ends., *The Argumentative Turn in Policy Planning and Analysis*, Frank Fischer and John Forester, eds., Duke University Press, Durham

Kaplan, Abraham. 1964. *The Conduct of Inquiry: Methodology for Behavioral Science.* Chandler Publishing Co., N.Y.

Kasinitz, Philip. 1986. Gentrification and Homelessness: The Single Room Occupant and the Inner City Revival. in Erickson and Wilhelm, Eds. *Housing the Homeless.* Rutgers University Press, New Brunswick.

Kassebaum, Gene, Ward, David and Wilner, Daniel. 1971. *Prison Treatment and Parole Survival: An Empirical Assessment.* John Wiley & Sons, Inc., N.Y.

Kaufman, Leslie and Flynn, Kevin. 2002. New York's Homeless, Back Out in the Open. *The New York Times*, October 13, 2002, Page 1.

Katz, L. 1966. *The Salvation Army men's social center: II results.* Quarterly Journal of Studies on Alcohol. 27(4), 636-647.

Kelly, Marisa and Steven Maynard-Moody. 1994. Policy Analysis in the Postpositivist Era: Engaging Stakeholders in Evaluating the Economic Development District's Program. *Research in Public Administration: Reflections on Theory and Practice*, Jay D. White and Guy B. Adams, eds., Sage Publications, Thousand Oaks, CA.

Kemeny, Jim. 1981. *The Myth of Home-Ownership: Private versus Public Choices in Housing Tenure.* Routledge & Kegan Paul, London.

Kemeny, Jim. 1992. *Housing and Social Theory.* Routledge, London.

King, Gary, Keohane, Robert O. and Verba, Sidney. 1994. *Designing Social Inquiry: Scientific Inference in Qualitative Research.* Princeton University Press, Princeton.

Kingdon, John W. 1995. *Agendas, Alternatives and Public Policies.* Little, Brown & Co., Boston.

Knight, E. M. 1943. Homeless and financially dependent adolescents as clients of a family agency. *Smith College Studies in Social Work 13, 40-73.*

Kovan, Steven G. 1989. Fighting the Drug Wars: Rhetoric and Reality. *Public Administration Review* Nov/Dec.

Kuhn, Thomas S. 1962. *The Structure of Scientific Revolutions.* The University of Chicago Press, Chicago.

Kunstler, James Howard. 1996. " Home From Nowhere: How to Make our Cities and Towns Livable." In *The Atlantic Monthly*, September 1996.

Lamb, H. R. 1986. Deinstitutionalization and the homeless mentally ill *Housing the Homeless*, J. Erickson and C. Wilhelm, eds. Rutgers Center for Urban Policy and Research, New Brunswick.

Lasswell, Harold. 1936. *Who Gets What, When and How?* McGraw Hill, NY.

Lauer, Quentin. 1965. *Phenomenology: Its Genesis and Prospect.* Harper & Row, NY. (originally published as *The Triumph of Subjectivity* in 1958).

Leusner, Donna. 1999. Advocacy Group to Sue State over Problems in Child Welfare. *The Star-Ledger.* August 4, 1999. Newark, NJ.

Levinas, Emmanuel. 1973. *The Theory of Intuition in Husserl's Phenomenology.* Northwestern University Press, Evanston, IL.

Levine, I. S. and Stockdill, J. W. 1984. Homeless: A National Problem Jones, B. E. ed., Treating the Homeless: *Urban Psychiatry's Challenge.* American Psychiatric Press, 1-16, Washington, D. C.

Levinson, B. M. 1955. The intelligence of middle-aged white homeless men in receipt of public assistance. *Psychological Reports 1, 35-36.*

Levinson, B. M. 1957. Use of the abbreviated WAIS with homeless men. *Psychological Reports 3, 287.*

Levinson, B. M. 1963. The homeless man: a psychological enigma. *Mental Hygiene 47(4) 590-601.*

Levinson, B. M. 1965. The homeless man. *Psychological Reports 17(2), 391-394.*

Levinson, B. M. 1966. Structural studies of homeless men. *Transactions of the NY Academy of Science 29(2), 165-182.*

Levinson, B. M. 1967. Mental deficiency on skid row. *Psychological Reports 20(1), 291-294.*

Levinson, B. M. 1967. Field dependence in homeless men. *Journal of Clinical Psychology 23(2), 152-154.*

Levinson, B. M. 1970. The New York City skid row Negro: some research findings. *Mental Hygiene 54(4) 548-552.*

Levison, D. 1988. *The Key to Equality: The 1986 Woman and Housing Survey*. Institute of Housing, London.

Levy, J. (1933) The homeless boys retreat. *Mental Hygiene 17:369-373*.

Lindblom, Charles E. 1990. *Inquiry and Change*. Yale University Press, New Haven.

Lindblom, Charles E. 1959. The Science of Muddling Through. *Public Administration Review 19:79-88*.

Linder, Stephen H. and Peters, B. Guy. 1985. From Social Theory to Policy Design. *Journal of Public Policy 4:237-259*.

Lipsky, M. 1980. *Street-Level Bureaucracy*. Russell Sage Foundation, New York.

Lovald, K. A. 1961. Social life of the aged homeless man in skid row. *Gerontologist 1, p. 34*.

Lowi, T. J. 1972. Four systems of policy politics and choice. *Public Administration Review 32:298-310*.

Lowi, T. J. 1964. American business, public policy, case studies and political theory. *World Politics 16:766-693*.

Lukes, S. 1974. *Power: A Radical View*. Macmillan, London.

Marcuse, P. 1988. *Housing the homeless*. Urban Affairs Quarterly 23, 647-656.

Marin, P. 1987. Helping and hating the homeless. *Harper's Magazine 274, 39-49*.

Marini, F., ed. 1971. *Toward a New Public Administration: The Minnowbrook Perspective*, Chandler, Scranton, PA.

Main, T. J. 1983. The homeless of New York. *Public Interest 72, 3*.

Main, T. J. 1986. The homeless families of New York. *Public Interest 85, 3-21*.

Martin, Daniel W. 1992. The Management Classics and Public Productivity. *Public Productivity Handbook*, Marc Holzer, Ed., Marcel Dekker, Inc., New York.

Maslow, A. H. 1943. A Theory of Human Motivation. *Psychological Review*, July 1943.

May, R. 1995. *1993 Poverty & Income Trends*. Center on Budget & Policy Priorities, Washington, DC.

McChesney, Kay Young. 1990. Family Homelessness: A Systemic Problem. *Journal of Social Issues*. Vol. 46, No. 4.

McGuire, Thomas G. and Weisbrod, Burton A. 1981. Economics and Mental Health. *Mental Health Service Systems Reports*. National Institute of Mental Health, Rockville, MD.

Mead, Lawrence M. 1999. The Decline of Welfare in Wisconsin. *Journal of Public Administration Research and Theory 9:4*.

Merton, Robert K. 1936. The Unanticipated Consequences of Purposive Social Action. *American Sociological Review*. Vol. 1, Issue 6, December.

Meyers, Roy T. 1994. *Strategic Budgeting*. The University of Michigan Press, Ann Arbor.

Miles, M. and Huberman, M. 1994. *Qualitative Data Analysis: a sourcebook of new methods*. Sage Publications, Beverly Hills.

Miller, Delbert C. 1991. *Handbook of Research Design and Social Measurement*. Sage Publications, Newbury Park.

Miller, Gerald J. 1992. Cost-Benefit Analysis. *Public Productivity Handbook*, Marc Holzer, ed., Marcel Dekker, Inc., New York.

Mishler, Elliot G. 1986. *Research Interviewing: Context and Narrative*. Harvard University Press, Cambridge.

Moffit, Robert. 1983. An Economic Model of Welfare Sigma. *The American Economic Review. 73:5*.

Molotsky, Irvin. 2000. Robust Economy is Contributing to a Loss of Affordable Housing. *The New York Times*, March 28, 2000.

Moore, R., et al. 1988. Characteristics of male and female residents of the New York City shelter system July 1988. Cited in Hopper, 1991.

Morgan, A. E. 1941. *The Needs of Youth.* Oxford University Press, New York.

Morse, Janice M. 1994. *Critical Issues in Qualitative Research Methods.* Sage Publications, Thousand Oaks, CA.

New Jersey, Department of Community Affairs. 2000. *State of New Jersey FY 2000 5-Year Consolidated Plan.*

New Jersey, Department of Community Affairs. 1999. *State of New Jersey FY 1999 Annual Consolidated Plan.* New Jersey Department of Health and Human Services. New Jersey State Plan for Temporary Assistance for Needy Families, Trenton.

New Jersey, Department of Community Affairs. 1985. *Homelessness in New Jersey: A Study of Shelters, Agencies and the Clients They Serve.* Bureau of Research Evaluation and Quality Assurance.

New York DMH. 2000. Admissions to and Resident Patients in All Programs at State Psychiatric Centers, United States and New York State, Selected Years 1949-50 – 1997-98. Bureau of Planning, Assistance and Coordination, State University of N.Y., Nelson A. Rockefeller Institute of Government.

New York City Commission on the Homeless (Cuomo Commission). 1992. "The Way Home: A New Direction in Social Policy."

Newman, Dorothy K. 1978. *Protest, Politics and Prosperity: Black Americans and White Institutions 1940-1975.* Pantheon Books, NY.

Newman, Maria. 1999. Rights Group Sues New Jersey Over Child Welfare System. *The New York Times.* August 5, 1999.

Nevitt, Adela Adam. 1967. *The Economic Problems of Housing.* St. Martin's Press, NY.

Noble, E. P. 1978. *Third Special Report to the U. S. Congress on Alcohol and Health. U.S.* DHEW Publication No. (ADM) 79-832.

Norris, Donald F. and Thompson, Lyke, Eds. 1995. *The Politics of Welfare Reform.* Sage Publications, Inc., Thousand Oaks, CA.

Nuttin, Jozef M, Jr. 1975. *The Illusion of Attitude Change: Towards a response contagion theory of persuasion.* Academic Press, NY.

O'Flaherty, Brendan. 1996. *Making Room: The Economics of Homelessness.* Harvard University Press, Cambridge.

O'Flaherty, Brendan. 1995. "An Economic Theory of Homelessness and Housing." *Journal of Housing Economics, 4:13-49.*

Oei, T. I. 1987. "Psychic Coping Behaviour and the Role of Social Support." *International Journal of Social Psychiatry. 33:1,* Spring, 5-12.

Okun, Arthur M. 1975. *Equality and Efficiency: The Big Tradeoff.* The Brookings Institution, Washington, D.C.

Orloff, Ann Shola. 1988. The Political Origins of America's Belated Welfare State. In *The Politics of Social Policy in the United States,* Ed. Weir, M, Orloff, A.S. and Skocpol, T., Princeton University Press, Princeton, NJ.

Orth-Gomer, Kristina and Unden, Anna-Lena. 1987. "The Measurement of Social Support in Population Surveys." *Social Science and Medicine 24:1, 83-94.*

Ostrom, V. 1974. *The Intellectual Crisis in American Public Administration.* The University of Alabama Press, Alabama.

Park, June. 2000. Increased Homelessness and Low Rent Housing Vacancy Rates. *Journal of Housing Economics* Vol 9, Issue 1-2, March.

Parsons, Wayne. 1995. *Public Policy: An Introduction to the Theory and Practice of Policy Analysis.* Edward Elgar, Cheltenham, U. K.

Pear, Robert. 1996. What welfare research? *The New York Times*, September 15, 1996, p. E4.

Piliavin, Irving, Wright, B., Mare, R. and Westerfelt, A. 1994. The Dynamics of Homelessness. *Institute for Research on Poverty*, Madison.

Powledge, Fred. 1991. *Free At Last?: The Civil Rights Movement and the People Who Made It*. Little Brown & Co., Boston.

Pressman, Jeffrey L. and Wildavsky, Aaron. 1973. *Implementation*. The University of Chicago Press, Chicago.

Pringle, K. 1960. 1909-1960: A half century of the White House conference. *Child Study 37 (1), 3-8*.

Prohl, S. J. 1977. The "discovery" of child abuse. *Social Problems 24, 310-23*.

Pynoos, Jon, Shafer, Robert and Hartman, Chester, W. 1980. *Housing Urban America*. Aldine Publishing Co., N. Y.

Pugh, Cedric. 1980. *Housing in Capitalistic Societies*. Gower Publishing, Southampton, England.

Quigley, John M. 1996. The Homeless. *Journal of Economic Literature*, Vol. 34, No. 4, December.

Quigley, John M. 1990. Does Rent Control Cause Homelessness? *Journal of Policy Analysis and Management*. Vol. 9, No. 1.

Quigley, John M. , Raphael, Steven & Smolensky, Eugene. 2001. Homeless in America, Homeless in California. *The Review of Economics and Statistics 83 (1): 37-51*.

Rabinow, Paul and Sullivan, William M. 1979. *Interpretive Social Science: A Reader*. University of California Press, Berkeley.

Rangarajan, Anu and Robert G. Wood. 1999. *How WFNJ Clients Are Faring Under Welfare Reform: An Early Look*. Mathematica Policy Research, Inc., Princeton.

Rank, Mark Robert. 1994. *Living on the Edge: The Realities of Welfare in America*. Columbia University Press, NY.

Rawls, John. 1971. *A Theory of Justice*. The Belknap Press of Harvard University Press, Cambridge.

Rich, Wilbur C. and Winn, Mylon. 1992. The Politics of Public Productivity. *Public Productivity Handbook*, Marc Holzer, ed., Marcel Dekker, Inc., NY.

Ricoeur, Paul. 1976. *Interpretation Theory: Discourse and the Surplus of Meaning*. Texas Christian University Press, Fort Worth.

Riis, Jacob A. 1890. *How the Other Half Lives: Studies Among the Tenements of New York*. Charles Scribner's Sons, NY.

Robbins, Tom. 1986. New York's Homeless Families. In Erickson and Wilhelm, Eds. *Housing the Homeless*. Rutgers University Press, New Brunswick.

Roman, Nan P. and Wolfe, Phyllis B. 1997. The relationship between foster care and homelessness. *Public Welfare, 55:1*, Winter 1997

Roman, Nan P. and Wolfe, Phyllis B. 1998. *The Children of the Poor*. Charles Scribner's Sons, NY.

Rossi, Peter. 1989. *Down and Out in America: The Origins of Homelessness*. The University of Chicago Press, Chicago.

Rourke, R. E. 1969. *Bureaucracy, Politics and Public Policy*. Little Brown, Boston.

Rowe, Peter G. 1993. *Modernity and Housing*. The MIT Press, Cambridge.

Rueschemeyer, Dietrich and Skocpol, Theda, eds. 1996. *States, Social Knowledge, and the Origins of Modern Social Policies*. Princeton University Press, Princeton.

Safdie, Moshe. 1970. *Beyond Habitat*. The MIT Press, Cambridge.

Sauer, Carl. 1956. *The Agency of Man on Earth*. The University of Chicago Press, Chicago.

Schmidt, Mary R. 1994. Grout: Alternative Kinds of Knowledge and Why They Are Ignored. *Research in Public Administration: Reflections on Theory and Practice*, Jay D. White and Guy B. Adams, eds., Sage Publications, Thousand Oaks, CA.

Schneider, Anne L. 1986. The evolution of policy orientation for evaluation research: a guide to practice. *Public Administration Review*, July-August 356-363.

Schneider, Anne L. and Ingram, Helen. 1993. Social Construction of Target Populations: Implications for Politics and Policy. *American Political Science Review 87:2.*

Schneider, Joseph. 1985. Social problems theory: the constructionist view. *American Review of Sociology 11, 209-229.*

Schon, Donald A. and Rein, Martin. 1994. *Frame Reflection: Toward the Resolution of Intractable Policy Controversies*. Basic Books, NY.

Schorr, Lisbeth B. 1988. *Within Our Reach: Breaking the Cycle of Disadvantage.* Anchor Books, NY.

Schutz, Alfred. 1967. *The Phenomenology of the Social World*. Northwestern University Press, Evanston.

Second National Conference on Housing (Proceedings). 1912. *Housing Problems in America*. The University Press, Cambridge.

Sen, Amartya. 1992. *Inequality Reexamined*. Harvard University Press, Cambridge.

Sexton, P. C. 1983. The life of the homeless. *Dissent 30* (Winter), 79-84.

Shane, P. G. 1991. An invisible health and social policy issue: homeless runaway youth. *Journal of Health and Social Policy 2(4), 3-14.*

Shlay, Anne B. and Peter Rossi. 1992. "Social Science Research and Contemporary Studies of Homelessness." *Annual Review of Sociology, 18:129-160.*

Simon, H. A. 1946. The proverbs of administration. *Public Administration Review 6, 53-67.*

Simon, H. A. 1957. *Administrative Behavior: A Study of Decision-Making Process in Administrative Organizations*. The Free Press, NY.

Simon, Julian L. 1969. *Basic Research Methods in Social Science*. Random House, NY.

Simpson, John H. and Kilduff, Margaret. 1984. *Homelessness in Newark: A Report on the Trailer People*. Newark Committee on the Homeless, Newark, NJ.

Sipes, Richard Grey. 1980. *Population Growth, Society, and Culture: An Inventory of Cross-Culturally Tested Causal Hypotheses.* HRAF Press, New Haven.

Skidmore, William L. 1975. *Sociology's Models of Man: The Relationships of Models of Man to Sociological Explanation in Three Sociological Theories*. Gordon and Breach, NY.

Skocpol, Theda. 1995. *Social Policy in the United States: Future Possibilities in Historical Perspective*. Princeton University Press, Princeton.

Skocpol, Theda. 1992. *Protecting Soldiers and Mothers: The Political Origins of Social Policy in the United States*. Belnap Press of Harvard University Press, Cambridge.

Slessarev, Helene. 1988. Racial Tensions and Institutional Support: Social Programs during a Period of Retrenchment. In *The Politics of Social Policy in the United States*, Ed. Weir, M, Orloff, A.S. and Skocpol, T., Princeton University Press, Princeton, NJ.

Snow, D.A. et. al. 1986. The myth of pervasive mental illness among the homeless. *Social Problems 33, 407-423.*

Solnit, Albert. 1992. *When Home is No Haven: Child Placement Issues.* Yale University Press, New Haven.

Sosin, Michael, Piliavin, Irving and Westerfelt, Herb. 1990. Toward a Longitudinal Analysis of Homelessness. *Journal of Social Issues,* Vol. 46, No. 4.

Spector, M. 1981. Beyond crime: seven methods to control troublesome rascals *Law and Deviance,* H. L. Ross, ed., Sage, Beverly Hills.

Spiro, Melford E. 1958. *Children of the Kibbutz.* Harvard University Press, Cambridge.

Stegman, Michael A. 1970. *Housing and Economics: The American Dilemma.* The MIT Press, Cambridge.

Stern, M. 1984. The emergency of homelessness as a public problem. *Social Services Review 58, 291-301.*

Stone, Marraccini and Patterson. 1971. "Some Observations on Behavior in Institutional Settings." *Environment & Behavior.* Vol. 3(1), 103-114, Mar. 1971.

Stoner, M. R. 1983. The plight of homeless women. *Social Services Review 57, 565-81.*

Straus, R. 1946. Alcohol and the homeless man. *Quarterly Review of Studies on Alcohol 7, 360-404.*

Straus, R. 1948. Some sociological concomitants of excessive drinking as revealed in the life history of an itinerant inebriate. *Quarterly Journal of Studies on Alcohol 9, 1-52.*

Straus, R. and McCarthy, R. G. 1952. Nonaddictive pathological drinking patterns of homeless men. *Quarterly Journal of Studies on Alcohol. 12, 601-611.*

Strauss, A. L. and Corbin, J. 1990. *Basics of Qualitative Research: Grounded Theory Procedures and Techniques.* Sage Publications, London.

Struening, Elmer L. and Padgett, Deborah K. 1990. Physical Health Status, Substance Use and Abuse, and Mental Disorders Among Homeless Adults. *Journal of Social Issues.* Vol. 46, No. 4.

Sweeney, J. L. 1974. Quality, Commodity, Hierarchies and Housing Markets. *Econometrica, 42.*

Sweeney, J. L. 1974. A Commodity Hierarchy Model of the Rental Housing Market. *Journal of Urban Economics 1, 288-323.*

Taeuber, Karl E. and Taeuber, Alma F. 1965. *Negroes in Cities: Residential Segregation and Neighborhood Change.* Atheneum, NY.

Taeuber, Karl E., Bumpass, Larry L. and Sweet, James A. 1978. *Social Demography.* Academic Press, N.Y.

Taylor, F. 1923. *Scientific Management.* Harper & Row, NY.

Timney, Mary. 1994. Do Physicists Use Case Studies? Thoughts on Public Administration *Research. Research in Public Administration: Reflections on Theory and Practice,* Jay D. White and Guy B. Adams, eds. Sage Publications, Thousand Oaks, CA.

Titmuss, R. M. 1951. *Problems of Social Policy.* British Information Services, NY.

Toulmin, S. 1958. *The Uses of Argument.* Cambridge University Press, Cambridge.

Tucker, William. *1992.* The Excluded Americans: *Homelessness and Housing Policies.* Regnery Gateway, Washington, D.C.

Tucker, William. 1991. How housing regulations cause homelessness. *The Public Interest.* 102 (Winter) 78-88.

Tucker, William. 1987. Where Do The Homeless Come From? *National Review.* September.

Tuckman, B. (1978) *A Distant Mirror: the Calamitous 14ᵗʰ Century.* Alfred A. Knopf, NY.

Turner, B. et al (1987) Between state and market: housing in the post-industrial era. Almquist and Wiksell International, p. 287.

United States CMHS. 1999. Mental Health: United States. Congressional Information Services, Washington, D.C.

United States Department of Health and Human Services.

1999. Mental Health: A Report of the Surgeon General.

1998. Child Maltreatment 1997: Reports from the States to the National Child Abuse and Neglect Data System.

1998. National Household Survey on Drug Abuse.

1996. DAWN Emergency Room Data.

1996. DAWN Medical Examiner Data.

1993. Centers for Disease Control, Reported Cirrhosis Mortality – United States 1970-Deaths and Hospitalizations from Chronic Liver Disease and Cirrhosis – United States 1980-1990; Morbidity and Mortality Weekly Report U.S. Government Printing Office, Washington, DC.

United States Department of Justice. 2000. Bureau of Justice Statistics, *Incarcerated Parents and Their Children, NCJ 182335*, August.

United Way of Essex and West Hudson. 1997. *The Tie that Binds Us*. Position Paper, Newark, NJ.

Van Til, Jon. 1994. Nonprofit Organizations and Social Institutions *The Jossey Bass Handbook of Nonprofit Leadership and Management.*, R. B. Herman, Ed., Jossey-Bass, San Francisco.

Veiller, Lawrence. 1914. *A Model Housing Law*. Russell Sage Foundation, NY.

Wagner, Richard V. and John J. Sherwood. 1969. *The Study of Attitude Change*. Wadsworth Publishing, CA.

Waldo, D. 1984. *The Administrative State*. Holmes & Meier, NY.

Wallace, S.E. 1968. The road to skid row. *Social Problems 16(1), 92-105*.

Wamsley, G. et. al. 1984. The public administration and the governance process: refocusing the American dialogue. *Dialogue 6(2), 1-17*.

Warner, R. 1989. Deinstitutionalization: How did we get where we are? *Journal of Social Issues 45(3), 17-30*.

Wattenberg, W.W. and Moir, J.B. 1954. *Counseling Homeless Alcoholics*. State Board of Alcoholism, Lansing, Michigan.

Weber, M. 1971. Bureaucracy. In *From Max Weber: Essays in Sociology*. Gerth, H.H. and Mills, C.W., eds., Oxford University Press, NY.

Weinberg, A. A. 1952. Mental health of transplanted and homeless persons. *Bulletin of the World Federation for Mental Health 3(4) 172-181*.

Weisbrod, Burton A. ed. 1965. *The Economics of Poverty: An American Paradox*. Prentice-Hall, Englewood Cliffs, NJ.

Weitzman, Beth C., Knickman, James R. and Shinn, Marybeth. 1990. Pathways to Homelessness Among New York City Families. *Journal of Social Issues. Vol. 46, No. 4*.

Welfeld, I. 1990. Our nonexistent housing crisis. *Public Interest 101, 55-61*.

Wells, Tim and Triplett, William. 1992. *Drug Wars: An Oral History from the Trenches*. William Morrow & Co., NY.

Westie, Frank R. 1967. "Toward Closer Relations Between Theory and Research: A Procedure and an Example." *American Sociological Review 22:149-154*.

Wheaton, William. 1947. Housing comes of age. *Public Administration Review 7, 284-291*.

Wildavsky, A. 1979. *Speaking Truth to Power: the Art and Craft of Policy Analysis*. Little, Brown, Boston.

Williams, Frederick. Ed. 1970. *Language and Poverty: Perspectives on a Theme.* Markham Publishing Co., Chicago.

Wilner, Daniel M. 1962. *The Housing Environment and Family Life: A Longitudinal Study of the Effects of Housing on Morbidity and Mental Health.* The Johns Hopkins Press, Baltimore.

Wilner, Daniel M., Walkley, Rosabelle Price and Cook, Stuart W. 1955. *Human Relations in Interracial Housing: A Study of the Contact Hypothesis.* Russell & Russell, NY.

Wilson, J. Q. 1994. Culture, incentives and the underclass. In *Values and Public Policy.* Aaron, Mann and Taylor, eds., The Brookings Institution, Washington, DC.

Wilson, William Julius. 1987. *The Truly Disadvantaged: The Inner City, the Underclass, and Public Policy.* The University of Chicago Press, Chicago.

Wilson, Woodrow. 1887. The study of administration. *Political Science Quarterly 2, 197-222.*

Wolch, J. R. et al. 1988. Explaining homelessness. *Journal of American Planning Association 54, 443-53.*

Wright, S. E. 1993. Presidential address: blaming the victim, blaming society, or blaming the discipline: fixing the responsibility for poverty and homelessness. *Sociological Quarterly 34, 1-16.*

Wright, James D. 1990. Poor People, Poor Health: The Health Status of the Homeless. *Journal of Social Issues.* Vol. 46, No. 4.

Wright, James D. 1989. *Address Unknown: The Homeless in America.* Aldine de Gruyter, NY.

Wright, James D. and Rubin, B. A. 1991. Is homelessness a housing problem? *Housing Policy Debate 2(3) 937-56.*

Yancey, W. L. 1971. "Architecture, Interaction and Social Control: the case of a large scale public housing project." *Environment and Behavior 3:1, March, p 3-22.*

Yanow, Dvora. 1996. *How Does a Policy Mean?: Interpreting Policy and Organizational Actions.* Georgetown University Press, Washington.

Yinger, John. 1995. *Closed Doors, Opportunities Lost.* Russell Sage Foundation, NY.

Zeller, Richard A. and Carmines, Edward G. 1980. *Measurement in the Social Sciences: The Link Between Theory and Data.* Cambridge University Press, Cambridge.

CHAPTER SIX

Financial Aid and Access In New Jersey

By
Robert P. Haney, Jr.

Executive Summary

Due to reductions in state support and increased costs, tuition and fees at public colleges and universities in New Jersey are skyrocketing. Even taking into account state and federal financial aid, public higher education has become unaffordable for low and lower middle income families, and threatens soon to become unaffordable for the middle class. Since higher education is a powerful generator of opportunity and increased wages, the state faces a tremendous loss due to its failing commitment to higher education.

Unreasonable tuition increases stem from a flawed year-to-year budget process where spending decisions and state aid are decided first, then college administrators are asked to fill in the gap by increasing tuition. Tuition increases should be capped at the rate of inflation, and the state should increase aid both generally for public higher education and to establish affordability standards for low and moderate income families who are already "priced out." The state must then focus on more efficient delivery of higher education to control increases in cost that threaten the long-term affordability of New Jersey's public higher education system.

Introduction

By relying on tuition increases to meet annual financial shortfalls, New Jersey's public higher education system has gradually become unaffordable for large numbers of students and their families. The average tuition at New Jersey state colleges and universities is approximately 50 % higher than the average for public institutions across the United States.[1] Even after taking account of

---

[1]   New Jersey's Colleges and Universities, 7th Annual Systemwide Accountability Report, New Jersey Commission on Higher Education, January 23, 2004, *available at* http://www.nj.gov/highereducation/ar07.pdf, at 3.

financial aid, the net cost is still higher than the national average,[2] presenting a severe challenge for qualified students and their families.

For many students, paying for college has proven overwhelming. While New Jersey leads the nation in sending its students to college, it also leads the nation in students who do not finish four-year programs within six years, an indicator of financial distress.[3] Students who can barely afford college may see their grades suffer when they work two jobs just to make ends meet.

New Jersey's Commission on Higher Education has acknowledged that higher education is barely affordable for many. In an annual report published last year, the commission recognized that "low income and lower middle income families still face formidable odds in meeting the costs of college attendance in the state."[4]

Higher education, however, is a key element in achieving the American dream and fulfilling our nation's promise of equal opportunity. It is essential to reducing poverty and improving standards of living. Those who earn college degrees can expect higher earnings and a "better" life. Moreover, an educated, highly productive population benefits New Jersey in the form of increased tax revenues and decreased spending on social programs such as welfare. Educated citizens also more informed health and retirement choices, further reducing the demand on public resources.[5]

Lack of access to higher education represents a major loss for individuals and the state as a whole. One report estimates that, in the year 2002, the educational gap for black students cost individuals and the state approximately $13.1 billion in lost income and $4.6 billion in lost tax revenue.[6] The New Jersey Commission on Higher Education reports that New Jersey exceeds the national average in personal and family income, in part because it has a larger

---

2   New Jersey's Colleges and Universities, 7th Annual Systemwide Accountability Report, New Jersey Commission on Higher Education, January 23, 2004, *available at* http://www.nj.gov/highereducation/ar07.pdf, at 3. New Jersey grant in aid for low-income students in the 2000-2001 academic year was 124% of federal Pell grants. States average 50% to 60% of federal dollars in need-based aid. During the fiscal year 2003, the state distributed $227 million in financial assistance to over 70,000 New Jersey- resident, undergraduate students. However, New Jersey has the seventh highest senior public college tuition rates for state residents and the ninth highest community college tuition rate. New Jersey's Colleges and Universities, 7th Annual Systemwide Accountability Report, New Jersey Commission on Higher Education, January 23, 2004, *available at* http://www.nj.gov/highereducation/ar07.pdf, at 3.

3   The National Center for Public Policy and Higher Education, Policy Alert, The Educational Pipeline: Big Investment, Big Returns, April 2004, *available at* http://www.highereducation.org/reports/pipeline.

4   New Jersey's Colleges and Universities, 7th Annual Systemwide Accountability Report, New Jersey Commission on Higher Education, January 23, 2004, *available at* http://www.nj.gov/highereducation/ar07.pdf, at 3.

5   The National Center for Public Policy and Higher Education, Policy Alert, The Educational Pipeline: Big Investment, Big Returns, April 2004, *available at* http://www.highereducation.org/reports/pipeline.

6   New Jersey's Colleges and Universities, 7th Annual Systemwide Accountability Report, New Jersey Commission on Higher Education, January 23, 2004, *available at* http://www.nj.gov/highereducation/ar07.pdf, at 10.

proportion of households and families headed by parents with college degrees; holding a college or more advanced degree boosts average household and family income by 35%.[7] New Jersey is the seventh largest net recipient of college graduates from other states, suggesting an economy that depends heavily on people with college degrees or better.[8]

Higher Education Is a Victim of Cyclical Spending

Our state risks squandering this advantage. Higher education is one of the largest discretionary spending items in most state budgets, and a target for cuts during budget crises.[9] New Jersey has followed other states in reducing its commitment to higher education as a percentage of its budget. During recessions, cuts in higher education spending are disproportionate. Faced with a budget deficit of more than $5 billion, one of James E. McGreevey's first acts as governor, when he took office in 2002, was to order a 5% cut in higher education spending.[10] Even during good times, spending does not keep up. During the 1990s, when higher education received funding increases, its share of the overall pie still shrank.[11] New Jersey's funding of public higher education actually declined by 8% in the 1990s, when corrected for inflation.[12]

As New Jersey reduces its commitment to supporting higher education, students and their families are picking up the slack. State support has declined steadily as a share of operating expenditures for senior public institutions, dropping from 64% in 1994 to 56% in 2002, with the percentage borne by students and their families increasing by a commensurate amount.[13] While funding of community colleges increased from 25% in 1994 to 29% in 2002, this

---

[7] New Jersey's Colleges and Universities, 7th Annual Systemwide Accountability Report, New Jersey Commission on Higher Education, January 23, 2004, *available at* http://www.nj.gov/highereducation/ar07.pdf, at 10.

[8] New Jersey's Colleges and Universities, 7th Annual Systemwide Accountability Report, New Jersey Commission on Higher Education, January 23, 2004, *available at* http://www.nj.gov/highereducation/ar07.pdf, at 10.

[9] The National Center for Public Policy and Higher Education, Losing Ground: A National Status Report on the Affordability of American Higher Education, 2002, *available at* http://www.highereducation.org/reports/losing_ground/affordability_report_final_bw.pdf, at 12.

[10] The National Center for Public Policy and Higher Education, Losing Ground: A National Status Report on the Affordability of American Higher Education, 2002, *available at* http://www.highereducation.org/reports/losing_ground/affordability_report_final_bw.pdf, at 12.

[11] The National Center for Public Policy and Higher Education, Policy Alert, State Shortfalls Projected Throughout the Decade, February 2003, *available at* http://www.highereducation.org/pa_0203, at 3.

[12] Council of New Jersey State College Locals, American Federation of Teachers, AFL-CIO, What Happened to Excellence? Financing Higher Education in New Jersey, March 2000.

[13] New Jersey's Colleges and Universities, 7th Annual Systemwide Accountability Report, New Jersey Commission on Higher Education, January 23, 2004, *available at* http://www.nj.gov/highereducation/ar07.pdf, at 9.

increase was offset by a steeper decline in county support, so overall public support still went down.

Not surprisingly, the cost of higher education for students and their families has skyrocketed. Graph 1 and Data Table 1 document the extent of this trend. Over the last 15 years in New Jersey, the average tuition at state colleges has increased 181.6% and the average community college tuition 98.9%. Annually, this represents a 7.1% increase in tuition at state colleges and a 5.0% increase in community college tuition. Inflation increased at an annual rate of approximately 2.7% over the same time period. The annual median income for a family, adjusted for inflation, increased 0.7% over a similar time period.[14] By any measure, public higher education has become substantially less affordable because of these trends.

The overall picture is clear. New Jersey is spending less on public higher education, leaving students and their families to pick up the slack in the form of higher tuition. This trend has made public higher education less accessible for middle and lower income families.

Graph 1

Average Resident (In-State) Full-Time Tuition Charges at New Jersey State Colleges and Community Colleges[15]

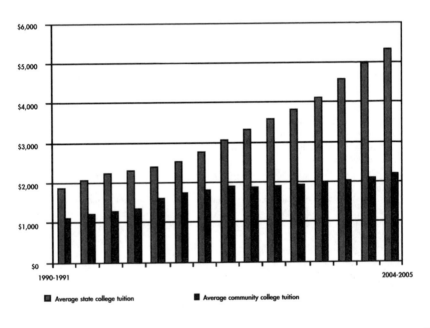

---

[14]   From 1990 to 2003. http://www.census.gov/statab/www/income.xls.
[15]   The information collected can be found at
http://www.nj.gov/highereducation/TUITweb04.htm. The site provides the annual tuition increases for each college.

Data Table 1

	State colleges[16]	Community colleges[17]
1990-1991	$1,901	$1,114
1991-1992	$2,092	$1,243
1992-1993	$2,248	$1,300
1993-1994	$2,311	$1,362
1994-1995	$2,422	$1,623
1995-1996	$2,552	$1,753
1996-1997	$2,780	$1,831
1997-1998	$3,063	$1,907
1998-1999	$3,347	$1,903
1999-2000	$3,586	$1,934
2000-2001	$3,833	$1,946
2001-2002	$4,138	$1,981
2002-2003	$4,580	$2,049
2003-2004	$4,990	$2,128
2004-2005	$5,353	$2,216
Total percentage increase (not adjusted for inflation)	181.6%	98.9%

The Inadequate Role of Financial Aid

State financial aid has increased, but at a slower rate, causing lower income students and their families to fall further behind. For the academic year 2002-2003, tuition increased 13% at public four-year institutions while total state grant aid increased 4%.[18] Over the years, these deficits have HAD a devastating impact on the tight budgets of those struggling to attend college.

---

[16] The state colleges are: New Jersey Institute of Technology, Rutgers University (average), the College of New Jersey, Kean University, Montclair State University, New Jersey City University, Stockton College of New Jersey, Ramapo College of New Jersey, Rowan University, and William Paterson University.

[17] The community colleges are: Atlantic Cape Community College, Bergen Community College, Brookdale Community College, Burlington County College, Camden County College, Cumberland County College, Essex County College, Gloucester County College, Hudson County Community College, Mercer County Community College, Middlesex County College, County College of Morris, Ocean County College, Passaic County Community College, Raritan Valley Community College, Salem Community College, Sussex County Community College, Union County College, and Warren County Community College.

[18] The National Center for Public Policy and Higher Education, Policy Alert, State Shortfalls Projected Throughout the Decade, February 2003, *available at* http://www.highereducation.org/pa_0203, at 8A. Per capita income rose 3% over the same time period.

There are many financial aid programs that help make college more afford-able for lower income families. Even all the programs put together are not enough to make higher education affordable for many qualified students.

Traditional Grants to Needy Students

Federal Pell Grants and New Jersey Tuition Aid Grants are the major forms of financial assistance for lower income New Jersey residents. The size of each Pell grant is based on a complex formula that determines each student's expected family contribution based on the parents' and the student's income and assets, the family's household size, the number of family members attend-ing higher education institutions, and basic living expenses. In fiscal year 2003, the maximum grant per year was $4,050 per student, and the average award was $2,457 per student.[19] The grants are not available to families with incomes above $45,000. The average grant range in 2004-2005 was from $400 to $4,050.

New Jersey Tuition Aid Grants (TAG) are the main form of state assis-tance; one out of every three full-time New Jersey students receives a TAG award. Eligibility is determined by consideration of many factors including family income and assets, family size and number in college, and the cost of the particular school the student plans to attend. For the school year 2005-2006, the maximum award for community college was $2,030, state colleges and uni-versities $5,220, Rutgers/University of Medicine and Dentistry School of New Jersey (UMDNJ) $6,792, and New Jersey Institute of Technology (NJIT) $7,918.[20] Currently about 60,000 students (of approximately 300,000 in the state system) receive TAG awards; the average grant is $3,400. TAG awards are subject to the vicissitudes of the state budget, and currently the state only funds 80% of awards for students who demonstrate eligibility.

Part-time Tuition Aid Grants for County College Students provide pro-rated awards for county college students who attend school part-time and are otherwise eligible for TAG grants. For the school year 2005-2006, the maxi-mum award for students enrolled half-time is $381 per term, and students enrolled three-quarter-time is $571 per term.[21]

Educational Opportunity Fund Grants are awarded to students with excep-tional need from educationally disadvantaged backgrounds. The Fund provides supplemental financial aid to cover college costs such as books, fees, room, and board that are not covered by the TAG program. Grants for college students range from $1,050 to $1,300 per year. The state offers several merit scholar-ships for distinguished students, but these may not be available to all hardwork-ing, qualified students who want to attend college but cannot afford it.[22]

---

[19] Information obtained from
http://www.federalgrantswire.com/federal_pell_grant_program.html.

[20] The information can be found at: http://www.nj.gov/highereducation/njhesaa.htm.

[21] The information can be found at: http://www.nj.gov/highereducation/njhesaa.htm.

[22] For a full list of scholarships, see http://www.nj.gov/highereducation/njhesaa.htm.

General Financial Incentives

Although many lower income students and their families struggle to afford college, much financial aid is targeted toward students in the middle and upper middle classes, many of whom are also having difficulty paying for higher education. After sharp tuition increases in the early 1990s, state and federal governments responded to middle class concerns by offering a package of tax credits and deductions, tax-sheltered savings plans, and merit aid programs.[23] These plans do not benefit many lower income families; even the federal tax credits can only be taken by those who earn enough to owe federal income taxes.[24]

Federal HOPE Scholarship Tax Credits are limited to students enrolled at least half-time and are in their first or second year of college. To be eligible for the maximum tax credit of $1,500, the student or family must owe at least $1,500 in federal income taxes, and pay at least $2,000 in tuition and required fees out-of-pocket. The student or family must earn no more than $50,000 per year if either is a single tax filer or $100,000 if a joint filer.[25]

Federal Lifetime Learning Tax Credits are limited to students who have completed two years of college, or who are in their first or second year of college and enrolled less than half-time. To be eligible for the maximum tax credit of $1,000, the student or family must owe at least $1,000 in federal income taxes, and pay at least $5,000 in tuition and fees. The student or family must earn no more than $50,000 per year if either is a single tax filer or $100,000 if a joint filer.[26]

Federal Income Tax Deductions of up to $3,000 are available to single tax filers whose adjusted gross income does not exceed $65,000 and to joint filers with incomes not exceeding $130,000.[27] All of these programs are,

---

[23] The National Center for Public Policy and Higher Education, Losing Ground: A National Status Report on the Affordability of American Higher Education, 2002, *available at* http://www.highereducation.org/reports/losing_ground/affordability_report_final_bw.pdf, at 10.

[24] The National Center for Public Policy and Higher Education, Losing Ground: A National Status Report on the Affordability of American Higher Education, 2002, *available at* http://www.highereducation.org/reports/losing_ground/affordability_report_final_bw.pdf, at 15.

[25] Information is for the 2001 tax year. The National Center for Public Policy and Higher Education, Losing Ground: A National Status Report on the Affordability of American Higher Education, 2002, *available at* http://www.highereducation.org/reports/losing_ground/affordability_report_final_bw.pdf, at 15.

[26] Information is for the 2001 tax year. The National Center for Public Policy and Higher Education, Losing Ground: A National Status Report on the Affordability of American Higher Education, 2002, *available at* http://www.highereducation.org/reports/losing_ground/affordability_report_final_bw.pdf, at 15.

[27] Information is from 2002 and 2003. The National Center for Public Policy and Higher Education, Losing Ground: A National Status Report on the Affordability of American Higher Education, 2002, *available at* http://www.highereducation.org/reports/losing_ground/affordability_report_final_bw.pdf, at 15.

of course, useful for middle income families who also face legitimate affordability concerns.

Making Higher Education More Affordable

Even in combination, these numerous programs do not succeed in making public higher education affordable in New Jersey. On average, even after taking account of financial aid, students (or their families) are required to spend 27% of their household incomes to pay tuition and expenses at four-year public institutions in NJ (the statistic for private colleges is over 50%). While precise information may not be fully reliable, the available data suggests that, for lower income families, the percentage likely exceeds 50%.[28] Nationally, even after financial aid, low income students on average are required to cover $3,800 in college-related expenses per year, leading to extremely high attrition rates.[29] Among low income students who start college after high school, only 7% graduated by age 24. By any reasonable measure, public higher education is no longer affordable for large segments of New Jersey's population.

Any package of reforms should address affordability for middle class as well as less fortunate students. A mixed package of keeping down tuition prices for everyone and increasing financial assistance for lower income families to cover tuition increases is the most fair solution.

Caps on Tuition Increases

Tuition and fees should be at the center of the debate. Under the present system, tuition and fee increases are the result of policy decisions focused on salaries, capital expenditures, and state budget contributions to higher education. After all these decisions have been made, the administrators of the various state colleges and universities are left to fill the remaining gaps by increasing tuition or cutting costs. Since most costs are fixed (i.e. teachers' contracts negotiated on a statewide basis), it is little surprise that students and their families are left holding the short end of the stick.

Setting caps on tuition increases at the rate of inflation (currently about 2.5% annually) at the beginning of the process would force the legislature and administrators to factor tuition into the equation earlier.[30] While it puts admin-

---

[28] Measuring up 2002: The State By State Report Card for Higher Education available at http://measuringup.highereducation.org/2002/stateprofilenet.cfn

[29] The Futures Project: Policy for Higher Education in a Changing World, Correcting Course: How We Can Restore the Ideals of Public Higher Education in a Market-Driven Era, February 2005, at 2-3

[30] In the past session of the legislature, Assembly Bill 3488 was introduced by Assemblyman Robert Morgan (D-Monmouth and Mercer) to limit tuition In the pastsession session of the legislature, Assembly Bill 3488 was introduced by Assemblyman Robert Morgan (D-Monmouth and Mercer) to limit tuition increases for already enrolled students to the CPIduring the four-years the student is enrolled. Asbury Park Press, August 14, 2005 "A year at a senior state college can run $17,000." The bill does not address funding this limitation.

istrators under pressure to control costs, it also strengthens their hand in budget discussions with the legislature (since they would be prohibited from increasing tuition beyond a specified rate). It pressures the legislature to fully fund any budget gaps and take responsibility for tuition increases.

Capping tuition increases at the level of consumer price inflation is a much more difficult goal to achieve than it might seem. The cost of labor, the single largest budget item for colleges and universities, is rising much faster than the rate of consumer inflation. During the current 2003-2007 contract, salaries for unionized professors will rise an average of 18.5% (including merit increases) similar to salary increases for most other highly trained professionals.[31] These contracts are negotiated on a statewide basis, and individual colleges have little control. If salaries and other costs rise at almost 5% annually and the legislature only increases state funding by 2.5%, tuition will necessarily increase at a rate much higher than inflation. Capping tuition increases will force the legislature and other participants in the system to make hard choices: hold the line on salary increases, allocate more money, cut funding for useful projects, or implement broad based administrative consolidation to cut costs. Capping also eliminates the easy solution of merely passing on a disproportionate share of the increased cost to students and their families in what amounts to a highly regressive tax. Ultimately, these problems can only be addressed by the legislature restoring public funding to prior levels and providing about 67% of the total cost for state colleges and universities.

Establish Affordability Standards for Low/Moderate Income Students

The second part of the policy would be to increase tuition assistance to maintain affordability. The legislature should adhere to the basic principle that affordable, public higher education is a right for all New Jersey citizens. All New Jersey residents pay for higher education through their tax dollars. It is not acceptable that working parents should be unable to send their qualified children to public institutions because they cannot afford the tuition. After all, these taxpayers have supported these institutions with their tax dollars for years.

One way to maintain affordability would be to fix the expected family contribution to a percentage of annual income, much as financial aid is currently calculated, but in much more systematic fashion. Data indicates that available financial aid programs do not make public higher education affordable for low and moderate income students. The impact of these programs is hit or miss, with many students falling through the cracks.

Legislators should consider reducing the expected family contribution to a lower percentage of income to make college a realistic possibility. Specifically, the legislation should establish affordability standards for higher education, which ensure that no family should have to pay an excessive part of its annual income for higher education. (The legislation would say, for example, that for

---

31   The Star-Ledger, June 18, 2004 "Rutgers Profs, Aides Due for Raise Under Tentative 4-Year Pact."

a family with an income between $25,000 and $30,000 should not have to pay more that 20% of its annual income for higher education. If tuition, less all other sources of financial aid, would require a greater family contribution, the state should step in and fill the difference.)

These two proposals will require a substantial additional financial contribution by the state. To mitigate this effect, the state should also enact comprehensive measures to control the cost of higher education in New Jersey.

Focus on New Initiatives To Control Cost

A key element of affordability will be to find new, more efficient ways to deliver higher education to students at public colleges while maintaining quality. This pressure on administrators and legislators to hold down tuition may lead to wiser spending decisions, counteracting the tendency to increase spending for higher education during good times, but in ways that do not reduce the cost of attending college.[32] State universities often compete for faculty and erect new buildings to attract students or improve the overall quality of the educational experience, sometimes at the expense of affordability.[33] With a cap on tuition increases, all participants in the budgeting process would be more accountable for their spending choices and more likely to search for ways to reduce the need for tuition increases, while maintaining high quality educational environment for students. College administrators might also take the following steps that the National Center for Public Policy and Higher Education has recommended:[34]

- Consider the potential of information technology for improving educational effectiveness and cost-effectiveness of on-campus and off-campus instruction;
- Reduce new research and graduate programs with ill-defined goals that result in "mission creep" and eat up significant funds;
- Encourage more high school programs that allow qualified students to obtain college credit while still in high school.

Other steps that college administrators might take to reduce costs include reducing overhead by eliminating duplicative offices at New Jersey's many public colleges.

---

[32] The National Center for Public Policy and Higher Education, Losing Ground: A National Status Report on the Affordability of American Higher Education, 2002, *available at* http://www.highereducation.org/reports/losing_ground/affordability_report_final_bw.pdf, at 4.

[33] The Futures Project: Policy for Higher Education in a Changing World, Correcting Course: How We Can Restore the Ideals of Public Higher Education in a Market-Driven Era, February 2005, at 3-4.

[34] The National Center for Public Policy and Higher Education, Losing Ground: A National Status Report on the Affordability of American Higher Education, 2002, *available at* http://www.highereducation.org/reports/losing_ground/affordability_report_final_bw.pdf, at 13.

Some of these programs are more straightforward (making college credit possible for more high school students), and others more controversial (cutting down on administrative overhead). Some of the proposals are likely to face considerable resistance, but may become realities if the ability to pass on excess costs to students and their families is constrained.

Conclusion

The current system of budgeting and paying for higher education simply does not work. It has led to unaffordable public education, which should be a contradiction in terms. The legislature should start by taking a new, comprehensive approach toward managing affordability and organizing the budget process around affordability for all of New Jersey's families. The social, political, and economic stakes are simply too high to let talented students miss their chance at the American dream. Establishing a minimum standard of affordability, capping annual tuition increases, and taking new initiatives to control costs would be the beginning of a policy to restore affordability to New Jersey's public higher education system.

Special recognition and thanks to Michael Stein, a Harvard Law School student and former summer associate at my law firm, Covington & Burling, for his research and writing assistance on this article.

CHAPTER SEVEN

How One District Responded To the No Child Left Behind Act

By
Thomas John Locke

The Story of the Research

Introduction

"The No Child Left Behind Act of 2001 (NCLB) is a landmark in education reform designed to improve student achievement and change the culture of America's schools" (U.S.D.O.E., 2003). While it remains unclear if either of those two intended goals is being achieved, it seems clear that school districts and communities have been deeply affected by this legislation. One of the cornerstones of the law is an increased accountability for student achievement. Each state must develop a plan to assess children's progress in meeting state standards in all of its public schools. Under the provisions of this law, students must be tested at least once a year for both language arts and mathematics in grades 3-8 and once again in high school. The results of these assessments will be disaggregated into various subgroups[1], and schools must make adequate yearly progress in meeting established benchmarks in each subgroup for the purpose of achieving 100% proficiency by 2014.

Schools that fail to make AYP (Annual Yearly Report) face increasing consequences. After receiving a warning in their first year, schools that do not meet all of the AYP benchmarks must offer intra-district school choice after the second year of failure. After three years, Title I schools must use federal funds to provide supplemental services to their most needy students. Schools may face more severe consequences in subsequent years, including restructuring or reconstitution. Each state must also set rewards for schools that regularly make AYP and begin to close achievement gaps.

As is the case with most states, New Jersey bases its accountability system on standardized tests, and this single measure largely determines a school's sta-

---

[1] "Assessment results and State progress objectives must be broken out by poverty, race, ethnicity, disability, and limited English proficiency to ensure that no group is left behind." (U.S.D.O.E., 2003)

tus. Schools can achieve AYP either by meeting the established benchmarks in all 40 categories[2] or by decreasing the number of students who did not reach proficiency by 10%. The latter provision ("Safe Harbor") is calculated by comparing the current students on a particular grade level to the previous cohort of students. The only other cause for exemption in New Jersey is if the number of students in a particular subgroup is below 20. This method of calculating school effectiveness differs vastly from traditional methods of simply reporting the information for general education students only. The state reports testing results annually in the state report card, which local newspapers publish.

Perception of the Impact

Many were shocked to learn that 271 of the 361 high schools in New Jersey did not make AYP in 2003. (N.J.D.O.E., 2003c). Schools that were always considered among the best in the state were, for the first time, labeled, "In need of improvement." This public accountability has sent many educators scrambling for solutions even though the consequences for most schools would not begin for another year or two. Because subgroups of 20 or fewer students are exempt, most small elementary schools have made AYP. The New Jersey Department of Education reported that only 20% of the state's elementary schools (275 out of 1,365) have been placed on the early warning list. (2003a). The real impact of the imposed consequences is still years away for most schools. In fact, the consequences truly affect only Title I schools, and, even so, the designation of Title I funds for supplemental services as a year three consequence does not seem to warrant the panic evident in the educational community.

National Reaction

"A small but growing number of school systems around the country are beginning to resist the demands of President Bush's signature education law, saying its efforts to raise student achievement are too costly and too cumbersome." (Dillon, 2004). In a political year, it was not surprising to see the rising criticism. *The New York Times* reported that many of the Democratic candidates for President in the 2004 election were criticizing the legislation, even though some originally endorsed it. Howard Dean led the way, claiming the law was "making American education worse, not better." (Zernike, 2004). The growing rebellion has extended far beyond rhetoric of politicians:

- Several districts in Vermont and Connecticut have refused federal funds rather than comply with all NCLB mandates. A district in Pennsylvania is suing the state over what it sees as inequities in the law.

---

[2]   The 40 indicators are as follows: 95% participation rate in language arts literacy and math tests, as well as meeting the Adequate Yearly Progress (AYP) benchmark target in the same subject areas. The 10 subgroups are: total school population, students with disabilities, limited English proficiency (LEP) students, white, African-American, Asian/Pacific Islander, American Indian/Native American, Hispanic, other, and economically disadvantaged. (N.J.D.O.E., 2003b).

- At least seven states have passed resolutions criticizing the laws or asking for federal waivers on some requirements.
- Maine is considering a bill, similar to one in Vermont, to prevent state funding of reforms.
- In Utah, a bill to opt out of NCLB entirely (and so forgo many federal funds) has passed the House education committee. (Paulson, 2004).

While many criticize the law, groups from both sides of the political spectrum are defending its merit and decrying its detractors. The former Secretary of Education, Rod Paige, was at the forefront, comparing this legislation to the historic Brown v. Board of Education decision, which outlawed segregation. "Because of the powerful sweep of this change, this revolution, there are some who resist it. And that's to be expected. The resistance to Brown was massive. It took decades and we're still moving forward. And so the resistance to the NCLB Act is to be expected. But those who fought Brown were on the wrong side of history. Just like those who fight No Child Left Behind will be judged so." (Paige, 2004). The organization, The Education Trust, "is soliciting signatures for a petition urging Congress to 'stay the course' on NCLB in the face of gathering calls that the law's accountability provisions be suspended or repealed." (Cardman, 2003). This debate will undoubtedly continue.

Research Questions

The increased accountability that has ensued seems to create daily headlines, debate, and reflection among educators and across society. An important question to consider is whether or not the changes that are taking place in states, districts, and schools are the type of changes we want for our students. In order to examine these changes and the resulting tensions embedded in the responses to NCLB, I conducted a case study of how the leadership team of a large, suburban school district in New Jersey responded to the legislation.

- Are the decisions that local educators make because of NCLB the types of changes we want for our students?
- To what extent does the rationale behind the accountability measures of NCLB mesh with educators' personal beliefs on the purpose of public education?
- How has NCLB affected the work of educational leaders?
- What are the tensions in the minds of educational leaders when making decisions related to NCLB?

Crucial to this study were the perceptions that each member of this leadership team had of the impact of NCLB on their day-to-day work. Equally important was studying their reflections on these changes. I was interested in examining whether NCLB had any significant impact, whether or not the impact was real or perceived, and how its philosophy aligned with the educational philosophy of each team member. The tensions involved in the local educational decisions are seldom uncovered, and so, through this research, I uncovered some of the unseen effects.

The notion that schools should ensure all children are learning is intuitive and seldom argued, but when issues of measurement and strategies for accountability are imposed on schools, the debate becomes more interesting. If the intent of the law is to hold schools accountable for the learning of all students, it is important to examine the actions of leaders at local levels to see if, indeed, there is progress towards this goal, and if the means of achieving this goal are educationally sound. The national debate has intensified over the last year, but the educational community needs to learn more about the smaller, district level directions as well as the day-to-day decisions that leaders are making in response to the federal legislation.

Context of the Setting

The Central Valley Public School District[3] serves over 11,400 students in 19 schools pre-K-12. There are 12 elementary schools, three middle schools, two comprehensive high schools, an alternative high school, and an early childhood center. This district is one of the 15 largest school districts in New Jersey, and it has grown 14% in the past five years. In the next two years alone, an increase of another 600 students is anticipated. The population in Central Valley is changing dramatically. Once a community comprised mostly of white students (90%), there are now rapidly growing populations of Asian, African-American, and Hispanic students. Student mobility is also increasing with a turnover of 18-20% annually, and more than 20% of the total student population receives free or reduced lunch.

Central Valley spends less than the average school district in New Jersey, but still maintains its position as one of the educational leaders in the state. Ninety-five percent of the graduates last year attended a two-year or four-year college, and the dropout rate is far below 1%. Central Valley offers the most Advanced Placement and International Baccalaureate courses in the state, and students are regularly honored for their achievements in athletics and the arts.

The district is led by a very progressive superintendent. He has been in the district for over seven years now, and, in that time, Central Valley has seen dramatic changes. The most obvious shift has been the reduction of class sizes. The board of education has placed a cap on class size of 20 in K-3 and 24 in 4-5. The five Title I elementary schools have class sizes of no more than 15 students in first grade. There is now open enrollment, so parents can choose either high school or any of the elementary schools provided there is space. The middle schools have also seen a major transformation with the opening of an International Baccalaureate magnet school, which caused a response of significant educational changes from the other two middle schools. An intense focus on professional development has meant that teachers have had to talk more honestly about their classrooms and work harder to learn the best practices of current research. The administrators all work under a performance-based contract with a portion of their salary increases tied to "key performance areas." All of this change has increased the stress level among employees in the dis-

---

3   Pseudonyms are used for the school district and all participants.

trict, and, so far, only the elementary schools have seen good results in student achievement gains.

The district is in its sixth year of a standards initiative that focuses on all students achieving. It has had a major impact on the daily lives of all the stakeholders. The basic plan for the district was to create standards and benchmarks for each subject area that were aligned to the standards of state, national, and international organizations. The second year focused on professional development so that teachers and administrators knew how to create standards-based classrooms and schools, and the third year focused on the creation of curricula. The district began disaggregating data by race and ethnicity several years before the advent of NCLB, and it was clear that, despite the reform, large achievement gaps existed between the performance of African-American and Hispanic students and the performance of their Caucasian and Asian peers.

A Minority Achievement Committee was created, and diversity training was provided for all administrators in the district. A teacher in the high school developed a course for Spanish heritage speakers, which provided a venue for conversation about achievement and advocacy within the context of Spanish instruction. A full-time student advocate was hired to help minority students and parents better navigate the school system. Minority teaching candidates were automatically granted interviews in an effort to increase the diversity of a mostly white staff.

While it is clear that Central Valley has adopted the goal of helping all students achieve,[4] it seems the fervor with which it pursues this goal has increased with New Jersey's implementation of the NCLB legislation. Both high schools and one of the three middle schools have been placed on the state's early warning status for failing to make adequate yearly progress.[5] And so now, a district known for its annual accolades finds itself publicly cited for lack of student achievement. The reactions have been swift and sweeping.

With the knowledge of achievement gaps and the mounting pressures of NCLB, the district leadership group has made several decisions that have disrupted the daily activities of traditional schooling. In January of 2004, the leadership group decided to create a major intervention program for students who were at risk for not passing the state assessments. Teachers were pulled out of class for intensive professional development around specific teaching strategies and "look-alike" test items. Students' schedules were shuffled to provide them with extra support and specific, intensive intervention programs. Students were selected using several criteria, including teacher recommendation, performance on previous standardized assessments, and performance on "look-

---

[4]   The board vision statement reads, "The Central Valley Board of Education commits itself to all children by creating an internationally benchmarked school district in which all students receive a preeminent education."

[5]   Central Valley North did not make AYP in the African-American subgroup in both language arts and math as well as the special education subgroup in language arts. Central Valley South did not make AYP in the special education subgroup in language arts. Oak Ridge Middle School did not make AYP because it did not meet the 95% participation rate in the special education subgroup in both language arts and math. It also did not make AYP in the African-American subgroup in Math.

alike" tests, which were created and administered in grades 3-11 math and language arts. Test preparation materials were purchased as the resources for these intervention programs.

In addition to this specific intervention, the district level leadership has required each school to create and maintain "at risk binders" that contain achievement data and other information on students deemed "at risk" by their teachers, counselors, or their performance on standardized tests. Part of each administrator's salary increase is now tied to the systems he/she puts in place to increase student achievement as well as to the actual scores on state assessments. Because the district did not want to wait until 2014,[6] school level benchmarks were created on these assessments to take each school from its current level to 100% proficiency by 2008.

There have been several meetings hosted by a central office administrator that focus on specific issues within special education. These have led to the elimination of certain math courses that do not focus on algebra or geometry, the inclusion of special education teachers in math and language arts professional development experiences, the elimination of I.E.P.[7] exemptions for state assessments, and the adoption of standard curricula for special education classes. There are additional plans over the next few years to reduce the amount of ability groupings in the high school.

Looking to the state level, central office leaders have applied and been accepted to two programs influenced by the NCLB legislation. Central Valley was named one of nine districts statewide to participate in a statewide initiative to pilot performance assessment. This program has the goal of creating a valid, performance-based assessment system that can be reliably scored at the local level. If successful, the state hopes to use this in addition to the more traditional assessments in determining AYP. On the other end of the spectrum, Central Valley has been approved as a supplemental services provider. Competing with private companies, Central Valley hopes to retain the Title I money that would be redirected to tutoring should a school fail to make AYP for three consecutive years.

Central office leaders have also begun to monitor the grade distributions of all secondary teachers, and improvement plans have been created for teachers with a high percentage of students receiving Ds or Es on their report cards. Lastly, the Superintendent has expanded the practice of student focus groups. Central office leaders now meet regularly with groups of students from the five secondary schools in order to get the students' perspective on their school experience. Sometimes the groups consist of targeted populations, such as school leaders or students of color, while other times the groups encompass a more eclectic population.

If one of the purposes of the NCLB legislation was to create change at the local level, it seems apparent that, at least superficially, it has attained its goal

---

[6] The year 2014 is when all students must be proficient as outlined in the NCLB legislation.

[7] Individual Educational Plans are legal documents that outline specific educational goals and supports that must be in place for students with disabilities.

in Central Valley. Whether or not student achievement will follow is still unknown.

Literature Review

The literature on accountability systems for schools can inform the discussion of NCLB. It is important to consider the purposes of accountability systems, their effectiveness and outcomes, their implementation, and the reactions of educational communities to them. The NCLB legislation has added to the growing number of standards and accountability policies across the nation, and these policies are dominating discussion at the local, state, and national levels. In order to analyze the quality and potential impact of these policies, it is important to take a critical look at the underlying assumptions upon which they are based.

Every day, a new article is published on the effects of this legislation, but there seems to be a need for a deeper examination of its impact on specific communities. Because accountability systems do not often specify how they will directly affect student achievement (Linn, 2001), they assume that they can improve schools by stressing the importance of outcomes. "The most common assumptions about outcome-oriented accountability systems appear to be that they will improve schools by:

- Informing students, parents, and teachers about student progress;
- Monitoring the learning process and holding students, schools, educators, and states responsible for attaining learning outcomes;
- Certifying teacher quality on the basis of student achievement;
- Evaluating the overall effectiveness of schools or reforms and assisting education policymakers and administrators with programmatic decisions;
- Ensuring that equitable opportunities to learn are available for students. (Goodwin, Englert, & Cicchinelli, 2003).

These goals align well with the rhetoric around NCLB, and while they may seem intuitive, it is important to look more deeply into the assumptions motivating accountability in general. In "Redesigning Accountability Systems for Education," Susan Fuhrman breaks down this theory of action into five major assumptions. (Fuhrman, 2003). Using them as a framework, I will compare the research and comment on the challenges of implementing accountability policy. Lastly, I will comment on some additional assumptions of the recent accountability policy.

The new accountability assumes that "performance, or student achievement, is the key value or goal of schooling." (Fuhrman, 2003). While this is a point that does not seem to be disputed among educators in the literature, I explore this concept with the leaders in Central Valley. Focusing on student achievement is clearly a departure from when states were "judging schools based on the number of books in the library and the proportion of certified staff." (Elmore, Abelmann, Fuhrman, 1996). While most schools spend resources attending to the affective side of children, they do so with the hope that if a child is happy and comfortable, he/she will learn more. The first part of this theory of action focuses appropriately on the end result. However, when we consider parents' point of view, there is tension implicit in this assumption. "For example, in 1999, ICR Research Group found that the public's top three concerns relative to schools in their communities were lack of parent involvement (55%), use of alcohol or illegal drugs (51%), and undisciplined and disruptive students (50%). In citing these findings, SEDL researchers (Pan, Mutchler, 2000) noted that 'these priorities contrasted sharply with the predominant education reform agenda which, since the 1980s, has focused solidly on defining and measuring student and school performance.'" (Goodwin et al., 2003). "The irony is that although the public seems to be generally in favor of accountability, they are generally opposed to more bureaucracy or large, seemingly impenetrable institutions controlling their schools." (Goodwin, Arens, Barley, & Williams, 2002). "Thus, a system that makes schools more accountable to state officials, instead of parents and local community members, may run counter to what parents and members of the public are demanding." (Goodwin et al., 2003). The tension between what policymakers and educators want is worth exploring in more depth. One of my research questions uncovered this tension: *To what extent does the rationale behind the accountability measures of NCLB mesh with educators' personal beliefs on the purpose of public education?*

Once achievement becomes the decided goal, the next premise assumes that "performance can be accurately and authentically measured by the assessment instruments in use." (Fuhrman, 2003). Many of the assessment tools come in the form of high stakes tests, which are a departure from "the flexibility and second chances that characterize the US educational system." (Smith, O'Day, 1990). Not only are many of these tests one-shot opportunities, but many states have built their accountability almost exclusively on the results of one test. Fuhrman argues that "additional information about the education system is necessary to interpret accountability system performance data." (Fuhrman, 2003). "It is important to look for other information that will either support or disconfirm the information provided by a single test score. The importance of obtaining other information to confirm or disconfirm the information provided by a single test score increases as the importance of the decision and the stakes associated with it increases." (Baker, Linn, Herman, Koretz, 2002). Sirotnik and Kimball would agree, noting, "Common sense suggests that scores on one test (which itself is only a sample of many possible performances) cannot possibly represent all that is going on in a school, any more than the temperature reading on a thermometer can represent all that is going on in a human body. (Sirotnik, Kimball, 1999). Mark Goldberg, in a recent *Phi Delta Kappan* article, sarcastically remarks, "We would give Roger Clemens a paper and pencil test on pitching and baseball because it would be easier to administer and grade such a test than it would be to evaluate several pitching performances over two or three seasons." (Goldberg, 2004). The counterintuitive nature of a single measure accountability system indeed caused tension with the belief systems of the leaders in my study.

Many researchers believe that other data need to be considered alongside this single test. "The most accurate and fair way to evaluate the performance of schools or districts is to consider multiple indicators, such as student achievement, attendance, drop-out rates, and graduation rates." (Stapleton, 2000). The researchers at the National Center for Research on Evaluation, Standards, and Student Testing (CRESST) agree that "other kinds of data about students should be considered, including information related to attendance, mobility, retention, dropouts, and graduation. (Goodwin et al., 2003). I suspect I may find that educators believe that even the addition of these factors may not be sufficient.

There are also concerns about the actual tests. Achieve, an independent organization, found that when tests cover standards, the "coverage is often superficial with tests measuring the least complex of the skills called for" (Fuhrman, 2003). In order to reach the higher order thinking skills, some states have incorporated more open-ended and performance-based assessments. When Kansas educators tried this approach, they found numerous problems, "including scoring reliability and validity, and various complaints about portfolios resulted initially in the state backing away from the more performance based features of the test." (Kannapel, Aagaard, Coe, Reeves, 2000). If the open-ended portions are reduced, the richness of the standards movement may be lost.

Even if the test is aligned to the standards and shown to be both valid and reliable, there are still concerns about how the data are interpreted. Many states do not use a value-added model, instead relying on comparing two different cohorts, who can have "very different characteristics. In addition, in areas with a lot of mobility, the turnover of students in a school could be responsible for performance changes, not learning" (Fuhrman, 2003). Additionally, there is always some sort of measurement error, and states must consider the possibilities for misclassification. New Jersey has favored a 5% margin of error applied across the board rather than implementing a more complex statistical formula. "Those responsible for the accountability system also have a responsibility to help ensure proper interpretation of the results and to minimize inappropriate interpretations to the extent possible. Efforts to assist the press in understanding the results, their strengths and limitations, and the legitimate and illegitimate interpretations can pay considerable dividends in improved coverage by the press and better understanding by the public" (Baker et al., 2002). Both the quality of the data and the interpretation of the data are crucial to an effective accountability system.

There is great variety in the implementation of this accountability among the states. "Each state sets its own minimum number of students that need to be tested before the group counts as a separate category for accountability purposes." (Hall, Wiener, Carey, 2003). This causes wide discrepancies over which students get counted. As more schools fail to meet adequate yearly progress, the assumption that we can measure performance accurately and authentically will be challenged. "Because of the central state and local role in education, AYP results don't allow apples-to-apples comparisons of student achievement from one state to another." (Hall et al., 2003). It may become difficult for parents and educators to digest the fact that their state has many schools failing, while another has very few. "In the end, we should resist the urge to compare states based on the number of schools that failed to make AYP this year. It's not a contest among states; it's a process for identifying individual schools and districts that need improvement." (Hall et al., 2003). This comparison may be inevitable though its value unclear.

Many states do not have the capacity to implement such dramatic increases in testing, and so they are left scrambling. The resulting shortcuts are giving critics plenty of ammunition. This is the area in which the accountability polices will be attacked, and until states can create challenging, well-aligned assessments that are both valid and reliable, there will be tensions among educators.

The third assumption in this area of policy is that "consequences, or stakes, motivate school personnel and students" (Fuhrman, 2003). Smith and O'Day question whether or not we can even implement real consequences in the first place. "We do a terrible job of holding anyone accountable . . . Occasionally, a principal or Superintendent is removed as a scapegoat, but rarely is the system altered in any significant fashion. In the worst case, the pressure to demonstrate improvement leads some educational personnel intentionally or unintentionally to manipulate the accountability system." (Smith et al., 1990). One study from the Consortium for Policy Research in Education (CPRE) found that, "Consequences for poor performance appeared limited to professional development, coaching, and mentoring." (Goertz, Duffy, 2003). "Many of the teachers in the CPRE study reported that their districts and states held schools more accountable for student performance than teachers." (Goertz, Duffy, 2003). While the scope of my study did not allow for an examination of the effect of consequences on teachers, it did include data from leaders that suggested the consequences of NCLB had a negative effect on one of the schools that failed to meet testing benchmarks. One of my recommendations focuses on the need to define and celebrate student growth in more meaningful ways than outlined in the accountability legislation.

Regardless of the implementation of the accountability systems, we must examine whether consequences (with some rewards) will actually motivate educators. Even in cases where teachers do appear to be changing practice, the inertia of the status quo is great. "The instructional changes Kentucky teachers have made appear to be in the direction of standards-based reform, but teachers are a long way from changing radically the way they instruct students." (Kannapel et al., 2000). Tenure laws and the fact that education has changed so little in the last thirty years suggest that consequences will not adequately motivate school personnel. Even if these measures are successful in holding students accountable, we will not make true progress until all adults feel genuinely responsible for the success of each and every one of their students. If these polices are going to truly effect change, the consequences need to be enforced, and the rewards need to be genuine.

"Research on school-based performance awards programs and other accountability policies also show that clear goals and incentives are necessary, but not sufficient, to motivate teachers to reach their school's student achievement goals." (Goertz, 2003). Motivation is also influenced by effective capacity building. (Goertz, 2003). The fourth assumption claims that "if teachers don't have the capacity necessary to respond to the accountability system incentives, it is assumed that the incentives are strong enough to motivate them and administrators to find it somehow." (Fuhrman, 2003). The craft of teaching is so complex even with a tremendous amount of supportive conditions, so I believe this is a mistaken assumption. Teachers need extensive professional development in multiple areas (e.g., curriculum, assessment, differentiated instruction), as well as adequate resources and data. "Because school accountability systems focus almost exclusively on outcomes, they produce little in the way of reliable information about classroom practice." (Fuhrman, 2003). It is in this area that we need data. The culture of isolation needs to be broken in order to build the necessary capacity to handle these complex issues. Even though the teachers in Kentucky have attempted to make great changes, "it comes as no surprise that Kentucky schools have not achieved the full range of curricular and instructional change that was envisioned." (Kannapel et al., 2000). This tension between short-term outcomes and the long-term sustainability of curricular and pedagogical change is explored in my study.

There are indeed some examples of improved student achievement in states of high accountability. In a cross state analysis, Carnoy and Loeb's results "suggest a statistically significant relationship between the degree to which states hold school accountable for student outcomes and their gains in NAEP scores at the end of the 1990's." (Conroy, Loeb, in press). The Kentucky study also showed gains in all academic areas, nearly doubling the results in math, reading, and science. (Kannapel et al., 2000). While these examples show promise, "the history of school reform demonstrates that even when standards are raised and more or better resources are allocated, little lasting change occurs in the classroom." (Smith, O'Day, 1990).

The final assumption that Fuhrman presents is the notion that the unfortunate, unintended consequences of these accountability policies, if they are operating as intended, will be minimal. (2003). I explored this assumption in depth throughout my research when I examined how NCLB had affected the work of these leaders and the tensions that resulted from decisions they made. One of the challenges to the assumption often comes with the argument that teachers will start teaching to the test. If the test is truly aligned with the standards, this could be a good thing. The danger comes when "teachers adjust their teaching to improve test scores, not by teaching the subject matter in more creative and productive ways but by tailoring their instruction to the form and nature of standardized tests." (Smith, O'Day, 1990). The program in Kentucky also had the unfortunate outcome of a shift in focus from learning to test scores. (Kannapel et al., 2000). Others argue that there will be additional fallout, such as increases in dropout rates and a dropin retentions. (Conroy, Loeb, in press). At the same time, these policies may wake us up to consider changing some older paradigms. "On one hand, researchers and reporters alike have lauded the success of states like North Carolina and Texas in raising the academic performance of their students and narrowing the performance gap between White students and students of color. (cf. Grissmer, Flanagan, 1998; Grissmer, Flanagan, Kawata, Williamson, 2000). On the other hand, civil rights advocates in New York and Texas have charged in court that high-stakes accountability systems discriminate against poor and minority students." (Goertz, Duffy, 2003).

These five assumptions serve as a useful framework for analyzing policy; however, we should continue to acknowledge other assumptions. For example, it seems that the new systems of accountability work on the assumption that the state level is the appropriate place for implementation of policy. An area of further study would be to look at district or national accountability systems. Another assumption is that accountability policy, or any policy for that matter, will work for all students. It would seem more intuitive that increased accountability will have different effects on different people.

While the research points out the flaws in the assumptions of these accountability systems, Goodwin, et al., recommend that "rather than flatly rejecting or discarding such systems altogether, educators and policymakers should work to improve accountability systems so that they truly encourage positive outcomes. At the same time, the negative consequences created by some of these systems should be honestly examined and corrected." (2003). In my study, I recommend that school districts need to learn from the decisions they make so that the negative consequences of NCLB can be reduced.

Over the next several years, the educational literature around NCLB will undoubtedly expand. To get to the depth of its effects, researchers will have to conduct thorough case studies. In January of 2004, the Center on Education Policy released its findings from its national study, which included 33 case studies. According to the center, "the case study reports presented here describe each district's progress in carrying out NCLB requirements, its challenges with implementation, and its strategies for addressing these challenges." (CEP, 2004). The center found many schools were increasing professional development, implementing new, research-based programs, and extending time for students. Schools report directing funding to "such strategies as increasing the use of student achievement data to inform instruction, matching curriculum with standards and tests, and using research to inform decisions about improvement strategies." (CEP, 2004). These studies focused on a broad study of implementations at the district level. However, those studies and the rest of the research fail to explore the tensions in the minds of local leaders as they make these changes. For example, discovering that districts are extending time for students is too broad to adequately examine the effects of NCLB. My study sought to find out why leaders decided to extend time for students, how they extended the time, and whether or not they believed that, ultimately, this change was in the students' best interest. There are few case studies in the research, and they did not explore whether or not local leaders felt the changes they had made were the types of changes they want for their students. I was more interested in the human level, where embedded tensions of human reaction and interaction told a different story of the effects of this legislation.

In fact, tensions exist throughout the literature between accountability systems and the NCLB Act. The way that Central Valley responded to this legislation demonstrated this tension. This experience was worth investigating, for it informs policy on one level, but it also serves a deeper purpose. When people confront their own educational philosophies, they broaden their own learning and begin to think quite differently about an institution that has changed very little in the last century. A deeper case study causes the type of reflection that leads to more prudent decisions within the school district and its surrounding community.

It was clear that my research needed to be narrowed, for the NCLB legislation deals more broadly with education than the areas I have discussed. While it may be interesting to study the effects of the highly qualified teacher provisions, for example, I was not able to attend to such breadth. This case study focused on the accountability component of the NCLB legislation. The research field will benefit from the findings of how a major suburban school district in New Jersey responded to this controversial legislation. The struggles this community muddled through are both interesting and informative to the larger educational and political society.

Methodology

In order to better understand the impact of NCLB and the embedded tensions it causes, I conducted a case study of how the leadership group of Central Valley School District responded to the legislation and the resulting feelings they have as to the value of these changes.

Site Selection

The Central Valley School District serves as a useful site for several reasons. Although large for New Jersey, Central Valley would be considered an average size school district in the country based on the size of its student population. With increasing levels of enrollment, diversity, and academic disparity, this district faces issues typical to those that many suburban districts are facing nationwide. This district is also similar to many that have enjoyed decades of praise for the quality of their performance, but now face public scrutiny with NCLB. Central Valley's response to this legislation may have significant impact on the rest of the state, for it has always been considered a progressive district, leading educational change.

On a practical level, this site offered tremendous access for me, for I work in this district as a member of the leadership team. I have already established a rapport of trust and candor with each member of this group, and, because I work with these people each and every day, I was able to collect data from various sources with greater ease than if I were an outside researcher. Personally, I am invested in the success of this school district, because, in addition to working in this district for the last five years, I grew up and currently live in Central Valley.

Research Subjects

For the purposes of this case study, I narrowed the subjects to the leadership group of the school district. Known as the "Superintendent's Council," this group meets weekly to discuss the important issues facing the district and make the decisions that determine the district's direction. This eclectic group brings a variety of experiences and expertise to the table, and it will be interesting to hear the different perspectives on the effects of the NCLB legislation on the district. The members of this leadership team are described below.

Superintendent: Steve Green

For the last seven years, this Superintendent has led Central Valley. A former English teacher, he has also been a High School Principal, Director of Curriculum, Assistant Superintendent, and the Superintendent of two other districts in New York and Connecticut. He is ultimately responsible for the direction of the school district. In 2004, he directly supervised eight of the twelve elementary schools.

Assistant Superintendent, Business: George Stanley

The business administrator heads all the financial divisions for the district as well as facilities and transportation. Serving the district for over 25 years, he is the administrative representative on the Board Business and Facilities committee.

Assistant Superintendent, Curriculum: Phil Jennings

Directly responsible for the supervision of the two comprehensive high schools and, in 2004, one of the elementary schools, this Assistant Superintendent was a former high school principal in the district. He serves also as the representative on both the Curriculum and the Policy and Legislation board committees.

Assistant Superintendent, Instruction: Pat Wilson

A former elementary and middle school principal in this district, she is directly responsible for the three middle schools and, in 2004, she was responsible for three of the elementary schools. Those who work on curriculum report directly to her.

Assistant Superintendent, Elementary Education and Professional Development: Morgan Phillips

A former elementary school principal in another district in the state, he joined the team in 2004 and supervises half of the elementary schools as well as the professional development for the district.

Assistant Superintendent, Elementary Education and Achievement Gaps: Jason Wilkens

A former elementary school principal from within the district, he joined the team in 2004 and supervises half of the elementary schools as well as the district's efforts to close the achievement gaps.

Director of Special Education and Student Services: Sam Wright
He supervises the Child Study Teams and all of Special Education in the district.

Director of Curriculum: Dan McLaughlin
Responsible for coordination and development of curriculum, he also supervises the subject area supervisors and the assessment department. Formerly, he was an elementary school principal and a middle school assistant principal in the district.

Supervisor of Professional Development: Melissa Harris
In 2004, she coordinated all of the professional development work in the district, including the work of outside consultants. A former colleague teacher in the district, she also supervised the Talented and Gifted program and served as the state liaison for the Pilot Performance Assessment Project. She retired after the 2004 school year.

Assistant to the Superintendent for Operations and Registration Services: Alex Walker
A non-certificated employee, he is responsible for the implementation of the district's technology plan. He also coordinates the open enrollment and magnet school application procedures.

Assistant to the Superintendent for Planning, Grants and Community Outreach: Robin Miller
A non-certificated employee, she coordinates the district's strategic plan as well as writing all of the grant applications. Working closely with various community groups, she has conducted many focus groups. She also serves on the Board's planning committee. She also worked closely with local legislators to influence state and national policy.

Director of Human Resources: Kathy Davis
A non-certificated employee, she is responsible for all personnel administration in the district.

Public Information Officer: Carol Martin
A non-certificated employee, she coordinates all of the district's work with the press. She handles questions from the public on all matters, and she writes most of the letters that are publicly distributed.

Role as Researcher

As the Director of Curriculum for the district, I serve as a member of the Superintendent's Council. Because of the intimate, often confidential discussion matters, it was important for me to get the approval of all the members of this leadership team for this study. They gave me permission to use data from various sources throughout this study. It was also important for me to maintain confidentiality and positive relationships with the members of this group.

Because my experiences and beliefs as a part of this group were crucial to this study, a fellow graduate student who was familiar with my research interviewed me. I reviewed the questions and interviewing strategies with him beforehand so that he could control the interview and conduct an interview similar to the others.

I faced many tensions throughout this study as I tried to navigate the roles of researcher and research subject. As a member of this leadership team, I clearly remember many struggles these leaders had with the changes we made in our district, but, when I began the interviews, I found that many of these leaders ignored those struggles, saying that they were quite comfortable with the NCLB legislation and the changes we made. My first concern was their ability to be candid with a colleague. Were the participants expressing their public stance as they would to a newspaper reporter? I was also concerned that the individuals in the group were adopting the district philosophy for their own without critical thought. It became necessary throughout the interview process for me to explore these concerns directly.

Reporting these data also became difficult because many of the more critical comments came from my own interview. It was a challenge to reflect the data I provided without over-representing my own point of view. Overall, there may have been harsher criticism of the district's direction had I conducted the interviews closer to the implementation of the changes. In my recommendations, I endorse this distance in order to make policy decisions with less emotion, but this same emotion may have added more pointed criticism. Ultimately, I think the interview data were accurately reflected with appropriate balance.

In early drafts I did not attribute the quotations in an attempt to achieve complete anonymity, but in the end I felt it was necessary to identify the speaker because it enriched the story of the data. The use of pseudonyms helped to preserve the confidentiality, but it was a struggle for me throughout my research.

I have also struggled with how I report the data back to this leadership group. While I am sure that a few members of the team would enjoy reading my work, I think it is more useful to present them with my recommendations chapter and the PowerPoint® presentation I created for my defense. While this is not a petty group, people might spend more time trying to figure out who said what than focusing on the learning that can be gained from my data analysis and ensuing recommendations.

While a researcher always learns from the research he/she conducts, I believe I learned more because of the nature of my situation. In addition to what I gained from the interview data, I grew as an educator in very practical ways because I had to navigate the challenges of studying a group of individuals with whom I worked on a daily basis. I feel closer to my colleagues, and I have an increased sensitivity to their individual perspectives.

Data Sources

The primary source for this qualitative study was the set of individual interviews of leadership team members. The interviews were divided into two groups. Preliminary interviews included a sample of the leadership group. This small group of five included both certified and non-certified personnel. I used the initial interviews to narrow down the various implemented initiatives to those most significantly cased by or related to NCLB. (See Appendix A). This narrowed focus allowed the second interviews, which was conducted with the entire team, to get into more depth on the most relevant issues.

These second interviews addressed the participants' perceptions of their roles as members of this leadership team, how they felt their jobs had been affected by the NCLB legislation, and their opinions of the resulting changes. (See Appendix B). The initial questions explored the purposes of public education and the perceived intent of the accountability measures in NCLB. A second group of questions asked how the participants see their roles as members of this leadership team, and what they saw as their particular responsibilities in addressing the accountability issues of NCLB. Another group of questions focused on the changes they made or observed because of the legislation. We discussed the genesis of each initiative, the process of implementation, and its perceived impact. These were followed up with questions that were designed to discern how well these changes are aligned with the participants' educational philosophies. All interviews were audiotaped and transcribed for analysis.

While the interviews served to bring out the voices in this case study, it was also important to study data from a variety of other sources. These data sources fall into three categories: communication among members of the leadership team; communication with other educators within the district; and communication with the board, public, and those outside the organization. In the first two categories I collected data that relate to school accountability from conversations, email, and internal documents (agendas, memos, notes, etc.). In the third category, I analyzed an eclectic collection of data that included press releases, program brochures, board presentations, testing reports, interview questions, and notes from conversations.

It was necessary in many cases to conduct the interviews in several stages because of the time required to cover a variety of topics. The discussion of district initiatives was time consuming. The length and number of interviews depended largely on the individual. For example, the Business Administrator had an interesting take on some of the issues, but he clearly has not been as involved in many of the educational initiatives, so his interview only lasted a little over a half-hour. In contrast, I needed to interview some members, such as the Director of Special Education several times, for their work is more directly affected by the accountability policy. Many of those interviews approached two hours in length.

Even though the specific initiatives covered in this study were implemented prior to the 2004-2005 school year, I included the two new Assistant Superintendents in the process. While they could not speak to the genesis of the initiatives, they did add deep reflections on the tensions inherent in these decisions.

Data Analysis

In analyzing the data, I tried to "identify salient sets of ideas, concepts, or issues and condense them into categories." (Stringer, 1999). Stringer's concept of analyzing the converging and diverging perspectives was especially useful here, for I believe that the tensions in the various perspectives offer insight into the core issue. Some of the diverging perspectives helped me to think of things I had not previously considered, and they sensitized me to some of the tensions not openly communicated. The analysis of converging perspectives either strengthened early convictions or emphasized issues to which I had initially attributed less relevance.

Moving Forward

Fifty years ago, schools had to be forced to integrate students with the Brown v. Board of Education decision. Today, with growing achievement gaps, schools have been forced to change again. NCLB has shaken up the public schools, and educators everywhere are debating the inherent challenges. Many are rebelling and some are rallying, but what seems consistent is that educators are indeed making changes. The key point is whether or not these changes are actually making public education better. Time will tell, but perhaps this close look into one district will help to inform the larger debate.

Findings

Are the decisions that local educators make because of NCLB the types of changes we want for our students? The following secondary questions provided context, depth, and insight that laid the foundation for the larger question:

- *To what extent does the rationale behind the accountability measures of NCLB mesh with educators' personal beliefs on the purpose of public education?*
- *How has NCLB affected the work of educational leaders?*
- *What are the tensions in the minds of educational leaders when making decisions influenced by NCLB?*

In order to identify the effects of the NCLB at more micro levels, it is important to assess to what extent the perceived purpose of the legislation meshes with the beliefs of educational leaders for the purpose of public education. When discussing accountability, philosophy is important. Participants were asked, "What is the purpose of public education?" and subsequently asked what they felt was the reasoning behind the accountability measures in NCLB. Once I understood the degree to which the purposes of public education and the rationale behind NCLB matched, I explored the pressures these leaders felt because of NCLB. In this line of questioning, I was also interested in understanding whether or not the pressures were a direct effect of the legislation or simply perceived. When studying the decisions that local leaders made, it was important for me to understand the forces that affected those decisions.

To expand the context and look for tensions, I asked each of the leaders if they had any mixed feelings about NCLB, and it was the combination of these thoughts with their earlier opinions that provided the landscape for an exploration of the major initiatives that were greatly influenced by the legislation. For each of the three major initiatives, I explored the purpose, the decision-making process, any debates that ensued, the perceived effects, and any unresolved issues. Throughout the questioning, I probed for tensions, perceptions, and opinions.

In my conclusion I will discuss the overall impressions of the study group members as they tried to reconcile whether or not the changes they made were educationally sound. I will highlight the salient concerns, and I will explore why this group felt it approached NCLB differently than most educators.

The Purpose of Public Education vs. The Purpose of NCLB

The creation of a level playing field, the preparation of students for the skills they will need in life, and the attempt to fix a system that was not working were the three major themes that grew out of the interviews. I will discuss how these leaders thought about each of the themes and to what extent they perceived the purposes of public education and NCLB to be aligned.

A Level Playing Field

Perhaps the greatest connection found in the data between the purpose of public education and the purpose behind NCLB accountability was the belief that public education as an institution had the responsibility for leveling the playing field for all students by "providing educational opportunities to any child regardless of their background, their capabilities, their abilities or disabilities, or their support at home." (C. Martin, personal interview, December 9, 2004). This was a particular point of passion, and it was clearly an issue about which this team of leaders had thought deeply.

> Public education serves a larger public good by taking absolutely everyone in and making sure that we do our best to challenge and support each and every child. And by that I mean to give them the very best education we can. We need to make sure we support kids who may need extra time, but that we don't lower our standards for kids. We need to build on their strengths and do everything we can to make sure they succeed, so that could mean all sorts of things in public education, but our goal is to bring every kid to a high standard. (D. McLaughlin, personal interview, December 9, 2004).

To some, this was important in order to serve a broad purpose. "If we have compulsory education for every student in the United States and every student gets a quality education, then we would expect that they would all have opportunities to go out and do wonderful things in their adult life." (P. Jennings, personal interview, December 9, 2004). But for others, there seemed to be a more personal responsibility.

> We've got the kids in our hands, and so, if we have that awesome responsibility, then it's our job to make sure that every kid is successful. I think that there are some injustices in the world, and public education can be the great equalizer. Kids of privilege and kids without privilege all deserve the same quality education, and I think public education can be a kid's way out to pursue the American Dream. (D. McLaughlin, personal interview, December 9, 2004).

Many felt there was no other reasonable option, and so the responsibility fell on the public schools. "I see it as a social need that public education serves, and so if we're not going to do it, then I'm worried who can" (D. McLaughlin, personal interview, December 9, 2004). "I think that's the difference between public education and private education. Private schools can turn kids away. They don't have to accept anybody and public schools do, and I think that's the cornerstone of our country." (C. Martin, personal interview, December 9, 2004). Certainly this responsibility comes with its challenges.

> Private schools can say, "Hmmm, no we don't want you here. If you start to misbehave, get out." They don't have to deal with all the family issues, the emotional issues, the baggage issues that come with the children growing up in a dysfunctional family or whatever it happens to be. Public schools have to deal with all of the youngsters, disadvantaged to advanced and everywhere in-between – from Special Education to the talented and gifted and in-between, unlike the private sector where you pick and choose. (G. Stanley, personal interview, December 17, 2004).

This reality was personal for many of the team members, because they saw themselves as "public educators," or as Jason Wilkens, an Assistant Superintendent for Elementary Education, shared,

> You are looking at one of the successes of public education. We believe that if this nation is going to be strong, then public schools are the one way of achieving that. I have worked in public schools all of my life and certainly worked in disadvantaged communities because I feel so very strongly about it. (personal interview, December 16, 2004).

This concept of leveling the playing field also permeated the group's opinions of the rationale behind NCLB. The Assistant Superintendent for Business added his thoughts.

> It must have finally dawned on someone on the federal level that, just as the term says, not all children were achieving, and they were not all [provid-

ed with] an equal opportunity to achieve...The NCLB legislation was based on the failures of both large and small school districts to address the needs of children of color, children who were socio-economically disadvantaged, or of children who were of a different cultural base. (G. Stanley, personal interview, December 17, 2004).

This reasoning resonated with the Assistant to the Superintendent. "We have to figure out if Johnny isn't getting it at the same rate as Mary, you have to adjust accordingly. It isn't "Today we're doing math for an hour, and we're going to take a test at the end and everybody should pass it.." (A. Walker, personal interview, December 16, 2004). The Assistant Superintendent for Elementary Education agreed. "The whole purpose was to make sure that when we talk about educating 'all' that it means 'all,' and that we have to disaggregate data and make sure that all of the subgroups are indeed achieving." (J. Wilkens, personal interview, December 16, 2004).

Preparation for Life

In many ways, these educators expressed that public education sought to prepare students for their lives after school, but with this theme there was a much weaker correlation to the ideals of NCLB. This concept of preparation for life meant different things to different people. For Steve Green, the Superintendent, this meant preparing students for life in a democratic society. "I think one of the core issues for public education is dealing with democracy, passing on democracy, understanding democracy, being a member, a participating member of a democratic society." (personal interview, December 16, 2004). He felt that sometimes students needed to deal directly with the history of democracy.

> I think it's important that we understand one another so that we can work together for a common cause, and the common cause happens to be a democratic principle. Democracy in terms of The Bill of Rights, Declaration of Independence, and our Constitution as framing documents that establish who we are as a people and all the literacies that go with them – we need to understand those. (personal interview, December 16, 2004).

Green did not see this perspective reflected in NCLB. "[NCLB] has defined [learning] in terms of mathematics and language arts, rather than saying there are some principles such as democracy, community service, and caring about one another that are also the fabric of what schooling is all about.." (personal interview, December 16, 2004).

Others, including the Assistant Superintendent for Middle Schools, saw the democratic role of public education as producing productive citizens.

> It's the whole basis of our society – of who we are – of what America is....I believe that because I think that when we look at a child's life, we probably spend the most time with them, so schools definitely shape children,

which means they shape the citizens of the future. (P. Wilson, personal interview, December 9, 2004).

Only the Superintendent saw any connection with democracy in the NCLB legislation.

> I think the intent, probably, as everybody in the world has said, is an honorable one, believing that there is some body of knowledge, some set of skills necessary to participate in this democracy, this society, and the idea of NCLB is to be sure that we have an educated society, citizenry, and can participate well. And it's not fair in a sense to have those who can and those who can't, those who can read and write and do math and those who can't. (S. Green, personal interview, December 16, 2004).

The Director of Curriculum struggled with making the connection to democracy.

> I guess as soon as I start to think about accountability, I think of accountability towards each child, so I don't think of accountability towards a larger democratic ideal. But in terms of thinking of the purpose of education, [NCLB] does have this kind of broader, democratic ideal, but I guess in my daily life and what dominates my thinking is the individual child. (D. McLaughlin, personal interview, December 9, 2004).

Most everyone saw skill development as one of the fundamental roles of public education. "We need to give them the critical skills – the academic skills and the life skills – that they will need in the public workforce." (D. McLaughlin, personal interview, December 9, 2004). Even when these leaders talked about "providing the basics," it was not for any inherent value of the skills themselves but more for the purpose of providing options. Robin Miller, Assistant to the Superintendent, explained, "We have to make sure they have the basics and very strong foundations so they can learn and move into areas wherever they want to go." (personal interview, December 12, 2004). The concept of "helping children create options in life" was prevalent in the thinking of many members. (M. Phillips, personal interview, December 21, 2004).

> In general, [the purpose of public education] is to prepare students for the next step in their life, so when they're ready to transition to adulthood that transition is in place, and it is a successful transition whether it be to the workplace, to college, the military – whatever those aspirations are, we've given the kids a great foundation to move them along. (S. Wright, personal interview, December 8, 2004).

The Director of Curriculum thought persistence and reflection played an important role.

> We need to give them the skills so that they know how to reach for more when they feel that they are at their end. We extend them to do things that they never thought were possible. We need to provide engaging, rigorous activities

and then also add reflective activities to let them know more about themselves. (D. McLaughlin, personal interview, December 9, 2004).

When discussing the rationale behind NCLB, the concept of skill development was less prevalent, but it did surface. The Assistant Superintendent for Middle Schools said, "I see the function of NCLB as establishing the minimal standards that kids need to meet, and those NCLB accountabilities help us to have benchmarks along the way to see if kids are making the progress that we need them to make." (P. Wilson, personal interview, December 9, 2004). But when asked if NCLB helped students to make choices in life, the Assistant to the Superintendent responded with the following statement.

No, there is nothing in there. We never do a pre and a post about that . . . . We never ask a child, let's say their freshman year, what they are thinking about. Are they thinking about going to college? If they are, what are they thinking about? What are some of their options or interests? So, I think that progress [in schools] is so much more significant than what is measured by NCLB. (R. Miller, personal interview, December 15, 2004).

For the most part, this group of leaders did not see the rationale of NCLB as focused on preparing students for life.

Broken System

After seeing an aligned rationale in "leveling the playing field," the group did not see as strong a connection between NCLB and the goals of preparing students for later life. Instead, the group felt strongly that part of the rationale of the accountability provisions in NCLB was to bring consistency and greater accountability to a public school system not meeting its potential.

"Part of the issue is the consistency from state to state." (C. Martin, personal interview, December 9, 2004). Alex Walker, Assistant to the Superintendent, thought it was the great variability that did not sit well with legislators.

My gut is that there was an obvious gap – that public education could be very different, not even just by state, by county, by district, by school, but within school districts. [The goal of NCLB] was to make it more standardized so that, if my child went to school here and I moved to Tennessee next week, there should be some sort of consistency. Things should feel the same. (personal interview, December 16, 2004).

Walker assumed expectations and programs were already consistent.

Before coming into education from the business world, I actually thought that it existed more – that things were more standardized. I thought if my child went to school and took math in eighth grade in [one town], and then I moved into Central Valley or [a neighboring town], maybe they'd be taking almost the same class. (personal interview, December 16, 2004).

In addition to the need for consistency, Morgan Phillips, Assistant Superintendent, thought NCLB attempted to bring more accountability to schools, especially in terms of fiscal responsibility.

> By and large, I think if you look at urban districts and districts that have a history of failing, I think those kinds of restraints and accountability systems need to be in place. I mean there was history in the larger urban districts where funds were misappropriated. Funds never got to the classrooms, and the funds that did get there didn't bring about the results that the folks expected [because of] the whole notion that money was going to change all of this. This was the catalyst behind putting the NCLB act into place. (personal interview, December 21, 2004).

The Director of Human Resources saw accountability operating as a simple business principle. "I mean businesses are all about a return on investment, and they want to know what the bottom line is." (K. Davis, personal interview, December 8, 2004). Because education "takes up a tremendous amount of the American budget," the public deserves more accountability. (D. McLaughlin, personal interview, December 9, 2004). Phillips, an Assistant Superintendent for Elementary Education, added the following statement:

> As long as districts were getting money and not necessarily having the reporting systems in place, it became very easy to point the finger and say, "Well look, we gave them all this money, and they're not bringing about the kind of results that we need, and children are stilling failing." (personal interview, December 21, 2004).

Money was not the only reason behind NCLB, according to this leadership group. "We needed to have solid measures that were comparable and that could be sustained over time to see if the districts' outcomes were going in the right directions." (S. Wright, personal interview, December 8, 2004). The Public Information Officer added the following.

> My understanding would be [that the purpose of NCLB] is to ensure that schools and school districts are reaching those benchmarks, those adequate yearly progress benchmarks, progressing along that continuum at an appropriate rate, and, if they're not, then [schools should be] doing some intervention to help [students] catch up. And if they're still not, then giving those students in those schools the opportunity to go someplace else. (C. Martin, personal interview, December 9, 2004).

The Director of Curriculum wondered if NCLB was a way for the outside world to simply ask, "How do you know the kids are learning? We need to know." (D. McLaughlin, personal interview, December 9, 2004).

Several members of the team intimated there might be more complex motives behind NCLB, as is described by the Superintendent in the following passage.

> I think there's a sub-rosa political reason – that there are many who

believe public education has not served us well, and so beyond making sure that there is an educated citizenry is the issue to force the hand of public education to change its ways. Some of the items on the agenda, such as charter schools, schools of choice, and changing some public funding into support of private, parochial schools are all part of that, because I think the argument goes that it doesn't matter from where the education comes as long as students get those skills that are necessary. (S. Green, personal interview December 16, 2004).

There was a level of cynicism in many of these leaders' minds. The Director of Curriculum explained:

In my most pessimistic view, I think there are some political forces that want to get rid of public education, and, while I don't believe the law is founded on that, I think there is some reasoning of bringing in private enterprise and the restructuring of schools. I think this opens the way to vouchers, and I think this allows public education to get knocked around a bit; so I am a little leery of some of the political forces behind it (D. McLaughlin, personal interview, December 9, 2004).

And even though NCLB offers the opportunity for schools to demonstrate effectiveness, the Assistant Superintendent for High Schools said, "I think there are those with an agenda that think we're not going to fix public schools and therefore we should go to some other form of education. (P. Jennings, personal interview, December 9, 2004).

And while this thinking was prominent in the minds of many of these educators, Jennings also offered the cause for this possible subversive movement.

It is clear that we did not clean our own house in public education. And I say that not from a perspective of where I work necessarily, but if you look at it broadly across the country or across the state, there are some islands of excellence, and then there are areas that, you know, why would you ever send your kid to that school or that school district? (personal interview, December 9, 2004).

Pat Wilson, Assistant Superintendent for Middle Schools, explained that this "mess" in public education was evidenced by the quality of the graduates. "It was because large urban centers were graduating kids that you, know, barely had proficiency in writing or didn't have proficiency in writing or reading." (personal interview, December 9, 2004). Phillips agreed.

It was because our schools were failing and business people were then reporting back, 'You're turning people over to us who aren't ready to work in the workforce.' The government said, 'Well this is what we need to do to put more sanctions on and try to control what was going on,' (M. Phillips, personal interview, December 21, 2004).

Beyond these anecdotes, leaders cited data from international studies that did not set the public schools from the United States in a very good light.

"Obviously, all the international forces of the competition of kids in other parts of the world, based on the TIMSS research and many other measures, do so much better than our kids. That had to be another influence on NCLB." (P. Wilson, personal interview, December 9, 2004).

> I think it's looking at other countries and then saying that our kids are not doing well enough in school. And I think that legislators see that really as the pressure, saying, "Wait a minute. Our schools aren't doing it, so we need to put more pressure on our schools and tell our schools they have to do a better job" (R. Miller, personal interview, December 15, 2004).

Sam Wright, Director of Special Services, felt that public schools did not respond well to the international reports. "We did not have evidence that what we were doing was having any positive effect on children. Our evidence was anecdotal. Our evidence was case-based." (personal interview, December 8, 2004).

When thinking about accountability, individual philosophy is important. If all of the personal ideals were perfectly correlated to the perceived ideals of NCLB, there would probably be less tension when it came time to implement the law, but clearly there is variability, which will undoubtedly cause some tension.

Mixed Feelings

It is reasonable to assume that these educators would have mixed feelings about the accountability measures in NCLB. Their perception that the law is aligned with their ideal of public education serving as the great equalizer helps them to digest the fact that they think the law was not designed to better prepare students for life, which was clearly important to them. Then there is the fact that many of them believed that NCLB was created to change, or even eliminate, a system that just is not working. This is the same system that these leaders have dedicated their lives to, so it was important to find out more directly about their opinions of NCLB and if they had any mixed feelings about the law. Unsurprisingly, the leaders talked about the tensions and struggles in thinking about the legislation.

Practical Issues – Is the law making a difference?

Similar to the educators who are having many conversations around the country, this group had its fair share of comments that demonstrated the belief that the intent of the law is good, but there were problems in the implementation. This was especially true for Morgan Phillips, who felt the law matched his own philosophy of education.

> I think when you go back to how the conversations began it was really about trying to make certain that all kids were getting appropriate educations.

But the reality of it is, because it's become so process orientated, it's really not, in many instances, affecting instruction. I think that principals are doing a lot more managerial stuff because of all the data collection, [which is important], but shouldn't they be in classrooms instead? (personal interview, December 21, 2004).

Clearly, Phillips is struggling with the amount of paperwork but admits the data the principals are working with are important. There is a tension here because he knows principals need to get into classrooms more to make a difference.

Alex Walker, Assistant to the Superintendent, who does not deal with the instructional side of the district, identified a similar struggle with the day-to-day hassles of implementing the law. "It seems like there's an incredible amount of money and time spent on people having to be obsessed with No Child Left Behind, and I guess I would just challenge is this the right way to put our energies and efforts." (personal interview, December 16, 2004)? In his next thought, Walker mentions some of the benefits.

I think the premise of having something more standardized than [what we had] makes sense. You can't cookie-cut every school in every district, and that is the beauty of having different schools in different areas of the country. But if a kid goes to a college or a university from Michigan, you would hope that someone who enters there is pretty well balanced or equal to someone that comes out of a school in New York or South Dakota. (personal interview, December 16, 2004).

In addition to finding some benefits in the law, which counterbalances this question of wasted resources, he also struggles with the balance between consistency and individuality.

The issue of whether or not these accountability measures are working also surfaced. Carol Martin, who is a parent in the district in addition to working at central office, explained her frustration.

It's not necessarily correcting any problems, resolving any problems. It's just identifying the problems perhaps, just not correcting them . . . the idea behind it is good, and I think it is important that if public schools are failing our students that we take measures to improve. I'm not sure how [NCLB] does that though. I'm not sure that offering choice because one school fails to meet one benchmark is going to solve the issue. (personal interview, December 9, 2004).

Clearly frustrated with the sanctions of a school failing to make AYP, she recognizes that something needs to be done. The Superintendent thought the consequences of NCLB not only were ineffective but also had a negative effect on part of the community.

[One of our schools] is a good example – a school that hasn't performed well and hasn't performed well for a long time on a comparative basis. You and I know, psychologically, you don't take something or someone that has not achieved well and beat the hell out of it. That's not how you improve performance; and so these poor people in that school, these poor people in that community now have this whole mentality, you know, 'We really are a failing school. We really are not that good.' And it sets up this whole range of community reactions that are off-base. It is not an appropriate way of improving schooling for kids. (personal interview, December 16, 2004).

Some saw it differently. Melissa Harris, who coordinated the professional development in the district, added her thoughts. "As much as you might hear a lot of people talk dismissively of NCLB, there is nothing wrong with being accountable." Beyond the accountability of the AYP benchmarks, the Assistant Superintendent for Middle Schools thought the law was having a deeper and more important impact, but even she admits to the hassles.

So, yeah, of course it's been a headache. But really what it has done for kids and programs for the most part – how it's played out in our district – I don't see it as being awful. I think it has helped us to move some important things forward that we probably would have taken more time to do. (P. Wilson, personal interview, December 9, 2004).

One of the other challenges to the practical aspects of the law is the doubt that the goal of 100% proficiency is a real possibility. In this passage, Robin Miller, Assistant to the Superintendent, offers her struggles and an anecdote that personalizes these tensions.

I almost have an internal fight, if you will, about [reaching 100% proficiency] because you want to believe that every kid can. You look at your own child, and even if you know that your child has a hard time in a certain area, you say I'm going to do everything I can to get them as far as they can go. I know that we have spoken to students, and I remember this one. We spoke with African-American students from [one of the high schools]. There was this one girl. She was in her freshman year. She'd already been in nine school districts, and she talked about how she would love to go to college. But she doesn't think she's ever going to get to college. And you know what? I wanted so badly to say to her, "You will, because you are going to come to my office every day after school, and I'm going to make sure you do your homework, and you are going to get there because you have so much drive, so much ambition, so much desire that you'll get there." And I swear to God, I wanted to pull her. You know you can't do that to every kid, so you want to believe that every kid can get there. I think, realistically, we know that not every kid will get there. I think more kids can, but there are a lot of problems just inherent in the system, in the public education system that is going to prevent us from getting there. (personal interview, December 15, 2004).

This type of honest reflection on the law and its potential, or lack thereof, demonstrates the tensions that leaders face every day at the local level.

Can the Test Measure Everything?

One complaint about NCLB was the limited nature of the accountability using standardized tests only in language arts and math. The Director of Curriculum explained his view.

> The fact that we are only testing math and language arts in grades three through eight and once in high school – I have real issues with that – because I also believe in creating students who are reflective and advanced critical thinkers. We need to push kids beyond what they normally can do. (D. McLaughlin, personal interview, December 9, 2004).

Only one member of the group, Kathy Davis, Director of Human Resources, was comfortable with this aspect of the Act. "I think that probably my perception is that math and language arts, reading, and writing are the core of everything – in that you need a really strong basis there in order to achieve other goals, and that's why it is narrowed down to those particular subjects." (personal interview, December 8, 2004). Other members, including the Superintendent, were not as understanding.

> The purpose in the [NCLB] definition of education is to get a set of skills, to learn something, to be able to regurgitate it in some kind of form of assessment, some kind of accountability measure, and I don't ever hear within that framework what the purpose of education is in general. If it's in the purpose to create a literate citizenry, that you need to participate actively in the democracy, then you might begin to think how you deliver that. (S. Green, personal interview, December 16, 2004).

He wants the legislation to define the role of public education more explicitly, for he believes there are indeed democratic ideals inherent in that role. This system of accountability is not an appropriate match. He continues, "So, the reason I think this is a fallacious argument is because it is so skill-based that it's not seeing the bigger picture. I think it's a very narrow, shallow sense of what the world is about and what public education is about." (personal interview, December 16, 2004). Even those who did not get as specific as the preceding argument made a broader complaint. "My biggest criticism of NCLB is there is more to a successful school or successful school district than just test scores, and that's all they're really taking into account." (M. Phillips, personal interview, December 21, 2004).

Focusing the accountability on one test was also an issue for many of the leaders. Robin Miller, who has children in the district, wanted to add some realism to the conversation. "Sometimes [students] are just not going to do well. Maybe something's going on at home. Maybe their parents are going though a divorce." (personal interview, December 15, 2004). Even without extenuating circumstances, she laughed at the reliability of testing adolescents with one measure.

An eighth grader? A fourteen year old? Please! You know on a given day that child is any person. Even from morning to night [they can change]. You know an eleventh grader. Think about all the things going on in their life and so to test them, to determine whether they made progress or whether a school district has helped them to get to where they need to be based on one test is really, really narrow-minded, because I don't think you can measure growth on one test. (R. Miller, personal interview, December 15, 2004).

If setting high expectations is more important than standardized growth, then the Director of Curriculum explains another problem of testing students with the same measure.

I think for some kids the tests are easy. I think for some kids, for some special education kids, who have worked real hard to be able to read a page, and now when they sit down and have to read a four-page story, and they break down in tears – I don't think that that is supporting kids the way we want. (D. McLaughlin, personal interview, December 9, 2004).

Thinking about the effects of NCLB on the student level was important to these leaders, and a few of them shared some real struggles. "I want desperately to have kids reach their potential, and for certain kids there is a disconnect between that child's potential and the high stakes test." (S. Wright, personal interview, December 8, 2004). Wright went on to explain that this disconnect becomes difficult when working with students directly.

I believe my role is to be a ceaseless encourager of children. So when something that I do doesn't appear to kids that way, it bothers me. So when I say to a child, 'I know you can write a little bit. I know you're working hard at it. I know this test is going to be hard, and I know you don't want to take it, but you still have to take it' – it really kills me. (personal interview, December 8, 2004).

This tension was particularly strong for him because he worked with so many students who have disabilities.

Look into the face of a kid who completes only six or seven items on the [high school test] and doesn't have a clue as to what the rest of it is about in any meaningful way. They're not feeling competent, and they're stressed out. Then ask yourself, 'What kind of use of this student's time is this? Isn't there a better way to spend this interaction with a student, and are there no other things of value that this child can show in his or her contribution?' I'm talking about a child who may be in a prevocational program where being an effective bagger and sweeper, or maybe a fruit guy, is maybe a satisfactory outcome, or even for that particular child a desirable outcome. (S. Wright, personal interview, December 8, 2004).

And as mentioned in the research, the concern of the tests themselves was an issue. "When you look also at the issue of strict accountability measures through tests, I think you are also setting up lots and lots of problems in terms of the validity and reliability of tests themselves." (S. Green, personal interview, December 16, 2004). This issue was not as prevalent in this group as it was in the research. Perhaps this relates to the perception that the tests in New Jersey are good assessments. The Assistant Superintendent for High Schools explained this commonly held view.

> I think here in New Jersey most of the educators in our community think the standards and the assessments are okay, pretty good, and [they are tests on which] we should have every kid be able to perform. So assuming that you have good standards and good assessments, and you can get past the point that this is hard work, I think that there are districts now that can demonstrate that it can be done. (P. Jennings, personal interview, December 9, 2004).

Whether or not one test can adequately measure learning progress was a concern, but, because there was general agreement from the curriculum leaders that the test is a fairly good measure, there was some tension around the issue.

We Can Do Better

Even though the criticisms abounded, these same educators expressed their comfort with the accountability measures. Phil Jennings, Assistant Superintendent for High Schools, talked of the need for more parent and student accountability. But when asked if he had any mixed feelings about the accountability for schools, he simply said, "No, not at all." (personal interview, December 9, 2004). The Director of Special Education explained how he made sense of it. "I'm not entirely comfortable with the fair application [of accountability measures] to individual cases, but I am very comfortable in that NCLB can be the rising tide that floats all boats – that it will make outcomes better for students over time." (S. Wright, personal interview, December 8, 2004). This comfort level comes with some tension, but, in his case, Wright accepted the pressure openly.

> I don't see how any educator can get up in the morning and look in the mirror and honestly give any kind of self-assessment of what you are going to do that day except to move every child towards a successful outcome. And if you really believe that, then you've got to be of a perspective of almost constantly looking into how can I do this better, and how, as part of a system, can I make this system better at achieving better outcomes for every student? (S. Wright, personal interview, December 8, 2004).

Even though they had some issues with NCLB, the group welcomed the call for more accountability.

> I think [accountability is] great. I do believe that we need to measure ourselves against means other than what we do internally. There has to be some external validation of your work, so I'm all for [the accountability of NCLB], and I think it has probably pushed even good districts to do things faster. (P. Wilson, personal interview, December 9, 2004).

The United States' lack of progress in the international mathematics scene reinforced this support for accountability.

> I think there was an article in the [newspaper] a couple of days ago saying that [the United States was] 18th out of 23 countries [in math achievement], which is still not any better after 20 years. What have we done for 20 years? We better catch up with the rest of the world. (G. Stanley, personal interview, December 17, 2004).

And even if the law is frustrating, there is something about the students that makes these educators accept NCLB. "You look at any child in any classroom, and you want to make sure they get to 100%. So I think that we can always do better." (R. Miller, personal interview, December 15, 2004).

Even when these educators felt that there needed to be "some adjustments in terms of special education children and in terms of ESL students," they still supported the call for accountability. (J. Wilkens, personal interview, December 16, 2004). The Director of Curriculum explained his point of view.

> While I have some problems with the way the accountability measures are structured, I think accountability in general, in something like NCLB, truly makes sense for public education. That is, if we are going to be the great equalizer, then getting every kid to 100% in math and language arts is a great first step for that. (D. McLaughlin, personal interview, December 9, 2004).

Every member was not ready to exclude special education from this accountability. The following passage exemplifies how an educator can be torn. Sam Wright, who oversees special education, considers some of the problems of individualizing the accountability.

> I'm referring to special education students who have exposure to the regular curriculum, but also have either physical or intellectual challenges that we currently don't have tools to address those needs to the level at which children will be highly proficient. We need to be very careful so as not to create yet another underclass of children who are exposed to rich curriculum but have not mastered it and [because of that] face some kind of penalty down the road by not being able to gain a diploma. Or I guess, depending upon in which state you live, being denied the diploma based on their disability – or having to receive some sort of diploma that is marked as somehow inferior. I think there are some bright light school districts out there that are showing us the way that even kids with challenging disabilities can, in fact, master difficult curriculum. (personal interview, December 8, 2004).

Clearly, for educators to accept the challenge of universal proficiency they will need models.

> One shining example is a district in New York State that has remarkably turned around the achievement levels of students with disabilities. As those districts publish their results and their efforts to move toward more staff training, and basically the will to do it – as that information becomes more wide-

ly available – I will be a little more at ease as an educator that we, too, can move in that direction. (S. Wright, personal interview, December 8, 2004).

Not In My Back Yard

While the acceptance of accountability ran through most responses, there were some, such as the Superintendent, who thought the federal government should not get involved. "It's a conflict of interest between states' rights and the federal government which has led us to many, many issues." (S. Green, personal interview, December 16, 2004). Phil Jennings, Assistant Superintendent for High Schools, who had previously voiced complete support of the accountability measures, struggled with the federal nature of the law.

> I think it's very troublesome when some leaders from Washington want to throw into the mix all kinds of other possibilities, like charter schools and religious schools, that consume public funding, because, every time you do that, it just takes away from a social experiment that still needs to be fixed a lot, but is probably better than in most parts of the world. (personal interview, December 9, 2004).

Carol Martin, Public Information Officer, agreed there were a lot of good things in public education, so the necessity of the legislation was not clear to her.

> [If I worked in] a state or a district where they weren't doing such a good job – one in which I didn't feel students were being prepared for the future, then I could see the value of [NCLB] . . . I just feel like, in our district, it's not something that we need to mandate. I think we have paid attention to these things all along. (personal interview, December 9, 2004).

This leadership team honestly struggled with the philosophical and practical aspects of NCLB. The positives and negatives are summarized in Table 1 below.

Table 1

Findings
Mixed Feelings about NCLB

Positives	Negatives
• Accountability is a good thing	• Waste of time and money
• Moved forward important initiatives	• Focus on sanctions
• Math and LA are critical	• Single measure
• Tests are pretty good	• Test reliability
• Raises expectations	• Focus only on Math & LA
• Morally right	• Students with disabilities
	• States' rights issues

Leaders must face these tensions each and every day as they try to lead their districts, always asking what is best for the students. Personal philosophy is only a part of the issue, and in the next section I will explore the additional pressures of NCLB on these local leaders.

Additional Pressure

After examining the extent to which the ideals of these leaders' beliefs about the purpose of public education mesh with the perceived ideal of NCLB, it is important to study the forces that affect the decisions of local leaders beyond those that emanate from a belief system. When considering these decisions, it is important to understand how these leaders perceive and think about the pressures associated with NCLB. This team discussed the various sources of this pressure and gave insight as to whether these pressures were actual or perceived. The Superintendent offered a candid statement on this issue.

> I think we feel a lot of pressures. You know we might pay some lip service and say [publicly] that we're not doing this because of NCLB, but, you know, to have one of our schools not make adequate yearly progress and face potential sanctions – I don't want that as a public school superintendent. (S. Green, personal interview, December 16, 2004).

The sanctions of NCLB were considered to be more of a perceived pressure by many, including the Superintendent. "[The pressures are] more perceived. Nobody is going to come in and smack our hands, and we're going to get very few people moving out of those schools taking advantage of the [school choice] sanctions. So, that's not real pressure." (S. Green, personal interview, December 9, 2004). The Director of Curriculum thought this thinking held true with the community as well.

> I have very few people knocking at my door saying that there is anything wrong, so a lot of it is perceived or internal pressure. You know, no one [from the state] is coming to take over our schools. No one is coming to shake up our district. We are the last person on their list. (personal interview, December 9, 2004).

He admitted that even though the official sanctions were not an issue, the public nature of NCLB caused some anxiety. "I don't like when our schools are labeled as failing in the newspaper. I do feel that pressure. I do have to defend that our schools are really indeed good schools." (personal interview, December 9, 2004).

A few of the leaders described the pressure in a positive context. Phil Jennings, the Assistant Superintendent for High Schools, noted, "So far it's been an enjoyable pressure. I mean if [the thinking behind NCLB] is something you embrace and believe in, then it really provides a mechanism to get this message out" (personal interview, December 9, 2004). Sam Wright agreed, but thought the pressure had some costs associated with it. "It's pressure that I crave, while simultaneously raising your blood pressure. You want the pressure of innovation. You want the pressure that it's never good enough." (personal interview, December 8, 2004).

Clearly, NCLB was causing pressure, but from where it was emanating was still elusive. "I don't feel pressure from the federal government or state government at this point, because I think our curve is further along than even the legislation is." (P. Jennings, personal interview, December 9, 2004). For most of these leaders, including the Director of Curriculum, the pressure was self-imposed.

When I see groups of African-American students doing significantly worse than white students, that's an issue for me. And I'm in a position to change that. I feel a lot of pressure with that, not because it would be in the paper, but, ethically, I have an issue with that. (D. McLaughlin, personal interview, December 9, 2004).

Phil Jennings thought of NCLB as he would with any challenge.

For me personally, it's a lot of self-imposed pressure. If [I am going] to do something, I want to do it well. I don't like to do something that's not done well. So, if you embrace the concept [of NLCB], you want to do the best work that you can. (personal interview, December 9, 2004).

The various sources of pressure were narrowed down to the ultimate focus of what is best for students.

I'm not the kind of person who would even want to deceive my boss with goals that aren't rigorous, so I think when I set a goal, it's a goal that's barely achievable because you want to challenge yourself, and hopefully you will do that because it benefits students. (S. Wright, personal interview, December 8, 2004).

The following summary statement by the Director of Curriculum truly encompassed both the range of pressures the group felt as well as the general sentiment.

I feel a lot of internal pressures. I do think that math and language arts tests that we give are pretty good tests, so I feel pressure for those kids to succeed. I feel pressure from the community that the parents want our kids to succeed. I feel pressure that I want to do better than the surrounding districts to show that we are the best. There is a competitive side of me that we can do a better job with public education. I feel pressure with providing kids the tools, so that when they sit for this test that they are comfortably prepared, that they feel we have given our client their money's worth, so to speak. I feel pressure from my Superintendent. He wants nothing more than to have 100% of these kids succeed. I feel internal pressure. I really feel that this is doable, and if we are going to do it – if someone is going to get to one hundred percent, it's going to be us. (D. McLaughlin, personal interview, December 9, 2004).

Even though these leaders did not feel most of their pressure from the legislation itself, the internal pressures from within the district and the self-imposed pressures certainly have affected them. NCLB is clearly impacting the decisions of these leaders. How these leaders, all struggling individually with the philosophy, come together as a team to implement the law, philosophically and practically, will be the focus of the next section.

Making Changes Independent of NCLB

My research questions focused on the changes that educational leaders make because of the accountability provisions of the NCLB legislation and the tensions inherent in these decisions. In order to bring depth and focus to this study, I decided to conduct a few preliminary interviews with representatives from the study group to identify the most salient changes this district has made in response to NCLB. It is important to distinguish between those changes made in response to the law and the changes that would have naturally occurred in the district.

When considering the range of initiatives the district has put forth to achieve 100% proficiency, leaders felt confident that they were already on the same path as NCLB. "I am inclined to think that all of [the changes we have made] would have happened anyway in this district. We are a district that is committed to continuous improvement for every child. I am not even sure that NCLB accelerated it." (C. Martin, personal interview, September 23, 2004). The Assistant Superintendent for High Schools pointed to similar initiatives that started prior to the legislation's inception, such as student focus groups.

> We had student focus groups prior to NCLB. They began as senior exit interviews with groups of seniors about what was working really well in our high schools and what needed improvement. I think we have expanded those to include more diverse groups of students in the high schools as well as middle school students. I think that was well underway prior to NCLB. (P. Jennings, personal interview, September 22, 2004).

Even the way the district looked at data has not changed. "We started disaggregating data before NCLB." (R. Miller, personal interview, September 24, 2004). The members of the Superintendent's Council saw influences other than federal legislation that affected local policy. The Assistant Superintendent for Middle Schools explained that perhaps the greatest influence was the Superintendent himself.

> I think you know he is very directive. He *will* drill down right to the school level, whereas some superintendents won't make a change in a high school. That's the way he leads. But that does go through Superintendent's Council, where people like the Director of Curriculum or Assistant Superintendents offer suggestions, but I believe if he has an idea of how he wants something attacked, he may listen to input, but I don't think that ever

alters his decision much. It may be shaped somewhat, but I think many times it's very directive. (P. Wilson, personal interview, September 15, 2004).

This strong leadership, however, was focused in what the study group felt was the right direction. "I think we are a district that has focused on continuous improvement and focused on individual students – helping them succeed – and I think everything that we have done since [this Superintendent arrived]…has led us in this same direction." (C. Martin, personal interview, September 23, 2004). It is this focus, the Assistant Superintendent for High Schools explained, that has led the district to make necessary changes.

> I think that the philosophy in our district that all students deserve a preeminent education came long before the pressures of NCLB. They fit nicely together, which was good for us, but I think our philosophy was in place before the federal government said, "This is what you need to do and here are your accountabilities" (P. Jennings, personal interview, September 22, 2004).

One of the district initiatives was to create a more diverse teaching staff, but again, NCLB was not the largest influence.

> There are probably nine or 10 legislations that can drive or push this, but certainly NCLB had some influence with the idea that a diverse teaching force is needed to be successful with student populations. In terms of the other things that we know that drive student achievement – attachment, feeling of isolation, and hopelessness – from what we have learned from student interviews, and what the minority achievement council has told us in meetings, having more minority teachers would be very helpful as long as they are appropriately qualified to teach to high standards as well as everybody else. (S. Wright, personal interview, September 22, 2004).

Some of these outside influences have made their impact, but the Assistant Superintendent for High Schools does credit NCLB for adding urgency.

> We have a very politically astute black community in Central Valley, and they keep some of those issues on the front burner for us, but, in terms of accountability which has driven a lot of our behaviors, I think without NCLB it wouldn't have happened so quickly or with such fervor. (P. Jennings, personal interview, September 22, 2004).

When the members of the study group were pushed to consider whether or not each initiative was a result of the pressures of NCLB, they held to their convictions. The common theme was that NCLB simply accelerated some changes. "Probably NCLB has served more as a catalyst for some of these issues as opposed to a progenitor for them. It might have speeded some things up that might have happened anyway. It just compressed the time." (P. Jennings, personal interview, September 22, 2004). "We would have gotten to [these changes]. Not at the same rate probably, but the changing demographics of our community would have forced us to examine these issues." (S. Wright, personal interview, September 27, 2004).

NCLB's Influence

Many of the district's initiatives were independent of NCLB, but three stood out as being either directly related to or greatly influenced by NCLB. The district first created "Six-Year Benchmarks" in order to accelerate progress toward the goal of 100% proficiency, and then tied student performance on these benchmarks directly to administrators' pay. In addition to these two, the initiative that caused the most conversation was "The Intervention," an eight-week intensive program providing extra support in math and language arts to students in grades 3, 4, 8, and 11 in the weeks preceding the state assessments.

The preliminary interviews helped to narrow the focus of the study and already revealed some tensions as to the role of NCLB in the decision-making process. While there were strong, consistent arguments that the district would have implemented many of these initiatives regardless of federal policy, there was ample evidence that the participants felt NCLB brought a greater urgency to their work. The specificity of the six-year benchmarks, the pressures of the performance pay, and the quick implementation of the "intervention" program all demonstrate NCLB's influence even in a district that aligns itself philosophically with the legislation.

A second, more thorough round of interviews explored these initiatives in order to inquire as to whether or not educational leaders believed that these are the types of changes we want for our students. We discussed the genesis of these initiatives, the decision-making process, the initial debates, the perceived effects of these changes, as well as any unresolved issues. Throughout these discussions, administrators honestly revealed their convictions and tensions around the changes they had made.

Six-Year Benchmarks

The first of the three initiatives I will explore in depth is the district's plan to speed up the federal accountability. While the federal legislation designed its accountability with the requirement of having 100% of students reach proficiency by 2012, this school district decided, in 2002, to adopt six-year benchmarks to reach 100% by the 2008-09 school year. The formula behind it is quite simple. After a "planning year" for which the target stays the same, there is a "five-year linear approach.... It's wherever [your current achievement level] is minus 100 divided by 5. That was your AYP." (P. Jennings, personal interview, December 9, 2004). Phil Jennings, Assistant Superintendent for High Schools, who came up with the idea, provided a sample scenario. "If 30% of your students were at the partially proficient stage this year, it's going to be 5% fewer next year and 5% fewer the year after until you get to all kids proficient." (personal interview, December 9, 2004).

Most of these leaders thought the six-year benchmarks were greatly influenced by NCLB, but the Assistant Superintendent for Middle Schools explained the district would have implemented accountability to test scores regardless of the law. "We would have created benchmarks anyway. I believe that about this district. We have always been pretty accountable." (P. Wilson, personal interview, September 15, 2004). This more aggressive timeline demonstrates that internal pressures may be stronger than those emanating from federal and state policies.

The general consensus of the group was that the specific six-year benchmarks may not have come into place so quickly if it were not for NCLB, but there definitely would have been some sort of direct accountability for standardized test scores. "Unless there is urgency about the outcomes, change doesn't happen anywhere near as quickly." (S. Wright, personal interview, September 27, 2004). Wright acknowledged that the public nature of NCLB reporting did cause some urgency. "I think that when people believe that their school district is a fine school district, and you see that slipping away by any measure, then the caring, intelligent professional says we have got to have more urgency about this." (personal interview, September 27, 2004). Carol Martin explained the benefits of this urgency at the classroom level.

> I still think that there are probably teachers out there that don't believe that every child can achieve and don't believe that is their role to support every kid. They would rather see a kid drop out of their honors level class than to try and make them succeed in it. That is the challenge...that challenge was there before...this accountability crystallizes it. (personal interview, September 23, 2004).

The philosophy of the district and that of the law seem to be closely married in many ways.

Purpose

The idea of the six-year benchmarks came to Phil Jennings as he was talking with some administrators about student achievement and NCLB. "It just so happened that the few of us who were talking were all of a maturity level that none of us thought we'd be around in 2014, so we began thinking, 'Wouldn't it be nice to accomplish this within our lifetime, or at least our careers.'" (personal interview, December 9, 2004)?

There were other reasons why the district decided to move in this direction, besides the fact that everyone would be retired by 2014. The main reason was described by the Superintendent. "We don't believe in discarded kids, we're not going to [reach 100% proficiency] tomorrow perhaps, but we are going to make a commitment to do it faster." (S. Green, personal interview, December 16, 2004). Wilson explains that it is a tough concept against which to argue. "How can you look at these kids and say you're not going to be proficient until 2014." (P. Wilson, personal interview, December 9, 2004).

Secondary reasons for implementation of this initiative were specific to the district. The Director of Curriculum noted that many of the scores were already high. "I think some of our schools were easily going to make the NCLB benchmarks, so what accountability do they have? So, this was a way to get a greater accountability for [those schools]." (D. McLaughlin, personal interview, December 9, 2004). The Assistant Superintendent for Elementary Schools said another factor was the district's relatively low mobility rate.

> In districts where the student population is pretty stable, I think it makes sense [to speed up the timetable], because if you know you have a history of kids who are in the same buildings for four to five years, then the cohorts are pretty much the same because it's the same teachers going though the same process – the same curriculum. You kind of know the kids are moving the way they should. So, in Central Valley it probably makes sense, but in most districts it doesn't. (M. Phillips, personal interview, December 21, 2004).

The Director of Curriculum thought the six-year benchmarks took on a more symbolic importance, one that needed to be shared with other districts.

> I think that there is a message that it sends, that regardless of whether or not we think we could get there in five or six years, the fact that we *say* we are going to do it sets a high expectation. And we'd rather have said it and push for it and not get there than to have never have pushed for it in the first place. So, I think there is a strategic side of things where we say we are going to do it. I think it sends a message not only to our district, but to every other district that hears of this that, 'We're doing this. Embrace this law. Embrace the spirit of this law, and let's meet it. Let's do something right for all kids.' (D. McLaughlin, personal interview, December 9, 2004).

Almost everyone liked the "optimism" of the plan. "The fact that we have adopted targets, six-year benchmarks, I think it is a credit to the district that we didn't take the 14-year route, and we took the six-year route." (S. Wright, personal interview, December 8, 2004).

Decision-Making Process and Early Debates

When examining the decision-making process, it was evident that the benchmarks caught on quickly. "When you work with a boss like our boss, you should never say you can do it in less time because that becomes your new parameter." (S. Wright, personal interview, December 8, 2004). Jason Wilkens, one of the Assistant Superintendents for Elementary Schools, added, "He's a very impatient man, and he's impatient because he thinks it's the morally right thing to do." (personal interview, December 16, 2004). Before it was implemented, Phil Jennings, the Assistant Superintendent for High Schools, worked with the principals first, but as he explained, there was not a lot of debate.

> There were those dissenters at first, and of course part of the issue of NCLB is you are testing a new group of kids [each year], and it's not truly value-added and all that kind of stuff. But once we got beyond that – because a test is what it is – we decided that if it could happen, it could happen in a district like Central Valley. We were going to hold our own feet to the fire and agree that we were going to do this in six years. (P. Jennings, personal interview, December 9, 2004).

The Superintendent thought the principals did not take the issue that seriously at first.

> [The principals were] having lots of conversations with [Phil], and they were all kind of passive about it, and I wonder at the time whether they were thinking . . .'This too shall pass. This is no big deal' because they were new to NCLB, and a lot of them weren't reacting the way they should have to the test data itself, and they weren't using it well. So, they didn't react at the time, and now [the benchmarks have] become a part of our district, and we're not going to back off it. (S. Green, personal interview, December 16, 2004).

The Director of Special Education remembers the genesis of this concept. "That was the defining moment when we all decided, yes, we are going to try to do this – this noble task, this essential task, the kind of task that we were sort of born and bred for. This is the mission we were going to undertake." (S. Wright, personal interview, December 8, 2004).

Not all of the conversations around the six-year benchmarks were as inspired, and, even though principals were involved, there were other points of view the group did not think were considered. The same people who provided the rationale for doing this initiative also had some concerns – the first of which was that the district jumped at this idea without any thoughtful planning. Pat Wilson explained, "My concerns [are] that we have not laid out clear plans to support the district to get there in six years." (personal interview, December 9, 2004). In fact, if teachers had been involved in the decision-making process, she thought they would have made some good contributions.

I think they would have said, 'We see where you're coming from. We believe that every kid coming out of school should be proficient, but here's the reality of where we are.' I just think they would have hoped for more vision of how they are supposed to get there with the teachers that they have and the resources that they have. (personal interview, December 9, 2004).

The Assistant to the Superintendent was growing tired of all the negative talk, especially from teacher unions, and did not feel they needed to be consulted.

> When they talk about No Child Left Behind, it's not about students and getting students there, it's about 'Let's blame it on the teachers.' 'We can't do this' and all the reasons why they can't do it. I'd like to see something on their agenda that says reasons why they can do it and what supports they need. (R. Miller, personal interview, December 15, 2004).

The Assistant Superintendent for Middle Schools thought seeking more input would have been valuable.

> We should [get to 100% proficiency] as fast as possible, but often when these decisions are made the people that make them haven't really walked in principal's shoes every day [for a while], so I don't know if they understand the implementation issues behind these grandiose ideas. (P. Wilson, personal interview, December 9, 2004).

She thought other background work was needed and that this issue was not thought out sufficiently.

> There isn't a huge staff development plan of how they will help teachers with pedagogy. Those pieces are not clear to people – 'How are you going to help me get there by 2009?' There is no clear road map; the only clear road map is that you just need to be 100%. (personal interview, December 9, 2004).

There was also some criticism as to the arbitrary nature of the six-year plan. "It really wasn't a scientific process that started this conversation." (S. Wright, personal interview, December 8, 2004). The Director of Curriculum had some concerns about the simplistic structure of the six-year plan.

> Statistically, this is just goofy. The fact that we were just taking the number they are at now and dividing by five – it just sounds so intuitive, but statistically I don't know if student growth works that way. They are different cohorts of kids. I don't know if it has any statistical responsibility. So the arbitrary nature of it was a real issue for me. Why five years? Why does it have to be linear? I don't think it *would* be linear. I think it would be some other kind of step function. It would have to be more complicated than the way we're seeing it. (D. McLaughlin, personal interview, December 9, 2004).

He went on to say that someone who knew "something about statistical growth should be involved." (personal interview, December 9, 2004). Again, there was some tension around process.

> There are people that can add to this conversation that we need to listen to. I know enough to say that I don't know enough about this, or at least I want to find out more about it before I make a decision like this. And we hadn't done that, so I had a real issue about it. We needed to talk to other people that could ask us questions to see if we thought through these things. (D. McLaughlin, personal interview, December 9, 2004).

On this issue, there was a good amount of tension among the administrators, some of whom ultimately agreed with the premise of the six-year plan.

> I don't think there was room for debate. We were told to do it and no one would argue with [the Superintendent] because really, he's right. We should be doing everything we can for kids. We would have just liked to have had the conversation in September and had some time to prepare something. (P. Wilson, personal interview, December 9, 2004).

The Director of Curriculum talked about a different, more personal tension. He explained his mental struggle in the following passage.

> I mean, publicly, I feel more comfortable about [the six-year benchmarks], but privately I am just concerned about our long-term sustainability and the amount of thoughtfulness we put into things . . . I had a real problem with it from the beginning. I don't know; now I question whether or not I sup-

port it, because I guess the tension I have is that sustainability issue. This puts us even more into that short-term mode, and it's an honest tension because I do see the good sides of it. I see the reasoning for high expectations, but I just don't see – maybe it's because I haven't seen it work before. Maybe we *can* do education like no one else has. I try to be open-minded to it. It just seems like we're putting way too much pressure on one test, and we're not giving thought [to the long term] – we're less likely to adopt things that will take time to do well (D. McLaughlin, personal interview, December 9, 2004).

When others were asked what they thought of the six-year plan, the group was divided. Several members thought it would be difficult because of the staff turnover. The Director of Human Resources said, "I'm probably not a great supporter of it. I think that it's stressful. I think it's great to want to be better earlier, but I don't know that its practical, especially because of the staff that we have that are so new and are adjusting." (K. Davis, personal interview, December 8, 2004). Pat Wilson agreed that the amount of new staff would make it challenging.

[It will be difficult] with new alternate route teachers who have never taught a day in their lives – with 50% of our work force non-tenured. Of our 1,000 teachers, almost 500 are non-tenured. These are huge implications of how much more difficult the work is going to be with a work force in that situation. Often we don't factor in all that when making decisions. (personal interview, December 9, 2004).

Alex Walker, Assistant to the Superintendent, who did not feel a part of the decision-making process, said jokingly, "I think you're nuts." (personal interview, December 16, 2004). He laughed and went on to explain his real concern.

No, that's not fair . . . I just think 100% is aggressive. I think it's good to set the bar high, but I think you have to balance out setting the bar high and what that does to your organization. How much does it stress out your organization. (personal interview, December 16, 2004)?

Three members mentioned that, privately, they did not think it was realistic to reach 100% proficiency. "I don't know how you could ever hit 100%. I just don't know how you're ever going to consistently hit 100%. I think it's great to shoot for that. Is it realistic? Probably not." (K. Davis, personal interview, December 8, 2004). Alex Walker just thought the field of education was too imprecise. "This isn't like a manufacturing plant where you can make 100% perfect widgets and, you know, tweak the manufacturing, and they come out to 100%." (personal interview, December 16, 2004). As with almost all the issues, these administrators struggled with their beliefs. "I think it's unrealistic. I think it's an admirable goal. I think I should live every day hoping I can get 100% of my kids. I would have no difficulty just following the federal legislation, though." (P. Wilson, personal interview, December 9, 2004).

The Superintendent, on the other hand, did not think the plan was too aggressive.

In six years, we should be able to put some immediate programs in place.

That is kind of saying, you know, you are discarding all the kids in grades 12, 11, 10, 9, 8, 7, 6, 5, 4 all the way down because you don't have sufficient time to work with them. I think six years is sufficient time to work with them and make a difference, or it's never going to work. I'm okay with it. (S. Green, personal interview, December 16, 2004).

So, after a quick review with the principals, this initiative was implemented, and many of the mixed feelings noted above were never uncovered, for there was very little formalized debate. A summary of these mixed feelings is listed below in Table 2. The impact of this initiative is the focus of the next section, as I sought to uncover the perceived effects of the six-year benchmarks.

Table 2

Six Year Benchmarks

Positives	Negatives
• Demonstrates commitment and leadership	• Lack of a support plan
• Good public statement	• Statisically unsophisticated
• Raises expectations	• Lack of capacity to implement
• Focuses on immediate improvements for students	• Overstressed organization
	• 100% unrealistic

Effects

Even with all the discussion mentioned heretofore, the six-year plan is not perceived as having any dramatic effect on the district. In fact, when coding the data, no distinct themes emerged. This situation is perhaps an area for further study, for the effects of the six-year benchmarks may be felt more strongly at the building level.

When I asked these leaders about the effects of these benchmarks, there were a few interesting findings. The Director of Special Education did make a comment of note that demonstrates, in his mind, it is important to keep sending the message that the goal is 100% proficiency because not everyone has gotten the message yet.

I think [universal proficiency] is possible, but I don't think the rank and file in our district thinks it's possible. My evidence for that is that they keep asking the wrong questions. Rather than framing questions like, 'I'm not getting through to my kids certain concepts' or 'I'm having difficulty in presenting or teaching this, and I'd like some help with it.' The questions I get are, 'Well, how many special ed. kids are allowed in my class anyway?' 'Do we have a compliance violation?' Although you patiently answer those because there are real compliance issues around the district, it's deeply disappointing that the questions aren't asked about learning. They're always asked about process and procedure, and they're the wrong questions. So we have a long way to go. (personal interview, December 8, 2004).

The Assistant Superintendent for High Schools explained that other school districts did not embrace this accountability either.

We have been asked to both personally and collectively present our plans at a number of state forums, and they have been well received, although when you begin talking about the fact that NCLB is not such a bad thing and how we go for six years rather than 14 years, you see people's eyes start to glaze over a little. A lot of people are still of the opinion that this is still going to go away if they wait long enough (P. Jennings, personal interview, December 9, 2004).

I will conclude this section by mentioning one other quotation, for in the end many of the tensions people had with the details have been reconciled with the larger ideal behind the six-year benchmarks.

I think it's a great thing to say to our community – we're not going to wait for kids to achieve. I think it's a great thing to say to other school districts that we're not going to wait for kids to achieve, and all of your griping – we don't want to hear it. We're going to do something different. We are going to do something better. I think it's a great leadership stance for us to take, and so other districts look at us like we're crazy. I'm really comfortable with that. I'm real comfortable saying we're going to do something better for kids. I don't know if we are going to get there. I hope we do and that gets down to some of the details of the law that probably aren't that important, but I think the idea that we are going to try to get there is a really admirable thing, and I think it says something positive to the community as a whole. (D. McLaughlin, personal interview, December 16, 2004).

Key Performance Areas (KPAs)

The second major initiative I explored relates directly to the first. The Central Valley Administrators and Supervisors Association has a current bargaining agreement that includes a three-tier compensation plan. The first tier is connected to satisfactory performance, and the third tier is tied to the board achieving its goals. Both of those percentages are small, so the bulk of an administrator's raise each year is based on the KPA described in the second tier. These individually designed performance objectives have now, in part, been tied directly with the performance of the students in their building on state tests. The six-year benchmarks are used to determine whether an administrator receives a certain percentage increase. This accountability system has been in place for five years now, but it was only last year when a portion of the KPAs were tied directly to performance on state tests. This was the same year the "Intervention" and the six-year benchmarks were implemented.

The question remains whether or not the connection between the administrators' and state test scores was a function of the pressures of the legislation. The Assistant Superintendent for High Schools explained the influences he sees. "The Superintendent has always been pushing for highly measurable quantitative KPAs or goals for people, and the principals have been pushing back just as hard for softer things that are more easily achievable." (P. Jennings, personal interview, December 9, 2004). The Superintendent was very clear on this issue and was adamant that NCLB was not the influence behind this initiative. The other leaders saw the connection of state test scores and salary as a direct result of NCLB, but the Superintendent disagreed. "No, that's not true, that's just not a good perspective." (personal interview, December 16, 2004). He provided several confidential examples, which covered over the last five years, of administrators who faced serious consequences because of poor performance on state assessments.

Purpose

This leadership team agreed that tying administrators' pay to student achievement was a great public statement for the district to make. "Tying a portion of people's KPAs to those goals was a way to say upper management and middle management are so committed to this that we are going to put real dollars behind it that has an accountability cost to it if we don't perform." (S. Wright, personal interview, December 8, 2004). The purpose was obvious for these leaders.

Decision-Making Process and Early Debates

There was some initial debate around the fairness of tying test scores to salaries.

> I think [the principals'] argument is, 'Do we as principals truly control how well kids do on a test . . . The clear answer is we don't have complete control, but we do have an awful lot of influence.' We listened to them and actually divided their performance compensation into two general areas. One dealt with the plan that they brought forward [to improve student achievement] and the implementation of that plan, and the second piece, which was a smaller piece, dealt with the actual test results. (P. Jennings, personal interview, December 9, 2004).

Unlike the other initiatives, the principals had more influence on the substance of this change. The Director of Curriculum discussed the result of that fact. "We kind of watered it down." (D. McLaughlin, personal interview, December 9, 2004). Even though the correlation of performance pay to test scores is not as strong as most central office leaders would like, they still see it as a step toward greater accountability for student achievement. "I think we're one of two districts in the state that have a performance compensation plan for administrators, so just talking about that is difficult." (P. Jennings, personal interview, December 9, 2004). Jennings went on to explain that it is more of an incentive system than a penalty. "Because of the way we have allocated resources to this, we have set up a scenario where a principal can make a lot of money if their performance is good . . . .We have come up with some rather creative ways of doing this so that people don't get killed in terms of their salary, and there is still that measurable accountability." (personal interview, December 9, 2004).

Even though there was unanimous support for this initiative, there was still tension in the minds of a few of these leaders. There were concerns over the potential negative effects at the building level.

> I think it's a fine line, because do we want an administrator in there teaching kids and leading the educational program that the kids will benefit from all around? Or building an education program only on the idea that students need to pass the test so that the principals can get their 2% salary increase. (A. Walker, personal interview, December 9, 2004)?

As with the six-year benchmarks, there was very little debate among the central office leaders. One difference, though, is the more perceived effects on the school district.

Effects

Several leaders acknowledged they knew that principals were "pretty aggressive with the teachers in the testing grades." (K. Davis, personal interview, December 8, 2004). The Director of Curriculum said, "The tension I'm uncomfortable with is when it gets down to the teacher or student level. I hear about one school abandoning the curriculum to do test prep. That's the kind of stuff that drives me nuts." (D. McLaughlin, personal interview, December 9, 2004). He offered a suggestion to reduce this negative approach.

> I think if we were reasonable, saying that some changes that we were implementing would take some time to see results – I think that if *any* of that language came forth from central office it would ease some pressure on the teachers and administration. They'd feel better about it. But because we want to implement these huge things and keep thinking short term, this is causing some tension for people. (D. McLaughlin, personal interview, December 9, 2004).

Tying performance pay to the six-year benchmarks has put more pressure on schools to meet the adequate yearly benchmarks. "It is one thing to read the newspaper that your school is in need of improvement because you didn't quite make the AYP. Okay, we will go on with business. It is quite another to have that tied to a salary increase every year. It is very personal for people." (P. Jennings, personal interview, December 9, 2004). Most of the leadership team, including the Assistant Superintendent for High Schools, saw the significance of this change more in its symbolism than its actual impact.

> Most people will offer an opinion that it is not about the money. For most of our administrators I think that it's, "Did I do a good job?' Sometimes that's measured by the amount of money you received. So, you know, whether a couple hundred dollars changes your lifestyle – it doesn't. Everybody wants to be [the best]. We have a group of administrators who want to work real hard and want to be acknowledged by their supervisors that they've done a great,

terrific job. And when you deal with measurable data, it does have a tendency sometimes to take everybody from the category of ten [on a scale of one to ten] and put them along a continuum. And that's difficult for some of our administrators and our administrator association to deal with. (P. Jennings, personal interview, December 9, 2004).

The Director of Curriculum explained that this situation has caused some tension between the administrator's association and central office. "I think the bitterness, in general, is that our administrators work hard. They take a lot of pride in what they do, and they don't like being told at the end of the year that they are getting points taken off." (D. McLaughlin, personal interview, December 9, 2004). He explained some of this tension, comparing the KPAs to NCLB.

I think that [the KPAs] really cause some tension [between principals and central office], and it really makes them think that all we care about are numbers and not qualitative results or whole child kind of stuff. I think we're constantly being defensive, but I think it's a real easy defense, in that we want all kids to achieve. And so when you go to the heart of what NCLB says, the rhetoric of it, you can't argue it. Because if you argue it, then tell me which three kids you want to leave behind. Tell me their names. No one wants to tell you that. So you almost don't have to defend it because it is what it is. You have to defend the details; just like the No Child Left Behind legislation has to defend its details. (D. McLaughlin, personal interview, December 9, 2004).

In many of these leaders' minds, this perceived tension may just be grandstanding on the part of the administrator association.

I think we may be pushing to the point where they don't approve a performance contract next time. They'd be silly not to. They get so much more money now. Rather than getting a 3% to 4% raise each year, they have a chance to get 7% or 8%. It's almost double, so it's in their best interest to keep this going. (D. McLaughlin, personal interview, December 9, 2004).

Even if the administrators may not like this increased accountability, the concept of performance pay plays well with many members of the community. Robin Miller, the Assistant to the Superintendent, who works closely with the community, explained, "You have to understand, I come from the corporate world, and I come from the sales environment where your performance was tied to your pay. So, I would like to see [performance pay] district-wide." (personal interview, December 15, 2004). Every one of the administrators was ultimately "comfortable with the KPAs," with the Assistant Superintendent for Elementary Schools adding, "I long for the day that we can tie teacher accountability to tests." (personal interview, December 16, 2004).

A summary of the leaders' thoughts about the KPAs are listed below in Table 3.

Table 3

KPAs and Test Scores

Positives

- Focuses on immediate improvement for students
- Unanimous support from Central Office
- Adds real accountability

Negatives

- Watered down
- Perception that principals were aggressive with teachers in testing grades
- Lack of support for long term initiatives
- Test prep
- Tension with Administrator Association

The six-year benchmarks and the performance pay that accompanies them have generated some reflection, debate, and tension, but, clearly, the initiative that has generated the most discussion is the "Intervention." In the next section, I will explore this initiative, which differs from the first two in many ways. Its decision-making process was more controversial, the debates were more intense, and the effects on the district were more dramatic.

The "Intervention"

The agreement was before we left for winter break that we would have an intervention program in place for hundreds and hundreds of kids throughout the district, and if it meant that students would not be in phys. ed. or an elective or whatever the case may be, we were going to do whatever it took, and we were going to provide resources to give every kid an opportunity to do well on this test. (P. Jennings, personal interview, December 9, 2004).

In December of 2003, plans were created for an eight-week intensive intervention for students who were at risk for not passing the math and/or language arts sections of the upcoming state assessments. In the preliminary interviews, many participants identified this move as a response to the pressures of NCLB. In order to understand the law's true effect, it is not only important to examine what this leadership team did, but why they did it, how they did it, and what the effects were.

Purpose: Why was it done?

The primary reason given for creating this intensive intervention program was that "kids were not achieving at the levels they should have been based on benchmarks the Superintendent had in his mind or the district had laid out. Indicators at that point in time in December said that they wouldn't be successful on a high stakes, very public test in March." (P. Wilson, personal interview, December 9, 2004). The Director of Curriculum was in on the conversation from the beginning and recalled how it evolved.

> That started one afternoon last December when the Superintendent asked two or three of us, 'Have we done everything we can to make sure that kids are going to pass these state tests?' Of course, the answer was no. You can always do more; and so that started an avalanche, which very quickly meant serious pull-out support during the day for math and language arts for our kids 6-12. It also meant schools changing what they do for K-5; but because our scores were pretty good there, we didn't think we were in as much trouble there, but in middle school and high school we were real worried that the long-term changes we made weren't going to have as much impact on the test. And we were pretty sure that a lot of kids weren't going to pass [the tests], and so if we were sure, basically, we came to the conclusion that we needed to do everything we could to make sure that the day after this test, we were out of breath, and we could look at ourselves in the mirror and say we did everything we could for these kids. (D. McLaughlin, personal interview, December 9, 2004).

He explained that the early conversation focused on the data.

> We weren't getting results from the [building] staff saying 100% of the kids were meeting [the standard] – that we are going to blow away these tests. We weren't getting that feeling from the buildings, and I don't even know if we believed that ourselves. Maybe we knew that some kids weren't going to make it, so maybe we knew internally that we weren't doing everything we could. (D. McLaughlin, personal interview, December 9, 2004).

The Superintendent's Perspective

When discussing the "Intervention" program, each of the members of Superintendent's Council mentioned the powerful impact of the Superintendent. When asked why the "Intervention" was implemented, the Superintendent had a much lengthier and sophisticated set of reasons. There were several conditions building up that led to this decision in his mind.

> I had seen some lack of energy and some flattening of scores coming into that school year. . . .There was a real heightened anxiety in my mind about how well we were doing as a district, because, here we are, Central Valley, spattering off all this stuff about 'all kids,' and when it came down to it, our scores weren't good – forget about NCLB. (personal interview, December 16, 2004).

In fact, the Superintendent felt this "problem" was less about NCLB and more about "our own history and our belief system and our own commitment" (S. Green, personal interview, December 16, 2004).

The second factor, according to the Superintendent, had to do with the fact that the district was undergoing some changes. "There was some staff turnover which included some principals and some Assistant Superintendents who were new to their positions, and, therefore, I think there was some slippage in terms of our attention to move the program and the details of the accountability ahead." (S. Green, personal interview, December 16, 2004). Because of that, the Superintendent became more directly involved with the principals and the data.

The third factor had to do with an emerging philosophy with which he could simply not agree. He explains how all these conditions came to a head.

> So, here I was – with heightened awareness and concern, starting in June – new staff, some people out, my additional connection to the details that I don't normally have, and then a conversation at the Superintendent's Council table which said the wrong thing. It said the wrong thing from a belief and mission statement point of view. It said, 'Let's be realistic, not all kids are going to make it.' I don't believe that. I just don't believe it in my being. If we don't believe we can make a difference, then why are we educators? 'Kids can go anywhere and just improve, and some of them won't make it,' but if we really believe they can make it, then we have to say we're serious about 100% of kids. (S. Green, personal interview, December 16, 2004).

So, between what was happening in the field and "what was happening philosophically" at central office, the Superintendent explained, "My leadership changed very quickly." (S. Green, personal interview, December 16, 2004). He described why this development became the tipping point.

> From what I heard at the table, we had crossed over to the non-negotiables, saying, 'It's okay for some kids not to make it.' And I heard that up and down the organization. And one administrator was very honest about it because he's very honest, but, when you pressed, everybody was really saying [that all kids were not going to achieve] – so I had to realign the school system. I had to do it and send a very clear message, and most, importantly, I had to make sure our kids had a chance to make it. The tests were good, and we just weren't preparing them for this test. We had failed along the curriculum, and I felt miserable about it. That's what made us get to that point. (S. Green, personal interview, December 16, 2004).

This very personal account demonstrates the complexity of the situation from the Superintendent's perspective. The reasons he felt compelled to make a change certainly influenced the process of making it happen in the schools.

Decision-Making Process

In order to analyze how this new accountability affects educators at the local level, it is not only important to look at what decisions they make and why they make them; even more can be learned from the process leaders go through to make these decisions.

Several of the leaders described the "Intervention" as being "designed top-down." "I don't think anybody would disagree with that." (S. Wright, personal interview, December 8, 2004). The same definitive statements were repeated by others. "It was truly top-down, and everyone still sees it that way." (P. Wilson, personal interview, December 9, 2004). Just as most of the leaders described it in these terms, at the same time, everyone also seemed quite comfortable with the top-down nature of the process.

> I think sometimes you have to [be directive]. I think that's the role of a strong leader and a strong leadership team – that sometimes you have to do things that people don't like. But if you do them for the right reasons, then you have to do them. (R. Miller, personal interview, December 16, 2004).

The Superintendent admitted the process was not typical.

> School systems sometimes want to roll up their sleeves and involve as many people as possible in making decisions, and we talk about all these processes. Well, hell, if it's good for kids and we all know it – .... In many ways, it destroyed every process that you could possibly think of, and yet it was the best thing we could have done. It was pure, because it was right for the kids. (S. Green, personal interview, December 16, 2004).

The Director of Special Education admits the fine line nature of this thinking, but agreed nonetheless. "I think it's dangerous to say that the ends always justify the means, but when you don't pay enough attention to results and don't make changes proportionate to the effort that's required because you're satisfied by the way things were, you are never going to change" (S. Wright. personal interview, December 8, 2004).

The decision-making process was not very inclusive. When discussing the fact that teachers were not involved in this decision, the Director of Special Education explained that the need for change became a focus.

> Some of our teachers still would maintain that it wasn't a valid way [of doing business] – to take their autonomy of their classroom away, which we did. But it sent a really powerful message that we need to be more introspective and more responsible. And if those results look like they're not going in the right direction, the people who are accepting responsibility, the Superintendent and the Superintendent's Council will act, and we'll do it again. I think that message came through very clearly. (S. Wright, personal interview, December 16, 2004).

The Director of Curriculum discussed one of the motives for this approach

> We also were just really unhappy with a lot of the pedagogy we saw and the lack of teachers and principals doing absolutely everything they can for kids. So, this was a way to say, hey, you are not getting it right. We are going to send a top-down message that you are going to change things, but also we are going to train you in some specific pedagogy to do this differently than what you have been doing. I think that's a pretty strong message to send to the schools. (D. McLaughlin, personal interview, December 9, 2004).

In the minds of these leaders, this intervention had to be done because the schools were not doing it themselves. "We were saying to people, 'You have the data, and you haven't paid attention to the data. If you were paying attention to the data, you would be way more desperate for change than you are.'" (S. Wright, personal interview, December 8, 2004). In fact, several members of the team, including the Assistant Superintendent for High Schools, turned the tables back on the buildings.

> Let me reverse it. Why didn't they come to the Superintendent and say, 'I've got three kids that aren't going to make it, and I want to do something?' So, if we were going to wait for something to bubble up, we might be old and gray by the time that happens, so some of the stuff is going to have to be somewhat draconian. (P. Jennings, personal interview, December 8, 2004).

It was clear that central office did not expect the principals to have all the answers, but they expected them to know their buildings and ask for help when necessary. "They should have come pounding at the door, saying, 'I need help. I need resources. I need time, because [we] have a group of kids who aren't making it.'" (S. Green, personal interview, December 16, 2004). But the principals did not come with those issues, and the decision was made without input from the buildings.

The other stakeholders were considered briefly during the process, but they were eventually dismissed. "There was no time to engage more focus groups; there was no time for any more debate. There was an urgency to get results and to force some change" (S. Wright, personal interview, December 8, 2004). The Director of Curriculum offered what various groups might have said if they were given input.

> I think people would have had a real problem with pulling kids out of electives and changing kids' schedules and changing teachers' schedules. Kids don't want to be pulled out of electives. Teachers don't want to teach additional classes or shift their schedules around. Principals don't want to deal with this nightmare. Parents either would go one of two ways: 'don't mess with my kid,' or Thank you for doing it.' If they thanked us, that's great, and if they said, 'Don't mess with my kid,' then we say, 'Tough, we want to mess with your kid.' So, I don't think Superintendent's Council wanted to hear any of this, because it just would have led to a fight anyway. I don't think it would have changed anything, so I don't know if their voice needed to be at the table. (D. McLaughlin, personal interview, December 9, 2004).

The Superintendent explained that they would have heard the same old answers from the buildings.

> They would have said, "We need more time. Let's look at the best programs. Let's do a pilot. Let's give this stuff all a chance to work. We worked so hard. You can't ask any more of us. The teachers are tired. What about this sense of reality?" I think all of that kind of rhetoric that we would traditionally hear, you would have heard at the table. And I think you would have heard the same from both [principals and teachers]. (S. Green, personal interview, December 8, 2004).

The Director of Curriculum thought the teachers would have argued that they were not doing business as usual.

> I think they would have said, 'This is crazy. I'm not disrupting my school. I'm not doing this much work for a test. We have done a lot for these kids. Our long-term interventions, the changes we made in curriculum, the changes we made in curriculum mapping, the changes we made in support for kids are going to work. So we don't need to do an eight-week intervention program; our kids are going to do fine on these tests.' (D. McLaughlin, personal interview, December 9, 2004).

The building-level educators were not the only ones who had a problem with the "Intervention." Pat Wilson, who was in on the discussion from the beginning, explained her early reaction. "I think at the time I also resented it because it disrupted my whole schedule, and it took a lot of time to make it happen, and it happened so quickly. That's the problem around here. [Everything happens] so quickly." (personal interview, December 9, 2004).
As the few administrators who made this decision looked back on this time, they had their share of regrets. The Superintendent offered his reflections.

> At that moment, I sat alone at the table saying, 'Damn it, this is what we have to do.' My will was not going to be broken on that. You know the whole district might have been ticked at me for eight or nine weeks, but it didn't matter. For me it was *that* important. So there was a sense of: How come I didn't create that culture and that capacity within everybody to jell at the time and say, 'This is the right thing? (S. Green, personal interview, December 16, 2004).

There was also some self-doubt from those whom he had to convince. The Assistant Superintendent for High Schools questioned, "Why didn't we think about things like this before? Why did it take a crisis to make us jump through these hoops to create these programs?' (P. Jennings, personal interview, December 9, 2004). Reflection brought out the learning that was gained for the Assistant Superintendent of Middle Schools as well.

> When I step back now and look at it, I knew it was right. I should have done what he did. I should have known that my schools hadn't done everything possible and been on it faster than he was, and I learned a lot and changed practice because of it the following year. So it was a good lesson for me. (P. Wilson, personal interview, December 9, 2004).

Inside the Debate

Even though everyone agreed that this was a top-down decision, it does not eliminate the fact that there were some heated debates at central office. There was plenty of tension around this decision. One of the early arguments from Phil Jennings was that there was already an aggressive plan in place.

> We had met with 19 principals, and we had convinced them that we

could do the No Child Left Behind scenario in six years rather than 14 years, and that took an awful lot of convincing because their question was, 'Why do it in six years rather than 14 years?' We had some compelling arguments. They had all bought into that and, indeed, had staked part of their salary to the benchmarks for those six years, and now as the district we're saying, 'Well, that's not good enough. We want all of our kids to be there this year.' So, I think if we really thought this out well, we should have gone to them about that premise initially, as opposed to doing something and working through almost a six-month process and then saying, 'Wait a minute, that's not good enough.' So I was struggling with the process. (personal interview, December 9, 2004).

This debate was described by a few members as "heated." The Superintendent explained his perspective. "That was a key issue. I didn't buy that even though I understood the practicality of it. I can't say that I believe it. I don't want anybody at my table saying that they believe in it." (S. Green, personal interview, December 16, 2004). Jennings explained how he came around.

I guess it was maybe a day or two later, I actually recognized that the two things we were talking about were not mutually exclusive. You can have accountabilities for principals, for schools, and for administrators that stick to that plan, and you can also do everything that's humanly possible to close gaps and see that every kid is not left behind immediately, knowing that you may not be 100% successful. (personal interview, December 9, 2004).

After first considering the idea of a massive intervention, the leaders harped on the logistical issues. The Director of Curriculum explained all the thoughts that were racing in their minds.

There was a lot of debate, even initially, in terms of can we pull this off? Can we stop the momentum of a district this size? What do you mean we are going to change kids' schedules right in the middle of the year? We're going to change teachers' schedules? And the answers were all, "Yes, we are going to do these things," and it just seemed so crazy of an idea to do at the time that we are going to disrupt a lot of what is going on at some of our schools. (D. McLaughlin, personal interview, December 9, 2004).

The minor details were at the forefront of everyone's minds. "Real basic things, like how can you get it done this quickly, how can we reschedule hundreds of kids, and how do you take kids out of electives or out of another subject?" (P. Wilson, personal interview, December 9, 2004). Teachers struggled with this idea as well when they first heard about it. "I think they were just afraid that they were up against such a short time, how could they create something that would have meaning?" (M. Harris, personal interview, December 22, 2004). The scope of the "Intervention" played a factor in the thinking as well.

Could we stop the momentum of a pretty large district that has 12,000 kids in it? An organization like that does have momentum, and it does have history. Could we stop that and say, "Time out. For the next six weeks, here is what we are doing." I think that was a huge issue that at least I struggled with initially (P. Jennings, personal interview, December 9, 2004).

Because everyone was mired in these issues, they had to find some way to make progress. The Director of Curriculum recalled the breakthrough.

> The logistics of this were a nightmare, and if we got caught up in that we would never get it done. So [the logistics] had to be off the table for the moment, and that one shift made it happen because we were able to think of this not in terms of the details, but in terms of what would we do with the time if we had the kids sitting in front of us. (D. McLaughlin, personal interview, December 9, 2004).

These debates still resonated with the group almost a year later. The Superintendent reflected on this point in time.

> How come we had to get to that point? What did I miss? How come we didn't do this in September? During the summer? How come we didn't have other kinds of programs naturally in place, rather than creating havoc in this school district? As nice as it is to say, you can stop a district on the dime; you shouldn't have to (S. Green, personal interview, December 16, 2004).

The group did eventually find a way to get through the logistics.

> It turned out that we could do it. It turned out that practitioners that we turned this over to did a great job and worked real hard, and in a period of two weeks provided us with a design that captured more kids and gave more kids the opportunity to do well than would have if we hadn't done anything. (P. Jennings, personal interview, December 9, 2004).

But the fact that these leaders still have some issues unresolved in their minds today indicates how difficult it was to make sense of these decisions at the time.

> I think it's something we needed to do at the time, but I think like everyone else felt; it's better built in from the beginning of the school year. One, so kids aren't identified and they don't feel that initial 'Oh, I'm a loser,' and then, two, the teachers. I mean teachers need to know what's expected so their year isn't interrupted. (R. Miller, personal interview, December 15, 2004).

Once the team tabled the immediate logistical issues, they began to debate the philosophical issue of which students should be included in the intervention.

> There was a significant debate as to which kids we could focus on....It was a serious argument. If we are going to do this, shouldn't we get the most bang for our buck with the kids that we know have a chance of passing this? Because some kids were so far behind that we didn't think they had a chance at passing the test. (D. McLaughlin, personal interview, December 9, 2004).

Phil Jennings, who initiated the conversation, explained how it was resolved.

> I was arguing that there are kids who just aren't going to pass the test regardless of what we do; however, [others argued] if we have to make them sit through this test, why don't we give them as much as we can to enable them to do as well as they can? For me, that was a pretty powerful argument. (personal interview, December 9, 2004).

Even though these students would not improve the test scores, the group saw this as an "ethical responsibility."

> If a kid is going to see a question in front of him, we need to do everything we can to give that kid the best opportunity to feel comfortable answering that question – to give him the best shot of answering that one more question. We had that ethical, moral responsibility, and so that became the thinking of the group, and [the person who disagreed initially had his mind changed], and he understood that this could be more than just getting ready for the test. It could be about helping a bunch of kids that were behind. (D. McLaughlin, personal interview, December 9, 2004).

While this all occurred eight weeks before the test, the district felt justified that it was more than just "test preparation" in response to NCLB. "These assessments stress the types of content and skills we value. Whether it is responding to text, writing a persuasive piece, or solving a higher order mathematical problem, our students need to have these fundamental skills." (D. McLaughlin, personal interview, December 9, 2004). The pressures of public accountability that come with NCLB might cause such dramatic changes, but many members insist the "Intervention" was inevitable. "The intervention initiative fell out of NCLB even though it is probably something we would have done anyway. Maybe we were more aggressive about it because of NCLB." (C. Martin, personal interview, September 23, 2004). Robin Miller, Assistant to the Superintendent, agreed. "I think the interventions would have been done anyway. Maybe they would have been held off until this year, but I still think they would have been done." (personal interview, September 24, 2004). The Assistant Superintendent for Middle Schools provided the reasoning. "I think down the road as the community continued to change we would have to change to meet the needs of our kids." (P. Wilson, personal interview, September 15, 2004).

Carol Martin, who is not a certified educator, saw the dramatic intervention program as the new way business would be conducted.

> I don't know a lot of what is going on in the classroom, but my guess is that the intervention effort last year was just the start of what we may have to do again. Our goal was that these kids get support all the time, every year, year after year. That certainly requires professional development, changes in culture – all of those things to make sure that the teacher in the classroom knows that it is not okay to grade on the curve and think that is a good way to do

things...that you need to now make sure all of your kids are achieving. (personal interview, September 23, 2004).

Programs like this are becoming more typical across the country.

> Districts with schools in need of improvement reported taking concrete actions in 2002-03 to improve student achievement in these schools, including extending school hours, notifying parents, strengthening professional development, changing curricula, and implementing research-based methods to improve student performance (CEP, 2004).

Many members described the passion of the Superintendent during this time.

> The Superintendent discovered that there were some students that we felt would fall in between the cracks, and the superintendent has a passion that no child will fall between the cracks, and he was determined to do all that he could do to make sure that did not happen. (J. Wilkens, personal interview, December 16, 2004).

The Superintendent worked hard to convince the team of the importance of this initiative.

> I remember him calling it triage; and I remember so clearly the analogy that he used that if you had seen any of these kids and they had fallen in the street – fallen off a bicycle, if they were hurt, if they were bleeding, you'd help them. So these are kids who, in effect, have fallen off their bicycles, and they need to be triaged. We're going to do it. And I thought that was a very responsive and courageous kind of thing, and it rallied people. And everyone was scared [of such a drastic change], but it empowered people to do something right for kids. (M. Harris, personal interview, December 22, 2004).

When asked if this intensity was the result of the Superintendent's concern for his job, the Director of Curriculum responded with the following statement

> No, that never came up. I mean I know Superintendent jobs are based on test scores a lot of places, but that was never debated. I think even though we had a bad year the year before, and that was killing all of us, and I know quite frankly that the political tide can turn on the Superintendent very quickly, and if we keep getting bad scores then he's on the hot seat, but I don't know....I just believe enough in our Superintendent – I mean he could get a job anywhere, so I don't really think it's about his job or even his ego. I just think he feels the same internal passion that we need to do more for our kids than we have been doing (D. McLaughlin, personal interview, December 9, 2004).

In fact, to many, this effort became much more than working toward improved performance on a test.

> And it was looking at test scores and saying, you know what, if we don't do something very quickly, these kids are never going to perform on these

tests, but I think there was also something, too, that was not just about the test, but that they were going to let them go on to the next grade level and they're never [going to catch up]. They're still going to be behind where they need to be. (R. Miller, personal interview, December 15, 2004).

A memo from the Director of Curriculum to the Superintendent and Board of Education outlined the district's public stance. "Even though many of our students are supported more than ever, we still know that some of our students are just not making it. From the data, we know that some of our students will still struggle on the state assessments this March." Through a series of very serious, intense meetings at central office, the following decision was made: "Because we have an obligation to do everything we can to help each child learn as much as possible, we have decided to make specific, short-term interventions over the next eight weeks to help close the gaps that still exist in math and language arts." Student and teacher schedules were adjusted in order to provide additional instruction; specific curricula were created and customized; and professional development was provided to the teachers.

There was not complete unanimity about the causes of the "Intervention" being a natural extension of the district's work. Pat Wilson put it very simply, "I think it stemmed from the fact that it looked like we wouldn't have good test scores." (personal interview, December 9, 2004).

> The intervention was clearly a response to NCLB and the accountability of a state standardized high-stakes test that we have never really given much credence to. [The tests] are getting better, and we think they measure the standards that they are supposed to measure, now. I guess, in retrospect, as the tests have improved, our responsibility to see that the kids have done well on them has increased, because they truly measure the standards. (P. Jennings, personal interview, December 9, 2004).

In an earlier interview, Phil Jennings was more direct, "If it weren't for NCLB, I don't think we would have had an intervention program." (personal interview, September 22, 2004). It may have been the short-term nature of the program that caused these dissenting opinions. "The one thing that probably wouldn't have happened would have been the stop-on-the-dime intervention." (S. Wright, personal interview, September 27, 2004). Credit was given to NCLB for causing this change. "While there is certainly a lot of things that could be improved with NCLB, I think it has really begun the conversation that, shame on us, we should have been having for years." (P. Jennings, personal interview, September 22, 2004).

This thinking helped get many people past the idea that this was only in response to NCLB, but a year later the group admits that it was, in many ways, about the test and about NCLB.

> There was some debate of whether or not we should do this. Should we do this because of the tests? We only did it in grades 3, 4, 8, and 11, so this was clearly NCLB-driven in my mind. And should we be disrupting education for this purpose? I think the answer to that question lies in the fact that these

tests are pretty good, and if we didn't have faith in the test I don't think we would have done the intervention program. (D. McLaughlin, personal interview, December 9, 2004).

This was a point that these leaders wrestled with, and the following passage demonstrates how the Superintendent has made sense of it.

> So it might be teaching to the test on a very short, narrow point of view, but, in the end, it's really preparing the kids and getting them ready to have skills necessary for school and life. And that's how I always looked at it; and I think that's a message that we tried to send out, although people probably still respond that we are teaching to test. Until somebody tells me that the tests are lousy, until somebody tells me that has nothing to do with the skills you need to succeed in school, I'm going to continue believing it wasn't teaching to the test; it was much broader and much deeper and much more important.. (S. Green, personal interview, December 16, 2004).

It was important at the time for the leaders to discuss this issue and its resulting perception.

> I think those of us at Superintendent's Council went through with the Superintendent why we are doing this. We made sure we repeated the language so we were all at the same page – that this wasn't about the tests. This was about doing what's right, giving these kids the important skills that they need. I mean if you look at the memos I've written, my name is on them; we are not doing this for NCLB. We're doing this because we think these are important skills for kids. (D. McLaughlin, personal interview, December 9, 2004).

> I guess the way I frame it in my mind [is], yes, we may have been teaching to the test, but the thing that the test measures is all the standards that we're responsible for teaching anyway, so if we disrupted instruction to ensure that kids are meeting the standards and benchmarks we set out by grade level, I don't have any problem with it. (P. Wilson, personal interview, December 9, 2004).

When pressed, though, many of these leaders did have some problems with it.

Not everyone agreed that this focus on the students who would be taking the test was the best thing for the district. The Assistant Superintendent for Elementary Schools, who was a principal in the district at the time of the intervention, recalled, "We nearly dropped everything else and concentrated on those kids who were going to be taking the test, and that meant that the other kids for three or four months did not get services, and there is something wrong with that." (J. Wilkens, personal interview, December 16, 2004). Pat Wilson thought this thinking had implications beyond the "Intervention."

> I do believe that because of all the high stakes and accountability and pressure from the federal government, from me, from the Superintendent, from all these powers, that we do get people that sacrifice the learning to teach

to a test sometimes, and that doesn't sit well with me. (P. Wilson, personal interview, December 9, 2004).

There was also the issue of taking some students out of the electives they loved. The Assistant Superintendent for High Schools had a different way of looking at his tension.

> We are always worried about kids' feelings good about themselves and their self-esteem, and in the United States our kids have the highest self-esteem in world. But what we want them to feel good about is reading and writing and maybe some of those more important things, so their short-term disappointment for long-term gain is really what you are looking at. (P. Jennings, personal interview, September 22, 2004).

The Director of Curriculum saw this debate as dependent on the quality of the teacher.

> The rhetoric is real strong. 'I don't care how the kid feels, I want the kid to achieve and want the kid to feel good about the achieving,' but if that's delivered by a bad educator, then you *need* to care how the kid feels….[When a teacher] says, 'I told you do it,' or 'Because I said so,' it's not going to make any sense to kids. (D. McLaughlin, personal interview, December 9, 2004).

That is why it is so important that the teacher genuinely cares about the students. "If it is delivered well and the teacher does care about a kid's achievement, then the kid will feel cared about. Kids feel good when they are pushed and are asked to do a lot work." (D. McLaughlin, personal interview, December 9, 2004). This makes it difficult for central office leaders to make broad decisions around situations that are sometimes personnel dependent.

This debate begs the question, though, by focusing so much attention on math and language arts – are the arts and other subjects ignored? This was an issue about which the team had thought deeply.

> We spent a lot of time talking about the asset versus the deficit model and tried to create a system, though I don't think we were entirely successful, which recognized that kids had some assets, that they liked music or shop in some cases, or whatever it may be, and we didn't always want to pull them out of those classes, so we recognized that. (S. Green, personal interview, December 16, 2004).

The Superintendent thought the "Intervention" fell far short of the sacrifices other districts were making because of NCLB. "If we look at this as an intervention program for a period of some time, it doesn't do what some districts end up doing, which is reducing the amount of time in art or music." S. Green, personal interview, December 16, 2004). The Assistant Superintendent for High Schools agreed that the short-term nature of the "Intervention" compensated for what might otherwise be lost, comparing it to missing school for an illness.

If they were in art, for example, they came out of that class for about six weeks and then went right back into it. We had agreements with teachers that they would not hold kids responsible for the work that they were not able to do because they were not there. So it was like they went on an extended vacation or had mono and were out for six weeks and came back. (P. Jennings, personal interview, December 9, 2004).

The Public Information Officer had no issue with pulling students out of electives because she thought that reading and writing simply needed to be a higher priority than the arts.

The fact is whatever you believe about kids getting that balance between math and English and the arts and all that other stuff – that's all well and good, but the fact is they have to pass this test to get out of high school, and if they're not going to pass it then so what if they're great artists? (C. Martin, personal interview, December 9, 2004).

The Director of Special Education acknowledged this tension but thought reading and writing were critical.

If you have a slew of Cs or Ds, and you are not proficient in reading and writing, are you going into the Moore College of Art? Tyler Art School at Temple? Penn to pursue your dreams? Rutgers? It is all a piece of the same pie. Yes, there is a risk of ignoring the affective domain, but we didn't stop school plays, we didn't stop athletics, we didn't put chorus to a halt. (S. Wright, personal interview, December 8, 2004).

George Stanley, the Business Administrator, added, "I think they could survive in the world without music; they cannot survive without math or English." (personal interview, December 17, 2004).

Considering all these issues was far from simple for these educators, and the tensions in their minds are real and often leave them searching for answers. When asked if the other subjects were taking a back seat to math and language arts, the Assistant Superintendent for Middle Schools explained the struggle.

I struggle with that every day. I struggle when we say in a meeting, 'Well they need more help in math and language arts, forget about history or world language.' Other countries never let go of their languages. It is critical to who their kids are when they graduate their schools, being fluent in multiple languages. Our state doesn't even believe it should be a requirement for graduation. How provincial, right? And so that doesn't sit well with me when I think about it. But I do think these thoughts, 'I'm accountable for math and English, so take away history time and give them more math. Take away more world language.' So that's very conflicting in my mind, but given the teacher contracts that we have and the fact that we can't extend the day or have other transportation for kids to get here before or after school, I don't know what other choices I'm left with (P. Wilson, personal interview, December 9, 2004).

Educators do make these types of decisions all the time in this era of accountability. Now, after studying all that went into this 'Intervention," it is important to look at the effects it has had on the school system.

Effects: Benefits and Costs

Of course, the most important effect that people considered was the change in actual achievement on the assessments. "I think test scores were affected. I mean you can't prove causation, but I definitely think this had an impact on test scores. Our test scores went up a lot, and I think this extra support really helped kids in terms of test scores." (D. McLaughlin, personal interview, December 9, 2004). One of the major groups affected was the special education population.

> It had massive effects in the district, all of which makes it, at least par- tially, if not totally, justified that we caused measurable student improvement that are measured on the NCLB accountabilities. In special education, stu- dents in the high school went from 33% in achieving proficiency to 55%. That really showed that what we were doing wasn't working and that when we did something else, kids had a better chance of making those milestones. (S. Wright, personal interview, December 8, 2004).

These special education students were included in the "Intervention" pro- gram, and many of their regular math classes were also changed. The Director of Special Education recalled why they were included.

> [The Math Supervisor] and I had a conversation last year, which I thought was pretty telling in that he said that he and the math teachers at [the high school] discovered that although learning-disabled kids were not able to master the entire part of the curriculum, what they were able to master was way more substantial than what they had assumed up front. I think that is kind of a change of reasoning opportunity, removing the glass ceiling from the learning disability population in particular. If you look at the standardized test scores that we got, you saw that there was a pretty huge jump. (S. Wright, per- sonal interview, December 8, 2004).

Even the "advanced proficient" scores increased, but equally important was the culture shift it made.

> More kids are taking higher-level courses, if not advanced courses. I think that's an important step in moving everybody to high-level achieve- ments. So, culturally there is a beginning of a change....We got results and maybe it's a bit Machiavellian, but when you look at what we were able to roll out by systematizing what we did in eight weeks. I don't think there is any- body that can really in their heart of hearts say that this district is not better and stronger. (S. Wright, personal interview, December 8, 2004).

Although the scores were generally positive, the other effects the "Intervention" had on students were certainly mixed.

> You know we have done this evaluation, and we heard from kids initial- ly. The cost for some of the kids is that they were very upset going into the

program, being singled out, being marked as a kid with potential failure. A lot of them were crying. (S. Green, personal interview, December 16, 2004).

Many of the administrators, including the Director of Curriculum, still struggle with this in their minds.

> I think there were some real negative effects on kids that were pulled from their electives. I think some of the reasons these kids come to school is for music or art or for band or for whatever, even if it's for an elective that we don't see as academic. It's an elective. They elected to be in it. They wanted to be there, and sometimes these kids come to school for that purpose; and to pull a kid out of that and to put a kid into something that they weren't having success with in the first place – I don't know how respectful that is for the kid. (D. McLaughlin, personal interview, December 9, 2004).

Pat Wilson agreed and wished there was a different way to get the students more support. "I don't think that's the right leverage for them to take away things that they love, so I think that could potentially be very problematic. " (personal interview, December 9, 2004). The parents of these students also raised their concerns at that time, which the Assistant to the Superintendent recalled.

> Parents were saying that it is not fair to kids. [They were] being singled out. [They were asking], 'Why do we need to do this?' We had the African-American community saying there was a high percentage of minority students in there, and they didn't like the way it was being done. We felt we were really in a crisis situation. We had to work to make the public understand. (R. Miller, personal interview, December 15, 2004).

The Director of Special Education recalled, "My phone certainly rang off the hook many times with angry parents asking, 'How could you make this change?'" (S. Wright, personal interview, December 8, 2004). The district tried to ameliorate many of these negative effects by offering incentives to students, such as field trips, and teachers were also provided with talking points to help deal with frustrated students.

Eventually, the help in math and language arts made a difference for both the students and their parents.

> I think parents, at first, were very upset, saying, 'What do you mean you're pulling my kid out? My kid feels like the dumb kid in the class now,' and I think parents realize now that it wasn't such a bad thing. The results were there for their own child....I've heard parents come back and say, "I didn't like this at first, but, you know, I see the benefit of it now." (R. Miller, personal interview, December 15, 2004).

Sam Wright resolved, in his own mind, the problem of students missing an elective.

> The perception that the only reason special ed. kids come to school,

sometimes, is for the electives – that turned out not to be true. Those kids might have griped about it, but even when we did the post-interviews, they all seemed to appreciate the academic progress. (personal interview, December 8, 2004).

The main reason student attitudes changed was because these students felt more prepared for the test. "The data we got from kids was, even though I hated it at the time, when I took that test I felt better than I ever did." (P. Wilson, personal interview, December 9, 2004).

Lessons Learned

The leaders in this district realized that it was critical to learn as much as possible from this process in order to make improvements in the educational program.

[There have been] tons of effects on teacher practice in the classroom. The way we have structured [teacher collaborative] time has changed. The conversation has changed to be driven more by student data and the changes in instruction that are needed because of that data. It's changed the awareness of the importance of the tests of kids and parents, especially eighth graders that now know if they don't pass the GEPA they don't get an elective in high school. Those kinds of mandates never were around, before so they could blow off that test because kids would say, 'What difference does it make.' (P. Wilson, personal interview, December 9, 2004)?

There were resulting programmatic changes. The Superintendent explained that the middle schools "created ongoing interventions, individualized around specific skills," which is "the real-time learning model [we had been looking for]." He said of the new model, "I think it is just brilliant." (S. Green, personal interview, December 16, 2004). The high schools also implemented changes using double periods of math and language arts for the students who need it.

I think we learned that the traditional curriculum and pedagogy that we have exposed all of our kids to, the one-size-fits-all, may not work well. Even though you might think that you tailor classroom instruction to the individual kid, it probably doesn't happen all that often in large group instruction, so we learned that small groups, small focused groups of kids with dedicated teachers can make wonderful things happen. (P. Jennings, personal interview, December 9, 2004).

The Director of Curriculum thought there were some lasting benefits gained from the "Intervention."

I think the way our middle school math intervention was done, where we took it as an opportunity to learn about our teachers and about learning, to learn about our pedagogy, to look at our curriculum in different ways. I think those are exactly the kinds of changes that we should be making.

(D. McLaughlin, personal interview, December 9, 2004).

There has been a cultural shift for the district because of the growth gained from the "Intervention."

> We now have in our school system a model, as screwy as it may be, in our pocket that says, 'You know, you really can stop the school district if it's the right thing to do for kids, involve the teachers, and get something into place. You can do that. It can be done' (S. Green, personal interview, December 16, 2004).

The Director of Curriculum explained that the district will no longer wait until September to implement a new program. "Well, I think it's helped us to think differently as a district. I think we've now gone into a mentality where, if something's not working, you don't wait until the end of the year, you stop and do something about it now." (D. McLaughlin, personal interview, December 9, 2004). And in terms of finding solutions, "We have learned that nothing is so outside the box that we shouldn't consider it." (P. Jennings, personal interview, December 9, 2004).

As empowering as a drastic intervention can be, some of the administrators were deeply concerned about the sustainability of these efforts.

> It caused a tremendous amount of stress on the lives of people, and, in one way, that can be good in terms of people realizing what they are capable of, but that pressure, that short-term pressure cannot be sustained in an organization. I firmly believe that people would quit. People would've said, 'I don't want to work in this kind of insanity.' (D. McLaughlin, personal interview, December 9, 2004).

The Superintendent was concerned about whether everyone really learned from the experience or simply survived it.

> I wonder about its lasting effects. I think there potentially are some lasting effects, but I think more of it is out of fear of it happening again, rather than people saying, 'You know what? I understand the message and I understand my responsibility. Now let me see what I can do for kids.' (S. Green, personal interview, December 16, 2004).

The Director of Curriculum questioned whether or not the district could handle the short-term thinking that NCLB causes, especially if there is a change in management.

> If NCLB makes us think, 'current moment,' all the time, we will never be thinking long-term for kids, and we'll never be putting systems in place that will make our organization run well. So what happens when the head leadership leaves, and some people in this room can't make this decision? What if [the next leader] comes in and isn't as aggressive? These things won't happen. You need to create mechanisms in this organization that are sustainable. (D. McLaughlin, personal interview, December 9, 2004).

Clearly, this leadership team has thought deeply about the "Intervention." The interviews were filled with tension and deep reflection. A summary of the positives and negatives of the "Intervention" appears in Table 4. This dramatic decision was heavily influenced, if not directly caused, by the NCLB legislation. One year later, these leaders are still struggling with the decisions they made.

Table 4

"The Intervention"

Positives
- Provided students with the best opportunity to succeed
- Created a new model
- Disrupted business as usual
- Provided new professional development
- Test scores went up
- Students felt they had learned
- Attention and support given to Special Ed students
- District learned from the process
- Long term changes initiated

Negatives
- Top down process
- Disrupted whole district
- Logistical nightmare
- Kids lost electives
- Teaching to the Test perception
- Teachers and students did not like it
- NCLB driven
- Diverted resources away from students in non-testing grades
- Short Term thinking

Conclusion

The No Child Left Behind legislation clearly has complicated the lives of local educational leaders. From the way they think about the philosophical stance of NCLB to the way they create and implement local policy, these leaders struggle with the tensions inherent in a climate of increased accountability. There were no definitive answers to any of the research questions, but there is much to be learned from this lack of clarity.

When looking closely at the extent to which the rationale behind the accountability measures of NCLB meshed with educators' personal beliefs on the purpose of public education, there were mixed results. The team thought there was strong alignment when thinking of creating equity for all students. One of the fundamental purposes of public education is to level the playing field, and the research group felt that was clearly part of the rationale of NCLB. A second purpose of public education focuses on preparing students with the skills they will need later in life. While the group felt that NCLB shared this goal to some extent, many felt that the law had defined these skills too narrowly. One of the perceived reasons behind the accountability provisions of NCLB was to bring greater accountability to a system of public education that was not meeting its potential. Some members agreed that this was necessary in order to improve the consistency of high expectations and achievement, but some others felt that NCLB overextended the federal role and was unfairly critical of public education.

Philosophically, this group would struggle less with the legislation if it broadened its definition of public education and made more of an effort to support, rather than solely critique, the public schools. Some of the logistical issues that have been raised nationally were also concerns of this team (e.g., one-shot testing, lack of flexibility for special education students).

The second research question focused on how NCLB has affected the work of these leaders. The new accountability had created additional pressures for them, but the sources and nature of this pressure were varied. The public nature of NCLB was one direct pressure, but mostly, the group perceived the greater pressure was to address the spirit of the law. For this team, there were many examples of individuals who put the pressure on themselves to improve, and every member cited the passion, commitment, and high expectations of the Superintendent as a source of additional pressure. The extent to which NCLB influenced the new initiatives was debated throughout the data, but each initiative clearly grew out of a sense of greater accountability to student learning.

The third question sought to surface the tensions these leaders struggled with when making decisions around issues associated with NCLB. Tensions were evident throughout the data. From the beginning, there were tensions around the motives behind NCLB. Team members questioned whether or not resources were appropriately directed, and some even questioned whether universal proficiency was even possible. The questions of the validity of the state assessments raised tensions for many when they created policy that focused on improving scores on these tests. The three initiatives on which this study focused were filled with tensions, some of which surfaced through open debate, while others just ruminated in the leaders' minds. Ultimately, these struggles helped to inform the overarching question of whether or not the changes these leaders are making are the kinds of changes we want for students.

Team members were asked to reflect and judge if changes this district had made (e.g., the "Intervention," the six-year benchmarks, the KPAs) were in the best interest of children. Two members were very clear that they thought the district was on the right path. The Assistant Superintendent for High Schools said, "I have worked on each of those components and have heard all the conversations. I am very solidly behind all of them." (P. Jennings, personal interview, December 9, 2004). Jason Wilkens, an Assistant Superintendent for Elementary Schools, thought these specific changes attended to issues beyond NCLB. "It's about what is morally right. " (personal interview, December 9 2004). And while the other leaders were not as decisive in their thinking as these two, there was a general optimism about the ongoing work of the district reflected in the following reflection by the Director of Curriculum.

> I think that when we talk about how special ed. kids have been learning
> about fractions and percentages in our high schools for the eighth year in a

row, because they've been getting it from third grade on without success, and now we are getting them some Algebra and Geometry – they are the things I think we should be doing for kids. I think getting administrators focused on the idea that their work needs to directly affect student achievement – I think that's the kind of work we need to be doing. I think those are educationally sound things, and I think that in some part those are driven by No Child Left Behind. I think publicly saying we're not going to wait – we're going to do things now. I think those are all great leadership pieces. I think giving kids the best chance that they can do on a test, I think attending to achievement gaps – those are great things. (D. McLaughlin, personal interview, December 9, 2004).

Not all of the final reflections were as positive, and one concern that was mentioned throughout the interviews surfaced as the most common tension when considering whether or not the changes they had been making were educationally sound. Many of the leaders expressed concern about the fact that NCLB has caused a short-term focus on achievement. "Some days it puts you in a mindset of desperation rather than creativity, and I think that's the newness of the effects of NCLB. Rather than being a reflective decision maker based on data gathering, we are likely to jump at solutions." (S. Wright, personal interview, December 8, 2004). This rush to solutions has had a perceived affect on the principals.

I think principals are more in a panic mode, where they are just trying to do short-term fixes to make sure kids reach every year, and I'm struggling to find the balance between short-term success and long-term sustainability. That's particularly difficult in this district that really values short-term results, and that's a tension for me. (D. McLaughlin, personal interview, December 9, 2004).

Finding balance has been difficult. "I think the pressure is okay, initially, to kind of jump-start some changes, but this fear – that's not going to make a difference in school's" (P. Wilson, personal interview, December 9, 2004). "I certainly feel that principals are in the short-term mode, but I think we put them in that mode" (D. McLaughlin, personal interview, December 9, 2004). In fact, the Director of Curriculum explained this tension in his own work.

I think I push a little too much short term. I think sometimes I'm uncomfortable with the amount of testing we do and the amount of class periods we take out for testing – the amount of time we ask people to create tests, those are things that I probably wouldn't do if I didn't feel the pressures for immediate student achievement. I would love to get to a place where teachers can make their own decisions in classrooms. But, on the other hand, I want consistency, and I want a guaranteed curriculum for kids. I really believe in that. But with the superstar [teachers] out there, I'm worried I'm limiting their potential. So, I struggle with that. (D. McLaughlin, personal interview, December 9, 2004).

The long-term effects are clearly more desirable.

> I'd like us to get to a place where our everyday instruction doesn't leave children behind, where we don't have to do supplemental interventions for kids as much or as frequently or with as many kids. So, if we don't get to that point, then we're not making educationally sound decisions. (D. McLaughlin, personal interview, December 9, 2004).

It is not easy to get to that point, and the Assistant Superintendent for Middle Schools discussed the problems of NCLB and the sometimes short term thinking of the district.

> I guess that the biggest struggle for me is that to do this kind of work, to reach every child with achievement gaps, with the differences kids come to school with, we need a lot of resources to support this work. And I just don't mean stuff; I mean professional development, manipulatives, assessments – and that takes money, and it takes teacher time, training, and I think that is the whole piece that the legislation didn't think about. If we don't think about how we implement [these changes], we will always be in a very similar situation. (P. Wilson, personal interview, December 9, 2004).

The Director of Curriculum thought balancing all of these tensions and making the best decisions for students were the responsibilities of the leadership team. "Superintendent's Council needs to find that balance between short term accountability and long-term sustainability. That's our challenge, and that is our responsibility." (D. McLaughlin, personal interview, December 9, 2004).

When federal policymakers create legislation that proposes to leave no child behind, it is difficult for them to conceptualize the complexity of its implementation at the district level. This study presents an example of intelligent, hard working, caring educators struggling to do what is best for all of their students. This work is difficult, and the issues are serious. Certainly there needs to be further study into the effects this legislation has at the building and classroom levels, but this study can begin to help educators and policymakers reflect on the direction of public education and how well it has maintained its focus on what is best for children in light of an increased accountability.

Recommendations and Implications

NCLB is dominating the educational agenda across the country. It is on the cover of every educational periodical, in the keynote address at every national conference, and in the marketing strategy of every educational product. It is the topic of debate in state legislatures, in local board meetings, and at school PTA functions. The research community has studied accountability systems, and certainly the academic community has looked at how states have been affected by NCLB, but there has been very little research down at the district level.

In January of 2004, the Center on Education Policy (CEP) released its findings from its national study, which included 33 case studies. It explains that, "the case study reports presented here describe each district's progress in carrying out NCLB requirements, its challenges with implementation, and its trategies for addressing these challenges." (CEP, 2004). What it found was hat many schools were increasing professional development, implementing new, research-based programs, and extending time for students. They were also tudying how NCLB affected the decision making at the local level.

My study addressed the same issue. In fact, one of my research questions vas, *How has NCLB affected the work of local educational leaders?* But I was particularly interested in what was going on in the minds of the educators making these decisions. I wanted to know the philosophical stance of local leaders vhen thinking about NCLB, so I explored the question, *To what extent does the ationale behind the accountability measures of NCLB mesh with educators' personal beliefs on the purpose of public education?* With these two questions, expected to provide a context for the study of the decisions that leaders made. Beyond the decisions themselves, I focused on the tensions in the minds of hese leaders. I wanted leaders at the local level to reflect and think deeply about the pressures of NCLB and the struggles around an accountability system that expects universal proficiency. My overarching question was, *Are the decisions that local educators make because of NCLB the types of changes we want for our students?*

NCLB has shaken up the public schools, and educators everywhere are debating the inherent challenges. Many are rebelling and some are rallying, but what seems consistent is that educators are indeed making changes. The key point is whether or not these changes are actually making public education better. Time will tell, but perhaps this close look into one district will help to nform the larger debate.

This paper seeks to present some of the findings of my research and its implications on the future work of the district. I will share what makes Central Valley different from most other school districts, and I will present a series of recommendations based on what I have learned from this research.

Why is Central Valley Different?

It seems most professional organizations, legislative bodies, and even nformal collections of educators are unabashedly critical of NCLB. The common line heard around the country is, "I like the idea behind NCLB, but the devil is in the details." This clichéd conversation has done little to help education move forward. The interviews I conducted in this study revealed a team of leaders with a different mindset. Even though there were many tensions and nherent criticisms associated with NCLB, ultimately this leadership team seemed comfortable with the legislation. While it was not related to my research questions or a part of the initial interview protocol, it became necessary to push theses leaders to think about why their district was different from others, in their minds.

At the most simple level, two of the members thought that the relative success the district has had eliminated some discordance. "I don't think we stand o lose as much as other districts." (M. Phillips, personal interview, December 21, 2004). He went on to describe the pressures on other districts.

> I think [NCLB] has huge ramifications on districts where children are not doing well, and I think [some districts] start losing the confidence of the public in terms of how [they] are preparing kids. It's almost impossible to gain that confidence back. So in that regard, I think there are some districts that are really behind the eight ball. (personal interview, December 21, 2004).

An Assistant Superintendent in the district thought "other environmental factors like a strong, supportive parental support and a number of parents with professional backgrounds" made the demands of NCLB easier to handle. (J. Wilkens, personal interview, December 16, 2004).

A second reason these leaders were comfortable with NCLB was that several of them thought there was a genuine connection in terms of mission. "I guess it's the fact that the ideals behind the legislation mesh so well with the underlying focus of our district, the underlying belief that all students can achieve." (C. Martin, personal interview, December 9, 2004). This was a belief that ran through all leadership levels.

> We might quarrel a lot and argue over the details, but, generally, I think the philosophical position of the administrative staff, even to the assistant principal level – they are really true believers....I think a lot of them ultimately believe in their heart in what we're doing. I think that makes a difference for our district. (S. Green, personal interview, December 21, 2004).

> Whether it was the 'proactive approach' or a work ethic in a district in which 'even the clock watchers work hard,' the answers were always connected to purpose. 'It's work ethic, but it's really based upon a more sophisticated level of sense of mission.' (S. Wright, personal interview, December 8, 2004).

In addition to an aligned belief that all children can learn, throughout every conversation, these leaders had a feeling of empowerment. "There is kind of like this self-fulfilling prophecy that if anything could be done, it could be done here in Central Valley. I think people really believe that, and that's kind of remarkable." (S. Green, personal interview, December 16, 2004). This feeling was revealed in many statements like the following, "I think this is a district that believes we can do it all." (D. McLaughlin, personal interview, December 9, 2004). When asked if this district was ultimately unaffected by NCLB, a senior leader explained his position.

> I wouldn't say it isn't a big deal. I think it is a very big deal, but I think we are positioned so that we are able to deal and cope with it. I think it is very much of a big deal, and I still think there are still conversations to go around the district about why are we doing this and why are we doing that, but when I think when you look holistically we're making progress and doing well. (P. Jennings, personal interview, December 9, 2004).

The Superintendent explained, "The feeling that we can do anything has served us well on taking on these really tough issues." (S. Green, personal interview, December 16, 2004). He then offered a concluding remark that came across with tremendous sincerity. "I think there is such a pride and profession-alism about our district that is almost emotional for a lot of people." (personal interview, December 16, 2004).

The last major reason this group perceives itself more differently than most is because it does not let the details of the federal legislation get in the way of the things it wants to do for students. The Director of Curriculum discussed how NCLB should not be a reason to limit education.

> I feel that, in my job, I'm able to push for the more holistic things, the more reflective things, and the more interesting things for kids. I am able to advocate for art in my position and for physical education and health. In my position, I'm allowed to have that voice, so I don't feel that No Child Left Behind makes me do too many things that I don't want to do. (D. McLaughlin, personal interview, December 9, 2004).

The strength of this district stemmed from the fact that it was not limited to the changes mentioned in this study. So, when thinking about whether or not these changes were good for kids, one leader offered this response.

> I want to see reflection and internationalism. I want to see inquiry. The same leaders that are bugging the heck out of people for 100% are also bug-ging them for these deeper things. So as long as we're doing that, I'm okay working in this environment. I know in other districts they are doing test preparation only. Those are not the kinds of things that we want for kids. (D. McLaughlin, personal interview, December 9, 2004).

Beyond the fact that this district's success kept some of the formal pres-sures of NCLB at bay, these leaders felt their belief system kept them from being distracted by the criticism of the legislation. Their belief system includ-ed an aligned vision of universal proficiency as well as the belief that they were empowered to actually make it a reality. Finally, the details of the legislation did not distract these leaders from defining quality education more broadly to provide more for students than proficiency in math and language arts.

Recommendations

Rather than focus on recommendations for changes to the legislation, I hope to offer suggestions to try and reduce the intra-district tensions involved in working with NCLB, so that leaders can implement the types of changes that are in the best interest of students. Accountability will inherently cause stress, but much energy can be wasted if a district spends its time solely working against the system. I do not pretend that the implementation of these recom-mendations will be uncomplicated or undemanding, but they should help ensure that the decisions leaders make at the local level are the types of changes we want for our students.

1. Focus on the intent of the law rather than the details of its implementation.

2. Broaden the way NCLB defines success, accountability, and the purpose of public education.

3. Implement short-term initiatives intended to immediately improve student Achievement, as well as long-term, systemic approaches that increase the capacity of the district to achieve universal proficiency f for its students.

4. Become a true learning organization.

These recommendations are meant to be thought of as a set, for they work together to help local leaders focus the conversation on what is best for the students. Each recommendation informs the others to create a systemic way to approach accountability sensibly and responsibly. The first recommendation sets the overall goal of universal proficiency, but relies on the second recommendation to define that vision in more meaningful and complete ways than the current legislation does. Recommendation three offers a framework for reaching this vision, but relies on the fourth to create a systemic, continuous improvement model that is always focused on what is best for the students.

Focus on the Spirit of the Law

There are plenty of groups criticizing the finer details of the federal legislation, but as educational leaders we must not buy into a "whining" mentality. Instead, we should focus on the intent of the law rather than the sometimes troubling details of its implementation. The rationale behind this recommendation is two-fold. First of all, too much time is wasted; and secondly, too many critical conversations are avoided with unnecessary and misplaced frustration.

While many educational leaders get bogged down in the details of the legislation, the leaders from Central Valley tried to see the larger picture. "I think we have a calling to follow the spirit of this law, so, yeah, there are some onerous details, but we're not going to focus on them." (D. McLaughlin, personal interview, December 9, 2004). Many of these leaders felt that it was important to look beyond the specific aspects of the legislation and the specific changes this district has made.

> I think the role of [the leadership team] is to think deeply about the issues. I think we need to make sure, policy-wise, we are covering all aspects of the law. I mean that's part of our job, but I also think it's to hold the district to a greater accountability to the spirit of the law (D. McLaughlin, personal interview, December 9, 2004).

The concept of increased accountability must be embraced. Even though there are many who believe NCLB is, in some ways, an indictment of public education, it is important for leaders to embrace accountability toward universal proficiency. Some of the leaders in this study gave strong reasons for this approach, the first of which argues that it is hard to improve while living in a vacuum.

I do believe that we need to measure ourselves against means other than what we do internally. There has to be some external validation of your work, so I'm all for [the accountability of NCLB], and I think it has probably pushed even good districts to do things faster (P. Wilson, personal interview, December 9, 2004).

Another leader admitted that the types of data most educators were collecting before NCLB were not sufficient. "We did not have evidence that what we were doing was having any positive affect on children. Our evidence was anecdotal. Our evidence was case-based." (S. Wright, personal interview, December 8, 2004).

Many would argue that the data NCLB calls for are insufficient. I will address this in the next recommendation, but we should embrace the NCLB data for what it is.

I think the intent, probably, as everybody in the world has said, is an honorable one believing that there is some body of knowledge, some set of skills necessary to participate in this democracy, this society, and the idea of NCLB is to be sure that we have an educated society, citizenry, and can participate well. And it's not fair, in a sense, to have those who can and those who can't – those who can read and write and do math and those who can't. (S. Green, personal interview, December 16, 2004).

One of the purposes of public education is to provide equity. NCLB must be viewed as a step forward.

While I have some problems with the way the accountability measures are structured, I think accountability, in general, in something like NCLB truly makes sense for public education. That is, if we are going to be the great equalizer, then getting every kid to 100% in math and language arts is a great first step for that. (D. McLaughlin, personal interview, December 9, 2004).

We have a responsibility not to let the criticisms of NCLB get in the way of the larger purpose. This is going to take some courageous leadership that challenges some of the conventional thinking. The type of leadership for which I am advocating does not take place behind a podium; it takes place each and every day wherever decisions are made that affect kids. In my study, the Superintendent shared his reaction to an unfortunately common belief.

'Let's be realistic; not all kids are going to make it' – I don't believe that. I just don't believe it in my being. If we don't believe we can make a difference, then why are we educators? But if we really believe they can make it, then we have to say we're serious about 100% [proficiency]. (S. Green, personal interview, December 16, 2004).

Educational leaders are not only responsible for managing the day-to-day decisions, we are also responsible for controlling the conversation and setting the agenda. If our advocacy for all children learning gets lost in the smaller criticisms of NCLB, we are sending the wrong message.

Broaden Your Definitions

I do not try and portray the NCLB legislation as beyond reproach. There are some serious concerns, and we can address many of them by working with our local communities to broaden the way NCLB defines success, accountability, and the purpose of public education. We can control the conversation by creating our own definitions.

Although the legislation recommends rewards for improved student performance, there are only a few schools that have received these distinctions. There are many more who have been publicly labeled as needing improvement. This approach is counterintuitive, and in some cases can harmfully impact expectations.

> [One of our schools] is a good example – a school that hasn't performed well and hasn't performed well for a long time on a comparative basis. You and I know psychologically you don't take something or someone that has not achieved well and beat the hell out of it. That's not how you improve performance, and so these poor people in that school, these poor people in that community now have this whole mentality, you know, 'We really are a failing school. We really are not that good,' and it sets up this whole range of community reactions that are off-base. It is not an appropriate way of improving schooling for kids. (S. Green, personal interview, December 16, 2004).

We know that high expectations affect student achievement, so it is our job to celebrate success and improvement. This may mean local rewards and recognition for growth on standardized test scores, even if schools fail to make AYP. It may mean recognizing growth in math and language arts by examining the quality of student work. We should not judge success or failure based on one assessment point, and, certainly, we need to recognize that achievement in these subject areas is not the only purpose of public education.

> [NCLB] has defined [learning] in terms of mathematics and language arts rather than saying there are some principles such as democracy, community service, and caring about one another that are also the fabric of what schooling is all about. (S. Green, personal interview, December 16, 2004).

At the same time, we cannot limit our definition of accountability to a linear progression of performance on standardized tests. The achievement gap issues are real, they are complex, and they extend beyond what is measurable on tests. In order to truly address the achievement gaps, we need to disaggregate all our data, including suspension rates, graduation rates, and numbers of students participating in high-level classes. In fact, we must look everywhere we can for the institutional barriers that prevent certain students from reaching their potential. We must hold schools accountable to provide the same type of education for all children that we would want for our own children.

By broadening these definitions we will be able to celebrate quality student work beyond that which is measured by the state assessments. We will be able to honor the arts and our efforts in character education in addition to our work in math and language arts. And lastly, we will hold ourselves accountable to providing the best for all children in all aspects of education.

Develop Both Short-Term and Long-Term Planning

As the pressures of accountability increase, either through the formal sanctions of NCLB or through the growing moral pressure to reach all students, the temptation to focus on short-term gains increases. In this study, the leaders in the district realized that some students were not going to do well on the upcoming state assessments. So they decided to implement a dramatic, short-term "Intervention."

> The agreement was before we left for winter break that we would have an "Intervention" program in place for hundreds and hundreds of kids throughout the district, and if it meant that students would not be in phys. ed. or an elective or whatever the case may be, we were going to do whatever it took, and we were going to provide resources to give every kid an opportunity to do well on this test. (P. Jennings, personal interview, December 9, 2004).

While many criticize short-term approaches like these as nothing more than hollow test preparation, the leaders in this study ultimately saw the issue as more complex, as the Director of Curriculum previous explained.

> If a kid is going to see a question in front of him [on a test], we need to do everything we can to give that kid the best opportunity to feel comfortable answering that question – to give him the best shot of answering even one more question. We have that ethical, moral responsibility. And so that became the thinking of the group, and [the person who disagreed initially had his mind changed], and he understood that this could be more than just getting ready for the test. It could be about helping a bunch of kids that were behind. (D. McLaughlin, personal interview, December 9, 2004).

But when leaders disrupt the school system for short-term fixes, educators begin to struggle in their minds with what is educationally sound. One leader shared the tensions that resulted from this short-term approach.

> I think principals are more in a panic mode, where they are just trying to do short-term fixes to make sure kids reach every year, and I'm struggling to find the balance between short-term success and long-term sustainability. That's particularly difficult in this district that really values short-term results, and that's a tension for me. (D. McLaughlin, personal interview, December 9, 2004).

If NCLB makes us think current moment all the time, we will never be putting systems in place that are sustainable. It is imperative that leaders find ways to address immediate needs of students and simultaneously pursue the long-term needs of the educational system. One way to do this is through professional development. Even if the district feels the need to provide extra supports for students through some sort of short-term intervention, their professional development plan needs to focus on developing the capacity in teachers to help students achieve real depth in their learning.

Many educators follow an imperative that says, for example, "This child only gets to be in fourth grade once, so we owe him everything to make it the best fourth grade experience." This same urgency must be balanced by the fact that the teacher of that student may be teaching fourth grade for 30 more years, and if the district does not want a curriculum based solely on test preparation, then it needs to invest in teacher learning to achieve success year after year. When teachers learn how to deliver a rich and well-rounded curriculum effectively, their expectations of what students are able to achieve increase, and these high expectations will ultimately mean fewer students will need short-term interventions.

Become a Learning Organization

Perhaps the greatest way to reduce the tensions associated with the difficult decisions surrounding NCLB is to make a commitment as a district to always learn from any action taken. If leaders make decisions to focus on the short-term, they need to simultaneously study whether or not these choices are having positive effects. If districts consistently and honestly reflect, the problems with short-term thinking can be transformed into long-term solutions.

In my study, the district made the decision to implement a dramatic, eight-week intervention for students at risk of failing the state test. Teacher and student schedules were changed, a short-term curriculum was created, teachers were trained, and administrators stopped all that they were doing in order to focus on successful implementation of this intervention. Although test scores improved, almost everyone involved agreed that stopping the district and making changes mid-year was not the best approach. The most successful aspect of this work was the fact that these leaders made a conscious decision to study and learn from the changes they made. They used the recommendations that resulted from the study of their short-term interventions to inform long-term programmatic changes as well as the professional development plan. When asked if the changes the district made that were influenced by NCLB were educationally sound, one leader responded with the following:

> I think the way our middle school math intervention was done, where we took it as an opportunity to learn about our teachers and about learning. To learn about our pedagogy, to look at our curriculum in different ways, I think those are exactly the kinds of changes that we should be making. (D. McLaughlin, personal interview, December 9, 2004).

Besides the lessons learned in curriculum and pedagogy, the district's efforts brought forward a feeling of empowerment to help all students. "We learned that small, focused groups of kids with dedicated teachers can make wonderful things happen. (P. Jennings, personal interview, December 9, 2004).

In addition to studying the effect on learning and student achievement, the leadership group looked at survey and focus group data from all the stakeholdrs. They discovered that students and teachers did not like the "Intervention," ut each group admitted it had a positive effect on student learning. (Coleman, 004). The formal study made several recommendations that have since been mplemented. Now the district has several improved systems in place for ddressing the needs of struggling learners. This step improved the district's fficiency, and because, the stakeholders had a voice in recommending nprovements, demonstrated the district's integrity. It is critical for education-l leaders to learn from the perspectives of those whom their decisions affect.

In my recommendation to reflect on decisions in order to learn from them, is important to point out that this reflection cannot be at the point of initial ebate or even soon afterward. Reflection needs distance in order to gain per-ective. One of the leaders in my study explained how this was especially true ith the parents of the students involved in the "Intervention."

> I think parents at first were very upset saying, "What do you mean you're pulling my kid out? My kid feels like the dumb kid in the class now," and I think parents realize now that it wasn't such a bad thing. The results were there for their own child....I've heard parents come back and say, "I didn't like this at first, but you know, I see the benefit of it now." (R. Miller, person-al interview, December 15, 2004).

The angry parents were not the only ones who came around. Many of the dministrators who struggled with the decisions they had made, thought, in the nd, they had done what was best for these students.

> When I step back now and look at "Intervention," I knew it was right.... I learned a lot and changed practice because of it the following year. So it was a good lesson for me (P. Wilson, personal interview, December 9, 2004).

The pressures of NCLB and public accountability only increase the need or districts to develop into learning organizations. And while this process usu-ly involves forming study groups and reading current research, a learning rganization, in this sense, is also one that values practitioner research, reflec-on, and the honest desire to improve.

onclusion

There are serious flaws in the NCLB, both in the details of its implemen-tion and in its definitions of success. When leaders make changes in practice order to comply with the law, they understandably struggle to insure that ey are doing what is best for students. It is easy to get frustrated and spend me complaining about some of the more ridiculous aspects in the details, stead of focusing on the intent of the law, and, by publicly supporting the oncept of universal proficiency. In fact, public educators should embrace ccountability and demand that we do a better job of reaching all students.

At the same time, that leaders embrace accountability, they must define is effort more broadly than the legislation does. In addition to an intense cus on math, language arts, and success on standardized tests, leaders should publicly support the arts, depth in learning, and character development. Local leaders also have the power to control the conversation in their districts, so instead of reacting to the negative labeling that results when schools do not meet the NCLB benchmarks, leaders should proactively define success more broadly. Success in school means much more than linear progression on snap shot assessments, and educational leaders are in a strong position to help their communities make more accurate evaluations of our progress. This means more than celebrating art shows, dramatic productions, and character education programs. Leaders must demand the best schooling experience for all students. So, as this definition of success broadens, so does the accountability. While this approach does not reduce the pressure on administrators, it should decrease the tensions when thinking about whether or not they are making the best choices for students.

Letting NCLB define the success of a school system opens the door for the temptation of focusing on short-term gains. Administrators think that by dropping everything and implementing a test preparation curriculum, they might get more immediate results, but they will sacrifice long-term success and sustainability. So, while immediate results are important, short-term interventions must be studied, and they must ultimately inform long-term professional development and systematic improvements. If leaders do not make these connections, they will soon discover increased teacher burnout, limited potential for growth in achievement, and many sleepless nights with the knowledge that they are depriving students of a complete education.

The tensions that result from short-term interventions can also be resolved with a commitment to learn from these experiences through reflection and careful study. The continuous cycle of improvement can transform short-term decisions into long-term, sustainable improvements. When conducting a self-study, it is critical to consider the voices of all stakeholders. District leaders must listen carefully to the recommendations of principals, teachers, parents, and students. This distinction between a study group and a learning organization can lead to a shared vision, a more collaborative effort, and more effective decision-making. The commitment to learn can mitigate much of the negativity associated with dramatic change.

These recommendations will not solve the problems of NCLB. They will not eliminate the tensions that leaders face when implementing the law. They will not lead to changes in the legislation itself. What these recommendations can do is help educators control the conversation and make changes that are in the students' best interest. They can help unite a school community to work for an accountability that makes sense and is greatly needed in public education.

Appendix A

Preliminary Interviews

1. What are some of the changes that have been made in this district because of the accountability provisions in NCLB? Who initiated these changes? What are some other changes? Are there any others?
2. Have you noticed any differences in the work you do that you attribute to the No Child Left Behind legislation? Why do you attribute these to NCLB?
3. What other changes needed to be made in order for the district to successfully meet the challenges of NCLB?
4. Were there any other changes created by Superintendent's Council?
5. Who was responsible for driving these changes? Why that person? How did they do this?
6. Which of these changes were you involved with? Why those? In what ways were you involved?
7. Would any of these changes not have happened if it weren't for NCLB? Can you explain why you feel this way?
8. Which of the changes influenced by NCLB generated significant debate/dialogue? Can you explain? (Explore both why it created dialogue/debate and what the debate/dialogue was)
9. Do you have any mixed feelings about any of these changes?
10. Here are some other things people have mentioned as changes made because of NCLB.
    *   Intervention
    *   Student focus groups
    *   Inspiring conversations
    *   Conversation about quality and external validity
    *   Look-alike assessments
    *   Six-year benchmarks
    *   KPA
    *   Student Advocate
    *   MAC
    *   Heritage Speakers Class
    *   African-American Speaker Series
    *   Application for Supplemental Services Provider
    *   Pilot Assessment Application
    *   Minority hiring

Now that you have seen these, were any of these more significant than what you have said?

Appendix B

Secondary Interviews

1. What do you see as the purpose of public education?
   Why do you believe this?
2. Why is this important? What is your understanding of the reasoning behind the accountability measures of NCLB? What drives this, in your opinion?
3. What do you think of these accountability measures? Do they mesh with your views of the purpose of public education? Do you have any mixed feelings about NCLB?
4. What have been the effects of NCLB on you and your work? Do you feel any pressure because of NCLB? (Explore to see if this is real or perceived pressure) What effects has the law had on Principals? Teachers? Students?
5. What do you see is the role of Superintendent's Council in meeting the demands of the accountability provisions in NCLB?
6. How would you describe your role as a member of Superintendent's Council?

The following protocol was followed for each of the following areas of change identified in the preliminary interviews.

- The "Intervention"
- Six-Year Benchmarks
- KPA – Tying student achievement directly to administrator pay

1. Tell me about the intervention program
2. What was the genesis of the intervention program?
3. Why was the intervention program implemented?
4. What were some of the issues debated when the intervention program was first considered? Tell me more about the debate or what was considered.
5. When discussing the intervention program, whose voices were not heard? What would they have said? Why would they have said that? What do you think about that?
6. What have been the effects of the intervention program? (Probe for benefits and Costs.) Who has this affected? How has it affected them? Why? What have we done to ameliorate any negative effects? Has it affected anyone else? What other effects can you think of?
7. Do you have any mixed feelings about the intervention program?
8. Now that the intervention program has been implemented, what are some things you think about? Are there any unresolved issues? Are there any ongoing debates?

To close the interview:

1. Now that we have talked about some of the major changes that are related to NCLB, I'd like you to think about whether or not these changes are educationally sound or good for students. What are some of the things you think about or struggle with?

2. Ultimately, do you believe these changes (i.e., the intervention program, the 6 year benchmarks, and the KPAs) are the kinds of changes we should be making for students? Why? Why not?

References

Baker, E. L., Linn, R. L., Herman, J. L., Koretz, D. 2002. Standards for Educational accountability. *CRESST Policy Brief, 5.*

Cardman, M. 2003. Ed Trust offers real-life rebuke to NCLB critics. *Education Daily.* November 10, 2003.

CEP. 2004. From the capital to the classroom, year 2 of the No Child Left Behind Act from http://www.ctredpol.org/pubs/nclby2/cep_nclb_y2_full.pdf

Coleman, A. B. 2004. An evaluation of the 2003-2004 8-week intervention program: Working towards a system of program implementation and evaluation. (Unpublished).

Carnoy, M., Loeb, S. In Press. Does external accountability affect student outcomes? In S. H. Fuhrman & R. Elmore (Eds.), *Redesigning Accountability Systems in Education.* New York: Teachers College Press.

Dillon, S. 2004. Some school districts challenge Bush's signature education law. *New York Times,* January 2, 2004.

Elmore, R. F., Abelmann, C. A., Fuhrman, S. H. 1996. The new accountability in state education reform. In H. Ladd (Ed.), *Holding Schools Accountable: Performance Based Reform in Education* (pp. 65-98). Washington D.C.: The Brookings Institution.

Fuhrman, S. 2003. Redesigning accountability systems in education. *CPRE Policy Brief*(Fall), 12.

Goertz, M. 2003. Implementing the No Child Left Behind Act: The potential for a "perfect storm." Paper presented at the American Educational Research Association.

Goertz, M., Duffy, M. 2003. Mapping the landscape of high-stakes testing and accountability programs. *Theory Into Practice, 42*(1).

Goldberg, M. F. 2004. The test mess. *Phi Delta Kappan, 85*(05), 361-366.

Goodwin, B., Arens, S. A., Barley, Z. A., Williams, J. 2002. Understanding No Child Left Behind: a report on the No Child Left Behind Act of 2001 & its implications for schools. Aurora, CO: Mid-continent Research for Education and Learning.

Goodwin, B., Englert, K., Cicchinelli, L. F. 2003. Comprehensive accountability systems: A framework for evaluation. Aurora, CO: Mid-continent Research for Education and Learning.

Hall, D., Wiener, R., Carey, K. 2003. What new "AYP" information tells us about schools, states, and public education. Retrieved 11/22/03, from www.edtrust.org

Hannapel, P., Aagaard, L., Coe, P., Reeves, C. 2000. The impact of standards and accountability on teaching and learning in Kentucky. *NSSE Yearbook on Standards-Based Reform.*

Linn, R. L. 2001. The design and evaluation of educational assessment and accountability systems. Los Angeles: Center for the Study of Evaluation, National Center for Research on Evaluation, Standards, and Student Testing.

N.J.D.O.E. 2003a. DOE announces nearly two-thirds of elementary schools meet NCLB criteria; Only 20 percent of all elementary schools placed on early warning status, from http://www.state.nj.us/njded/news/2003/1119acc.htm, November 19, 2003.

N.J.D.O.E. 2003b. DOE releases list of 271 "early warning" high schools Commissioner Librera supports NCLB goals; Questions implementation, 'failing label, from http://www.nj.gov/njded/news/2003/1003ews.htm. October 3, 2003.

N.J.D.O.E. 2003c. McGreevey demands changes to No Child Left Behind, from http://www.state.nj.us/cgi-bin/governor/njnewsline/view_article.pl?id=1445. October 10, 2003.

Paige, R. 2004. Remarks of Secretary Paige at The American Enterprise Institute. In T. A. E. Institute (Ed.).

Pan, D. T., Mutchler, S. E. 2000. Calling the roll: Study circles for better schools. Austin, TX: SEDL.

Paulson, A. 2004. An education rebellion stirring. *Christian Science Monitor.* February 11, 2004.

Sirotnik, K. A., Kimball, K. 1999. Standards for standards-based accountability systems. *Phi Delta Kappan, 81,* 209-214.

Smith, M. S., O'Day, J. 1990. Systemic school reform. In S. Fuhrman & B. Malen (Eds.), *The Politics of Curriculum and Testing* (pp. 233-267).

Stapleton, J. 2000. Standards-based accountability systems. *Policy Brief.*

Stringer, E. T. 1999. *Action Research* (2nd ed.). Thousand Oaks, CA: Sage Publications.

U.S.D.O.E. 2003. Introduction: No Child Left Behind. Retrieved December 15, 2003 from http://www.ed.gov/nclb/overview/intro/index.html

Zernike, K. 2004. Attacks on education law leave Democrats in a bind. *New York Times.* January 12, 2004.